ALTERNATIVES
to
ECONOMIC
ORTHODOXY

m

ALTERNATIVES
to
ECONOMIC
ORTHODOXY

A READER IN POLITICAL ECONOMY

Edited by
RANDY ALBELDA
CHRISTOPHER GUNN
WILLIAM WALLER

M. E. SHARPE, INC.
Armonk, New York
London, England

Copyright © 1987 by M. E. Sharpe, Inc.
80 Business Park Drive, Armonk, New York 10504

Available in the United Kingdom and Europe from M. E. Sharpe,
Publishers, 3 Henrietta Street, London WC2E 8LU.

Library of Congress Cataloging-in-Publication Data

Alternatives to economic orthodoxy.

    1. Economics. I. Albelda, Randy Pearl.
II. Gunn, Christopher Eaton. III. Waller,
William, 1956–
HB171.A47 1987   330   86-33899
ISBN0-87332-409-9
ISBN 0-87332-413-7 (pbk.)

Printed in the United States of America

Contents

HB171
.A47
1987

I. Introduction

II. Post-Keynesian and Neo-Ricardian Political Economy

III. Institutional Political Economy

IV. Marxist Political Economy

Preface

This book reflects the way in which its editors approach economics. Each of us underwent markedly different university training in economics, but all of us began teaching and writing in the discipline with a clear commitment to political economy. We have worked with colleagues at Hobart and William Smith Colleges to make the study of political economy an integral part of our students' training, and an appropriate part, we think, of their liberal arts education. This book has grown out of our desire to present readers with a clear and concise introduction to the rich diversity of this subject. It is intended as an anthology that can stand on its own, or one that can be fruitfully incorporated into the syllabi of college and university courses in political economy, micro- and macroeconomic theory, or the history of economic thought. Our hope is to clarify issues under debate, and to facilitate further development of alternatives to orthodoxy.

This collective work has enabled us to enjoy both shared responsibility and a product in common. In addition, we were able to draw on the labor and thoughts of many colleagues and friends. First and foremost we would like to thank our managing editor Hazel Dayton Gunn. She typed, edited, cajoled, handled correspondence, and enforced deadlines with competence and grace. Our second debt goes to Hobart and William Smith Colleges, where we found financial and intellectual support. Our colleagues in the economics department were particularly encouraging and helpful. Our work for this reader was informed in important ways by our classroom experiences, and for that we also thank our students. Colleagues here and friends in other parts of the country offered extensive comments and suggestions. We thank Jerry Newsome, Ann Jennings, Michele Naples, Bernadette Lanciaux, and Cihan Bilginsoy. We also appreciate the enthusiasm and support of the staff at M. E. Sharpe—in particular that of Arnold Tovell, former editorial director, and David Biesel, current editorial director, both of whom provided substantive and editorial advice. Our copy editor, Anita O'Brien, did an excellent job of preparing the manuscript for publication. Finally, we want to thank the group that Keynes calls "the brave army of heretics," the people who struggle with the hard questions rather than accept the easy answers. We also appreciate and realize the importance of journals that publish and reproduce work by political economists: *The Review of Radical Political Economics, The Journal of Economic Issues, The Journal of Post Keynesian Economics*, and *The New Left Review*, to name a few.

We ask our readers to share with us their responses, suggestions, and criticisms concerning this reader. Should we develop a later edition, your comments will be invaluable. Please send them to us via M. E. Sharpe, Inc.

I
Introduction

The Resurgence
of Political Economy

Political economy, a term dating from the fifteenth century, today represents both conservative and radical perspectives of economic, political, and social phenomena. This anthology explores the parameters of political economy as it has developed from the work of Marx, Veblen, Keynes, and Sraffa. By political economy we mean an analysis that looks beyond the construction of a model built upon the desires of individual consumers and firms pursuing individual interests. The political economy of concern to us is an interdisciplinary study of the simultaneous and dynamic changes in economic, political, and social institutions and relations. It meters historical time rather than logical time as its frame of reference. Its basic units of analysis are individuals with interrelated and interdependent interests that act as groups or classes in conflict, not as harmonious, autonomous individuals. People's ideological and material existences are endogenously produced in systematic ways. The role of political economy is to define the groups, their systemic interrelations, and their consequent impact on political, economic, and social structures, practices, and outcomes. Some of the more salient commonalities and dissimilarities will be explored later in this introduction.

As the title of this reader suggests, what follows is an introduction to and a representative sampling of different frameworks that are currently being developed within the economic profession—Post-Keynesian, Neo-Ricardian, Institutionalist, and Marxian approaches to political economy. Their most striking similarity is their adherence to a political, social, and economic analysis that questions, critiques, and provides alternatives to orthodox economic theory. By economic orthodoxy we mean the current prevailing theories within economics, largely a resuscitated Neoclassical orthodoxy and its immediate precursor referred to as the Neoclassical-Keynesian synthesis. Neoclassical economics approaches economic problems as a balancing of individuals' choices translated into market mechanisms. Supply-side economics, monetarism, and rational expectations are all adjuncts of Neoclassical economics. Microeconomics is the textbook version of this line of orthodoxy. The Neoclassical-Keynesian synthesis, once referred to by Joan Robinson as ''bastard Keynesianism,'' is the peculiar amalgam of a static interpretation of John Maynard Keynes's work and Neoclassical price theory. Macroeconomics courses most often present this analysis.

The terrain of economic theory is currently a contested one. Today Neoclassical economists control most methods of disseminating economic ideas (editorial positions on journals, economic advisers, funding from political parties and businesses, senior academic positions), but their hegemony is not complete; their wisdom is by no means unquestioned. In the lead essay, ''The Poverty of Economics,'' Robert Kuttner exposes economic orthodoxy for what he and others see as a powerful misperception of economic reality. Kuttner argues that the analysis provided by political economists cannot replace Neoclassical economic orthodoxy. We disagree. Political economy, in all its forms discussed here, is providing a powerful analysis of contemporary society, and a basis for progressive economic and social change.

Since the late 1970s and early 1980s policy makers and theoreticians have recognized that policies and theories of the past have not worked. Crisis in the economy has been accompanied by turmoil in economics. Certainly one response to the failure of conventional economic theory and the economic crisis has been a move to a more conservative economic theory which tries to simplify the economy and present an ideological position of status quo. These theories are fond of reclaiming Adam Smith and the invisible hand—as if not to recognize the crucial role of the government in promoting postwar growth and likely their own economic well-being. This response relies on the individual as the unit of analysis and decries government intervention in the economy as the cause of the crisis. An unfettered market is again posed as the only solution to economic stagnation. Keynesian ''fiddling'' with the economy has brought about the mess, and a new laissez-faire economics is needed. This is the current Neoclassical economics, and for now it maintains a firm foothold in academia and government.

In hopes of explaining and solving the current crisis in economic behavior and theory, many scholars, including economists, have been dusting off volumes of Marx and Veblen. Students are entering graduate schools intent on developing alternative treatments of their disciplines. Many are seeking an economic analysis that is more inclusive of the concerns of women, people of color, the environment, and international justice. Neoclassical theory is premised on a harmony of interests abstracted from reality. Economists critical of this perspective have been reclaiming Institutionalist and Marxian frameworks to understand and correct these problems, while exploring more deeply the works of Ricardo and Keynes to build analyses of instability and disequilibrium. The failure of the economy and economic theory has precipitated the revival of political economy.

Common Elements in Political Economy

We have sketched the broad parameters of political economy. There is room within these flexible boundaries for tremendous diversity and considerable disagreement. To understand this diversity it is necessary to explore those elements of each school of thought that place it within these parameters. Then we can explore the differences that separate the various schools.

We count five basic areas of agreement among political economists. These are:

1. Explicit theoretical recognition of the complexity and systematic interrelatedness of social phenomena;
2. Explicit theoretical recognition of social conflict and its historical occurrence;
3. Explicit recognition of the constancy of change;
4. Recognition that modern industrial economies require some type of planning to perform in a satisfactory manner;
5. Agreement on the need for the democratization of economic decision making.

Each of these common elements will be discussed separately. Note that there is considerable diversity of interpretation within the common elements.

The Complexity and Systematic Interrelatedness of Social Phenomena

The observation that societies in general and modern industrial economies in particular are extremely complex is not a particularly profound one. This observation becomes a defining characteristic of political economy because it is an integral part of the theoretical structure. In some sense, this is a return to the boundaries of the discipline as developed by Adam Smith. It is an explicit rejection of the narrow disciplinary categorization of economic and noneconomic phenomena that have characterized and dominated orthodox Neoclassical theory.

Political economy emphasizes the social and cultural character of all economic activity. Moreover, political economists attempt to incorporate social and cultural analysis within their various theoretical frameworks in a systematic way, not as ill-fitting appendages to be discarded when the "real" analysis begins. This is what gives political economy its interdisciplinary character; it allows the practitioner to take full advantage of the knowledge of and advances made by other social and behavioral sciences. It also serves as a check against which theories in political economy can be evaluated, and it helps avoid perpetuation of misinformation within economics due to ignorance of advances made in other disciplines. Much of the criticism of orthodox economics made by political economists is of this type.

This emphasis on the social and cultural character of human behavior is a rejection of individualism. Orthodox economic theory is based upon individual human behavior *sans* society: all social and cultural influences are assumed away or taken as given. The nature of these influences is considered improper subject matter for economists. Political economy completely rejects the atomistic individual as the level of analysis appropriate for understanding the economy. It unequivocally rejects the possibility of individuals in a state of nature, or individuals taken separately, or any other notion that examines socioeconomic behavior in the absence of accounting for the culture in which it takes place.

This broader interdisciplinary perspective has resulted in political economy rejecting the positive-normative dualism as a meaningful distinction in social inquiry. This is not to say that political economy is ''normative'' economics to be contrasted with ''positive'' Neoclassical economics. It is a rejection of the very idea that scientific analysis of any type can be value-neutral. Political economists generally recognize that the choice of a subject of inquiry and the separation of available information into relevant and irrelevant are value judgments. As a result, all science is a value-laden process.

The explicit recognition of the complexity of social phenomena is a tremendously important characteristic of political economy. The recognition expands the boundaries, redefines the appropriate level of analysis, and rejects both the philosophical and methodological foundations of the discipline of economics as defined by orthodox economics.

Conflict in Society

Again this is not simply the pedestrian recognition of obvious social phenomena. It is a characteristic of these schools of thought that they include social conflict of some type within their theoretical structures.

Class conflict is particularly prominent in Marxist theory. This is not a crude theory of physical conflict. Instead it recognizes that different socioeconomic classes pursue different interests—the ability of one class to achieve its goals inhibits the ability of members of the other classes to achieve their goals. In addition, this has nothing to do with the malevolent intent of individuals in any class. Class conflict is seen as a pervasive phenomenon and the single most important catalyst of social change. It is present on the day-to-day level in the workplace, in conflicts over the conditions of employment, and it is a dominating element in political activity within established governmental structures and processes. Members of the class on the exploited side can eventually recognize their plight; they might perceive that actual physical struggle for the purpose of changing the nature of society is the only way to eliminate their oppression.

Conflict in Institutionalist theory is between ceremonially warranted behavior and technologically warranted behavior. Ceremonially warranted behavior is justified on the basis of authority, tradition, and myth. Technologically warranted behavior is justified on matter-of-fact, cause-and-effect grounds. This is referred to as the Veblenian dichotomy. In the context of a problem either type of behavior may be used. Certain groups in society may benefit from the status quo and will employ ceremonial behaviors to inhibit change. Others will seek to use technological behaviors to solve the problem. If those who use ceremonial behaviors succeed the status quo remains, and the problem goes unsolved. If this pattern is typical for a society it declines. If those who use technological behaviors succeed the problem is solved. If this is the typical pattern for a society it has the potential to progress.

The preceding discussion of conflict was intentionally kept abstract to illustrate two things: this is a theoretical construct systematically using conflict as an explanation of social and economic change; and this theoretical construct can be applied to societies other than those designated as capitalist. This is not an ad hoc generalization, but a theory of competing interests and their resolution.

Post-Keynesian economic theory incorporates conflict in the context of divergence in the public interest and the private interest of individual economic decision makers. The primary concern is with the need of the macroeconomy for investment to ensure adequate performance. But this investment in capitalist economies is controlled by individual economic actors (persons or firms) who make decisions to invest based on their perception of their personal well-being and profit. This may or may not coincide with the needs of the macroeconomy and society for investment at any particular time. Given the inherent uncertainty of unplanned behavior, it is virtually impossible to predict. Moreover, the type of investment that a society needs or desires may not coincide with the interest of individual investors in the absence of perfectly competitive capital markets. It is the case that Post-Keynesian conflict theory, unlike our previous examples, restricts itself to capitalist economies.

Conflict is also a salient feature of Neo-Ricardian analysis. Like Marxism, the focus of its theory is on understanding the generation and distribution of the surplus and the inverse relation between profits and wages. Although the extent or nature of class conflict is assumed in the generation of Neo-Ricardian results, it is an important starting point for the analysis—as workers and capitalists have different interests and receive different shares depending upon their relative strengths.

There is an element implicit in all conflict theories that is absent in Neoclassical theory. The resolution of any conflict depends upon the relative power of the groups involved. All of the schools of political economy discussed in this anthology recognize the role of power in the economy. Each tries to account for power within its theoretical framework, rather than treating it as an exogenous force or ignoring it, as does most Neoclassical theory. With this inclusion of conflict and power comes a rejection of the implicit "natural harmony of interest" doctrine in Neoclassical economics. The notion of a natural harmony of interest is a quasi-religious vestigial remain of the natural right philosophy that was contemporary with the classical economist, and that continues to infect the core of Neoclassical orthodoxy.

Change as a Constant

There is no "natural" tendency to any predetermined place of rest from which the system will move if "disturbed" or "interfered" with. There is no meliorative trend to a predetermined equilibrium. It is striking to note that the rapidity of economic and social change may be the most dominant characteristic of our society in the twentieth century. It is an equally striking fact that this dominant characteristic is treated as a temporary aberration from the normal state of affairs by Neoclassical economics. Political economy not only recognizes change as the normal state of affairs, it also treats change and the factors that bring it about as the single most important phenomenon that economic theory must account for. Thus all schools of political economy attempt to explain the process and mechanism of change from within their theoretical structures. In Neoclassical economics change, when addressed at all, is the result of exogenous forces, disturbing factors, or improper interference in naturally equilibrating markets.

Since political economists treat change as ongoing, they are forced to think in processual rather than static terms. This means the emphasis has been on explaining development as qualitative and quantitative change rather than growth as strictly quantitative change. Since change is not an occasional aberration in these schools of thought, considerable effort is directed at explaining the cumulative and synergistic effects of change on the social and economic system, and on individuals as well.

The importance of the cumulative effects of constantly changing circumstances, whether they be the result of technology, changing climate or environmental factors, or cataclysmic political occurrences, forces the analysis of political economists to be historically based. A historical basis underlies the theoretical structure of each school. Neoclassical economists tend to focus on logical time rather than historical time. Obviously many economic historians are Neoclassical economists. However, economic historians usually apply Neoclassical economic theory to past circumstances, whereas in political economy the historical analysis is an integral aspect of the development of the theoretical structure. Moreover, the historical basis is brought to bear on the application of theory to contemporary issues. This is not to say that the history precedes the theory or that the theory is really only a historical generalization. They are inseparable. In studying developmental systems you must have a sense of where you have been to get any understanding of where you are going.

The recognition of change and its incorporation into the theoretical structures of these schools of thought has led each of them to develop their own particular theory of economic crisis. All of these schools treat the periodic recessions and depressions of capitalist economies as the result of the usual operation of the capitalist system. The attitude of political economy in general was well summed up by Veblen when he characterized capitalism as chronic depression and crisis occasionally interrupted by expansion.

A Role for Planning

The fourth defining characteristic of political economy is the recognition that modern industrial economies require some form of planning if they are to perform adequately. There is no consensus among political economists with regard to what type of planning is preferred. Further, disagreements over appropriate types of planning do not neatly correspond to the divisions between schools of thought within political economy. Therefore, we will look at three general types of planning and try to indicate which schools' members tend to prefer each type.

At one end of the planning spectrum we find comprehensive economic planning. This involves the near elimination of the market mechanism for the purpose of allocating resources. The market as an allocative device is replaced by some sort of governmental structure that is responsible for economic decision making in the forms of investment, production, and distribution decisions. Different economists have different preferences for centralized vs. decentralized planning, but most would insist that the economic goals and methods of decision making be decided upon in an open and democratic process. Although we remain cognizant of the dangers of making broad generalizations, most Marxists, Neo-Ricardians, and some Institutionalists and Post-Keynesians prefer this approach to planning.

A second type of planning is indicative planning. Basically this refers to the government being responsible for setting overall economic goals and using the powers of government to achieve them. It is not just Keynesian stabilization policy that is intended here. Indicative planning includes comprehensive wage and price controls, large-scale income redistribution policies, and an expansion of government regulatory activity. Moreover, the market would be used as an allocative device only when it served the larger economic goals. When the outcome of market transactions conflicted with the overall economic goals the government would step in and either regulate or carry out the problematic activity itself whether this involved investment, production, or distribution. The market is viewed as just one of a variety of social mechanisms that can be used to address economic problems. If it works, fine; if not, it can be dispensed with. There is no ideological attachment to the market mechanism.

Indicative planning is most frequently associated with Institutionalists. This grows out of their treatment of the economy as a complex evolving system. The complexity of the economy leads them to an incremental problem-solving approach. They see making change in the system as disruptive and involving real social cost, thus change should be made when it will solve some problem. This is referred to as the principle of minimal dislocation. Because of the high cost and unforeseen consequences of social change, their preference is for incremental rather than systematic change, a preference shared by some Post-Keynesians. Some Marxists would think of indicative planning as an improvement over capitalism and may even see it as an intermediate step in the transition to a socialist system; however, indicative planning would not be many Marxists' first choice.

At the opposite end of the spectrum from comprehensive economic planning is an expanded notion of macroeconomic planning. Basically what is meant by this is greater use of the tools of monetary and fiscal policy, including wage and price controls, for the purpose of creating full employment and controlling inflation. An incomes policy might be considered to alleviate the worst ravages of poverty, but the market remains the prime mechanism for allocating resources. This minimal view of planning is probably the least any political economist would consider. Most Post-Keynesians would fall somewhere between the minimal view of planning presented here and indicative planning.

Democratization of the Economy

Political economists advocate wider participation and democratization of economic decision making at all levels. At the governmental level this is intimately related to the belief in the necessity of planning by political economists. The ethical justification of the market system by orthodox theory includes organizations of production activity on the principle of one-dollar, one-vote. For political economy, democratization can include decisions on what to produce and how to produce it, the actual division of work within the firm, investment decisions, and appropriate compensation. This view of democratically organized production is seen as equally applicable to production within the home. The household, largely ignored by orthodox economists, is recognized as an extremely important productive unit in our society. The lack of democratic participation in the typical patriarchal family structure mirrors the antidemocratic hierarchy to be overcome in the economy and polity in general.

Democracy is essential in a planned economy to help ensure that the goals pursued and the policies implemented genuinely reflect the public interest. Only if all members of society participate in the discussion of goals and the design and implementation of policy can there be any assurance that all essential needs are met and all points of view are heard. Democratic participation increases the likelihood that all possibilities will be explored. It ensures that institutional inertia does not perpetuate a narrow perspective or stifle innovation from outside the formal bureaucratic structure.

Diversity in Political Economy

These five characteristics are the broad defining boundaries of political economy. These boundaries are both flexible and capable of allowing much diversity. It is to this diversity that we now turn. Each school of thought within political economy sees itself as fundamentally different and separate from the others, and all of them are critical of one another. It is beyond the scope of this introduction to explore in detail the various schools' disagreements with one another; rather, our approach will be to point out the areas of disagreement and briefly present each school's point of view. The readings that follow provide fuller insight into these differences.

The six basic areas of disagreement are listed below. Each school of thought:
1. Uses a different theoretical conception of the nature of human behavior;

2. Has a different theory of the mechanisms of social and economic change;
3. Uses different units of analysis;
4. Has a different theory of value;
5. Has its own distinct philosophical foundation;
6. Has its own perspective on public policy questions.

This list of disagreements is by no means exhaustive or definitive. It does represent, in our view, the crucial differences that serve to differentiate and define these schools of thought. Some of the differences are more important between some schools of political economy; others represent minor, insignificant departures.

Each school of thought has a set of working rules for analysis. These working rules are really core hypotheses about how societies work. In most inquiry these hypotheses are treated as assumptions or premises from which analysis begins. These are not thought to be a priori truths since they are themselves subject to critical analysis and inquiry. They are hypotheses, considered to be warranted because of their success in previous application.

The Nature of Human Behavior

Differences in each school's perception of the nature of human behavior result in different perceptions of the appropriate level of analysis for economic inquiry. Marxists are interested in the impact of the productive and reproductive process on human behavior. They see the social relations associated with the dominant ways in which production is organized as the most important. The relations between the class that controls production and the class that actually carries out the productive activity, and relations within each class, are seen as the appropriate levels of analysis for economic inquiry. Neo-Ricardians sidestep the issue of human behavior in their model of capitalist production and reproduction by using a physical quantity approach. In this way they focus on technical relations in the determination of value, leaving social relations to be determined separately. Institutionalists treat economic behavior as taking place in a cultural context where both the technology of production and traditional ceremonial patterns of behavior and beliefs define the general parameters of human action. Thus the process of acculturation and technological development are crucial to understanding human behavior. Culture is an ongoing process; the appropriate level of analysis for the Institutionalists is the existing social hierarchy, its evolutionary origins, and its current impacts on development and progress. Post-Keynesians concentrate their attention on the macroeconomic aggregates that were so crucial in Keynes's *The General Theory*. The foundations of these aggregates are an area of dispute. Some Post-Keynesians implicitly accept the microfoundations of Neoclassical orthodoxy. Others adopt a position somewhat akin to that of the Institutionalists. Often this foundation is left unexplored.

Theories of Change

We have already discussed the fact that political economists see change as normal. Each school has its own view as to the mechanism that causes this change to occur. Dialectical materialism provides the mechanism of change in Marxist thought. The source of change comes from within the thing or process; it is the struggle of opposites, the contradiction inherent within the thing or process. The cause of qualitative change and social transformation is an ongoing resolution of contradictions and creation of new ones. Institutionalists see the mechanism of change as the result of the application of new technology to production or social problems, or put simply, applied intelligence in action. The nature of the change is incremental and evolutionary. The analysis focuses on its cumulative effect. Post-Keynesians also recognize the importance of change and development. The role of expectations and their accompanying uncertainty leads them to concentrate their efforts on disequilibrium analysis. Since disequilibrium is the norm for Post-Keynesians, their analysis is one of the constant flux and change within market economies. Neo-Ricardians rely on the nature of class relations to facilitate change in their model. What changes class relations is at present left unspecified.

Units of Analysis

The units of analysis used by Post-Keynesians are the factors of the Neoclassical synthesis—land, labor, and capital—as both productive and distributive categories. They accept Keynes's definitions of consumption, investment, and saving in their analysis; however, their focus on the dynamic nature of market economies, rather than static equilibrium, has resulted in important and innovative contributions to both the theories and definitions of production and capital. Marxists use some of this same terminology, but in a radically different way. The productive factor for Marxists is labor. What is sold by workers in labor markets is the commodity labor power—the capacity to do work. Workers, lacking access to their own or to socially owned means of production, sell their labor power in order to live. Capital has several meanings. It refers to plant and equipment (embodied labor), to finance capital (value in liquid form), and to *the class* that reaps surplus value because it owns and controls the means of production. Capital is both something tangible and a specific set of social relations. These categories are used in elaborating the class analysis that is the centerpiece of Marxist thought. Although Neo-Ricardians use the same units of analysis as Marxists, they do not claim that labor is the only productive category. Their analysis focuses on understanding the relative contributions of physical quantities to production and corresponding distribution of surplus. Institutionalists reject the Neoclassical factors of production of land, labor, and capital as meaningless taxonomy. They treat production as an integrated technological process. Resources are productive when used together, and their contributions cannot be meaningfully discussed except in terms of the integrated process. Institutionalists see these factors as distributional. Actual distribution of goods and services is determined by the existing social hierarchy, whether on the basis of need or the result of force and fraud. This cultural issue is the subject of inquiry.

Value Theory

Each school of thought has a different value theory that is performing a different role in its theoretical structure. The Post-Keynesians' position here is not well defined. In some respects they are stuck with the utility theory of value which equates value with the price determined by competitive markets, which are in turn the result of utility maximization by individuals. This tautological conception of value is seen by many political economists as an obfuscating leftover from Keynes's inability to discard his Marshallian heritage. It is this remnant that left the door open for the Neoclassical synthesis Post-Keynesians regularly vilify. In actual practice Post-Keynesians seem to adopt a pragmatic problem-solving value theory that is largely borrowed from the Institutionalists.

Marxists use a variant of the classical economists' labor theory of value. Value theory is not used in Marxist thought as merely an explanation of price. Productive labor embodied in a commodity determines the commodity's value. The capitalist sells the product for its full value, pays the worker less than the amount paid in wages for the use of the worker's labor power, and expropriates the resulting surplus value. This expropriation of surplus value is what defines the conflicting interest of the capitalist and working class. It is also a major source of the working class's alienation. Thus value theory is at the very core of Marxian analysis. In recent years some Neo-Marxists in their analysis of monopoly capitalism have added a new dimension. They have included an explicit analysis of relative power in the determination of the market price charged for a commodity.

The discussion over value theory is clearly the major contribution and focus for Neo-Ricardians. This work is fueled by the exploration of the determination of prices—profits, wages, and rent—employing a value theory that is based not merely on labor's contribution but accounts for the contribution of all physical quantities to production. It is here that Neo-Ricardians differ significantly from Marxists' adherence to the labor theory of value and converge with Post-Keynesians' cost of production analysis. Neo-Ricardians have claimed to solve the problem of transformation of values to prices which has bothered Marxists and critics of Marx for years.

Institutionalists treat the value of an economic good in a problem-solving context. This means the value of a good or service depends on what it is used for. Put simply, the value of a plunger is related to whether or not your sink is plugged up. This is not an explanation of market price. It is concerned with the ability of a good or service to contribute to the life process. Value in exchange is determined by the exercise of power within the social hierarchy. There is some affinity here to the explanation used by Neo-Marxists.

Philosophical Foundations and Perspectives on Public Policy

These last two areas of disagreement are so broad that even a superficial discussion of the issues involved could fill many volumes. As a matter of fact, the discussion of some of these issues will fill the rest of this anthology.

The philosophical differences between these schools of thought are profound. Each school originated from a different philosophical tradition. They have been influenced by differing views of appropriate methodological approaches for the social sciences. They disagree on methods or tools used in analysis, and on appropriate standards of verification of hypotheses. These issues are by no means settled; they make up the substance of some of the most spirited exchanges between economists generally and political economists in particular.

The areas of disagreement with respect to public policy are also large. They grow out of the other theoretical differences. Each school of thought defines "which direction is forward" differently. Definitions of what constitutes progress and development depend on how each school defines the economic problem in the first place. This determines how they pose policy questions, which leads to defining problems and potential solutions within their own framework. Fortunately, this does not mean these schools never address the same issues, they just approach them differently.

The schools of thought represented in the literature that follows have, in most cases, a long history. Even a summary history of economic thought would exceed the strict space limitations we face in writing this introduction. For readers not familiar with the development of political economy, we recommend the reading of at least one good book on the subject. Our own inclinations are to Guy Routh's *Origins of Economic Ideas* (Vantage, 1975) or E. K. Hunt's *History of Economic Thought: A Critical Perspective* (Wadsworth, 1979).

The following chart, risky as such a schematic presentation can be, serves at least to locate some of the principal actors in this history. It also helps delineate the schools of thought to be explored in the readings to follow. Dates accompanying names are those of an individual's major publication.

The spectrum of schools of thought at the contemporary end of this chronological sequence is arranged in a generally suggestive array from left to right in the political spectrum. It is intended not as a categorization of all the ideas and theories of any one school, but as a general indication of a school's substantive position on the desirability of private enterprise, free market capitalism.

A TABLE OF POLITICAL ECONOMY

Early Contributors

Plato — Aristotle — St. Augustine

Authors of 17th- & 18th-century pamphlets and essays on Political Economy

J. Locke
B. Mandeville
R. Cantillon
D. North
W. Petty
D. Hume

Mercantilists

J. B. Colbert
T. Mun
D. Defoe
J. Steuart

Physiocrats

S. P. de Vauban
P. le P. de Boisguilbert
P. S. Dupont de Nemours
F. Quesnay
A. R. J. Turgot

Classical Political Economy

A. Smith 1776
J. Bentham 1780
J. B. Say 1803
J. C. L. S. de Sismondi 1803
D. Ricardo 1817
T. R. Malthus 1820
N. Senior 1836
J. S. Mill 1848

Neoclassical Economics

W. S. Jevons 1871
C. Menger 1871
L. Walras 1874
A. Marshall 1890

Marxist Political Economy

K. Marx 1867

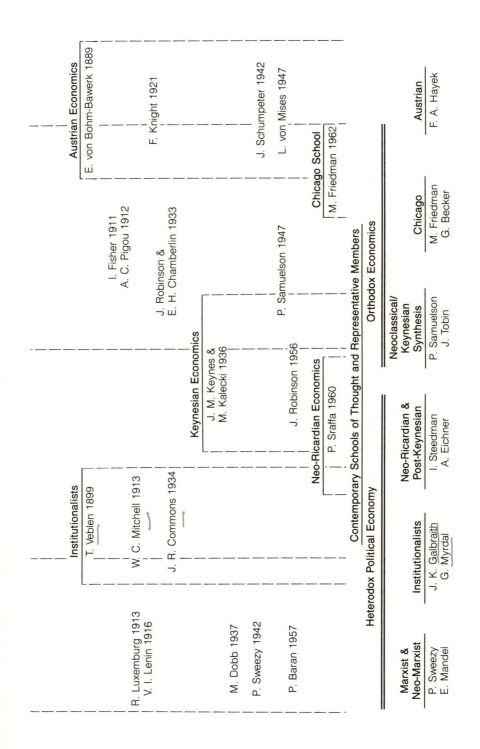

Contemporary Schools of Thought and Representative Members

The Poverty of Economics

ROBERT KUTTNER

Events have been unkind to the economy, and unkinder still to economists. Twenty years ago the age-old problem of boom and bust seemed to have been solved; the ideological schisms that had long plagued economics had been melded into a "Neoclassical synthesis" that reconciled the classical economics of the invisible hand with the inspired heresies of John Maynard Keynes. In the 1961 edition of his famous textbook Paul Samuelson could write with some confidence that the body of Neoclassical theory "is accepted in its broad outlines by all but a few extreme left-wing and right-wing writers."

During the 1970s the world's industrial economies not only faltered but faltered in ways that confounded received theory. As the economy became the paramount political issue in country after country, economists gained notoriety and lost their compass. The business community, a principal consumer of economic forecasting, became increasingly skeptical about the ability of economists to call the turns in the economy. Governments found economists urging politically suicidal austerities.

Within the profession itself the consensus of the sixties fragmented into Chicago monetarists, Post-Keynesians, Neo-Marxists, Neo-Institutionalists, Neo-Austrians, and a new fundamentalist strain, the rational-expectations school. Since 1970 an outpouring of serious and ideologically diverse articles and books has pronounced that economics is in a state of severe, perhaps terminal, crisis. Some titles convey the sentiments: *The Crisis in Economic Theory, Economists at Bay, What's Wrong With Economics, The Irrelevance of Conventional Economics,* ← No No→ *Why Economics Is Not Yet a Science, Dangerous Currents: The State of Economics,* Had even a scholarly article titled "Let's Take the Con Out of Econometrics."

One hears critical comments not only from Samuelson's "extreme left-wing and right-wing writers" but also in annual addresses by incoming presidents of the American Economic Association. Yet despite the apparent soul-searching, the teaching of economics, the hiring of young economists and the granting of tenure, the financing of research, and the pages of prestigious "refereed" journals all evidence deep resistance to change.

Neoclassical economics, the reigning school, marries the assumptions of the classical invisible hand—the principle of a self-regulating economy—to the Keynesian insight that macroeconomic stabilization by government is necessary to keep the clockwork operating smoothly. In method, standard economics is highly abstract, mathematical, and deductive, rather than curious about institu-

Robert Kuttner, "The Poverty of Economics," *The Atlantic Monthly* (February 1985), pp. 74–84.

tions. Neoclassical economic theory posits an economic system of "perfect competition." All transactions in the economy are likened to those that occur in simple marketplaces, like fish markets, in which prices rise or fall exactly enough to move the merchandise. As economists say, adjustment of price based on supply and demand serves to "clear the market." That is, if there is an oversupply of herring on a given day, the shrewd fishmonger will lower his price; otherwise the market will fail to clear and the fish will rot. If there is high demand for lobster but short supply, the fishmonger will raise his price; otherwise there will be too many willing buyers. From this stylized picture of a small market, standard economics projects a "general equilibrium" that is said to characterize the entire economy. Perfect competition, in a sleight of epistemological hand, is said to describe the best possible as well as the actual world.

The model also assumes that markets are composed of many sellers and many buyers, who individually have too little market power to dictate prices or to manipulate choices, and can only offer or accept bids. As economists say, each seller is a price taker, not a price maker—for otherwise there could not be perfect competition.

Perfect competition requires "perfect information." Consumers must know enough to compare products astutely; workers must be aware of alternative jobs, and capitalists of competing investment opportunities. Otherwise, sellers could charge more than a competitive price and get away with it, and workers could demand more than their services were worth. Moreover, perfect competition requires "perfect mobility of factors." Workers must be free to seek the highest available wage, and capitalists to shift their capital to get the highest available return; otherwise, identical factors of production would command different prices, and the result would be a deviation from the model. Economists argue that monopoly prices or wages cannot last very long, because some entrepreneur soon perceives an opportunity, enters the market, and forces prices back into equilibrium.

The introduction of concrete social institutions like banks, corporations, currencies, and the modern state complicate only the details, not the fundamentals. Likewise, deviations from perfect competition in actual economic life require embellishments of the model, not a revision of its premises. With Keynes, standard theory conceded that disequilibria might intrude upon the economy as a whole, but it held that these could be remedied by judicious stabilization of aggregate demand—that is, combined government and consumer purchasing power.

The Neoclassical model assumes that economic behavior is based on the concept of "marginal utility": individual consumers express choices by continually calculating and refining their preferences "at the margin"—the point at which they have extra dollars of income or hours of time to spend—and firms likewise make adjustments at the margin to maximize their profits. We know these things by assumption and inference: an individual who did not maximize his well-being would be behaving irrationally, and a firm failing to maximize profits would fall by the wayside. In most models the state of technology is assumed to be constant, and so are cultural and institutional environments. Technological, cultural, and institutional changes that do occur over time result from individuals' constantly adjusting their preferences at the margin. If individuals have cultural attachments, and motivations other than utility maximization, these are not of theoretical significance. Charles Schultze, a senior fellow at the Brookings Institution and a recent president of the AEA, says, "When you dig deep down, economists are scared to death of being sociologists. The one great thing we have going for us is the premise that individuals act rationally in trying to satisfy their preferences. That is an incredibly powerful tool, because you can model it."

When the standard model is presented in the classroom, an impertinent freshman invariably protests that it is plainly unrealistic. The professor has heard the complaint before. He tells the student that we must walk before we can run, that we must oversimplify for the sake of analytical clarity, and that after the student is more accomplished in analytic technique, refinements will be added to adjust the model to the nuances of economic reality. The model indeed becomes more elaborate, yet the basic assumptions persist. By then the student either will have decided that the entire exercise is unrewarding and moved on to history or sociology, or will have mastered the difficult mathematical proofs and acquired a certain fondness for deductive logic, as well as a professional loyalty to the discipline.

Neoclassical economic analysis grows out of the Enlightenment mentality, which substituted a scientific natural order for a metaphysical one. An invisible hand that shaped individual egoism into general harmony reconciled the Enlightenment predilections for personal liberty and natural laws. Adam Smith's concept of equilibrium in market economics is also a variation on eighteenth-century Newtonian mechanics. Physics has served ever since as a model to which economics should aspire.

The difficulty is that economic phenomena are neither so universal nor so predictable as physical phenomena. If, for example, most actual markets do not automatically clear according to price, then standard economics is building elaborate models of a world that does not exist. As Lester Thurow observed in *Dangerous Currents*, some markets, such as the stock market, do roughly bear out the classical assumption that markets clear on the basis of adjustment in price, while others, such as the market for labor, do nothing of the sort, and still others, such as the market for automobiles, are somewhere in between.

It is not unusual for laymen to fault academic experts for playing in a sandbox of abstraction, but such criticism is especially justifiable when it applies to economists, for they, unlike literary scholars, operate in two worlds. They are, as the radical economist Samuel Bowles once observed, both priests and engineers. Their sandbox is the economy. When economists are relied upon for practical advice, the consequences of faulty theory are real.

Of several major theoretical problems the most basic is that economic theory reasons deductively, from axioms. An axiom, said the English economist Peter Wiles, is "only a premise one is not allowed to question, dressed up as something grand." The world of perfect competition posited by Neoclassical economics may be so far from the world in which we live that it is not a useful basis for theory or policy advice. Certainly, if the world were literally like the theory, daily life would be anarchic. Thorstein Veblen wrote: "If, in fact, all the conventional relations and principles of pecuniary intercourse were subject to such a perpetual rationalized, calculating revision, so that each article of usage, appreciation, or procedure must approve itself de novo on hedonistic grounds of sensuous expediency. . . it is not conceivable that the institutional fabric would last overnight."

By reasoning deductively from axioms economics confuses the normative with the descriptive. Theory stipulates, a priori, that perfect competition is both a description of the optimal world and a useful approximation of the actual world. When it is pointed out that high unemployment, or segmented labor markets, or oligopolistic corporations, or national economic-development strategies, or big public sectors, or regulated banks, or protected agricultural markets—or the logic of social organizations in general—suggest a world very far from the textbook picture of perfect competition and self-correcting markets, the economist has essentially two choices. He can turn pamphleteer, as so many economists do, and insist that the world would be a better place if it did conform to the textbooks. (As the Cambridge University economist John Eatwell has said, "If the world is not like the model, so much the worse for the world.") Or he can scrap the formalism, get out of the office, and study the profane world of real institutions. There are some economists of this sort, but they are mostly of an older generation—men like Herbert Simon, of Carnegie-Mellon University, and Albert Hirschman, of the Institute for Advanced Study, who challenge the psychological assumptions of the orthodox model. However, you will find very few under age fifty in tenured chairs at major universities, or in the prestigious economic journals; and you will not find work of this kind in the body of theory taught to aspiring young economists.

The deductive method of practicing economic science creates a professional ethic of studied myopia. Apprentice economists are relieved of the need to learn much about the complexities of human motivation, the messy universe of economic institutions, or the real dynamics of technological change. In economics, deduction drives out empiricism. Those who have real empirical curiosity and insight about the workings of banks, corporations, production technologies, trade unions, economic history, or individual behavior are dismissed as casual empiricists, literary historians, or sociologists and marginalized within the profession. In their place departments of economics are graduating a generation of *idiots savants*, brilliant at esoteric mathematics yet innocent of actual economic life.

In a spoof titled "Life Among the Econ," published in 1973 in the *Western Economic Journal*, the Swedish-born economist Axel Leijonhufvud proposed

that the methods of the economics profession might be best understood anthropo-
logically, as the rituals of a primitive tribe: ''Among the Econ . . . status is tied to
the manufacture of certain types of implements, called 'modls.'. . . most of these
'modls' seem to be of little or no practical use, [which] probably accounts for the
backwardness and abject cultural poverty of the tribe. . . . The priestly caste (the
Math-Econ) [ranks higher] than either Micro or Macro. . . . The rise of the Math-
Econ seems to be associated with the previously noted trend among all the Econ
towards more ornate, ceremonial modls.''

The habits of the Math-Econ are perplexing to the laity, not only because the
math itself is technical but also because economists use statistics and mathematical models in several distinct ways, each with its own pitfalls. Some mathematical models are pure theory; they use algebra only to manipulate assumptions.
This is true of general-equilibrium theory, and also true of many lesser topics
explored in journal articles. For example, a characteristic article titled ''A Model
of Housing Tenure Choice,'' by J. V. Henderson and Y. M. Ioannides, which
appeared in a recent issue of *The American Economic Review*, inquired how
wealth, income, ''life cycle,'' and other variables influence the decision whether
to buy or rent a house. For the sake of analysis the model assumed, among other
things, that housing markets are ''in equilibrium.'' The model went on to deduce
algebraically what consumers do (in theory) given different market circumstances. The authors then reported certain conclusions, such as ''Renting becomes more attractive if housing is subject to random capital gains or losses and
consumers may also invest in a capital market at a fixed rate of return.'' In other
words, consumers will prefer a sure thing to a gamble. What is striking about the
article, and others of its genre, is that it contains no data and no indication that the
authors have ever studied an actual housing market. The article is pure manipulation of assumption and inference, using mathematical logic.

A quite different use of mathematics is econometric modeling, which can be
heavily empirical. Commercial consulting firms such as Wharton Econometrics,
Chase Econometrics, and Data Resources, Inc. (DRI) have devised complex
models of the economy, which may use upwards of a thousand equations, linked
by means of a computer program. By collecting data over a long period of time
and tabulating correlations, an econometric modeler attempts to predict how
variables will influence one another in the future—assuming of course that the
patterns of the recent past persist. For example, if the federal deficit is $200
billion and monetary policy is tightened, unemployment (according to past correlations) might rise to 8 percent and interest rates might be 12 to 13 percent.
Different models use different assumptions of causality. A supply-side model
might make savings rates paramount; a monetarist model, money supply; a
Keynesian model, the size of the public deficit.

The difficulties with such models are that there are always more variables than
the model considers and that the past does not necessarily foreshadow the future.
In recent years the major influences on macroeconomic climate have been exter-

nal variables (the OPEC price increase, for example) and structural changes in the system (the globalization of technology and finance). Further, an econometric model cannot read the mind of the Federal Reserve Board or Congress. The latest DRI forecast predicted fairly stable economic growth through the late 1980s, but the forecast could be derailed by financial panic, political deadlock over deficit reduction, the course of the Iran-Iraq war, or unexpected structural influences stemming from banking deregulation. After a period of rapidly increasing popularity in the 1970s, the big economic forecasting models have fallen somewhat from favor. ''We subscribe to DRI,'' says the president of Cyclops Steel, William Knoell, who is also the chairman of the board of the Cleveland Federal Reserve Bank. ''We consider them as one more input, as a baseline against which you have to apply common sense. But if you look at their forecasts in steel over the past few years, they weren't all that good. Economists generally missed the enormous rise of the dollar. They missed the recent drop in interest rates. There are just too many imponderables.''

A number of fledgling econometric firms went out of business in the early 1980s. DRI—which has hundreds of commercial clients and total billings in excess of eighty million dollars a year—and the other big firms are moving away from the megamodels, into more customized models that project a client's sales using a variety of macroeconomic scenarios. The crystal ball has given way to the more modest tool of contingency planning.

A different and even more controversial use of econometric techniques is in the testing of algebraically modeled hypotheses. A mathematical technique known as multiple linear regression allows the testing of several variables that might have a cause-and-effect relationship, by considering them one at a time. If wages are thought to be influenced by occupation, education, IQ, sex, and race, econometric techniques can determine how strongly each factor correlates with variations in wages; the researcher can then attempt to impute causality.

This brand of econometric testing, however, brings manifold problems. In economic life cause-and-effect does not happen instantly; there are delays before influences are felt. The last refuge of an economic scoundrel is the time lag. By manipulating time lags the determined econometrician can ''prove'' almost anything. Moreover, though many economists argue that the fair way to test a theory is to specify the hypothesis, and run the regression equations once, it is common practice to keep fiddling with the equations, manipulating lag times, lead times, and other variables, until the equations more or less confirm the hypothesis. Some correlations, of course, may be just coincidence; other apparent correlations may disguise real causes that have been overlooked.

The computer has made it simple for researchers to run an almost infinite number of equations, using standard software packages. Rather than serving as a tool of empirical scrutiny, this technique can turn the economist into a pure technician—or a pure ideologue. Recent innovations, such as ''vector auto regressions'' and ''multivariate auto-regressive integrative moving average'' models, in effect have the computer go on automatic pilot and search for correlations, almost at random. ''The risk of cheap computing,'' says Roger Brinner, the chief domestic economist at DRI, ''is the assumption that the machine can provide the intelligence. Researchers make the error of failing to test competing theories against each other; instead you spend all of your time plugging away at the terminal, trying to get your data to fit your theory.''

One celebrated methodological and ideological controversy raged over work by Martin Feldstein, a professor of economics at Harvard and a former chairman of President Reagan's Council of Economic Advisers, on the influence that Social Security has on savings rates. In a series of journal articles Feldstein reported econometric findings that Social Security had depressed savings by about 50 percent, which would have depressed GNP by many hundreds of billions of dollars. But at the 1980 meeting of the AEA two relatively unknown researchers, Dean Leimer and Selig Lesnoy of the Social Security Administration research staff, presented a paper showing a serious technical error in Feldstein's equations. When the error was corrected, the model Feldstein had used showed absurd results. *Without* Social Security, savings would have been negative. Feldstein ultimately revised his own equations to reconcile them with his hypothesis. But the affair was considered damaging to Feldstein's prestige and a good object lesson in the hubris of econometrics.

Among the most astringent critics of the overmathematization of economics is one of the profession's most notable mathematicians, Wassily Leontief. In his 1970 AEA presidential address, Leontief, the first economist to work with computers and the inventor of mathematical input-output analysis, which won him the 1973 Nobel Prize, decried the increasing ''preoccupation with imaginary, hypothetical, rather than with observable, reality,'' and described a ''Darwinian'' process by which pure theorists drive out those who study the actual economy. By 1982 Leontief had so despaired of his profession that he had ceased publishing in economics journals. In a letter to *Science* magazine Leontief wrote, ''Page after page of professional economic journals are filled with mathematical formulas leading the reader from sets of more or less plausible but entirely arbitrary assumptions to precisely stated but irrelevant theoretical conclusions.''

A good empiricist, Leontief tabulated recent articles in *The American Economic Review*. In the period from March 1977 to December 1981, Leontief found, 54 percent of *AER* articles were ''mathematical models without any data.'' Another 22 percent drew statistical inferences from data generated for some other purpose. Another 12 percent used analysis with no data. Half of one percent of the articles used direct empirical analysis of data generated by the author. Leontief says that a more recent tabulation finds the trend unabated. ''We found exactly one piece of empirical research, and it was about the utility maximization of pigeons.''

Another critic of the mathematical approach was the late Oskar Morgenstern, the coinventor of games theory and an economist and mathematician loosely

identified with the conservative Austrian school. Morgenstern, in a splendid
nontechnical book titled *On the Accuracy of Economic Observations*, pointed out
the unreliability of most economic statistics. For one thing, people responding to
official questionnaires often lie, out of fear of government scrutiny or a desire to
mislead the competition. "Nothing like this occurs in nature," Morgenstern
said. For another, economics is notorious for using secondhand data, collected for
other purposes, whose logic may be legal or bureaucratic rather than economic.
Profits reported on balance sheets for tax purposes have little to do with real
profits. Many official statistical series are completely incompatible with one
another. In international trade statistics one nation's import figures invariably fail
to conform to the trading partner's export figures.

Morgenstern went on to explain how the mathematical manipulations of data
that are imperfect to begin with compound statistical errors, leading to wildly
inaccurate results. If a regression equation shows the absence of a correlation, it
may be because no real relationship exists or because the statistics are incorrect,
and the economist has no way of telling which is the case. The more complex the
equation, the greater the possibility of cascading errors. Moreover, if the economist is consciously or unconsciously tailoring the equation to what turns out to be
false data, the equation can produce truly absurd results when correct data are
substituted. That tendency does not mean that researchers are dishonest; it means
that the whole method is suspect. Lester Thurow has written, "If Newton and his
contemporaries had behaved as the economics profession is now behaving and
had access to the modern computer, it is likely that the law of gravity would never
have been discovered."

The mathematical language and the deductive method tend to give economists
a certitude that theirs—and theirs alone—is a "hard" social science. At the
December 1983 annual gathering of the AEA, George Stigler, a Nobel laureate
and a leader of the Chicago school, began a lecture by remarking that a colleague
in political science had inquired why there were no Nobel Prizes awarded in the
other social sciences. "I told him," Stigler said, "that they already had a Nobel
Prize in literature." In the same vein another economist says archly, "Political
scientists think the plural of anecdote is data."

The most frequently cited defense of mathematical, deductive reasoning was
offered more than thirty years ago in Milton Friedman's *Essays in Positive
Economics*. It does not matter, Friedman argued, whether an assumption is
empirically true so long as it is internally consistent and the model is not refuted
by data. Thus, even in a world where competition is far from perfect it is valid to
model economic activity "as if" it conformed to the axioms of classical economics. Friedman used an analogy of a hypothetical expert billiards player:

> It seems not at all unreasonable . . . that the billiard player made his shots *as if*
> he knew the complicated mathematical formulas that would give the optimum
> directions of travel, could estimate accurately by eye the angles . . . could make

lightning calculations from the formulas, and could then make the balls travel in the direction indicated by the formulas. Our confidence in this hypothesis is not based on the belief that billiard players, even expert ones, can or do go through the process described; it derives rather from the belief that, unless in some way or other they were capable of reaching essentially the same result, they would not in fact be *expert* billiard players.

It is only a short step from these examples to the economic hypothesis that under a wide range of circumstances individual firms behave *as if* they were seeking rationally to maximize their expected returns . . . and had full knowledge of the data needed to succeed in this attempt; *as if*, that is, they knew the relevant cost and demand functions.

Pursuing Friedman's metaphor, Professor Richard Thaler, of Cornell University, suggests that a better analogy is to a novice billiards player, who has perhaps had a few beers. "The novice will use little or no 'english,' will pay little attention to where the cue ball goes after the shot, and may be subject to some optical illusions that cause him to systematically mis-hit some other shots." No formula can accurately predict the amateur's shots, and the real economy contains far more novices than experts.

It matters that economists are trained to view the world the way they do. Lately, almost all public-policy questions have been defined as economic ones. The experts with the professional authority to pronounce on such questions are, of course, economists. Civic issues of public values, political power, the nature of democratic society, are mistaken for narrowly technical issues, with conclusions ordained and alternative solutions foreclosed.

An equally serious consequence of the professional obsession with model making is that the most pressing *economic* questions lie outside the frame of reference. The issues that standard economics cannot explain and does not address are of far greater moment than the ones "solved" by the formal proofs. A noneconomist reading the economics journals is struck mainly by what is left out. The literature of standard economics recalls Tom Stoppard's *Rosencrantz and Guildenstern Are Dead*. Minor subjects have usurped center stage, while the truly important ones remain tantalizingly out of view.

One could imagine a wholly different sort of economics, which empirically investigated when the assumptions of the standard model apply and when they do not. How do technological and institutional changes influence economic growth? What institutional circumstances merit public intervention? What are the links between economic performance and cultural and political values? When is the famous trade-off between equality and efficiency a genuine imperative, and when is it only a rationalization for privilege? Which markets behave like the textbook market? Under what cultural, technological, and institutional circumstances does interference with the market allocation of capital investment produce dynamic gains? What really accounts for the wide disparities in the degree of technological success achieved by different nations in different historical eras? What practical costs and what benefits to dynamic efficiency do different forms of redistribution incur? What really motivates human behavior, and under what circumstances are impulses cooperative and altruistic as well as self-interested?

Adam Smith wrote, in a famous passage celebrating economic egoism, "It is not from the benevolence of the butcher, the brewer, or the baker that we expect our dinner, but from their regard to their own interest." But are there any circumstances under which cooperation is more "efficient" than the pursuit of self-interest? If so, what are they? Why are some labor unions in some nations friendly to productivity and technological progress and wage restraint, while others are obstructionist and self-seeking? Which sorts of deregulation lose in stability what they gain in innovation? Maybe it is appropriate to deregulate airline routes but not aircraft safety. Maybe trusting market discipline to deal with bank failures produces a loss to institutional stability that outweighs the gain to allocational efficiency. These subjects are seldom treated in the economics journals, except at impenetrable levels of abstraction and assumption.

To the extent that observation challenges theory, real empiricism becomes a thorn in the side of the deductive method. Richard Freeman and James Medoff, economists at Harvard, have assembled data indicating that the actual influence of trade unions on productivity depends on institutional particulars. Some unions, by providing workers a voice and a fair grievance procedure, apparently improve output. Others depress it. Getting down to cases suggests that orthodox theory has ignored the crucial variables of worker motivation and labor-management interaction. The most common dismissal of work like Freeman and Medoff's is "That's very interesting—but it isn't economics."

The puzzle of persistent episodic unemployment opens another revealing window on the way orthodoxy deals with evidence that does not fit the standard paradigm. The market for labor is the largest and most important market in the economy: about three quarters of all costs are ultimately wage costs. But this market chronically fails to clear—that is, it fails to equilibrate changes in supply and demand with marginal adjustments in price. Some workers remain arguably overpaid, while others have no jobs. In theory, if the market paid workers exactly their "worth," there would be enough work to go around, and no unemployment. But that does not happen. And it does not help to attribute unemployment to the distortions introduced by governments and unions, because business cycles were around long before trade unions or big-spending governments were.

If labor markets do not clear, something is fundamentally wrong with the classical paradigm of perfect competition. Keynes devised a plausible explanation for boom and bust—the tendency of aggregate demand to fluctuate—but he never produced one for what economists like to call the "stickiness" of wages: that is, their tendency not to fall with rising unemployment.

During the past decade an anti-Keynesian school, the rational-expectations school, has proposed a radically classical explanation of the sticky-wage puzzle:

involuntary unemployment is an illusion. Rational-expectations economists, such as Robert E. Lucas, Jr. of the University of Chicago and Thomas Sargent of the University of Minnesota, argue that economic man acts rationally but sometimes suffers misperceptions. Thus, unemployment is caused by the misperception that if you quit your job you will find a better one elsewhere, or by the refusal of workers conditioned to accepting high wages to take more realistic ones. A related theory is that unemployment is nothing more than the search for better jobs. This analysis is not implausible—high-wage workers often do refuse to take available low-wage jobs—but it does not fully explain the failure of wages to adjust or the cyclical variations in unemployment.

To borrow an observation of Lester Thurow's, the Great Depression was not just a decade of worker misperceptions about job opportunities. Few workers refused to take lower-wage jobs; many of the unemployed were desperate for any job. And the full-employment experience of the Second World War was the result not of sudden clarity in perceptions but of large-scale government spending. Real wages *rose* sharply during the war, and so did employment. The basic Keynesian view may not explain sticky wages, but it convincingly explains periodic unemployment.

Another recent line of analysis has begun to get at why labor markets fail to clear. Interestingly, this approach is more sociological than economic. A number of labor economists have observed that it is rational for a firm to pay its employees more than a market-clearing wage, for reasons of stability and motivation. A slight wage premium engenders loyalty and effort; it produces a more stable, more productive work force; it decreases turnover and reduces training costs. Other violations of the axiom of pay based on marginal productivity, such as seniority, make for a more secure and hence more cooperative work force. Digital Equipment Corporation and some other firms have a practice of never laying off workers; this incurs short-run costs, but these are compensated for by high morale.

Moreover, if employers paid their workers a narrowly market-clearing wage, wages would have to rise and fall almost daily. Unemployed people would regularly show up at factory gates to underbid the wages of the employed. No journeyman worker would ever train an apprentice, lest the apprentice underbid him for a job. In theory older workers are paid more than younger ones because they are more productive. But in practice productivity peaks early in midlife; older workers are often slower and less adept. They are paid better for the sake of the workplace as a social system and our conventions of fairness, not because they have higher marginal productivity. In short, it is not *homo economicus* who finds it efficient to pay salaries above a market-clearing wage but *homo sociologus*.

The standard economic literature also produces little useful insight into the sources of technological innovation and dynamic gain, because that is not how the problems are posed. According to the prevailing definition, economics is the study of the allocation of scarce resources: how free markets steer resources to their optimal use. But, to take a historical example, economic resources in the United States on the eve of the Second World War were lying fallow, because unemployment was high, purchasing power was depressed, and firms—already experiencing a lack of customers and substantial excess capacity—were (rationally) failing to invest capital. Along came the war, causing the government to raise taxes, to increase public borrowing, and abruptly to invest about a third of the gross national product in war production. The result was a drop in unemployment from 15 percent to 2 percent, a growth rate that averaged 11 percent a year throughout the war, the development of new advanced technologies (many with postwar civilian applications), and the training of a generation of skilled industrial workers. By 1944 the war had so revived the slack economy that civilian disposable income exceeded 1940 levels, notwithstanding the vast outlays of money devoted to military purposes. Surely there is in this experience a pattern of dynamic gain worth investigation.

Seemingly, the Second World War would be a laboratory case of the effects of deflecting a market economy from its true path with substantial planning and government control of investment, to say nothing of wage and price controls. Yet professional economists have not paid much attention to the war years. On the contrary, in practice econometric modeling often discounts the war experience because it tends to curdle the equations.

Orthodox economics has little appreciation for dynamic growth of the entrepreneurial, Schumpeterian variety, either. One finds extensive abstract debate in the scholarly literature about production functions, capital reswitching, labor productivity, and capital-output ratios but precious little concrete information about the rapid development of aircraft technology after the Second World War or the engineering advances and marketing strategies with which the Japanese machine-tool industry overtook its American counterpart.

In this last case economics knows only that Japanese economic planning did not help, because it could not have, a priori. Professor Paul Krugman of MIT, formerly the specialist on international trade for the Reagan Council of Economic Advisers, disposes of Japanese planning by the usual deductive method: ''By the early 1960s the Japanese steel industry would have had a competitive advantage over the U.S. industry even if the Japanese government had kept hands off. The same technological 'book of blueprints' was available to both countries, access to raw materials was no longer a crucial factor, and labor costs were much higher in the U.S. Capital was becoming steadily more available in Japan, thanks to a high savings rate. Quite independent of industrial targeting, Japan was gaining a comparative advantage in steel, while the U.S. was losing one.'' But did Japanese planning, *empirically*, make any difference? It must have made some difference. Does the Japanese government's coordinating role in the social system enhance Japan's dynamic efficiency and growth? Does Japan perhaps have a comparative advantage in, of all things, planning? That question is inadmissible.

As Thomas Kuhn observed in *The Structure of Scientific Revolutions*, scholarly conflict is always most intense along the boundaries of an established scientific paradigm challenged by anomalous observations. The "overthrow" of a scientific paradigm, Kuhn said, is much like a political revolution, which aims "to change political institutions in ways that those institutions themselves prohibit." The mistrust of empiricism in economics is a sure sign of an insecure regime.

Lately, a mood of self-doubt has even crept into the economics journals. In a wonderfully rich recent article in the *Journal of Economic Literature*, titled "The Rhetoric of Economics," Donald McCloskey of the University of Iowa wrote that economics is adrift in metaphors that have no application to empirical reality but are taken literally because they happen to be in the language of mathematics: "To say that markets can be represented by supply and demand 'curves' is no less a metaphor than to say that the west wind is 'the breath of autumn's being.' . . . Each step in economic reasoning, even the reasoning of the official rhetoric, is metaphor. The world is said to be 'like' a complex model, and its measurements are said to be like the easily measured proxy variable to hand."

Quoting the literary critic I. A. Richards, McCloskey defined a metaphor as "a transaction between contexts." Modern economics is in many respects metaphor run wild: it not only stylizes and misstates what occurs in narrowly economic realms but also extends its theory of the rational, utility-maximizing *homo economicus* to areas of life in which values other than material maximization plainly apply, and about which it has no data. An example is economic theories of the family that consider children to be material goods. McCloskey added:

> Metaphors, further, evoke attitudes that are better kept in the open and under the control of reasoning. . . . the invisible hand is so very discrete, so soothing, that we might be inclined to accept its touch without protest. . . . The metaphors of economics convey the authority of Science, and often convey, too, its claims to ethical neutrality. . . . "Marginal Productivity" is a fine, round phrase, a precise mathematical metaphor that encapsulates a most powerful piece of social description. Yet it brings with it an air of having solved the moral problem of distribution facing a society in which people cooperate to produce things together instead of producing things alone.

The study of who gets what and why, unlike the study of plants or planets, cannot help being an ideologically charged undertaking. Despite the laborious techniques and scientific pretensions, most brands of economics are covertly ideological. Marxian economics, with its labor theory of value, assumes the inevitability of class conflict, and hence the necessity of class struggle. Keynesianism, with its conviction that industrial capitalism is systemically unstable, offers an equally "scientific" rationale for government intervention. Neoclassical economics, with its reliance on the efficiency of markets, is a lavishly embroidered brief for laissez-faire.

There is certainly congruence between the current political swing back toward laissez-faire policies and the intellectual swing toward an idealized free market purged of institutional complications. But the model-building in economics is more than an apologia for the market, and the criticism of it is not limited to liberals.

Professor Israel Kirzner, a Neo-Austrian, writes, in an observation that might have come from a Neo-Keynesian, that the equilibrium model of competition is "obviously . . . unrealistic, and unhelpful in understanding markets," but "instead of dismantling the elaborate equilibrium models of which Neoclassical economics consists—and appreciating the subtle processes of spontaneous learning made possible by market interaction under imperfect knowledge, the new work seeks to address the problems by constructing even more complicated equilibrium models."

Professor Joseph L. Bower, a practitioner of the famous case method of the Harvard Business School, has called the Neoclassical model "wildly unrealistic," writing that the standard economic "theory of the firm, so called, is in fact elegantly developed surmise. The literature of the field has something of the character of a chain letter. The journal articles relate well enough to each other; it is only the reality that is difficult."

Today there are two quite opposite trends in economics. One is centrifugal; there is a flowering of epistemological doubt. There are anguished essays like McCloskey's in the *Journal of Economic Literature* (which, though published by the AEA, has served as a tolerant outlet for heretics) and even an occasional one in *The American Economic Review* itself. And there are those presidential addresses at AEA conventions. At the same time, there is a strong centripetal impulse. Economics *as practiced* is unchanged, and the resistance to real diversity within faculty ranks and classroom curricula is fiercer than ever. The debates are for the college of cardinals, not for the parish flock.

A generation ago economics was far more committed to observation, disputation, and its own intellectual history. The lions of the midcentury had lived through depression and war, had watched real economic institutions totter, had worked in economic agencies, and had appreciated the power of wartime statecraft. Most of them are now gone. In the 1920s and 1930s an eclectic school of economics known as Institutionalism flourished. Inspired by Veblen, Institutionalists were committed to the empirical study of corporations, banks, labor unions, and so on as concrete social organizations. Ironically, they were displaced partly by econometricians, who promised a more rigorous empiricism. Institutionalists still exist; they have their own professional guild, the Association for Evolutionary Economics (after a word favored by Veblen, who argued that economic institutions evolve). They still have strongholds in economics departments at state universities in the South and Midwest. But few Institutionalists are to be found at the fifteen or twenty elite graduate schools that turn out tenured faculty for one another. The very term has become a pejorative.

The other two main schools that today compete with Neoclassicism—Neo-

Marxism and Post-Keynesianism—are intellectually lively but effectively isolated from mainstream economics. The Neo-Marxists have their own professional association, the Union for Radical Political Economics, and have strongholds in a few graduate departments, but they hold, by my count, only four or five tenured positions at the elite universities, have only token access to the major journals, and receive little research funding. Ten years ago the Harvard economics department created a furor when it refused to grant tenure to the leading young Neo-Marxist Samuel Bowles, even though the appointment had the support of such senior luminaries as John Kenneth Galbraith, Leontief, and Kenneth Arrow. Bowles decamped to the University of Massachusetts at Amherst, where he and colleagues have built one of three major graduate departments offering Neo-Marxist curricula. Another of the three, the University of California at Riverside, recently had its graduate program threatened with elimination, though the program is now expected to survive in truncated form. Harvard's sole tenured radical economist, Steven Marglin, was far more orthodox at the time he was granted tenure.

Neo-Marxists study what mainstream economics overlooks: the organization of production, the influence of technology on work, the impact of the globalization of finance. A "social conflict" model of productivity slowdown by Samuel Bowles and colleagues was sufficiently plausible when rendered econometrically that it was accepted for publication in the *Brookings Papers on Economic Activity*. However, Marxism is at once a mode of scholarly inquiry and a revolutionary ideology. In America any form of Marxism is hopelessly distant from the political mainstream. Moreover, although economists have the distinction, rare among scholars, of influencing policy, few American policy makers will look for advice to economists who call themselves Marxist. Neo-Marxism is thus precluded from serving as a convincing alternative to the dominant Neoclassical school.

The third dissenting school, the Post-Keynesian, is the weakest and apparently the most despised of all. The Post-Keynesians want to rescue Keynes from the Neoclassical synthesis—which Keynes's disciple Joan Robinson has called "bastard Keynesianism." They, along with the Institutionalists, insist that large corporations and labor unions are major facts of economic life and that economic intercourse cannot be modeled as mechanical transactions in equilibrium. But Neoclassical economists are mostly contemptuous of the Post-Keynesians. A few Marxists, apparently, can be tolerated. But those claiming to be the true heirs of Keynes are regarded as economic Anabaptists, a historically curious theological mistake that will not go away. Even at Rutgers University, which is tolerant of Post-Keynesianism, the two tenured Post-Keynesians are not permitted to teach the basic courses on economic theory; they are treated as oddities whom career-minded graduate students would do well to avoid.

At its 1982 convention the AEA sponsored a session on Post-Keynesianism—and invited no Post-Keynesian panelists. The National Science Foundation, which awards about nine million dollars a year for economic research, has told

Post-Keynesian applicants that the economics division is interested primarily in mainstream research. The one well-entrenched center of dissenting research in the spirit of Keynes, the Cambridge Economic Policy Group, in England, has lost all of its British government funding.

In the interstices between the schools are a handful of brilliant eclectics—an older generation, including Galbraith, Leontief, Albert Hirschman, and Herbert Simon, and a few people in their thirties and forties like Lester Thurow, James Medoff, Richard Freeman, George Akerlof of Berkeley, and Michael Piore of MIT. Piore's recent book, *The Second Industrial Divide*, which he wrote with the political economist Charles Sabel, painstakingly reexamines technological innovation throughout history and concludes that the present macroeconomic woes are due in part to unsettling changes in the organization of corporations, financial systems, technologies, and consumer markets. This sort of insight depends on the concrete study of institutions.

The difficulty is that eclecticism, no matter how brilliant, does not add up to a contending school. The great idiosyncratic economists of the last generation, like Galbraith and Simon, disseminated their work to a broad audience but left few spores within the profession. In recent years the fields of inquiry that deal with applied economics have been driven from the standard curriculum. Thirty years ago an economics student took courses in money and banking, labor economics, economic history, and perhaps industrial organization, economic development, and international trade. All of these courses grounded the grand theory in a sense of how actual economic institutions operate. Today these are considered remnants of an older, not quite scientific tradition. A student looking for the fast track to a tenured position at a prestigious university tends to avoid them.

Most economists accord scholars who are trained in other disciplines but who investigate economic phenomena all the respect that M.D.s show for chiropractors. At a Federal Reserve Board conference last year on the merits of industrial policy, the work of Robert Reich, the author of *The Next American Frontier*, came up. Reich teaches public policy and was trained as a lawyer. One prominent economist, late of the Council of Economic Advisers senior staff, dismissed Reich thus: "He doesn't even believe in general equilibrium!"

The economic historian Robert Heilbroner titled his book on the history of economic thought *The Worldly Philosophers*. As a description of the moral philosophers of the Enlightenment who abandoned metaphysics for the investigation of commercial life, the phrase fit perfectly. As a description of today's economists, however, Heilbroner's title would be a misnomer. Economists have become the least worldly of social scientists. At a time when the other social sciences—sociology, psychology, political science, history—are letting many flowers bloom and many schools contend, only economics has such fear of dissension. "There is a profound weakness at the core of Neoclassical economics," Heilbroner says. "It can't answer the most basic questions. What is a price? What is money? What killed full employment? What is the boundary between economics and politics, or society? It has become like medieval theology. Before economics can progress, it must abandon its suicidal formalism.''

Yet mainstream economics is doing nothing of the kind. Virtually all of the heretics I have talked to agree that if they were young assistant professors attempting to practice their brand of economics today, they would not get tenure. The most frequently repeated insight of Thomas Kuhn's is that a paradigm cannot be displaced by evidence, only by another paradigm. And no dissenting paradigm seems able to gain a foothold within economics. Thus the economic orthodoxy is reinforced by ideology, by the sociology of the profession, by the politics of who gets published or promoted and whose research gets funded. In the economics profession the free marketplace of ideas is one more market that does not work like the model.

The Scope and Method
of Economic Science

PHYLLIS DEANE

The methodological debate between deductive theorists and empiricists in the late nine-teenth century and J. N. Keynes's resolution of this debate is the subject of Phyllis Deane's article. She characterizes Keynes's "resolution" as more of an agreement to disagree than an agreement or compromise over the actual methodological differences.

The title I have chosen to sail under on this occasion is a deliberate echo, modified in one particular only, of the title John Neville Keynes gave to the monograph that was designed to signal the end of the methodological crisis that developed in the 1870s.[1] For there is a parallel, it seems to me, between the crisis of confidence in the central tenets of their discipline that afflicted the intellectual community of economists a century ago and the current disarray on questions of economic method. Then, as now, economists seemed to feel that the glaring lack of consensus on fundamental principles compromised the scientific status of their discipline, and there were strong professional and public pressures to establish a new orthodoxy that could speak authoritatively on economic matters. The interesting question is how far did our predecessors succeed in reconciling their deep methodological differences and how far did they merely stop quarrelling about them?

A hundred years ago it was classical political economy that was under fire from a variety of directions. Nineteenth-century social reformers confronting the policy problems of an industrializing society were repelled by what they saw as its doctrinaire adherence to the principles of laissez-faire, its arid detachment from all ethical issues, and its narrow focus on a mythical economic man. Conservatives were uncomfortable with the stark conflicts of interest between capital and labor which the socialists were able to infer from Ricardo's theory of income distribution. Academic economists found their authority as teachers undermined, and undergraduates lacked confidence in the discipline of political economy, when its leading theorists differed on matters of principle. But it was not until 1869, when the most prestigious social scientist of his generation, John

Phyllis Deane, "The Scope and Method of Economic Science," *The Economic Journal* 93, 369 (March 1983), pp. 1–12. The essay was presented as the presidential address to the Royal Economic Society, July 21, 1982.

Stuart Mill, publicly recanted the Ricardian wage-fund doctrine, that the façade of orthodox classical political economy cracked wide open.

The substantive issue in question was whether trade unions could actually influence the level of real wages or whether that was predetermined by the capital funds available for investment. The central economic theory at stake was the cost of production theory of value on which the whole system of classical ideas seemed to rest. Mill's well-known assertion—"Happily there is nothing in the laws of value which remains for the present or any future writer to clear up; the theory of the subject is complete"[2]—still stood, unrevised, in the 1871 edition of his *Principles* after the ground had evidently been cut from under it. The "last of the classical economists," J. E. Cairnes, did not have Mill's magisterial authority, and his attempts to shore up what he himself described as "the present vacillating and unsatisfactory condition of the science in respect of fundamental principles"[3] were unconvincing in the face of the forceful arguments of those who insisted that if political economy were to qualify for scientific status it needed to acquire a more convincing method of inquiry.

In the methodological debates of the 1870s and 1880s the polar extremes were represented by the historicists on the one hand and the mathematical school on the other. The historical school had already established for themselves a distinguished academic reputation in Germany and spoke from the vantage of a respectable empirical research program. Their contempt for the characteristic deductive technique of Ricardian theorizing gathered conviction when the world trade boom of the 1850s and 1860s ran out of steam and the midcentury moves toward freer international trade lost momentum everywhere but in Britain. Confidence in what critics of classical political economy called "hypothetical science" depended on the manifest success of its predictions, and when the mid-Victorian boom turned into the Great Depression the introspectively based postulates of armchair economics lost much of their credibility. Meanwhile, current views of the Baconian inductive procedures that were supposed to characterize all the natural sciences[4] provided a justification for the empirical bias of the historicists.

At the other methodological extreme the abstract theorists succeeded in capturing the imagination of a rising generation of economists with the aid of an analytical tool based on the calculus. The marginal technique of analysis could be used to reconstruct the weakest link in the classical theoretical system—the cost of production theory of value—without denting the hard core of orthodox classical doctrine. It was a particularly attractive development for economists who had ambitions to mimic the methods of the natural sciences for three sorts of reasons: first, because the most progressive natural sciences were obviously benefitting from mathematical tools of analysis; second, because retention of the hard-core doctrine of the self-regulating economic system under competitive conditions implied the continuity of classical and Neoclassical economics and made it easier to believe in the cumulative advance of economic theory; and third, because the independent application of the marginal technique in three separate geographical locations in the early 1870s[5] gave the intellectual community of economists a sense of international consensus that is rare for social scientists.

Arguments about fundamental principles tend to acquire the bitter and divisive qualities of theological disputes, and the methodological divisions of the 1870s were no exception. Jevens's angry reaction against the "noxious influence of authority" and the "monotonous repetition of current questionable doctrines" is well known.[6] The historical economists condemned the hypothetico-deductive method of the classical economists as being hostile to empirical research, irresponsibly speculative, and, most wounding of all, ideologically biased. In effect, the classical economists were accused of devising amoral (if not immoral) theories involving implicit presumptions in favor of a laissez-faire stance in economic policy at a time when ethical considerations demanded a program of legislation to protect the underprivileged sectors of the economy. Then, as now, ideological preconceptions concerning the appropriate agenda for government economic policy were often the key to an economist's choice of sides in the methodological debate.

This was the background against which J. Neville Keynes began his attempt to clarify the scope and method of political economy roughly a century ago. He wrote essentially for undergraduates confused by the tendentious arguments of leading economists quarrelling about the basic nature and validity of economic knowledge. Neville Keynes's main strength as a teacher of political economy was a clear, logical mind and a capacity to detach himself from the partisan passions aroused by the current methodological debates. He had already published a successful undergraduate textbook on formal logic,[7] and his *Scope and Method* grew, as so many textbooks do, out of a course of lectures.[8] When he announced to his friend and contemporary, J. S. Nicholson, that he proposed to develop the lectures into a book, the latter (as reported by Keynes in his diary) said scornfully that "anyone could write such a book as that. He says he is sick of disquisitions on method and that what we want is useful *applications* of the right method."[9]

As it happened, however, the time was ripe for a book of the kind Keynes contemplated. For the marginal techniques of analysis were steadily gaining international acceptance, the economic historians were producing impressive research results of obvious relevance to applied economics,[10] and Marshall was already writing what was to be the bible of a new economic orthodoxy, Neoclassical economics. Evidently there was more than one progressive research program on the march, and a new generation of economists was persuaded that important advances were taking place in economic knowledge.

In the event, Keynes's *Scope and Method* and Marshall's *Principles of Economics* proceeded side by side, with each author systematically reading and criticizing the other's chapter drafts or proofs. They were published within half a year of each other, Marshall's *Principles* in mid–1890 and Keynes's book in January 1891. The latter was accepted by a majority of reviewers as being the definitive methodological text for the new political economy (in Britain identified with Marshall's *Principles*), and as ending the long and tedious *Methodenstreit*. Edgeworth, for example, who reviewed it twice (in *Nature* and in *The Economic Journal*) said in *Nature* "on a subject which it is undesirable to be always re-opening it may be hoped that Mr. Keynes's work will prove final."[11] James Bonar, reviewing it in *The Academy*, said (in a passage Keynes was proud to transcribe into his diary): "In a sense it is true that his book simply sums up the views about scope and method which have in the last twenty years been gradually taking shape in the minds of English and American economists under the influence of Jevons, Marshall, and Walker."[12] Nor was it only English-speaking economists who were already adopting deliberately noncontroversial views on scope and method. Similar ideas were appearing in the methodological pro-nouncements of leading continental writers such as Cossa in Italy or Wagner in Germany or Böhm-Bawerk in Austria.[13] Suddenly, it would appear, there was a consensus on the methodology of economics.

At the heart of the consensus was a determination to reestablish the scientific credentials of a discipline that had been publicly discredited by internal dissen-sion on fundamental principles. The scientific validity of the "new political economy" was accordingly justified along three main lines: (1) by tracing its continuity with classical political economy, so as to establish the cumulative quality of progress in economic knowledge; (2) by accepting that the inductive-empirical researches of the historical school and the deductive-analytical re-searches of the mathematical school had complementary roles to play in further-ing economic knowledge; and (3) by insisting that the basic postulates of the discipline were value free, that they were objectively given by the industrial and organizational conditions of modern society to which the resulting economic analysis was intended to be applied.

The first route involved a blurring of the methodological differences between the old and the new political economy and a systematic interpretation of radical changes in economic theory as being evolutionary rather than revolutionary. It was an interpretation that sat easily in the intellectual environment of the second half of the nineteenth century, buzzing with Darwinian or Spencerian ideas of natural selection, social evolution, and unity of the sciences.

The second route involved recognition of different types of economic inquiry and turned away from the narrow-minded intolerance inherent in the *Methoden-streit*. Neville Keynes, for example, distinguished between three kinds of eco-nomics, a positive science, a normative or regulative science, and an art. "The object of a positive science is the establishment of *uniformities*, of a normative science the determinants of *ideals*, of an art the formulation of *precepts*.[14] Adolf Wagner, writing from a different tradition, envisaged a division of labor between economists:

Nothing is, in my opinion, more harmful for the true advance of a branch of knowledge than that a given tendency in it, which happens to fit the abilities, the turn of mind, the training of individual scholars, which may indeed be fruitful and necessary, is carried so far as to demand for itself an exclusive control and to pretend that in it is the only true science. . . . The result is that a valuable line of thought, first entered on by great leaders, continues to be followed mechanically by a set of commonplace imitator—men it may be, of high technical training and the more arrogant for that. . . . The truth is that there are minds that tend to deductive reasoning, to systematic exposition, to generalizing and dogmatizing; there are other minds of a more ''historical'' bent that turn to induction, to historical and statistical investigation. . . . Each tendency has its strengths and weaknesses, its merits and defects.[15]

The third route to consensus involved denying that the classical assumption of perfect competition and the associated bias toward laissez-faire policy prescriptions were essential features of the more general, positive, kind of economic theorizing that was rising on the shoulders of the old orthodoxy. Thus Neville Keynes defended the traditional postulates on two ostensibly objective grounds: first, in relation to perfect competition, because ''it is best to take the simplest case first''; and second, because ''in modern economic societies laissez-faire has been as a matter of fact the general rule.'' But as ''a maxim of conduct'' he dismissed laissez-faire as being irrelevant to the pure economics that he equated with positive economic science and relegated it to the art of political economy.[16] Marshall, who seems to have been more sensitive than Keynes to the charges of ideological bias that were often levelled against economists, was prepared to go still further, both in disowning the convenient concept of the economic man and in throwing overboard the utilitarian heritage. The account of his speech seconding the vote of thanks for Goschen's presidential address to the Royal Economic Society reported Marshall's assertion that ''the economists of today dispensed with the economic man altogether'' and also that classical political economy was ''wholly independent of the utilitarian doctrine: it was, when rightly understood, common property to all ethical creeds.''[17]

In effect, then, the academics who embraced the ''new political economy'' of the late nineteenth century justified their claims for the scientific status of their discipline by distinguishing an abstract deductive core of ''pure'' economics aimed at explaining the logic of economic behavior in the market place without prejudice from its ethical or political implications. Accusations that political economy was speculative or unethical or biased toward the preservation of a particular economic system could be brushed aside from the objective core of economic *science* on the grounds that questions of empirical validity or distributional justice or policy desiderata simply did not arise at the theoretical level. They could be relevant only within the more flexible periphery of applied economics.

Acceptance of the idea that there was a central core of continuously evolving economic theory, insulated from irreconcilable conflicts between ethical or political value systems, represented a victory for the theorists over the antitheorists, the historicists. For although the leading theorists acknowledged the necessity for increased research in applied economics, they left little doubt that progress in economic science (as opposed to political economy) could take place only at the theoretical core where they focused most of their own research efforts.

Walras, for example, had originally set himself a research program that involved the writing of three volumes of basic economic principles—the first on pure economics, the second on applied economics "or the theory of Agricultural, Industrial, and Commercial Production of Wealth," and the third on social economics "or the Theory of the Distribution of Wealth via Property and Taxation."[18] The first book came out in two installments in 1874 and 1877, and he spent most of the rest of his life improving on it. The research projects that were to have underpinned the second and third books were never developed, though he published two books of essays under these titles. Similarly Marshall, who spoke strongly in favor of applied economics and put a great deal of historical and empirical material into the first edition of his *Principles*, went on steadily shifting the balance toward pure theory in each successive edition of this his major work.[19]

The effect of thus lifting the central body of economic theory out of the arena of ethical and political debate was twofold. It narrowed the scope of the theoretical core of the economists' research program so that it was largely reducible to a theory of exchange under competitive conditions; and at the same time it took the passion and the point out of the debates on method that had characterized the 1870s and 1880s. It did not eliminate all methodological differences: for example the debate on whether pure economics should become an essentially mathematical science continued. But such arguments were more decorously conducted in correspondence between individual economists or in the pages of the learned journals. They did not shake the foundations of the discipline. Indeed, the fact that leading theorists such as Marshall openly downgraded the role of mathematics enabled the largely innumerate rank and file of professional economists to retain a sense of confidence in their own scientific contribution.

There remained, of course, an "awkward squad," mainly composed of economic historians, which was not able to accept the terms of the consensus and persisted in raising questions of scope and method which the new school of economic science did not wish to know about. In particular, the economic historians continued to balk at the idea that abstract economic theory, or "pure economics" as it was commonly labelled, was the sole source of the discipline's scientific progress. Leaving aside the traditional historians such as Archdeacon Cunningham, for whom the study of economic history was a branch of political history, and who had little interest in, or understanding of, either classical or Neoclassical political economy,[20] there was emerging a new breed of economic historians, such as Thorold Rogers or William Ashley, for whom the study of economic history was a branch of applied economics. The new economist-historians had their own followings in the academic community of economists and were as capable of assessing the strengths and weaknesses of the new political economy as the innovating theorists themselves. Ashley, for example, in a careful exegesis of Ricardo's labor theory of value, provoked by the first edition of Marshall's *Principles*, effectively demonstrated the distortions involved in the latter's attempt to establish a classical pedigree for the marginal revolution.[21]

Some sixteen years later in his presidential address to Section F of the British Association, Ashley reviewed the international revolution in economic ideas that had taken place over the previous two decades and sharply criticized the oversimplifications and the limitations of the marginal analysis. "Instead of leading us to the very heart of the problem—the doctrine of marginal value seems to me to remain entirely on the surface: it is not much more than a verbal description of the superficial facts at a particular point of time."[22] He also pointed out that the consensus was only skin-deep, being limited to a common belief in the value of abstract, general reasoning "and the common employment of a few specialist terms. . . . So long as the student keeps to a particular set of writings, he may cherish the impression of a triumphant analysis, solving all difficulties for intelligent men in the same way; when he extends his reading, he will find that there are at least three main groups, following respectively the lead of Cambridge, of Vienna, and of New York; while among the younger men there are all sorts of ingenious but mutually irreconcilable attempts at eclectic compromise."[23]

Nevertheless, economists who were prepared to narrow the scope of their "science" to some aspect of the theory of markets operating under perfect competition, were able to convince themselves that they were engaged in a progressive research program, for which the Neoclassical orthodoxy supplied the necessary paradigm.

Those whose inquiries took them in directions where the theory of money was relevant found (then as now) that they had no such disciplinary consensus from which to begin. [. . .]

None of these doubts, however, was allowed to threaten the analytical core of "pure economics," and for several decades the dominant belief inspiring the intellectual community of economists was that they shared a common nucleus of views in the scope and method of economic *science*. They could go on teaching successive generations of undergraduates from the same, or similar, textbooks of economic theory and could assume that, whatever the intractability of the problems posed in the applied areas of their discipline, they were building on virtually impregnable analytical foundations. There *were* methodological differences between theorists, but they could be regarded as differences of degree rather than of substance; and they could be subsumed in the narrower or broader conceptions of the *scope* of the discipline adopted by different theorists.[24]

The reason why the economic historians found it impossible to observe the truce on scope and method was that they started from the belief that economic theory should illuminate the study of history, and they were dismayed therefore

by the gap that seemed to be widening between theoretical and applied economics. So in 1922 Clapham tried to confront the leading theorists on their own
ground with his article on "empty economic boxes."[25] The main burden of his
argument was that the strategic concepts of economic theory were empty of
relevance to the real world; that even Marshall and Pigou could make little
practical use of the abstract items of "mental furniture" on which the contemporary consensus in economic theory rested. "I think a great deal of harm has been
done," he complained, "through omission to make clear that the Laws of Returns have never been attached to specific industries; that we do not, for instance,
at this moment *know* under what conditions of returns coal or boots are being
produced."[26]

Pigou wrote a suitably crushing reply in the next issue of *The Economic
Journal*.[27] He began by distinguishing two sorts of knowledge: "pure" knowledge such as is sought in mathematics and logic; and realistic knowledge concerned with subject-matter presumed to be central, such as is sought by physi-
cists. "Within the second sort of knowledge must be further distinguished
knowledge that cannot and knowledge that can give us direct help in the practical
conduct of affairs. This second distinction seems to be somewhat blurred in Dr.
Clapham's mind."[28] The gap was maintained then between pure and applied
economics, and a further ditch was dug between applied economic research
which could not be justified in terms of its applicability to practical policy
problems (of which research in economic history was a telling example) and a
vaguely defined but evidently limited area of directly useful knowledge. Pigou
concluded by pouring scorn on the idea that economic theory was useless because
its concepts could not clearly be related to the real world: "It is as though Dr.
Clapham, in choosing between two suits of clothes (he will forgive the horrible
suggestion that he might buy such things ready-made) should refuse to inquire
which of them will fit him best, because there is another consideration also
relevant to his choice, namely the amount of money that they respectively
cost."[29] In short, Clapham was firmly put down for being confused and naive and
above all for wasting time in quarrelling about methodological issues that he did
not properly understand.[30]

Still, Clapham did make it into *The Economic Journal*, and he did rate a reply
from high authority. Other critics of orthodox economic theory found it hard to
attract any sort of response. I have found no evidence, for example, that Ashley's
lecture on Evolutionary Economics, written in 1923 for the Birkbeck College
Centenary, drew any response from the theorists though it argued more systematically than Clapham, and in terms that now seem persuasive, for "new theoretical ways of looking at things."[31] Ashley's argument was that insofar as economics could lay claim to being a scientific body of knowledge, its validity depended
on its capacity to adjust its assumptions, concepts, and analytical apparatus to
changes in the institutional and organizational context of industrial and commer-

cial behavior; and he listed a number of obvious ways in which the existing corpus of economic theory was plainly out of date. Of these the most important was in its clinging to the assumption that competition was the "normal" state of affairs in an industrial world where "it is almost as true to say that our condition is one of various degrees of combination checked by competition as to describe it as one of various degrees of competition checked by combination."[32] But, persuasive or not, it was easy to ignore such criticisms of established economic science when they were being levelled by those whose researches were confined to the fringe areas such as economic history or the "art" of political economy.

In Britain, the pure theoretical research tradition continued to dominate through the 1920s and the early 1930s while resisting externally generated winds of change.[33] The demonstration by Piero Sraffa that there were logical inconsistencies in the laws of returns[34] had more effect than the applied economists' complaints of unrealism in stimulating the search for new models based on the assumption of imperfect competition; and it was not until Maynard Keynes published his *General Theory* that the central assumption of the self-regulating market economy came under direct fire again. This time it was not too easy to paper over the methodological divisions that resurfaced. True there was a golden decade or so of superficial harmony when Keynesian macroeconomic theory and Neoclassical microeconomic theory inhabited separate compartments of the post-World War II textbooks, and while the growing army of professional economists in the service of national governments and international agencies was given credit for a prolonged postwar boom. When stagflation reared its ugly head, however, bringing with it a nasty mixture of high unemployment and high inflation for which neither Keynesian nor Neoclassical theory had a plausible explanation, a new crisis of confidence developed. The methodological debates flared up again, and economists began to reconsider the terms on which their discipline could lay claim to scientific status. The fact that the philosophers of science have also been reconsidering the demarcation lines between science and nonscience, and the nature of scientific progress generally, has added new dimensions to these debates.

This background noise of dissent dividing the leaders of the discipline on fundamental issues does not constitute a comfortable working environment for the would-be *normal* practitioners, and there is no lack of external as well as internal pressures to encourage the search for a new consensus. The difference today, however, as compared with a hundred years ago, or even fifty years ago, is that there is now a plethora of "new theoretical ways of looking at things," and it is not going to be as easy in the 1980s as it was in the 1880s to pretend that there is a hard core of cumulative economic knowledge to which—if it is defined carefully enough—the majority of economists could confidently subscribe. Econometricians are stuffing suitably trimmed empirical data into the new economic boxes almost as fast as the theoretical innovations appear in print, though it is not obvious that the recent explosion of quantitative research in mathematical models has improved the explanatory or predictive power of the economist's "engine of thought."

In the end, however, it is the external pressures for consensus that are likely to be most potent. For economics is more vulnerable than most other sciences to the immediate practical demands of social policy. To quote one of the most distinguished of twentieth-century econometricians, Ragnar Frisch: "at the global level the goal of economic theory is to lay bare the way in which different economic factors act and interact on each other in a highly complex system, and to do this in such a way that the results may be used in practice to carry out in the most effective way, specific desiderata in the steering of the economy."[35] It is here, in its implications for policy prescriptions, that dissension among economists is most disturbing.

The lesson, it seems to me, that we should draw from the history of economic thought is that economists should resist the pressure to embrace a one-sided or restrictive consensus. There *is* no one kind of economic truth that holds the key to fruitful analysis of *all* economic problems, no pure economic theory that is immune to changes in social values or current policy problems. The scope and method of our discipline needs at all times to be defined in relation to the social problems that give purpose to it, and there is room for more than one progressive research program in operation at the same time. We ought indeed to profit from the divergent approaches of leading theorists, provided that they and their disciples avoid the kind of arrogance of which Wagner complained a century ago and are scrupulously open-minded in the conduct of the necessary debates. In any case, there is now no prospect of fudging the difficult political and ethical issues by drawing a distinction between the science of pure economics and the art of political economy. For it is evident that designing economic models for direct use in the process of policy formulation is a research activity that is as likely to suggest fruitful "new theoretical ways of looking at things" as is fundamental theoretical research of a primarily abstract nature.

If economics is a science—and it is not as clear as it used to be what *that* is—it is evidently a science whose powers of prediction and control are limited, largely because the phenomena it seeks to explain are subject to persistent change and often for reasons that may lie outside the traditional boundaries of the discipline. In these circumstances successful explanation, or prediction, must depend on the economist's willingness to renew, discard, and adapt theories, concepts, and analytical techniques and even to adjust the boundaries of the discipline. What we need is not a new orthodoxy on scope and method but a readiness to listen seriously to our colleagues who take opposing views on fundamental principles and to admit to the natural scientists, or the politicians, or the students, who are crying out for economic truth, that the right answers are unlikely to come from any pure economic dogma.

Notes

1. J. N. Keynes, *The Scope and Method of Political Economy* (1st ed., 1891; 4th ed., 1930).

2. J. S. Mill, *Collected Works*, vol. 3 (Toronto ed.), p. 456.

3. J. E. Cairnes, *The Character and Logical Method of Political Economy* (1888 ed.), p. 21.

4. It was, of course, a myth that natural sciences did not use deductive procedures.

5. W. S. Jevons, *Theory of Political Economy* (1871); Carl Menger, *Grundsätze der Volkwirtschaftslehre* (1871); and Leon Walras, *Eléments d'économie pure politique* (1874–77).

6. See, for example, the preface to the 1879 edition of his *Theory of Political Economy*: "When at length a true system of Economics comes to be established, it will be seen that that able but wrong-headed man, David Ricardo, shunted the care of Economic Science on to a wrong line, a line, however, on which it was further urged towards confusion by his equally able and wrong-headed admirer John Stuart Mill."

7. J. N. Keynes, *Studies and Exercises in Formal Logic* (1st ed., 1884; 4th ed., 1928).

8. When Marshall left Oxford in January 1885 to take up his Cambridge chair, Keynes lectured in his place (but on a subject of his own choosing) for the rest of the academic year.

9. J. N. Keynes, *Diaries*, Cambridge University Library Add. MSS. 7834, 2-6-85.

10. In the early 1880s Arnold Toynbee gave his remarkable Oxford lectures on the industrial revolution (published posthumously in 1884), Cunningham's *Growth of English Industry and Commerce* appeared in 1882, Seebohm's "English Village Community" in 1883. These were the first of a stream of exciting new works by economic historians. Most significant of all perhaps, an economic historian, Thorold Rogers, was elected to the Drummond Chair of Political Economy at Oxford in 1888.

11. Keynes reproduced this passage in his diary for February 28, 1891, Add MSS 7841. The *Economic Journal* review appeared in 1891, pp. 420–23. It was longer and more critical as befitted a professional audience but equally determined to stress the book's "finality" on the methodological issues "on which authorities appear to be substantially, if not in phrase, agreed" (p. 423).

12. J. Bonar, *The Academy*, March 7, 1891, p. 227.

13. See, e.g., L. Cossa, *Guide to the Study of Political Economy* (1880), translated by W. S. Jevons from the 2d Italian edition (1878); "Wagner on the Present State of Political Economy," *Quarterly Journal of Economics* (October 1886); and E. Böhm-Bawerk, "The Historical vs. the Deductive Method in Political Economy," in *Annals of the American Academy of Political and Social Science* (October 1890).

14. Keynes, *Scope and Method* (1930 ed.), p. 35. The distinction between political economy as an art and political economy as a science goes back to Bentham.

15. Translated by C. F. Dunbar, "Wagner on the Present State of Political Economy."

16. J. N. Keynes, op. cit., pp. 66–67.

17. *Economic Journal* (September 1893), p. 388.

18. Leon Walras, *Elements of Pure Economics or "The Theory of Social Wealth,"* trans. W. Jaffé (1954), p. 35, quoting from the preface to the 4th ed. (1900).

19. There is a significant passage, in one of his letters to Neville Keynes, on the question of the reform of the Cambridge Economics Tripos to the effect that: "Gradually I have been forced to the conclusion that unless the empirical treatment of economics is completely to oust the scientific and analytical—to which you and I are almost the only elderly middle-aged English economists who are perfectly loyal (I don't count Edgeworth

because he is so extreme) we must throw over the mischievous and untrue statement that according to the classical economists 'it was only on the assumption of free competition that their principles and technology could apply.' '' *Marshall Papers*, Marshall Library, Cambridge.

20. Cunningham was a waspish critic of Marshall but his attacks were rarely on target for he did not understand what the new political economy was all about. See, e.g., W. Cunningham, "The Perversion of Economic History," *Economic Journal* (1892), and Marshall's reply in the same volume.

21. W. J. Ashley, "The Rehabilitation of Ricardo," *Economic Journal* (1891). See, for example, the last paragraph which, after freely acknowledging that "The *Principles of Economics* . . . casts into the background almost all that has been written in England since John Stuart Mill; it sums up the economic movement of the last forty years, and furnishes the point of departure for a new and fruitful development," concluded "The economic historian, we are told, is apt to be confused in theory; I am afraid we must add that the sympathetic theorist runs the risk of being unhistorical."

22. W. J. Ashley, "The Present Position of Political Economy," *Economic Journal* (December 1907), pp. 476–77.

23. Ibid., p. 478.

24. For example, when Wicksteed, in his 1913 presidential address to Section F of the British Association, restated the essence of the marginal theory of value in Jevonian terms, which were markedly narrower than the Marshallian version, the result was simply that it led him to restrict the scope of political economy (in relation to sociology) more narrowly than mainstream Neoclassicals would have done. P. H. Wicksteed, "The Scope and Method of Political Economy in the Light of the 'Marginal' Theory of Value and Distribution," *Economic Journal* (March 1914). See, e.g., p. 785: "the so-called supply curve is simply a part of the total demand curve"; or p. 784: "the better we understand the true function of the 'market' in its widest sense, the more fully we shall realise that it never has been left to itself, and the more deeply shall we feel that it never must be. *Economics must be the handmaid of sociology*" (my italics).

25. J. H. Clapham, "Of Empty Economic Boxes," *Economic Journal* (September 1922).

26. Ibid., p. 312.

27. A. C. Pigou, "Empty Boxes: A Reply." *Economic Journal* (December 1922).

28. Ibid., p. 458.

29. Ibid., p. 464.

30. Clapham's rejoinder, also in the December 1922 *Economic Journal*, showed that he was sensitive to the rebuke "whose point is sharpened by the references to ready-made clothes and 'a certain naivete' '' but he claimed his right to raise the issue of economic method: "Mounted on the smoothly running machine which he handles with such incomparable skill Professor Pigou may be a trifle impatient of suggestions that a differently constructed model might have a longer and more useful life; but that is no reason why the suggestions should not be made, even by a much less expert driver."

31. Sir W. Ashley, "Evolutionary Economics," *Birkbeck Centenary Lectures, 1823–1923* (1924).

32. Ibid., p. 60. Among the other changes in the nineteenth-century economic environment which Ashley identified as calling for radical reconstruction of orthodox economic theory were the increasing capital intensity of industrial production (calling for new approaches to the "study of the relations between Capital and Labour," to the theory of price formation, and to the theory of saving and investment) and the dropping of the gold standard (calling for a revision of the Quantity Theory of Money as an explanation of inflation).

33. In the United States the Institutionalists' revolt against the doctrine that abstract theorizing was the main source of scientific progress in economic knowledge seems to have had more impact on economists generally than did the economic historians in Britain. No doubt this was largely due to the personal qualities of Wesley Mitchell and to the fact that he concentrated his research efforts on the most pressing economic problem of the early twentieth century—business cycles. But it probably owed a great deal also to the human and financial resources of the National Bureau of Economic Research, through which Mitchell was able to mount an impressively fruitful empirical research program.

34. P. Sraffa, "The Laws of Returns under Competitive Conditions," *Economic Journal* (December 1926).

35. R. Frisch, Nobel Prize Lecture, "From Utopian Theory to Practical Applications: The Case of Econometrics." Reprinted in *American Economic Review* (December 1981), p. 6.

The Futility of Marginal Utility

EZEKIAL H. DOWNEY

The role of utility theory is to explain consumer behavior and price determination. Downey argues that marginal utility is a seriously flawed concept which does not explain human behavior. In addition, Downey shows it does not succeed at the simpler task of explaining market prices.

Marginal-utility economics has nothing to say of the genesis, growth, or current working of economic institutions.[1] Its deliverances, accordingly, are futile for the problem of social betterment, since social betterment is a matter of the adjustment of institutions to changing circumstances and changing ideals. But the marginal-utility doctrines are likewise futile for the purposes of the limited problem to which they are applied. That problem is the explanation of market value (price) as the resultant of individual (subjective) valuations expressed in market bids and offers. To be competent such an explanation must comprise (1) a psychologically tenable analysis of the process of individual valuation, and (2) a practically useful account of the market situation through which individual valuations are conceived to eventuate in market price. The marginal-utility theory fails in both particulars. (1) It is not psychologically tenable because it is essentially and irremediably hedonistic, whereas the human mind is perversely and persistently nonhedonistic. (2) It is not practically useful because it does not offer, in any concrete case, an explanation of price, but only restates the price problem in language which is unintelligible to the layman, and which is meaningless even when understood.[2]

I

That the marginal-utility theory usually has been formulated in hedonistic terms is pointed out at length by a recent profound and sympathetic critic of that theory[3] and is, indeed, too well known to require particular citation here. It is just as little open to question that hedonism is hopelessly discredited by modern psychology.[4] The frailty of this outworn psychological doctrine as a foundation for economic theory is sufficiently patent. Yet, just because hedonism does underlie what is termed "modern" economics, a brief review of the hedonistic doctrine and of

Ezekial H. Downey, "The Futility of Marginal Utility," *The Journal of Political Economy* 18, 4 (April 1910), pp. 253–63.

some of the cardinal objections thereto may not be out of place.

The hedonism here criticized is the theory that human conduct is guided by a rationalistic calculation of self-interest in terms of "pleasure" and "pain" (pleasantness and unpleasantness).[5] To apply this hedonistic calculus to everyday economic affairs requires no small dialectical finesse, but the marginal utilitarians—to coin a not inappropriate phrase—are quite equal to the feat. Starting with the desire for wealth as the immediate motive of economic acts, these economists point out that wealth is desired because it represents command over "enjoyable (pleasure-giving) goods and services." But wealth can be acquired only at the cost of painful effort (labor and "abstinence"). So economic activity comes to be rationally directed with a view to obtaining the maximum of wealth with the minimum of effort. Seen in this light, pecuniary loss and gain are convertible with pain and pleasure. Pecuniary gain is looked upon as an intermediate object only, the ultimate object in all cases being "psychic income"—the pleasurable effects anticipated from acts of consumption.[6]

The objection to all this is its want of verisimilitude, and that in two respects. (1) It assigns too large a place to reflective choice as an element in human conduct, and (2) it misconceives the basis of choice.

1. Deliberation, reasoned choice, plays but a minor part in the affairs of men.[7] (a) Habit, not calculation, governs the greater part of all our acts. Even such calculating and choosing as we do is done only upon the basis and within the limits of habit.[8] Moreover, the habits of thought which count for most in shaping choice are not the result of prevision, but are of the nature of conventions uncritically accepted by virtue of membership in a particular group. It is these conventions, far more than rational appraisal by individuals, that determine the relative "utilities" of "consumers' goods." The "utility" of diamonds or dress suits, for example, is purely conventional. If the price of these objects depended upon serviceableness for the life-process, or even upon aesthetic appreciation, their power-in-exchange would be small indeed. They owe their market value to the convention of pecuniary emulation which gives them a high "utility" as evidences of their wearers' ability to pay. To ignore this conventional value and explain the high price of diamonds and dress suits by their "marginal utility" as objects of use and beauty[9] is to lose sight of the main factor in the case. (b) Those acts which are not merely habitual quite as often result from suggestion as from choice (comparison of ideas and selection among them). This would appear to follow as an easy corollary of the economists' postulate that we seek our ends by the easiest path (with the smallest possible effort).[10] Calculation is difficult work. It is much easier to act on a suggestion than to weigh alternatives. The path of least resistance in buying a necktie is to enter a shop where neckwear is attractively displayed and select the cravat insinuatingly recommended by the engaging salesman. To make an exhaustive canvass of shapes, colors, prices, and of alternative uses of the purchase-money is far more tedious and wearisome. Whatever be the merits of the least-resistance theory, it is, at any rate, a fact of

observation that the human mind is extremely responsive to suggestion. The effectiveness of advertising, of window displays, and of salesmanship mainly depends upon this principle. A "catchy" advertisement fixes the attention upon a single idea to the exclusion of all others. It is effective in proportion as it precludes comparison and selection. Similarly, the commercial value of such phrases as "It floats" or "There's a reason" lies in their power to produce an unreasoned conviction as to the superior merit of the commodities with which these phrases are associated. The high "marginal utility" of very many articles of commerce is created by similar devices.

What has just been said as to the influence of habit and suggestion is, of course, a recital of psychological commonplaces. The recital is important only as tending to show that a theory of valuation that places the emphasis upon rationalistic appraisal overlooks the most important features of the process it seeks to explain.

2. So far as men take thought for the future they habitually do not think in terms of anticipated feelings. It is probable, indeed, that feelings cannot be imaged: hence, that they cannot be anticipated: hence, that anticipated feeling cannot serve as a motive.[11] The sounder view appears to be that the idea (image) of the thing anticipated is *accompanied* by a feeling of pleasantness or unpleasantness. I anticipate an approaching meeting with a long-absent friend. The thought of the meeting is presented to my mind as a vivid image—the friend's appearance, voice, manner, greeting—and this image, or group of related images, is accompanied by a rush of joyous feeling. The pleasure is *felt*, not *anticipated*, at the moment of anticipating the meeting. Doubtless this concomitant pleasure strengthens my desire to see my friend, but the pleasure is the result, not the cause, of the desire.

But apart from this question of anticipated feeling, it is clear to modern psychologists that men do not "strive after happiness"[12] or "satisfaction" or any other all-inclusive object of desire, but after definite, concrete, realizable objects—a college degree, a political office, a million dollars, the control of a railway.[13]

It is these concrete objects, and not the remote reasons for desiring them, which are the effective motives of action and which, consequently, are to be appealed to for the explanation of acts so motivated. It is notorious, for example, that the accountancy employed by business men runs in terms of money, not in terms of "consumption goods" or of "psychic income." The habitual resort to the pecuniary accountancy would require to be explained in a genetic account of business enterprise, but for the study of current business traffic it is to be taken as a datum, analysis of which would be irrelevant to the problem in hand. To resolve this money accountancy into terms of anticipated "gratification," after the fashion of marginal-utility theorists, is worse than useless: it is a false explanation of, or rather an attempt to explain away, the phenomenon in question.

The foregoing brief review should serve to make it clear that the hedonistic theory of "reasonable conduct" is a psychological misconception. Few economists of the marginal-utility persuasion are notable for their acquaintance with modern psychology; yet certain disciples of even this school have latterly come to feel that the ancient standpoint no longer affords a secure basis for economic analysis. But these doubters have not thereby been led to relate their economic speculations to more tenable psychological views. Instead they (1) have sought to escape hedonistic implications by a change of phraseology without substantial change of content, or else (2) they have denied that the soundness of hedonism is essential to the validity of doctrines based on hedonistic postulates. These two lines of defense against the antihedonistic protest require separate consideration.

1. A good illustration of the pious effort to modernize an antiquated system of doctrine by slight alterations of terminology is Professor Fetter's use of the term "gratification."[14] That this word, as used by Professor Fetter, carries a hedonistic content is sufficiently apparent from the following passages: "The [rationally conceived] purpose of industry is to gratify wants."[15] "The substitution of goods in men's thought is the shifting of the choice from a good that does not give the highest gratification economically possible at the time to another good that does."[16] "Time-discount" (interest) is an "anticipation of the difference between present and future gratifications."[17] "The value of all things must be traced back to gratification, to the relation of goods with psychic income"[18]— psychic income being the flow of pleasant feelings experienced or anticipated from the act of consumption.[19]

2. Some adherents of the marginal-utility school insist that the whole issue between hedonists and antihedonists is irrelevant to value theory. Admitting that marginal utilitarians usually have been hedonists they deny that the marginal-utility doctrines stand or fall with hedonism. Those who take this position—and their number includes the chief apostle of the faith[20]—assert that economics is concerned only with the fact of choice between goods or between alternative activities, and not with the basis of choice.[21] But if this be true, all talk of "gratification," "psychic income," or the "balancing of utilities" must be thrown out of economic discussion—whereupon the whole literature of marginal utility reduces itself to a meaningless jargon. For if choices are really made between goods and not between the "utilities" represented by the goods, why talk of "utility" at all? And, if it be admitted that economic choice is more frequently the outcome of habit, suggestion, and the like than of a rationalistic weighing of alternative gratifications, the marginal-utility analysis of price loses all its significance.

That the disavowal of hedonism does deprive marginal-utility economics of its whole content may be shown by applying the expurgated theory to a single concrete case. At the town where this paper is being written, pork chops are selling for eighteen cents a pound. The most naïve explanation of this fact, in terms of the marginal-utility theory, is that some portion of the whole supply of pork chops offered for sale possesses a "utility" to the purchaser precisely equal to the "utility" of the "marginal increment" of some other good procurable for the same money outlay. Hence, if the price should rise by even a fraction of a cent, some portion of the supply would be left unsold, since the "marginal purchaser" might then procure a greater "utility" by an equal money outlay for some other commodity.[22]

All this is intelligible enough if a hedonistic content be given to "utility." To a hedonistic man "the pleasure and benefit" of a barrel of apples may be comparable with "the pleasure and benefit" of a hat or a theatrical performance.[23] Moreover, since the hedonistic man is, *ex hypothesi*, endowed with a high degree of foresight and hindsight, it may be assumed that his "marginal purchase" of pork chops in the winter exactly balances in respect of "utility" his "marginal purchase" of underclothing the preceding autumn, or of peaches the ensuing summer. For hedonistic men, accordingly, the comparison of the utility of different goods, at different times, or even to different persons, presents no insuperable difficulty.

But the case is otherwise when the theory attempts to take account of (nonhedonistic) human beings. A restaurant-keeper, in the course of a morning, orders pork chops for his kitchen, coal for his furnace, and a box of cigars for himself. Possibly he hesitates between a prime cut of pork costing $1.80 and an inferior grade costing $1.55, between Missouri coal for $2.75 and Illinois coal for $3.00, between one brand of cigars at $3.25 and another at $3.50. Here are three "marginal increments" of the same price magnitude. Can it be said that they represent the same utility magnitude, as the theory would require? The caterer may compare the two brands of cigars in respect of the pleasure felt as he imagines himself smoking the one or the other. Most likely he compares the two sorts of coal in respect of fuel value, dirtiness, and the like without thinking of these qualities in feeling terms. It is almost certain that he will decide in favor of one or the other grade of meat according to his expectation of profit and that he will not resolve this prospective money gain into consumption units of any sort. Can quantitative equivalence be predicated on things so disparate as pleasant feelings, fuel value, and money gain? Clearly this cruder formulation of the utility theory necessitates some common denominator of "utility," such as the pain-pleasure jelly of unrefined hedonism.

The more sophisticated formulation of the doctrine does, indeed, escape the necessity of finding a common denominator of "utility," but it does so only by becoming inconsequential. This formulation runs that the market price of pork chops is fixed at eighteen cents because to the "marginal purchaser" of the existing supply the "subjective significance" of a pound of pork chops is greater than the "subjective significance" of eighteen cents' worth of any other good but less than the "subjective significance" of eighteen-and-a-half cents' worth of some other good.

What precisely does this mean? The "subjective significance" of pork chops may be an estimate of their food value, or a mental picture of pork chops and gravy on the supper table, or again, it may be merely the recollection of Mary's request to bring home pork instead of beef. The "marginal purchaser" may compare a quarter's worth of pork chops with a pound of sirloin steak, or with two cigars, or, as is most often the case, with nothing in particular. The "marginal purchaser" will, indeed, buy a greater quantity of pork chops at eighteen cents than he would at fifteen cents a pound—otherwise he would not be a "marginal purchaser"—but his decision to take two pounds instead of three is much more likely to be based on a vague conviction that he "cannot afford" to spend more than about so much for a mess of pork than upon any comparison of pork chops with other goods. For "marginal purchases," like others, are made with very different degrees of deliberateness. A business man's "marginal" investment in his business will commonly be made after a careful canvass (in pecuniary terms) of alternatives; his "marginal increment" of restaurant service is likely to be purchased in quite unreflective response to the suggestion of an expectant waiter or the example of his dinner companions. To speak of a "balancing of utility" in such a case of unreflective purchase is simply absurd—there being no balancing of "utility" or of anything else in the case. And unreflective buying of "consumption goods," if not "normal," is, at least, fairly common.

If, then, all hedonistic implications be disavowed, what is the significance of saying that the "utility" of a pound of pork chops is only just greater than the "utility" of eighteen cents' worth of something else? The statement can mean only that the pork is, at the moment of purchase, preferred by the purchaser to anything else (perhaps nothing) with which it is, at the moment, actually compared—otherwise it would not be bought. The pork is purchased because it is preferred—the proof of the preference being the fact of purchase. All of which is unilluminating enough as an explanation of the "marginal purchaser's" preference.

And it is equally unilluminating as an explanation of the price of pork. In the last analysis it says only that pork chops sell at eighteen cents because some portion of the supply in the market would remain unsold at any higher price. It was already observed by them of old time that the sales of a commodity commonly fall off when its price rises relatively to the prices of other commodities. It adds nothing to the older doctrine to say that sales fall off because some persons buy other things or keep their money in their pockets.

To conclude this stage of the argument: If the marginal utility theory be interpreted hedonistically it is psychologically invalid. If the theory be deprived of its hedonistic content it is reduced to the unobjectionable statements: (1) that men will not buy a thing unless they want it; (2) that a commodity cannot be sold for more than somebody is willing to pay for it; (3) that in a perfect market no one will pay more for a given commodity than anyone else. Surely it needed no bulky volumes and a profusion of obscure terminology to tell us this.

II

Our second proposition is that, quite irrespective of its psychological inadequacy, the marginal-utility theory falls short of practical usefulness. It does not solve concrete problems of price, but only translates them into a jargon hard to be understood. If this proposition can be established the futility of the theory will be sufficiently shown.

Men need to understand market price as a guide to either individual or social action. To cite a single instance, farmers and meat-packers wish to predict the price of hogs in order that they may shape their business operations in accordance therewith. The "consuming public" also is interested in the price of hogs, not merely as an aid in forecasting the probable future price of hog products, but as throwing light on the question how far the high price of meat is due to the cost of growing and packing hogs and how far to causes susceptible of social control. The first requisite to the intelligent handling of either problem is evidently an analysis of the forces at work in the hog market. Does the marginal-utility theory afford such an analysis?

The average price of hogs at Chicago was $8.10 on October 4, 1909, and had fallen to $7.53 on October 14. How is this to be explained? The marginal-utility theory has it that the price, on any given day, is fixed at a point between the "marginal price-offer" and the "marginal refusal price"—by which terms is meant the money expression of the "subjective value" of hogs to the "marginal buyer" and "marginal seller" respectively.[24] It is clear, then, that the price of hogs fell because the "marginal price-offer" and the "marginal refusal price" simultaneously declined.

But is this anything more than a puzzling restatement of the problem? It says only that the "marginal buyer" was disposed to pay less, and the "marginal seller" willing to take less, on October 14 than on October 4. As to the reasons for this change of heart we are left completely in the dark. And we are just as little enlightened as to the forces which fix the price on any given day. The "marginal price-offer" is simply the lowest offer any buyer can make without being outbid by other buyers. Likewise, the "marginal refusal price" is simply the highest price any seller can ask without being undersold by other sellers. If there is a "perfect market," so that all hogs of a given grade are sold for the same price— which, of course, never occurs—"marginal price-offer" and "marginal refusal price" will coincide, or nearly coincide, with each other and with market price. But the "marginal" bid and offer are only in an infinitesimal degree the *cause* of the market adjustment; they count for no more in that adjustment than do any other bids or offers.[25] The "margin" of price-paying or price-refusing disposition is what it is only because of the action of all the buyers and sellers in the market. And the action of buyers and sellers is what it is only because of all the forces which bear upon hog supply, on the one hand, and upon the demand for hogs, on the other. That is to say, the "margin" is the resultant of all those forces which fix market price. The "margin" is, indeed, a purely a posteriori fact. Barring omniscience, there is no way to ascertain the position of the "margin" until the "going price" has been established. To say that the price of hogs fell because the "marginal price-offer" for hogs declined is, therefore, to say that the price fell because it fell. Hogs sold at $7.53 because they did not sell for more.

Nor, seemingly, is the marginal analysis capable of carrying us much farther than this. Utility theorists would, indeed, point out that, hogs being an "intermediate good," their value is "reflected back from the value of hog products"—ultimately from the "gratification" afforded by the consumption of meat and lard. It would appear, then, that hog buyers anticipated an approaching fall of some 7 percent in the "marginal want-gratifying power" of hog products and reduced their "marginal price-offers" accordingly. But the "marginal want-gratifying power" of hog products exists only with reference to a given quantity and only because of all those facts—dietary habits, customs, climate, and the like—which create the demand for pork. "Marginal want-gratifying power," accordingly, requires to be explained by showing how the demand for, and the supply of, hog products come to be what they are. And the effect of changes in the estimated future "marginal want-gratifying power" upon the present price of hogs can only be explained through an analysis of the hog market. The net result of all this talk of "ultimate want-gratifying power" is to call attention to the fact—which was in no danger of being overlooked—that the estimated future price of hog products is one of the elements in the present demand for hogs.

Thus the marginal analysis leaves the problem just where it was at the outset—the fall in the price of hogs is still to be explained. Price can no more be explained by saying that it tends to coincide with "marginal price-offer" than by saying that it is such as to equate "demand and supply." Indeed, the older phraseology is to be preferred as being more familiar. The choice of phraseology is, however, a minor matter. The important question is an explanation of price movement, and this is to be found, not in a phrase which describes the outcome, but in an analysis of the market forces which make the outcome what it is.

In the present case, all would agree that the *general level* of the price of hogs is determined by the relative demand for hog products over against the relative scarcity of hogs. Both these factors require detailed analysis. But, for the present purpose, it is sufficient to point out that between the hog grower and the "ultimate consumer" intervenes a complex market organization capable of producing quite wide variations in the price of hogs without any marked change either in the pork-eating habits of the population or in the aggregate supply of hogs. It is to this market organization that attention must be directed if either the rapid fluctuation of livestock prices or the wide margin between these prices and the retail cost of meat is to be explained.

Such a study as is here suggested—but which, of course, cannot here be carried out—would probably show that drovers, commission men, and speculators[26] serve to increase the margin between what the farmer receives and what the consumer pays. It would show that the same result is powerfully furthered by an understanding or "community of interest" between the large packers who are almost the sole buyers of hogs. Further, it might appear that the short-term fluctuations in live-hog prices are largely produced by the concerted action of the packers. They cannot keep the price of hogs too low without disastrously affecting the supply, any more than they can push the price of meat too high without disastrously restricting sales. But, from time to time, they can force a reduction in price by "staying out of the market," so that a large number of hogs are left unsold in the pens and a sharp decline occurs.[27] When receipts begin to fall off, an advance is permitted until conditions again become favorable for a "raid." The average price is, in this way, kept considerably below what it would be in a competitive market, but it is kept so by wider and more frequent fluctuations than would probably otherwise occur. But, if some price fluctuations are to be thus accounted for, others are due to more fortuitous occurrences—a railway wreck delaying deliveries, an unexpectedly large or small "run" of hogs (sometimes willfully), erroneous estimates of the day's receipts. Lastly, it is a well-known fact that quite different prices are paid, even at the same moment, for equally desirable "lots" according to the market information, the judgment, the anxiety to buy or sell, the "bargaining ability," the business connections, and even the luck of different buyers and sellers.

Correctness, much less adequacy, is not claimed for the foregoing analysis. The point intended to be made, by way of illustration, is that some such detailed analysis is indispensable to the proximate solution of any price problem. The marginal analysis gets nowhere precisely because the margin, whether of utility or of cost, is fixed by the very forces which determine price. [. . .]

Hence analysis of these factors is necessary in order to ascertain the position of the margin, either of utility or of cost. But these are just the factors of market price, so that analysis of them will give the solution of the problem for the sake of which alone the position of the margin is sought to be ascertained.

It may be thought that all this insistence upon detailed analysis is uncalled for—no theorist ever supposed that general principles could be applied to particular cases without due allowance for the circumstances of each case. But, in the view here spoken for, it is just these "particular circumstances" and not the "general principles" that are of chief consequence for the problem of market price. It is not "the value problem whole—all commodities in their interrelations of exchange"[28]—much less the ultimate ground of value, but particular prices—the money exchange relations of particular commodities at particular places and times—the movements of prices, the amenability of prices to social control—to which practical interest attaches and with which economists must concern themselves, if their "science" is to be more than an intellectual pastime. Now, price in this sense is always a particular case, explicable only by the forces at work in this particular situation. These price-determining forces are so numerous, and they vary so much, both in number and in relative importance, from one situation to another, that no generalization about price which is of much significance can be true. It is, to be sure, often convenient to comprehend the multitudinous price factors in some general formula—as that price depends upon the demand and supply forces in the particular case, together with the relative "strategic" position of buyer and seller. But such a formula has meaning only as content has been given to its terms by previous analysis; and it is applicable to any concrete case only in the sense of pointing to the need of specific analysis.

The marginal-utility theory aims at showing, not how price is determined in any actual case, but how price would be determined if men were to act in certain ways under certain assumed circumstances. This mode of theorizing is grounded upon the assumption that the behavior of men in any given situation can be predicted from elementary human nature. It appears that adepts of the theory have misconceived human nature, and that the situation in which they assume market price to be worked out never actually occurs. But the decisive objection to this whole line of doctrine goes to the basis upon which it is built up. Elementary human nature may (or may not) be fairly uniform, but it functions through institutions, and these are not uniform. The behavior of men can be neither predicted nor understood apart from their habitual modes of thought and from the institutional situation in which they act. It is not surprising, therefore, that a century and a quarter of diligent research into "labor-pain," "abstinence," "marginal utility," and the like should have contributed substantially nothing to "the increase and diffusion of knowledge among men."

Marginal-utility economics is an admirable body of dialectics—scarcely surpassed for subtlety, reach, and want of content by the finest products of medieval scholasticism. It affords unrivaled opportunity for the pursuit of refined distinctions between elusive ideas and for the multiplication of strange-sounding terms. "Economics" of this type strongly attracts men of a metaphysical turn of mind, and will doubtless continue to be cultivated. But it has not contributed, and it cannot contribute, to the elucidation of any practical problem.

Notes

1. Veblen, "The Limitations of Marginal Utility," *Journal of Political Economy* (November 1909); "Professor Clark's Economics," *Quarterly Journal of Economics* (February 1908).

2. Carlile, "The Language of Economics," *Journal of Political Economy* (July 1909).

3. Davenport, *Value and Distribution*, pp. 304ff.

4. For criticisms of hedonism see Fite, "The Place of Pleasure and Pain in the Functional Psychology," *Psychological Review* (November 1903); Fite, *Introductory Study of Ethics*, ch. 8; Dewey and Tufts, *Ethics*, pp. 269–75; Dewey, *Study of Ethics, A*

Syllabus; Irons, *Psychology of Ethics*, passim; McDougall, *An Introduction to Social Psychology*, ch. 1; MacKenzie, *Introduction to Social Philosophy*, pp. 215, 216; James, *Principles of Psychology*, vol. 2, pp. 549–59.

5. Bentham and his followers meant by "pain" both the sensations now so termed and the affective tone now known as "unpleasantness." But political economists have generally understood "pain" in the sense of "unpleasantness," as is shown by their use of such expressions as "labor-pain," "pains of abstinence," and the like.

6. "The truth is—and it should never be lost sight of—that business men conduct their business with an eye always to enjoyable income" (Fisher, *The Rate of Interest*, p. 241). The "truth" is, of course, that the larger business men rarely think of converting their gains into "enjoyable income." Not enjoyable income but pecuniary rating, magnitude of capitalized wealth, is the object of large business operations.

7. "Mankind is only a little bit reasonable and to a great extent unintelligently moved in quite unreasonable ways." McDougall, *An Introduction to Social Psychology*, p. 11.

8. For a discussion of this point see Judd, *Psychology*, ch. 8.

9. Compare Böhm-Bawerk, *Positive Theory of Capital*, p. 153.

10. Oft-quoted statements of the "economic motive" are: "To satisfy our wants to the utmost with the least effort" (Jevons, *Theory of Political Economy*, p. 37); "Men follow the line of least motive resistance" (Davenport, *Outlines of Economic Theory*, p. 33).

11. That feeling cannot be imaged appears to follow from the modern theory of affection. But even if it be granted that pleasantness-unpleasantness can be imaged, it seems certain that the image, if obtained, cannot act as a motive. For, in order to react to the image, we must attend to it, and this, as Titchener has pointed out, is impossible. "We cannot attend to affection at all; if we attempt to do so, the pleasantness or unpleasantness eludes us and disappears" (*Text-Book of Psychology*, p. 231). Further, proof of the reality of a feeling-image appears to be impossible. There is no way of discriminating, introspectively, between an incipient or other feeling and the alleged image of the feeling. That is, there are no qualitative marks of the feeling itself by which the feeling and its image can be differentiated.

For this last point, as also for much helpful criticism, the writer is indebted to Mr. J. G. Scott, a graduate student at the University of Missouri.

12. Böhm-Bawerk, *Positive Theory of Capital*, p. 9.

13. Compare Dewey and Tufts, *Ethics*, p. 270; Dewey, *Psychology*, pp. 361, 362.

14. Of the same character are Professor Carver's "satisfaction of desire" and Professor Fisher's "psychic income."

15. Fetter, *Principles of Economics*, p. 9.

16. Ibid., p. 27.

17. Ibid., p. 150.

18. Ibid., p. 277.

19. More naïvely hedonistic expressions are not wanting in Professor Fetter's writings. Thus: "Our economic bookkeeping can be made to balance only when real income be looked upon as a flow of pleasure in all cases" (*Quarterly Journal of Economics*, vol. 15, p. 27).

20. Böhm-Bawerk, *Grundzüge der Theorie des wirtschaftlichen Werts*, pp. 49–50.

21. Davenport, *Outlines of Economic Theory*, pp. 305–11, esp. p. 306.

22. Clark, *Essentials of Economic Theory*, ch. 6.

Some careless statements of the Austrian doctrine imply that value is proportional to "marginal utility," or even directly proportional to "utility." Thus Professor Carver writes: "the value of a transferable thing depends upon how much it is wanted in comparison with other transferable things," which he terms an "obvious assumption." ("Diminishing Returns and Value," *Rivista di Scienza*, vol. 6, no. 12.) That is, a six-dollar pair of shoes is wanted twice as much as a three-dollar hat—which to the writer appears to be an obvious absurdity. The statement in the text above is not accurate Austrianism (see below), but it is believed to represent Professor Clark's analysis at its best.

23. Clark, *Essentials of Economic Theory*, p. 98.

24. Böhm-Bawerk, *Positive Theory*, book 4, ch. 4.

25. Compare Davenport, *Outlines of Economic Theory*, pp. 548, 549.

26. Refers, of course, to persons technically so termed in the livestock market.

27. See *Chicago Daily Tribune*, October 13, 1909.

28. Davenport, *Outlines of Economic Theory*, p. 33. The passage cited refers to Ricardo's conception of the value problem.

The Disintegration of Economics

JOAN ROBINSON

Joan Robinson criticizes the two schools of economic orthodoxy, Neoclassical economics and the Keynesian-Neoclassical synthesis (described in textbooks as microeconomics and macroeconomics). She calls into question the basic assumptions of these schools: the ahistorical nature of their analysis; the inability of either school to pose the most important questions about economic systems—in particular capitalism; and their refusal to change in the face of irrevocable evidence and recognized theoretical inconsistencies posed by other economic theories.

Professional economics grew and flourished on an unprecedented scale, especially in North America, after the end of World War II. At the same time, the Western industrial nations were enjoying a period of continuous growth and high employment, interrupted only by brief and shallow recessions and accompanied by only a mild rate of inflation in the price level. The central teaching of orthodox economic theory was the natural tendency to "equilibrium" in the free market system, and this did not appear to be in obvious contradiction to the facts of experience.

Since 1974, the occurrence of a serious worldwide recession accompanied by increased inflation has left the economists gaping. Orthodoxy has nothing to offer, and all kinds of fanciful notions are floating around.

Hollow Orthodoxy

However, it is not only the slump that has exposed the bankruptcy of academic economic teaching. The structure of thought it expounds was long ago proved to be hollow. It consisted of a set of propositions that bore hardly any relation to the structure and evolution of the economy they were supposed to depict. The reason for this intellectual aberration seems to have been that the very notion of an economic system, as a particular historical phenomenon, developing through time, was associated with the doctrines of Marx. The aim of teaching was to build up a screen to prevent students from glancing in that direction. This was reinforced during the McCarthy period by the fear of being suspected of dangerous thoughts. Thus the academics were anxious to present the economy in a pleasing light and did not care to examine it to see what it was actually like.

As a matter of fact, a very robust defense of capitalism can be derived from

Joan Robinson, "The Disintegration of Economics," in *What are the Questions? and Other Essays* (Armonk, N.Y.: M. E. Sharpe, 1980), pp. 96–104.

Marx's analysis. Exploitation, that is the payment as wages of less than the value of the net proceeds of industry, is necessary for the emergence of profits. Profits provide both the motive and the means for the accumulation of capital, and the competitive struggle among capitalists to accumulate leads to technical innovation which "ripens the productive power of social labor as though in a hothouse."

The academics (except for Joseph Schumpeter) did not follow up this line. They pretend that the Marxian "labor theory of value" means that workers have the right to the whole product industry—the view of the Utopian socialists whom Marx despised—and protest that capital also produces value and has a right to its share.

Before the great slump of the 1930s, Alfred Marshall was the dominant influence on economics in the English-speaking world. He was a subtle thinker who allowed for exceptions to every rule that he propounded, but the effect of his doctrines as they were generally interpreted was to support laissez faire—government intervention in economic life, however well-intentioned, will do more harm than good; belief in a natural tendency to equilibrium in the free-market economy at a level of real wages consonant with full employment of the available labor force; the beneficial effects of free trade; the defense of the gold standard and of sound finance. Many arguments drawn from this complex of ideas are being trotted out again now, as they were in the 1930s; for instance, the view that there cannot be any "involuntary" unemployment, because any individual could always get a job by offering to work at less than the going wage rate, or that government borrowing draws upon a given fund of savings (or is it of finance?) and so "crowds out" private-sector investment. However, during the great debate that was broken off by the war in 1939, the arguments of Keynes were gradually prevailing over orthodoxy, and by the end of the war Keynes had become orthodox in his turn.

In the course of his endeavor to understand the causes of unemployment, Keynes had reintroduced the concept of capitalism as a particular economic system, evolving through history. He saw it as containing an essential flaw—its inherent instability and chronic failure to make full use of its potential resources—but he thought that his theory showed how this could be patched up, and in any case, as an economic system, it "was the best in sight."

This was not good enough for the new orthodoxy burgeoning in the United States. The subject was split into two parts; Keynes was safely corralled in the section called "macro economics" while the mainstream of teaching returned to celebrating the establishment of equilibrium in a free market.

This section of theory was described as "micro economics," that is, the study of prices of particular commodities and the behavior of individual sellers and buyers; however, it is obviously impossible to discuss the behavior of individuals in a vacuum without saying anything about the legal, political, and economic setting in which they are to operate. The setting in which the equilibrium of supply and demand is analyzed has no resemblance to modern capitalism. It is suited, rather, to the discussion of a rural fair where independent peasants and artisans meet to exchange products that are surplus to their own requirements.

A great point is made of the freedom of the consumer to choose what commodities to consume, according to his individual "tastes," but obviously the main influence upon the pattern of demand for commodities is the distribution of purchasing power between families. Nothing is said about this except that each individual has an "endowment" of some "factor of production," such as the ability to work, or property in land, or (though this is scarcely consistent with the rest of the story) property in various types of industrial equipment.

In the old Marshallian theory there had been a discussion of "welfare," and it was admitted that a given flow of production of commodities would provide more "satisfaction" to a given human population the more equally it was distributed among the consumers concerned. Marshall himself favored a more equal distribution of national income provided it could be brought about without any revolutionary upheaval. This whole question, however, was eliminated from the analysis of the equilibrium model, first by passing very lightly over the question of the relative amounts of "endowments" possessed by different individuals while concentrating on the determination of the relative price per unit of the various "factors"; second, by concentrating upon the choices made by a single consumer under a "budget constraint," that is, with a certain amount of purchasing power to spend. When it has been shown that his "tastes" and the prices of the commodities determine what he buys, the suggestion is slipped in that the choices of consumers in the aggregate determine what is to be produced. In acclaiming the "sovereignty of the consumer," the problem of distribution of consuming power among the population somehow gets lost to view.

The great claim of equilibrium theory was that it showed how scarce means are allocated between alternative uses in accordance with consumers' tastes. The existence of scarce means (materials, energy, cultivable land) has recently come very much to the fore in public discussion, while consumers' tastes run to large cars, overheated rooms, and an excessive consumption of meat. The central doctrine of orthodox economics is the defense of the freedom of anyone who has money to spend, to spend it as he likes.

Smothering Keynes

In the other department, so-called macro economics, the discussion is all about instability and how slumps could be prevented by applying Keynes's conceptions of demand management. This complete break, like a geological fault, between the two departments of economic theory makes it impossible for students to form a coherent view of what it is all about. If there is a natural tendency in the free-market system to equilibrium with full employment, why do we need Keynes; and if Keynes was right, that the capitalist system is inherently unstable, why do we have to spend so much time working out the mathematics of an equilibrium system? Such doubts, however, were smothered by reducing "Keynesian" theory to a kind of equilibrium in its turn and swallowing it up in the "neo-Neoclassical synthesis."

Keynes himself, when he had worked out the argument of the *General Theory*, was startled by the indictment of the free-enterprise system that it seemed to represent, and he wrote the last chapter in a very mollifying style which made it possible for orthodoxy to accept it and to pass very lightly over the awkward questions that earlier chapters had raised.

The synthesis was very soothing. A natural tendency to steady growth took the place of equilibrium. The subject split up into a number of compartments—business economics, labor economics, urban economics, and so forth—which provided many fields of work for academics to burrow into without questioning the central structure of theory. The elaboration of mathematical theorems (though devoid of empirical content) kept many brilliant practitioners happily occupied. When some dissidents tried to attack the basis of orthodox doctrines from a Marxist point of view, they were absorbed into the profession; now "radical economics" is one of the standard compartments of the subject along with the rest.

Under this cover a great deal of work has been done and a mass of information collected, much of which is of great interest, but it has been confused and distorted by the need to stuff it into the restricting frame of equilibrium analysis.

A case in point is the so-called theory of the firm. Marshall was a great moralizer. His aim was to justify the ways of Mammon to man. The laborer is worthy of his hire, and the capitalist is worthy of his return. The interest received by a rentier is the "reward of waiting," that is, of keeping his wealth intact. For an entrepreneur it is the reward of "business ability in command of capital."

Marshall knew that the main source of finance for the growth of a business is reinvestment of its own profits, but he refused to accept the corollary that any business which gets a good start will go on growing indefinitely. He maintained that there is an upper limit to the size of firms so that every market will normally be served by a sufficient number of sellers to ensure competitive pricing.

His theory is one of the fossils of nineteenth-century doctrine that has been carried down till today in mainstream teaching. The mutation in capitalism which has come about with the establishment of the great, and still growing, multinational corporations is largely ignored. Kenneth Galbraith has examined the characteristics of the *New Industrial State*, but as he writes in a bright, readable style, his views need not be taken seriously. Many realistic studies of actual business performance have been made, but they are excluded from the mainstream textbooks which still depict competitive industries composed of a large number of firms each unable to grow beyond the equilibrium size.

Another Version

There was a serious weakness in the neo-Neoclassical synthesis to which most of the profession seems to have been oblivious. The theory of market equilibrium, with given "endowments" and given "tastes" for a specified list of commodities, is essentially static. It can accommodate accumulation and change only by making the assumption that buyers and sellers have "correct foresight" of the future course of prices. A world of correct foresight is not the world in which human beings live. From this point, the argument takes off into an elaboration of mathematical structures which have no point of contact with empirical reality. But if steady growth had been substituted in the synthesis for static equilibrium, it was obviously necessary to discuss accumulation. This required an account of the nature of capital and of the generation of profits.

There had been another version of the central theory derived from Marshall, often mixed up in the textbooks with market equilibrium. In this, the "factors of production" are not individual endowments but the total amounts available to the economy as a whole, of land, labor and capital. When all are fully employed, each receives a "reward," rent, wages, and interest, according to its contribution to the product of industry. This doctrine was propounded in the United States by Professor J. B. Clark at the beginning of the present century. Thorstein Veblen immediately pointed out that the "capital" which receives interest is rentier wealth that can be lent to business or to government, while the "capital" that contributes to the product of industry is the technology embodied in equipment and stocks that permits labor to produce output. But no one from the orthodox camp deigned to answer him. Veblen (the most original economist born and bred in the United States) was a maverick whose views could be laughed off.

When the question was raised in Cambridge (England) twenty years ago, the orthodox answer was: let us pretend that "capital" consists of a physical substance that is just like finance so that the problem does not arise. It is homogeneous, divisible, and measurable, and can be embodied in any variety of equipment, instantaneously, without cost and without change in the initial quantity. The distinction which Keynes had drawn between interest—the price of loans—and profit—the return on investment—was muddled up again, and the rate of interest was taken to measure the productivity of this imaginary substance.

Orthodoxy seemed to be quite content with this concoction, until the publication by Piero Sraffa of a book with the eccentric title *Production of Commodities by Means of Commodities* roused a sharp controversy. Cambridge (Massachusetts) challenged Cambridge (England) and failed to win the point. Professor Samuelson very candidly admitted that his system did not hold water. This knocked the bottom out of the logical structure of orthodox theory, but mainstream teaching goes on just the same.

The Present as History

Piero Sraffa's formal analysis reestablished (though in a somewhat cryptic manner) the classical doctrine that the rate of profit on capital depends upon the technical structure of production and the share of wages in net output. The classical economists, such as Adam Smith and Ricardo, had naturally thought in terms of accumulation as a historical process. (The equilibrists are fond of claiming Adam Smith as the founder of their school, but he certainly did not intend to set up a static model of an exchange economy.)

Keynes abused Ricardo for neglecting the problem of effective demand, and he had no time for Marx, but he himself instinctively thought in the classical manner of the institutions of capitalism evolving through time. His own analysis was confined, for the most part, to strictly short-period problems, but it fits into a classical, historical approach. (Modern attempts to force Keynes into the equilibrium mould are causing a great deal of unnecessary confusion.) By acknowledging that life is lived in time and that today is an ever-moving break between the irrevocable past and the unknown future, he had shattered the basic conception of equilibrium, though he sometimes felt a nostalgic reluctance to give it up.

When we view our problems in historical terms, it is obvious that the twenty-five years of continuous growth after the end of the Second World War was a special epoch (indeed, every decade in the history of capitalism is a special epoch). It was characterized by the rise to dominance of the United States over the free-enterprise world economy, with the cold and hot wars that that entailed. Keynesian doctrines had very little to do with its success, except, first, that the monetary authorities had learned how to prevent a recession in industry from developing into a severe credit crisis, and second, that deficit finance had been made respectable; this was an important contribution to the development of the military-industrial complex, to which President Eisenhower vainly attempted to alert public opinion in America.

The high rate of consumption of natural materials entailed by the growth of industrial production gradually caused demand to overtake supply so that the terms of trade were turned against manufacturers. The uneven development of the free-enterprise nations set intolerable strains on the world financial system, and the attempt by Nixon to devalue the dollar in 1971 was a further shock. Trying to counter an incipient recession due to rising costs by cheap money led to a wild inflation in 1973. Then OPEC threw a spanner into the works and the long boom finally collapsed.

Now there is a revulsion against Keynes, and the popular view seems to be that it was really all his fault.

Inflation

The characteristic of the present slump which makes it markedly different from the slump that Keynes was trying to diagnose in the 1930s is that it is accompanied everywhere by a greater or less degree of inflation, that is, by worldwide rising price levels. During the long run of high employment, as Keynes predicted, there was a tendency for money-wage rates to rise faster than the general productivity of industry, and so for prices to rise to cover rising costs. This experience led to the concept of a "payoff" between unemployment and inflation. Some rather slapdash historical research produced a statistical "law" showing an inverse relation between the level of unemployment and the rate of rise of the price level. The concept of a payoff is typical of the way economists argue from statistics without thinking about human beings. Clearly, the cost of unemployment falls mainly upon workers, while the inconvenience of inflation is felt mainly by the middle class. The economists do not hesitate to tot them up and set one against the other. When the "law" broke down in the late 1960s, with inflation and unemployment rising together, the economists proclaimed that the terms of the payoff had shifted, and it was necessary to have more unemployment to keep inflation in check. This is how the matter rests at present (1980).

During the long boom, while "Keynesian" policies seemed to be working satisfactorily, a dispute developed between two schools of thought as to whether monetary policy, operating through the banking system, was to be preferred to fiscal policy operating through central and local budgets. The prevalence of inflation has given a great boost to the monetarists, who flourish particularly in Chicago, for traditionally inflation was always regarded as a "monetary" problem. The strong point in their case is that a rise in the value of transactions, due to increased activity at rising prices, generally cannot take place without an increase in the stock of money. The weak point is that for the authorities to prevent the quantity of money from increasing requires a severe credit squeeze, which acts directly upon industry, causing bankruptcies and reducing employment, and only indirectly, if at all, on the level of prices.

The monetarist argument supports the idea of a "payoff." If a high level of unemployment can be maintained for long enough (some say two years, some say five), the rate of inflation will gradually fall until stability is established (does this include the price of oil?). Meanwhile, the stock of industrial equipment would be degenerating for lack of investment, and the labor force would be degenerating as juveniles fail to get jobs. But that does not matter. Inflation, to the monetarists, is the worst of all evils, and there is no remedy for it but keeping production low.

Business opinion seems rather to favor fiscal policy and hopes for an injection of profits into industry through enlarged expenditure on armaments. In a wider context, it might be argued that this remedy is worse than the disease.

Permanent Unemployment

The immediate problem of unemployment is serious enough, but the long-period problem lying behind it is still more menacing. Industrial technology is continually developing and continually reducing the requirement for manual labor. From one point of view, of course, it is a benefit to humanity to reduce the burden of heavy toil, but for the individual, the purpose of work is to earn money, and it is no benefit to him to reduce the burden of toil if it reduces the possibility of earning a living at the same time.

It is true that modern technology is very destructive of amenities, including fresh air, but the individual would prefer to earn money in the smog rather than not earn it at all.

No less an authority than Arthur Burns (in *Challenge*, January/February 1976) has pointed out that American industry, at its most flourishing, offers employment to a limited number of highly skilled workers. (He might have added that, when the great corporations do require unskilled labor, they often prefer to get it in South Korea and Taiwan, where wages are lower and trade unions not allowed.) Even if growth could be started up again at the old rate, there is no possibility of reaching full employment in the long-period sense, that the economy provides everyone with the opportunity to support himself without resorting to crime.

The most pertinent question to ask is: What characteristic of the private enterprise system is it that condemns the wealthiest nation the world has ever seen to keeping an appreciable proportion of its population in perpetual ignorance and misery?

The professional economists keep up a smoke-screen of "theorems" and "laws" and "payoffs" that prevents questions such as that from being asked. This situation is, I think, inevitable. In every country, educational institutions in general, and universities in particular, are supported directly or indirectly by the established authorities, and whether in Chicago or in Moscow, their first duty is to save their pupils from contact with dangerous thoughts.

The Nature of Labor Exchange
and the Theory of
Capitalist Production

HERBERT GINTIS

In this article the contemporary Neoclassical theory of the firm is subjected to critical analysis that leaves little doubt about its weaknesses. In contrast to an orthodox world of atomistic preferences and exogenous technology, Gintis argues that a Marxist analysis provides for a clearer and more realistic inquiry into the nature of capitalist production.

Introduction

This paper contrasts two perspectives on the organization and structure of the production process, Neoclassical and Marxist, defending the latter as a more accurate portrayal of capitalist production. Neoclassical theory, in capsule form, views the organization of the capitalist enterprise as the solution to the problem of finding a least-cost technique of production given an array of factor prices. Marxist theory views this organization, rather, as the outcome of a struggle (albeit an unequal struggle) between capital and labor over the rate of exploitation of labor.

For Neoclassical economics, the essence of capitalism is its sphere of exchange relations. Capitalism reduces all essential economic relations to independent exchanges among freely acting and mutually benefitting firms and households. These firms and households are in turn treated as "black boxes" whose internal structures (production functions and preference structures) are determined outside economic theory by the state of science and the psychology of the individual. Thus the Neoclassical analysis of capitalism reduces to the examination of market relations among technologically and psychologically determinate actors. Were this methodology valid, the Neoclassical theory of production would follow as a matter of course.

In Marxist theory, however, the social relations of capitalism cannot be reduced to exchange relations. The essence of capitalism is the exploitation of labor through the private ownership and control of capital on the one hand, and the system of wage-labor on the other. The key concept in Marxist theory delineating

Herbert Gintis, "The Nature of Labor Exchange and the Theory of Capitalist Production," *Review of Radical Political Economics* 8, 2 (Summer 1976), pp. 36–54.

the essential nonexchange relations of the capitalist economy is the labor/labor-power distinction. This concept is the methodological basis of volume 1 of *Capital* and was developed by Marx in *Theories of Surplus Value* as the prime weapon in the critique of classical political economy.

According to this conception, there is no quarrel with treating goods, services, raw materials, and capital goods as commodities. But labor cannot be so treated: the commodity which is exchanged on the market (labor power) is *not* the entity which enters into the production process (labor). Labor power is a commodity whose material attributes include the capacity to perform certain types and intensities of productive activity. Labor itself, however, is the active, concrete, living process carried on by the worker; its expression is determined not only by labor power but also by the ability of the capitalist to exploit it. Surplus value appears when the capitalist is able to extract more labor from the worker than that embodied in the value of labor power (the wage).

If labor cannot be analyzed as an exchange relation, neither can it be subsumed under the category of technological data. The labor forthcoming from a worker depends, in addition to his or her biology and skills, on states of consciousness, degrees of solidarity with other workers, labor market conditions, and the social organization of the work process. Thus labor can be reduced neither to commodity relations nor to technology alone; rather it must be accorded a separate status as a social relationship. Thus there is a fundamental gap in any economic theory which attempts to abstract from productive relations in an effort to comprehend capitalist development. Nor can the dynamics of class struggle be relegated to the political sphere, however extensive the impact of state activity or the cohesiveness of the workers movement.

Indeed, Marx argues, the basic categories of profit and wages cannot be understood outside the social relations between capitalist and worker in the production process itself. The sphere of exchange, which *appears* to condition all economic activity, actually masks the underlying structural relations embodied in the social relations of production.

From the labor/labor-power distinction, it follows that the organization of production in the capitalist firm must reflect essential elements of class struggle. Work organization is the historical product of a dynamic interaction between technology and class relations. Not only must such traditional issues as the length of the workday and the division of revenue between capitalist and workers be understood in terms of the extraction of surplus value, but also the structure of hierarchical authority, job fragmentation, wage differentials, racism, and sexism as basic characteristics of the capitalist firm. In this paper I shall sketch such an analysis.

The Marxist theory of work organization, which in modern corporate capitalism shades into a theory of bureaucracy, is by no means adequately developed. In addition to chapters 13–15 of Marx's *Capital*, there have been several important contributions, historical, heuristic, or speculative in nature [12; 21; 28; 29; 32;

33; 45; 51; 64]. What is needed as well is a structural theory which explicitly links the development of worker consciousness at the point of production to the organizational means of reproducing capitalist hegemony. I shall here offer such a theory by introducing two conceptual elements: the structure of *influence* in work relationships and the dynamics of *legitimation*.

The Marxist approach begins by affirming that we cannot abstract from labor as a social process. From this critical perspective, the Neoclassical theory is a failure indeed. The order it imposes on reality is a reification of human relationships which reduces the rich variety of social relations in production to triviality and assigns to residual categories fundamental aspects of modern society whose understanding is crucial to the prospects for human liberation. The reification imposed in Neoclassical theory is not simply arbitrary and short-sighted, but rather follows the actual process of reification imposed by the capitalist mode of production—the reduction of all social relationships to exchange relations. In the words of Marx [47, p. 120]: "The value of the worker as capital rises according to demand and supply, and even physically his existence, his life, . . . is looked upon as the supply of a commodity like any other."

Marxist theory recognizes at the same time, however, that the worker is *not* a commodity, and that the contradiction between worker as commoditized object and conscious, human subject is the driving force of class struggle in capitalist society. Thus the capitalist economy both *is* and *is not* reduced to exchange relations, in a dialectic we must capture. The principal contradiction in capitalist production is between capital and labor, between labor as the object of profit and domination and labor as self-actualizing subject. The firm as an organization can only be understood as an institution *mediating* this contradiction in the interests of profit, and *reproducing* when possible the forms of consciousness and social relations upon which the integrity of capital is based.

The Neoclassical Description of Production: Empirical Anomalies

The Neoclassical theory of capitalist production views each worker both as endowed with a preference ordering over all jobs in the economy and as capable of performing at higher or lower levels of productivity in each. These preferences are aggregated into supply curves for each possible job, in terms of which the entrepreneur chooses a cost-minimizing job structure using one of the available techniques of production. Labor is thus treated as a commodity like any other factor of production. Through the consequent blurring of the labor/labor-power distinction, three implications are derived of basic socio-political importance. First, *the resulting job structure will be efficient.*[1] That is, any alternative to the observed job structure which increases both output and worker satisfaction must also increase costs. Second, wage differentials reflect relative job desirability and unequal skill requirements. In particular, wage differences between two workers (say a black and a white) reflect differences in either their level of skills or their individual job preferences.

Third, *worker sovereignty* will obtain in the same sense, and under the same conditions, as the more traditional consumer sovereignty.[28] That is, the overall constellation of jobs will reflect the trade-off of workers between wages and job satisfaction. For instance, if a group of workers desired more satisfying work, they would offer their services at a lower wage. A profit-maximizing capitalist would search for a job structure embodying this type of work which would become profitable at the lower wage rates. Thus the supply would increase to meet the demand at the lower equilibrium wage.[2]

These three propositions illuminate some of the most fundamental perspectives of Neoclassical theory on capitalist society. The first implies that the sphere of production is socially neutral in the sense that it is independent of property relations, class structure, and the mode of social control of economic life. The second implies that wage inequality results from the difference in technically relevant attributes of individuals. In particular, capitalism exhibits a strong tendency toward "meritocracy," whereby individuals attain economic positions based on their "achievements" alone, and independent of such ascriptive characteristics as race, sex, social class background, ethnic origin, etc. Thus persistent differences in economic outcomes across ascriptively distinct groups are due to differences in tastes, abilities, or opportunities of skill acquisition. The third implies that the historical development of work corresponds, within the limits imposed by science and technology, to the preferences of workers. If work is less than satisfying, it is because most workers prefer higher incomes to more satisfying jobs.

Is the capitalist firm technically efficient? A fundamental characteristic of modern capitalist production is the hierarchical division of labor, according to which ultimate power is vested in the apex of the organizational pyramid and radiates downward. Associated with this is the specialization, fragmentation, and routinization of tasks, and the development of a finely articulated pattern of pay, prerogatives, and status. This organizational pattern is usually explained in terms of efficient technology, which in turn dictates strongly centralized control mechanisms for purposes of coordination. The experimental literature in industrial social psychology and sociology is, however, considerably more circumspect, and indicates a *mutual interdependence* of control mechanisms and the division of tasks. Thus Vroom reviews an extensive body of literature, concluding that the evidence indicates that "decentralized structures have an advantage for tasks which are difficult, complex, or unusual, while centralized structures are more effective for those which are simple and routinized" [65, p. 243]. Hence task fragmentation and routinization cannot be taken as the cause of the hierarchical control structures of the enterprise. *However* the hierarchical structure of power fits into the logic of profit maximization, task fragmentation will follow as a result. All that we can derive from this experimental literature is that *if* centralized control is posited, *then* the "minute division of labor" will be relatively productive.[63]

Indeed, it appears that in the course of development of capitalist enterprise, the hierarchical division of labor *preceded* technical innovation and accounted for the early success of the factory system over its traditional rivals [45] in the course of the British Industrial Revolution. Early factories employed the same techniques of production as putting-out and craft organization, and there were no technological barriers to applying them to these more traditional forms. The superior position of the capitalist factory system in this period seems to derive not from its efficiency sense, but its ability to control the work-force: costs were reduced by drawing on child and female labor, minimizing theft, increasing the pace of work, and lengthening the work week.[45] Of course, given the hierarchical structure of control as a temporal antecedent, the minute division of labor follows, and as new technologies are developed, they may be tailored to this division of labor. Thus prima facie observation cannot determine that the organization of the enterprise is an adaptation to superior technology.

Finally, there have been numerous attempts to replace the hierarchical division of labor by systems of worker control, team production, and job expansion. Fairly intensive attempts in China, Yugoslavia, Italy, Cuba, and Chile demonstrate higher productivity and work satisfaction.[11; 33] More moderate experiments have taken place in capitalist countries themselves.[3] [11; 66; 67] As Blumberg concludes: "There is scarcely a study in the entire literature which fails to demonstrate that satisfaction in work is enhanced or . . . productivity increases accrue from a genuine increase in worker's decision-making power. Findings of such consistency, I submit, are rare in social research. . . . The participative worker is an involved worker, for his job becomes an extension of himself and by his decisions he is creating his work, modifying and regulating it."

Yet a shift toward participatory relationships is scarcely apparent in capitalist production,[67] and small moves in this direction are generally interpreted as attempting to avoid severe labor antagonisms, rather than to increase profit under normal conditions of operation.[33; 60] These observations are not compatible with the Neoclassical assertion as to the efficiency of the internal organization of capitalist production.

If profit maximization does not entail efficiency, clearly the wage may represent the worker's "marginal contribution to profit" without representing his or her "productivity." Indeed, the very concept of marginal productivity is theoretically dubious, as it cannot be easily disengaged from the total Neoclassical framework. Empirically, we may obtain various indices of skills and abilities, supervisor ratings and behavior records. But these are distressingly indirect. Even when precise output measures are available (e.g., salespeople, taxicab drivers, baseball players), they do not capture the effect of the individual or the productivity of other members of the group. Moreover, individuals with widely varying "productivities" in this sense will often occupy the same positions at the same wage.[8; 12; 66] In this situation, evidence bearing on the adequacy of the marginal productivity assertion must be critically interpreted. Nevertheless, evidence does seem to contradict the theory where the two intersect.

To begin, as we have noted, the marginal productivity doctrine implies that over time differences in the economic attainment of workers with distinct ascriptive traits should decline, unless attributable to differences in acquired skills. Yet available evidence indicates that differences in economic success based on race, sex, and social class background have not significantly declined over time [3; 5; 12; 31; 36; 39; 69] and cannot be explained by differences in innate ability [13] or the acquisition of marketable skills.[10; 34; 36; 56; 59]

This suggests that skills may not adequately capture the value of a worker to the employer. This seems to be the case. Neither IQ nor measured cognitive skills have much independent explanatory value in income determination,[12; 29; 36; 59] and only a small portion of the association of education with economic position can be accounted for by the contribution of schooling to cognitive skills.[29] Within occupational categories, moreover, these attributes do not go far in explaining either supervisor ratings or observed promotions.[8; 21]

Indeed, hiring and promotion involve far more than the assessment of skills.[12; 51] Capitalists assess, in addition to possession of adequate skills, (a) ascriptive characteristics; (b) work-relevant personality traits; (c) modes of "self-presentation," including manner of dress, speech, and personal interaction, self-concept, and social class identifications; and (d) credentials, of which formal education is the most salient. How these factors relate either to profits or to productivity is complex. As a whole, however, their prominence tends to contradict a simplistic marginal productivity theory and indicates massive deviations from "meritocratic principle."

Additional evidence can be gleaned from investigations of the wage and hiring policies within individual firms.[e.g., 20] First, marginal productivity theory suggests that wage rates should adjust flexibly to changing market conditions. This is not the case. Within a firm the wage structure is quite rigid and ordinarily well-buffered from market forces.[20, part 1, pp. 13–90] Clear preference is ordinarily given to existing workers for filling job openings, as opposed to reliance on the market. A well-articulated "internal labor allocation process" arises in which worker productivity is but one factor. In particular there is a tendency for the number of individuals qualified for a position to exceed the number of jobs available, in which case seniority and other administrative rules are used to determine promotion. Hardly do workers compete for the job by bidding down its wage. Finally, job ladders artificially isolate individuals from skill-learning opportunities which might lead them to challenge their existing positions in the organization.[32]

Of course, if profit maximization does not entail technical efficiency, and if the doctrine of the equality between wages and marginal productivity is false, then worker sovereignty will not obtain. That is, the historical development of work will not conform to the manifest preferences of workers, even when weighted by skill differentials among workers. If the hierarchical division of labor is necessary to the extraction of surplus value, then worker preferences for jobs threatening capitalist control will not be implemented. In addition, there is to my knowledge no evidence that the historical evolution of work is brought into conformity with individual preferences via the wage structure mechanism. Rather, this evolution seems due to changes emanating from the *demand* side of the labor market (shift from entrepreneurial and craft organization to corporate enterprise, the expansion of the state sector), to which supply is brought into conformity.

In sum, the Neoclassical theory of production generates fundamental propositions which seem controverted in fact. This, I shall argue, is due to its faulty handling of the labor exchange.

The Nature of the Labor Exchange

The Neoclassical theory of production is based on the crucial assumption that the labor exchange (the social process whereby the worker exchanges his or her labor for a wage) can be treated solely as an exchanges of commodities. This treatment appears most clearly in mathematical formulations of general equilibrium theory. Thus in Debreu's *Theory of Value* [18], labor services and goods differ only in the algebraic sign of the variables quantifying them. Other mathematical formulations [e.g., 2] are only slightly more complicated. The standard microeconomic textbook presentation differs but in degree of sophistication.

This assumption is prima facie incorrect. In fact, the hallmark of the capitalist firm is its reliance on the *authoritative* rather than the *market* allocation of activity. As Coase noted in his classic article "The Nature of the Firm" [15, p. 333], "If a workman moves from department Y to department X, he does not go because of a change in relative prices, but because he is ordered to do so. . . . Outside of the firm, price movements direct production, which is coordinated through a series of exchange transactions on the market. . . . Within the firm . . . is substituted the entrepreneur-coordinator, who directs production."

Indeed, Coase proceeds to argue that the efficiency of the profit-maximizing firm rests securely on the *distinction between* the market and authoritative allocations. Certain allocations are more efficiently executed via authoritative decree than via market transactions. The profit-maximizing entrepreneur will determine exactly which ones these are. The efficiency of market exchanges is owed to the agglomeration of certain allocations within the productive unit, where they can be handled efficiently *through the mechanism of entrepreneurial authority*. Economic theory, dealing with exchange relations, can then treat the firm as a "black box" of authoritative allocations.

Coase's argument provides a sophisticated validation of the market character of the labor exchange as embodied in formal mathematical treatments. Thus in the Debreu model we need only note that the profit-maximizer *chooses* a production point which includes not only the market exchanges he makes, but the allocations of inputs (raw material and labor) as well. The latter are clearly authoritative allocations. But the question of the nature of the labor exchange then arises in a different guise. *Can the profit maximizer's "choice" concerning the disposition of nonhuman factors of production be treated symmetrically with that concerning human labor?* If so, the labor/labor-power distinction is clearly invalid.

Neoclassical economics has generally overlooked this critical question. But Coase attempts to repair the gap.[15] He begins by stressing the difference between an employee and an independent supplier of a service (an "agent"). Suppose an entrepreneur requires electrical repairs in the factory. He or she may either engage an independent electrician to perform a specific task (e.g., repair an outlet), or employ a worker skilled in electrical work. The entrepreneur will choose the most efficient solution. From *employing*, he or she secures the flexibility of obtaining a series of "electrical services" when needed, without having continually to recontract with an independent agent. The worker exchanges a wage for the *disposition* over work activities. Paraphrasing Batt (quoted in Coase, p. 350): "The employer must have the right to control the employee's work, either personally or by another employee or agent. It is this right of control or interference, of being entitled to tell the employee when to work (within the hours of service) and when not to work, and what work to do and how to do it (within the terms of such service) which is the dominant characteristic in this relation." That is, the essence of the employer-employee relationship lies in the latter's relinquishing *complete disposition* over his or her activities, subject to agreed-upon limitations and restrictions. The worker is then a passive agent who can be treated, from the employer's perspective, no differently from other commodities.

This conception of the labor exchange has been vigorously formalized by Herbert A. Simon.[61, ch. 11] Simon postulates a set A of activities the worker is capable of performing. He will supply each at a price p(a) for a ξ A. This describes his position as an independent agent. But he may contract a fixed wage w, in return for which the employer can *choose* any a $'<$ A, where the definition of A $'$ is part of the labor contract. Simple equations can be formulated to exhibit under which conditions one or the other exchanges will be acceptable to both parties. This model gives the Neoclassical conclusion as to the efficiency of the profit-maximizing solution for the firm.

The major objection to this approach is both simple and yet absolutely fundamental. The theory assumes that once the contract between capitalist and worker is completed, the question of who has power over whom is solved. The capitalist simply tells the worker what to do and the worker either does it or finds another job. Yet in fact the power relations within the enterprise are *not* solved through these market exchanges at all.

We may note that taking power relations as exogenous data in economic analysis is basic to the methodology of Neoclassical theory. The theory of the firm is merely a case in point. Indeed, Abba Lerner has astutely noted that Neoclassical economics is predicated on the prior solution of political problems: "An economic transaction is a solved political problem. Economics has gained the title of queen of the social sciences by choosing *solved* political problems as its domain."[43, p. 259] The most conspicuous examples are the treatment of property rights and contractual obligations, on which market transactions are predicated as "solved political problems." And with some validity. The security of property in factors of production, goods, and capital is based on the legal rights of ownership, guaranteed ultimately by the coercive power of the *state*. Exchanges of property, like all legal contractual obligations, are simple extensions of property rights, and are similarly secured by the state. Exchange relations involve "solved political problems" in that the coercive (i.e., political) instruments guaranteeing the binding character of the social relationship lie predominantly *outside* the jurisdiction of the exchanging parties. Thus it is often permissible to take these power configurations as exogenous for the purpose of economic analysis.

Clearly the Neoclassical assumption can be extended to hiring the services of an independent agent. If hired, the agent contracts to supply a particular service for a price. Failure to provide the service entitles the user to withhold payment, and perhaps also sue for damages. The contract is guaranteed by an external political power (the juridical system), and the exchange can be treated symmetrically with other market transactions.[4]

The essence of these various market exchanges is a legally enforceable quid pro quo. Not so in the case of wage labor, where in return for a wage (quid), the worker normally offers only to submit to the political authority of the firm. When a specific quo is in the form of labor services, the individual is an independent agent, not a wage laborer. What the worker must do in order that profits accrue goes far beyond the terms of legal contract. The legal contract will in general specify the hours of work, the meeting of certain health and safety conditions, limitations on what the worker can be asked to do, the wage rate, pensions, etc. While the state may in dire situations interfere in favor of the capitalist, he cannot in general be satisfied with the fulfillment of the *legally enforceable* conditions of the labor exchange. For instance, in the case of hiring an electrical worker, the exchange relations do not guarantee that *a particular range of services* will be offered (e.g., that x number of outlets will be repaired per day, or y number of panels installed, or z number of switches replaced). The latter can be guaranteed only by *the particular way* the employer exerts control over the worker.

In terms of the Simon model, the fault is simply this: the worker receives a wage, and can perform any act in set A, but what determines that the capitalist can *choose* any a ξ A'? The worker may *allow* the capitalist to do this, or the capitalist may somehow *induce* the worker to perform (a), but this is certainly not guaranteed by the contract. Power enters into the organization of the firm in a sense far beyond the "authoritative allocation of value" in the Coase-Simon sense. Power must be used to *evince* worker behavior not guaranteed by the labor exchange (the contractual obligations). Indeed, a common form of worker insubordination is "working to rules," whereby workers undermine the production process merely by doing exactly and precisely as they are required, not by contract, but by regulation.

This basic Neoclassical fallacy is *precisely* the blurring of the distinction between labor and labor power. The labor exchange involves the exchange of one commodity (labor power) for another (the wage). But the concrete substance of labor which actually enters into the production process is conceptually distinct from labor power and must be analyzed in fundamentally different terms. Actual labor is *not* exchanged for a wage according to market principles. Thus power relations between capitalist and worker are *resultants* of economic organization, and cannot be taken as given prior to economic analysis. On this point the Neoclassical theory of the firm founders. This fact bears several implications which we proceed to investigate.

Consciousness and Capitalist Production

The first implication of our analysis is that the profitability of production will depend intimately on the consciousness of workers. In this sense the labor exchange differs radically from a true market exchange, in which parties are concerned with only the attributes of the things exchanged, and not with the personal attributes of the other parties themselves. The labor/labor-power distinction, however, implies that capitalist production will be organized not only to produce a marketable commodity but also to reproduce, from period to period, forms of worker consciousness compatible with future profits.

This assertion can be demonstrated in the following manner. By the very nature of the labor exchange, a broad range of behaviors are available to the worker at any time, all of which are compatible with the legally enforceable aspects of the employment contract. Within this range we may view the worker as acting to pursue his or her own goals, subject only to the constraints the capitalist can place on the worker's choices. Depending then on the consciousness of the worker, the imposition of these constraints will be more or less costly to the capitalist and the worker will be more or less "valuable," quite independent of his or her skills or the legal contract between the two.

Suppose, for instance, the extreme case of the worker whose only goal is furthering the profits of the organization. Then the capitalist need only appraise this worker of the "needs of the organization" to elicit optimum behavior. Coercing or convincing each worker to contribute maximally to the enterprise is unnecessary.[5] At another extreme, we have the worker whose only goal is to maximize job satisfaction. Here the only constraints open to the capitalist involve the direct tailoring of job contents to the needs of the worker—presumably a costly endeavor.

In general, how might capitalists place constraints on workers? As we have seen, turning to the coercive power of the state for compliance is altogether too crude. Nor do they have the power to whip the worker, mutilate the worker's children, or burn down the worker's house. The historical development of political rights in capitalism has curbed these options. What powers do capitalists have? First, they may increase the worker's *accountability* by imposing a suitable number of supervisory and mechanical checks on performance. They may use the information gained to alter the conditions of the worker over which the capitalists possess legal control. These include pay, working conditions, and position in the organization. They may also apply moral pressure.

This simple argument provides several immediate conclusions. First, the value of a worker to the capitalist depends integrally on the former's *personal characteristics*, in addition to his or her productive capacities. This is in direct contradiction with the Coase-Simon model. Second, the actual quid pro quo in labor exchange depends on several organizational variables at least partially under the capitalist's control: (a) extent and character of accountability; (b) manipulation of worker consciousness; (c) pay scales and criteria of promotion and dismissal. These organizational factors replace the external political authority of the state in enforcing the labor exchange and constitute the power configuration of the capital-labor relation.

Important implications of these observations will be systematically developed in the course of our argument. First let us consider a firm where the cost of replacement of workers to the firm, and the cost of job transfer at the market wage to the employee, are both zero. The Neoclassical theory of the firm here implies that the wage rate associated with each job will be the going market rate for labor possessing the appropriate skills. The model we have presented indicates, on the contrary, that the market wage represents a *minimum* which will normally be exceeded. For in this situation, at the market wage, a major instrument of the employer in evincing appropriate worker behavior—the threat of dismissal—is absent. Raising the wage *above* the market rate, however, restores the threat of dismissal, and hence is part of a profit-maximizing strategy. Thus the "market rate" which equates supply and demand will not actually be observed on the market! This implication of our model, seemingly paradoxical, actually corresponds to real social conditions: capitalists have always acted to create reserve armies of labor on all levels, and yet continue to pay wages in excess of those which would allow all markets to clear. Moreover, the individual capitalist is more likely to use this strategy when the cost to the firm of inadequate worker performance is high. Indeed, it has often been noted that an increase in the "responsibility" of an employee is normally accompanied by an increased wage, even when no additional skills are required and the desirability of the job is enhanced.[20, pp. 66–68]

In this same situation, Neoclassical theory implies that job openings will be filled partially either by promoting existing workers or by bringing new employees into the firm. However, abjuring "special privilege" for existing workers eliminates the second major instrument of the employer for extracting labor from labor power—the control over advancement in the organization. Our model, on the contrary, predicts a strong preference for promotion within the ranks, a formalized series of "job ladders," and an articulated internal labor market. This of course agrees with the facts. [38; 20, part 1]

In the general case, where worker replacement and job transfer costs are not zero, the analysis is somewhat more complicated, but can easily be supplied by the reader. We should note that there are clearly specifiable conditions under which the employer-employee relationship shades off into the "independent agent" relationship, where the Coase-Simon argument applies. These include (a) low costs of accountability of worker performance; (b) low worker replacement costs to the firm; (c) high job transfer costs to the worker; (d) low firm costs associated with inadequate job performance (e.g., little responsibility); and (e) standardized and measurable worker services. An example combining (a), (b), (d), and (e) might be the supply of female labor to a company typist pool, and more generally jobs with secondary labor market characteristics.[56]

From this example we may draw several general conclusions. First, wage scales will in general deviate from the supply and demand analysis of Neoclassical theory, because the manipulation of wage scales is an instrument ensuring the integrity of the labor exchange. For similar reasons a well-articulated "internal labor market" will develop alongside the traditional labor market, differing qualitatively from a market exchange. Thus wage differentials are in no way captured by technical capacities of workers: workers at different wage rates may be equally capable of executing the same tasks; and worker productivity at a given job will in general be a function of the wage rate and consciousness of the worker, which may depend on the overall organization of the firm and the overall wage structure. Thus a reorganization of wage differentials which lowers profits may increase efficiency.

Second, the phenomenon of job tenure appears even where the firm faces perfect labor markets. In the traditional theory of the firm the work force can be "turned over" in each production period, subject only to replacement costs (recruitment and specific training). Our analysis indicates an additional and quite basic source of endurance in the capitalist-worker relationship: threat of dismissal and possibilities of promotion are basic instruments ensuring the integrity of the labor exchange.

Third, the labor exchange normally embodies another property not shared by pure market exchanges, which are "impersonal" in a sense accurately described by Arrow and Hahn [2, p. 23]: "The decision to supply a good in a perfectly competitive economy is not a decision to supply so-and-so much to such-and-such agents, but simply to exchange so-and-so much of the good for other goods." For the profit-maximizer must take into account in his choice of work organization, job staffing, and wage differentials *the effect of his or her actions on the consciousness of the workers*. Since the labor exchange depends on the preferences of workers in addition to their capacities, since the employer-employee relationship tends to endure over many production periods, and since the experience of workers in the production process will affect their consciousness, the simple one-product firm faces a joint-product production function: the inputs are raw materials and workers with a certain consciousness and the outputs include both the good produced and "new" workers with transformed consciousness. Many of these "new" workers will be inputs at the next stage of production. This observation alone invalidates the Neoclassical assertion as to the Pareto-efficiency of profit maximization. Moreover, in a general equilibrium system in which all of the usual conditions for efficiency hold, the economic configuration will not in general be Pareto-satisfactory. For there will be a substantive interdependence of the production-possibilities set and the preference functions of individuals.[2, ch. 6, sec. 2] In particular, forms of work organization which tend *not* to reproduce worker consciousness appropriate to further profits will not be introduced, however strongly desired by workers and however materially productive. In this sense the Pareto-inefficiency of capitalist production is rooted in class struggle. [. . .]

Collusion, Legitimacy, and "Divide and Conquer"

Extraction of surplus value is thwarted when worker solidarity is sufficiently high. But solidarity involves not only common interests and mutual influence, but *joint action* as well. Thus the capitalist must organize the production process to minimize the formation of worker coalitions.

The threat of worker collusion represents a major reason why the labor exchange cannot be conceived as an exchange of commodities and lends additional substance to the labor/labor-power distinction. The labor exchange differs from pure market exchange in the way the capitalist may affect the extent of collusion among the individuals (workers) with whom he exchanges. In the case of market exchange as codified in Neoclassical theory, collusion among the trades is handled by an *external authority*—the state. In the case of the labor exchange, however, recourse to the legal system covers only the most manifest and overt forms of worker collusion (e.g., wildcat strikes). In general, mechanisms minimizing collusion must be built into the organizational structure itself.

Collusion between superiors and subordinates, and among coworkers, can swiftly render ineffective the structure of accountability, destroy the downward transmission of directives, and render inoperative the upward transmission of information. Sanctions that can effectively control the behavior of individual workers may be useless when a group of workers is acting in concert. The mechanisms the firm employs to avoid collusion will include the repertoire of devices analyzed in preceding sections. The solidarity of a worker coalition depends on the degree of commonality of interests, the benefits accruing to an individual from withdrawing from the coalition, and the severity of the (usually informal) sanctions the coalition can impose on deviant members. The employer can then prevent coalition formation by fragmenting work groups, increasing the "social distance" between superiors and subordinates, and routing decision-making power through superior hierarchical levels to minimize the degree of control a group of workers may exercise over a co-worker.

But we must add another dimension to our analysis of capitalist production to capture the role of ideology and custom in the reproduction of the social relations through which labor is exploited. We must introduce the additional concept of *legitimation*, characterizing an aspect of the production process as legitimate when it conforms to the norms and expectations of participants. Thus legitimacy is an aspect of social consciousness which changes and develops through the substantive experiences and social relations of workers.

The failure of legitimacy within a group increases the possibility of collusion. Commonly perceived injustice increases solidarity, and increased solidarity leads to increased effective power. Such collusion thwarting the objectives of the employer may call forth extraordinary measures in the form of increased accountability and punishment. These measures may in turn be viewed as illegitimate, thus increasing the solidarity of the coalition and calling forth an additional set of extraordinary measures on the part of the employer. A downward spiral of legitimacy occurs.[26; 66] It follows that the capitalist will normally go to great lengths to avoid the appearance of illegitimate situations, and to provide regularized channels for their correction.[66, ch. 9, 11] This objective is reflected in the organization of production as a whole.

We begin by offering certain generalities concerning the structure of legitimacy. First, the cultural norms of the larger society may supply an overarching pattern of legitimacy orientations which are held more or less firmly by all members of the enterprise. [. . .]

Second, general legitimacy orientations in the larger society may vary systematically across different segments of the work force.[6; 17, p. 170] Thus individuals of a particular race, sex, ethnic or religious origin, age, or class background may consider certain patterns of reward and authority perfectly acceptable which a member of a different group would find intolerable, demeaning, or offensive.[40; 65] [. . .]

Third, specific legitimacy orientations will tend to coalesce around the immediate context of the enterprise and its economic environment. [. . .]

We apply these considerations to some concrete processes within the capitalist enterprise. These include (a) the legitimacy of the actions of superiors, co-workers, and subordinates; (b) the legitimacy of the processes whereby workers are assigned to positions in the organization; (c) the legitimacy of the global distribution of prerogatives, benefits and duties among organizational positions; (d) the legitimacy of the concrete process whereby the worker's own position and those of his or her immediate superiors, co-workers, or subordinates have been attained, as well as the particular criteria on which their prerogatives, duties, and chances for advancement and dismissal are based.[12]

We begin by investigating the global processes whereby individuals are assigned to positions in the enterprise. Most advanced capitalist societies possess a political system based on and reinforcing values of formal equality and representative democracy. The hierarchically ordered capitalist enterprise, however, represents the antithesis of those values, as ultimate decision-making power is held by the few and compliance expected by the many.[54] Thus hierarchical organization in the enterprise requires special legitimating mechanisms. Among these are hierarchically organized educational institutions which inure youth to the social relations of capitalist production [12; 27] and the promulgation of a "technocratic ideology," whereby hierarchical organization and unequal reward are deemed necessary by the nature of advanced technology.[12] Given that the hierarchical structure is legitimated, the legitimacy of the assignment of positions remains problematic. In a situation where a great deal of upward organizational mobility is feasible, this problem is minimal. Such a situation will obtain only when the ratio of the number of workers on successive hierarchical levels is large, a condition normally not obtaining.[6] At this point, the strategy of divide and conquer applies in full force. The profit maximizer will attempt to limit mobility by erecting barriers at fixed intervals in the vertical hierarchy, thus giving rise to stable comparative reference groups. Within these segmentations he will create meritocratic distinctions of pay and prerogatives while maximizing the lines of vertical mobility. Thus, "job ladders" appear for reasons of legitimacy.

Job ladders and segmented mobility patterns are also explained by the Neoclassical theory of the firm in terms of on-the-job training.[20] This theory predicts, however, that the pattern of internal mobility will follow cost-minimizing skill-acquisition opportunities. This need not be the case. Thus, in capitalist societies, entry into a particular segment (at so-called points of entry [see 20, pp. 43–49]) is based on the possession of educational credentials even when these credentials fail to increase worker productivity [8; 32] or when the concrete skills involved could be feasibly obtained on the job.

Much of the above analysis applies to the local situation of the legitimacy of the assignment of a worker and his or her superior to their respective positions. New elements also enter in, however, which bear some treatment. First, the supervisor's effective authority depends on the legitimacy of his or her incumbency in the eyes of subordinates.[14; 22; 62] Without this buttress, subordinates will frequently collude to render ineffective the supervisor's power. Second, the ideologies of "technocracy" and "meritocracy" which guide the perception of global legitimacy have much less sway in the local and concrete experience of a worker interacting with a supervisor. Thus particularistic orientations are likely to be involved in the legitimation of the incumbency of a superior. For instance, norms derived from class segmentations in the larger society may be brought to bear on the legitimate forms of supervisor-subordinate incumbency. In American society the authority of women over men, blacks over whites, younger over older, less educated over more educated, and lower status over higher status (in terms of modes of dress, speech, and demeanor) is generally unstable. Relationships of this type will therefore be discouraged in the capitalist's staffing of jobs.

These mechanisms account for a portion of sexual, racial, and social class discriminations. The Neoclassical theory of the firm treats the staffing of positions in terms of purely "technical" attributes of individuals (e.g., skills and knowledge). When applied across the economy as a whole, this implies the gradual elimination of economic discrimination based on nontechnical characteristics (race, sex, social class background, etc.)[7] This prediction has not been born out. According to our model, however, the decisions of the firm may indeed tend to *stabilize* these differences over time, as the capitalist draws on the segmentations of the larger society in staffing positions in the enterprise. [. . .]

Conclusion

Throughout this essay—in the critique of Neoclassical axioms, in the presentation of an alternative model, in the drawing out of its implications, and in exhibiting their concordance with empirical research—we have focused on the treatment of the various anomalies presented in the introduction.

Our fundamental observation is that in a correct formulation of the theory of the firm, profit maximization entails divergences from Pareto-efficiency which can be understood only in terms of class analysis. Without looking at the inner workings of the firm, we may attribute this to the fact that the real wage and the intensity of labor are effectively endogenous in the capitalists' decisions, the market being only one determinant. That is, the total wage bill is affected not only by the market, but the employer's choice of work organization. The employer can increase the piece of the pie accruing to capital and management by reducing the size of the pie to less than its maximum. Workers would gain by reorganizing production to increase output, work satisfaction, and wages. Indeed, they could compensate the capitalist for his or her losses and still be better off—but of course once they had power there would be no reason for them to do so.

This endogeneity of the real wage has several roots. First, assuming the *money* wage as given, the intensity of labor is not determined by market conditions. This is the failure of the Neoclassical model of the labor exchange. The intensity of labor is the *outcome* of the capitalists' choice of work organization: alongside the problems of allocating given amounts of work is that of eliciting those amounts. Second, even the *money* wage is not determined by market conditions. Not only will the employer voluntarily raise wages selectively above their "market minimum," but he or she may be forced to increase the wage bill should workers acquire sufficient power and solidarity. Since the work force cannot be turned over in each production period, and since wage structure decisions of one period have a strong influence on such decisions in the next, the endogeneity of the wage bill is a real and concrete contingency of profit maximization.

In our model the enforcement of the labor exchange lies within the enterprise. Hence it is not surprising that the most manifest inefficiencies deal with the interaction between productive techniques and control techniques. In the Neoclassical perspective the ''minute division of labor'' is in itself more productive and admits the more flexible introduction of new technologies. The hierarchical structure of control is then necessary to coordinate the atomistic and decentralized activity of a number of fragmented workers. While not denying the need for coordination and control in production, the Marxist model dramatizes the converse: given that profits depend on the integrity of the labor exchange, a strongly centralized structure of control not only serves the interests of the employer, but dictates a minute division of labor irrespective of considerations of productivity. For this reason, the evidence for the superior productivity of ''worker control'' represents the most dramatic of anomalies to the Neoclassical theory of the firm: worker control increases the effective amount of work elicited from each worker and improves the coordination of work activities, while increasing the solidarity and delegitimizing the hierarchical structure of ultimate authority at its roots; hence it threatens to increase the power of workers in the struggle over the share of total value.

In addition, our model, based on the labor/labor-power distinction, is capable of explaining racism, sexism, and the intergenerational transmission of status. While considerations of technical efficiency dictate the staffing of positions on the basis of technical attributes, legitimation dictates the reflection in the enterprise of culturally dominant sexual, racial, and social class ascriptions. There is no prima facie reason for the aggregated actions of individual employers to alter those over time. Nor is it to be expected that differences in mean economic position among various ascriptively identifiable groups will be based on productivity-related attributes. Indeed, our model of the firm places such attributes as one among a number of sets of profit-relevant personal characteristics, others of which include modes of self-presentation and interpersonal behavior, class identification, ascriptive traits, and credentials. Hence it is less than surprising to find the relatively small independent value of IQ and cognitive test scores in predicting economic success, the inability of cognitive differences to explain the association of education with economic success, and the wide variety of criteria actually operative in hiring and promotion.

Finally, our model sheds light on the failure of ''worker sovereignty'' to describe the historical development of work. The symmetry of the labor exchange with commodity exchanges in Neoclassical theory implies that the wage structure will reflect the job preferences of workers, just as the price structure reflects the commodity preferences of consumers. Our model predicts, however, that no set of worker preferences will be reflected in production which threatens the secure capitalist control of the organization, however cheaply labor could be acquired. A group of workers may agree to work under satisfying conditions (e.g., where they control their activities) for diminished wages, but there is no guarantee these wages would prevail in future periods, where worker solidarity and control is deeply embedded in the organizational structure.[7]

I conclude that a Marxist theory of production in which class relations in general, and the labor/labor-power distinction in particular, play a fundamental role provides an excellent basis for understanding the social relations of the production process. This paper, of course, provides only a few of the insights necessary to turn such a theory into a potent tool of socialist strategy. The general organizational issues we have discussed must in the future be supplemented by extensive historical and comparative studies.[14; 45; 57; 64]

Notes

1. By the term 'efficient' in this paper I shall mean Pareto-efficient; i.e., no reorganization of the work process or allocation of economic activity within that process can increase output without in the long run increasing objective or subjective costs of production. Thus the efficiency criterion is judged within the framework of existing technologies and worker preferences. While thereby limited and ahistorical in nature, the concept will be sufficient for our purposes.

2. This standard Neoclassical theory of job structures may not be familiar to some readers, as it is not normally presented in standard microeconomic texts. For a full treatment, see [2, 18].

3. For an extensive bibliography, see [67].

4. Of course if either the supply curve facing the user or the demand curve facing the supplier is not perfectly elastic the exchange may involve elements going beyond the legally enforceable contract. For instance, in a "buyer's market" the supplier may offer increased service in the hope of gaining further contracts with the user, and conversely in a "seller's market." The reader can easily show that this represents a case of limited monopoly or oligopoly, and "power relations" enter into the economic analysis even in Neoclassical theory. For this reason (according to Lerner's reasoning), the assumption of extensive competition becomes integral to traditional economic analysis.

5. This is the case of the so-called Economic Theory of Terms—cf. [46].

6. This condition may hold for certain sectors of the enterprise, such as middle and upper management, and within a hierarchical level, such as apprentice II mechanic —> apprentice I mechanic —> master mechanic. Hence they present problems of legitimacy.

7. It may be asked why, if observed organizational forms are not efficient, they are not competed out of existence. Our argument shows clearly why capitalists do not seek alternatives in competition with one another. But why, for instance, do not workers hire capital and institute their own organization? I take this to be an open question. It may be that workers simply do not have the collateral to borrow large amounts of capital, or that if several workers did decide to "go it on their own" they would hire labor as well as the other factors and in effect cease being workers. It must be stressed, however, that the answer is to be found in the nature of the capitalist economy, rather than an error in the model presented herein. For the same problem arises independent of the efficiency of the capitalist enterprise and its responsiveness to worker preferences. Suppose profit maximization entails efficiency and workers act to maximize their incomes. Let us also accept that

profits of efficiently managed firms are significantly positive, after making all factor payments (including interest on capital borrowed). Then any group of workers has an incentive to opt out of a firm, hire capital, raw materials, and appoint a manager—thereby capturing the surplus generated in production, while maintaining exactly the same internal organization of the firm. Yet workers do not do this. If the conditions of "optimality" in the competitive model held, we would observe a large number of ownership patterns of firms. While there is a large number, scarcely any involve hiring capital. If there were no "barriers of entry" into firm control, we would see some firms in which capital hires managers and labor, some in which managers hire capital and workers, and some in which workers hire managers and capital. The market would bid up the price of "managerial talent" so that net profits would be eliminated. Yet this does not occur. Thus some of the competitive conditions must be violated.[1] Whatever restricts workers from hiring capital and managers simply to capture profits also will operate to restrict them from improving their job characteristics.

Sources

Kenneth Arrow, "The Firm in General Equilibrium Theory," in R. Morris and A. Wood, *The Corporate Economy*. Cambridge: Harvard University Press, 1971.   [1]
Kenneth J. Arrow and F. H. Hahn, *General Competitive Analysis*. San Francisco: Holden-Day, 1971.   [2]
Orley Ashenfelter, "Changes in Labor Market Discrimination Over Time," *Journal of Human Resources* (Fall 1970).   [3]
Chester I. Barnard, *The Functions of the Executive*. Cambridge: Harvard University Press, 1966.   [4]
Alan B. Batchelder, "Decline in the Relative Income of Negro Men," *Quarterly Journal of Economics* (November 1964).   [5]
J. C. Baxter, J. M. Lerner, and J. S. Miller, "Identification as a Function of the Reinforcing Quality of the Model and the Socialization Background of the Subject," *Journal of Personal and Social Psychology* 2 (1965).   [6]
Gary Becker, *The Economics of Discrimination*. Chicago: University of Chicago Press, 1957.   [7]
Ivar Berg, *Education and Jobs: The Great Training Robbery*. New York: Praeger, 1970.[8]
Peter L. Berger and Thomas Luckmann, *The Social Construction of Reality*. Garden City, N.Y.: Doubleday, 1967.   [9]
Barry Bluestone, "The Tripartite Economy: Labor Markets and the Earning Poor," *Poverty and Human Resources* (July/August 1970).   [10]
Paul Blumberg, *Industrial Democracy*. New York: Shocken, 1969.   [11]
Samuel Bowles and Herbert Gintis, *Schooling in Capitalist America*. New York: Basic Books, 1975.   [12]
Samuel Bowles and Valerie Nelson, "The 'Genetic Inheritance of IQ' and the Intergenerational Reproduction of Economic Equality," *Review of Economics and Statistics* (1974).   [13]
Harry Braverman, *Labor and Monopoly Capital*. New York: Monthly Review Press, 1974.   [14]
R. Coase, "The Nature of the Firm," *Economica* 4 (November 1937), reprinted in *Readings in Price Theory*. Chicago: Irwin, 1952.   [15]
Lester Coch and J. R. P. French, Jr., "Overcoming Resistance to Change," *Human Relations* 1, 4 (August 1948).   [16]
Barry E. Collins and Bertram H. Raven, "Group Structure: Attraction, Coalitions, Communication, and Power," in *The Handbook of Social Psychology*, ed. Gardner Lindzey and Elliot Aronson. Reading, Mass.: Addison-Wesley, 1969.   [17]
Gerald Debreu, *Theory of Value*. New Haven: Yale University Press, 1959.   [18]

Peter B. Doeringer, "Low Pay, Labor Market Dualism, and Industrial Relations Systems," Harvard Institute for Economic Research Discussion Paper no. 271 (April 1973).   [19]

Peter B. Doeringer and Michael J. Piore, *Internal Labor Markets and Manpower Analysis*. Lexington, Mass.: D. C. Heath, 1971.   [20]

Richard C. Edwards, "Alienation and Inequality: Capitalist Relations of Production in a Bureaucratic Enterprise," Ph.D. diss., Harvard University, July 1972.   [21]

Amitai Etzioni, *A Comparative Analysis of Complex Organizations*. Glencoe: Free Press, 1961.   [22]

Leon Festinger, "A Theory of Social Comparison Processes," *Human Relations* 7 (1954).   [23]

J. R. P. French, Jr., "Field Experiments: Changing Group Productivity," in *Experiments in Social Process*, ed. J. G. Miller. New York: McGraw-Hill, 1950.   [24]

Maurice A. Garnier, "Power and Ideological Conformity: A Case Study," *American Journal of Sociology* (September 1973).   [25]

Carl Gersuny, *Punishment and Redress in a Modern Factory*. Lexington, Mass.: D. C. Heath, 1973.   [26]

Herbert Gintis, "Welfare Criteria with Endogenous Preferences: The Economics of Education," *International Economic Review* (June 1974).   [27]

Herbert Gintis, "Consumer Behavior and the Concept of Sovereignty," *American Economic Review* (May 1972).   [28]

Herbert Gintis, "Education, Technology, and the Characteristics of Worker Productivity," *American Economic Review* (May 1971).   [29]

Erving Goffman, *The Presentation of Self in Everyday Life*. Garden City, N.Y.: Doubleday, 1959.   [30]

Marilyn Goldberg, "Economic Exploitation of Women," in D. M. Gordon, *Problems in Political Economy: An Urban Perspective*. Lexington, Mass.: D. C. Heath, 1971. [31]

André Gorz, "Technical Intelligence and the Capitalist Division of Labor," *TELOS* 12 (Summer 1972).   [32]

André Gorz, "Le Despotisme de l'Usine et ses Lendemains," *Les Temps Modernes* (September-October 1972).   [33]

Bennett Harrison, *Education, Training and the Urban Ghetto*. Baltimore, 1972.   [34]

Herbert H. Hyman and Eleanor Singer, *Readings in Reference Group Theory and Research*. New York: Free Press, 1968.   [35]

Christopher Jencks et al., *Inequality: A Reappraisal of the Effects of Family and Schooling in America*. New York: Basic Books, 1972.   [36]

Harold H. Kelley, "Two Functions of Reference Groups," in *Readings in Social Psychology*, ed. Guy E. Swanson, T. M. Newcomb, and E. L. Hartley. Holt, Reinhart, and Winston, 1952.   [37]

Clark Kerr, "The Balkanization of Labor Markets," in *Labor Mobility and Economic Opportunity*, ed. E. Wight Bakke et al. Cambridge: Technology Press of MIT, 1954.   [38]

Dean D. Knudsen, "The Declining Status of Women," *Social Forces* 48, 2 (1969).   [39]

Melvin L. Kohn, *Class and Conformity: A Study in Values*. Homewood, Ill.: Dorsey, 1969.   [40]

Melvin Kohn and Carmi Schooler, "Occupational Experience and Psychological Functioning," *American Sociological Review* 38 (February 1973).   [41]

L. C. Lawrence and P. C. Smith, "Group Decision and Employee Participation," *Journal of Applied Psychology* 34 (1955).   [42]

Abba Lerner, "The Economics and Politics of Consumer Sovereignty," *American Economic Review* (May 1972).   [43]

Mao Tse-tung, "On Contradiction," in Stuart R. Schram, *The Political Thought of Mao Tse-tung*. New York: Praeger, 1969.   [44]

Stephen Marglin, "What Do Bosses Do?" *Review of Radical Political Economics* 6, 2 (Summer 1974). [45]

Jacob Marschak and Roy Radner, *The Economic Theory of Teams*. New Haven: Yale University Press, 1972. [46]

Karl Marx, *Economic and Philosophical Manuscripts*, ed. Dirk Struick. New York: International, 1969. [47]

J. L. Meij, *Internal Wage Structure*. Amsterdam: North Holland, 1963. [48]

R. K. Merton, *Social Theory and Social Structure*. New York: Free Press, 1957. [49]

Nancy C. Morse and E. Reimer, "The Experimental Manipulation of a Major Organizational Variable," *Journal of Abnormal and Social Psychology* 52 (1956). [50]

Claus Offe, *Leistungsprinzip und Industrielle Arbeit*. Frankfurt: Europaische Verlaganstalt, 1970. [51]

Talcott Parsons and Edward A. Shils, *Towards a General Theory of Action*. Cambridge: Harvard University Press, 1951. [52]

Martin Patchen, "The Effect of Reference Group Standards on Job Satisfactions," *Human Relations* 11 (1958). [53]

Carole Pateman, *Participation and Democratic Theory*. Cambridge: Cambridge University Press, 1970. [54]

Michael J. Piore, "The Role of Immigration in Industrial Growth," Department of Economics Working Paper no. 112, MIT, May 1973. [55]

Michael Reich, David M. Gordon, and Richard C. Edwards, "A Theory of Labor Market Segmentation," *Proceedings of the 25th Industrial Relations Research Association*, December 1972. [56]

Carl Riskin, "Incentive Systems and Work Motivations," *Working Papers* 1, 4 (Winter 1974). [57]

Fritz J. Roethlisberger and William J. Dickson, *Management and the Worker*. Cambridge: Harvard University Press, 1967. [58]

William H. Sewell, Archibald O. Haller, and Alejandro Portes, "The Educational and Early Occupational Attainment Process," *American Sociological Review* 34 (February 1969). [59]

Harold L. Sheppard and Neal Herrick, *Where Have All the Robots Gone?* New York: Free Press, 1972. [60]

Herbert A. Simon, *Models of Man*. New York: Wiley, 1957. [61]

Herbert Simon, *Administrative Behavior*. New York: Free Press, 1957. [62]

Arthur L. Stinchcombe, "Bureaucratic and Craft Administration of Production: A Comparative Study," *Administrative Science Quarterly* (September 1959). [63]

Katherine Stone, "The Origins of Job Structures in the Steel Industry," *Review of Radical Political Economics* (Summer 1974). [64]

Victor Vroom, "Industrial Social Psychology," in *The Handbook of Social Psychology*, ed. G. Lindsey and E. Aaronsen. Reading, Mass.: Addison-Wesley, 1969. [65]

William F. Whyte, *Money and Motivation*. New York: Harper and Row, 1955. [66]

Work in America, Report of a Task Force to the Secretary of Health, Education and Welfare. Cambridge: MIT Press, 1973. [67]

Dennis Wrong, "The Oversocialized Conception of Man in Modern Sociology," *American Sociological Review* 26 (April 1961). [68]

H. Zellner, "Discrimination Against Women, Occupational Segregation, and the Relative Wage," *American Economic Review* (May 1972). [69]

Economics:
The Revival of Political Economy

EDWARD NELL

Edward Nell argues that Neoclassical economics fails to explain one of the most important functions and outcomes of economic systems—the distribution of income. The reason, Nell claims, is that orthodox theory has completely displaced the concepts of property and power by assuming these relations away or subsuming them into a static misinterpretation of technology. He further asserts that the current challenges posed by political economy can in fact provide more substantial explanations.

Since the latter decades of the nineteenth century orthodox economic theory has made its main business the demonstration that a well-oiled market mechanism will produce the most efficient allocation of scarce resources among competing ends. This preoccupation has in turn dictated a characteristic mode of analysis, in which the economy is divided horizontally, so to speak, into "agencies," or institutions, which whatever their other differences, always operate on the same side of the market and so respond in roughly similar ways to market incentives. Thus Rockefellers and sharecroppers are both households, GM and the corner grocery are both firms. Households demand "final goods" and supply labor and other "factor services" (meaning the use of capital and land); firms demand labor and other "factor services" and supply "final goods."

This way of subdividing the economy fits neatly into the framework of "rational choice." Firms supply goods and demand factors in the amounts and proportions that will maximize their profits, given their technical possibilities and opportunities. Households supply factor services and demand goods in the amounts and proportions that will maximize their "utility" (most perfectly satisfy their preferences), given their "initial endowments," a polite and covert way of referring to property holdings. The amounts finally chosen, the equilibrium supplies and demands, will be simultaneously compatible solutions to all these different individual maximizing problems.

The task of high theory, then, is twofold: first, since the models are complex, *to show that there are, indeed, such simultaneous, mutually compatible solutions.* This is not obvious, and in fact not always true. Second, of equal mathematical and of greater ideological importance, are what might be called the

Edward Nell, "Economics: The Revival of Political Economy," in *Ideology in Social Science*, ed. Robin Blackburn (Isle of Man: Fontana/Collins, 1972), pp. 76–95.

Invisible Hand Theorems, which *show that the system of market incentives will direct the economy toward the equilibrium prices, supplies, and demands.* In other words, the theorems demonstrate that the system is automatically self-adjusting and self-regulating.

Orthodox economic theory has many strengths. Market incentives often *do* direct the system in various predictable ways. Maximizing is, under some conditions, an indispensable part of rational behavior, and so must be spelled out. That it is all done at an exceptionally high level of abstraction is not only no objection, it may be a positive merit. The analysis is not cluttered with irrelevancies.

But when all is said, apart from defending the freedoms appropriate to private enterprise from harebrained schemes of social reform, the theory of the optimality of competitive markets has never provided much practical insight into the working of the economy. Since it presupposes effective market incentives and institutions devoted to maximizing behavior, it cannot easily be applied to the study either of premarket economies or of postmarket ones—i.e., ideal communist (or anarchist) societies. Still, traditional theory could probably be forgiven these shortcomings if it provided a good model for studying the working and misworking of present-day capitalism. Unfortunately, it is not even a good model for this, and for a very simple reason.

Basically, orthodox theory is a theory of markets and market interdependence. It is a theory of general equilibrium in *exchange*, extended almost as an afterthought, to cover production and distribution. It is not a theory of a social system, still less of economic power and social class. Households and firms are considered only as market agents, never as parts of a social structure. Their "initial endowments," wealth, skills, and property, are taken as *given*. Moreover, the object of the theory is to demonstrate the tendency toward equilibrium; class and sectoral conflict is therefore ruled out almost by assumption.

As a result, the orthodox approach has comparatively little interesting to say about such important socioeconomic questions as the distribution of wealth and income. It cannot say how these came about; it cannot say how different they might be under another kind of economic system, and it cannot describe the evolution and development of the institution of private property.

It does, however, have one major claim to social and historical relevance. It offers a definite though limited theory of the division of the value of net output between land, labor, and capital. This is known as "marginal productivity" theory. Briefly, it states that each agent in the system will tend to be rewarded in proportion to and—as a limiting case—in direct equivalence to the contribution it makes to output. Thus a man earns what he (literally) makes; a landlord reaps what he (metaphorically) sows.

But with the revival of interest in the great problems of political economy in recent years, this central claim has come under increasingly heavy attack. Moreover, in the last few years, this attack, which began in particular objections to specific orthodox doctrines, has developed into an alternative conception of the economic system. It is no longer simply a rival theory of growth and distribution—a "non-Neoclassical" theory—nor can it be regarded merely as a return to the approach of the Classical Greats, Smith, Ricardo, and Marx. It is both of these, but it is considerably more. In currently fashionable terminology, it is the emergence of a new paradigm.

To see this, let us contrast the emerging view of income distribution with orthodox marginal productivity theory. At first glance, marginal productivity theory appears eminently sensible. As we have seen, it states that "factors"—land, labor, and capital—will be hired as long as they produce more than they cost to hire. Since expanding the employment of any one factor, the others held constant, will (the theory assumes) cause the returns on the extra units of that factor to decline (it having proportionately less of the others to work with), extra employment will cease when the declining returns just equal the cost of hiring the factor. The total earnings of any factor will then be equal to its amount times its marginal product, summed up over all the industries in which it is used. Clearly the relative shares of "factors," land, labor, and capital, depend on the technology (which determines how rapidly returns diminish) and on the supplies of the factors available.

So far so good. To be sure, this story depends on the existence of markets, specifically on markets for labor, land, and capital, so that the theory will not be much use in examining the emergence or abolition of the market system. But also, in a sleight of hand so deft as to have passed virtually unnoticed for an intellectual generation, it attributes responsibility for the distribution of income (under market competition) wholly and solely to the impersonal agency of *technology*. No man, nor god, least of all politics, in this most political of economic affairs, has decreed what the shares of labor and capital are to be in the total product. They are the accidental, but inescapable, and unalterable, consequence of the technology we happen to have. Only through technical changes, inventions which alter the engineering possibilities, can relative shares be changed. For if income shares are to change, the ratio of the proportional changes in the marginal products must differ from the ratio of the proportional changes in the amounts of factors employed. Which is to say that everything depends on how rapidly marginal returns to the different factors diminish, relative to one another, and this is a matter which depends only on technology.

So the class struggle is an illusion; unions are valuable only as mother-substitutes—providers of security and a sense of identification. Minimum-wage legislation, by restricting the level of employment offered, and in no other way, may or may not raise wages—if the marginal product rises proportionately more than the employment falls such legislation *could* raise labor's share. But in both cases the effect will depend wholly on what the technology permits. Only moves that change the relative marginal products of labor and capital can affect income distribution (though even they might not if, for example, the movement in the relative amounts of labor and capital employed just offsets the changes in marginal products). For whereas profits and wages depend to some extent on the available amounts of labor and capital, they hinge chiefly on the technical opportunities, which determine what the marginal productivity of each factor will be. Indeed, the influence of factor supplies is felt through, and only through, marginal productivity. Hence *technology* is what finally determines income distribution. Aggregate demand, monetary policy, inflation, unions, politics, even revolution, are, in the end, all alike, irrelevant.

That the technical possibilities available influence income distribution is surely undeniable. Clearly, if it is known that a machine can do a certain job, the laborer now doing it would be unwise to ask, and unlikely to get, more in pay than it would cost to install and run the machine. But this in no way depends on diminishing marginal returns; substitution of machines for men and *vice versa*, although what marginal productivity theory is talking about, can be examined without its straitjacket.

In any case, the technical possibilities of substitution are only one set of influences among many which bear upon the division of national income. For example, the orthodox story in singling out the influence of technology neglects that of, say, differential rates of inflation. This is not a merely accidental oversight. Ideologically significant choices are never simple and, while they may occur, in the first instance, by chance, it is not by chance that they get incorporated into the textbooks, even if the motivation is seldom explicit or conscious. Here the ideological content could hardly be clearer. No one is responsible for technology (so the story goes); it is "given"—the result of cultural and historical influences quite separate from the economic system. But if technology is the chief determinant of income distribution, then apart from its influence, only minor changes are possible. Even monopoly power and the influence of the state make only a marginal difference. The theory, in short, relieves politics and property of any responsibility for the existing division of earnings and patterns of consumption, no small coup in the ideological fray.

Socialist and New Left economists, indeed social critics generally, have always gagged on this. Property and power, they maintain, are the essential elements in class struggles and sectional conflicts; it is ridiculous to say they do not matter, that the outcome, given the competitive market, is predetermined by the accidents of technological inventiveness. From their vantage point, income distribution, the division of society's annual product among the members of society, is *the* central question. By way of contrast, for the orthodox economists the problem of *allocation* stood at the center; their questions were how the members of society choose to spend their incomes, and how suppliers adjust to this. But if we put income distribution at the center of the stage, these questions seem relatively minor. The framework of rational choice looks flimsier and more makeshift; essentially a consumer theory, it has come to resemble so many consumer products, ingenious, brilliant, but unsuited to human needs. Like the automobile, its surface dazzles, but its functioning can be destructive.

This is not to say that the political economist rejects the theory of rational choice outright; he rejects it merely as an appropriate framework for the analysis of production and distribution in the aggregate. The appropriate framework is one which reveals the *links* between sectors and classes, how the products of one industry or set of industries are used as inputs by other industries, whose products, in turn, are used by still others; how the earnings of one class are spent supporting production in some sector or industry. Interindustry and intersectoral relations are crucial to understanding how changes in demands or in technology transmute themselves into prosperity for some, disaster for others. Links between revenue from sales, social classes, and spending are crucial for understanding how the distribution of income is established and maintained in the face of considerable changes in the composition of output and in government policy.

The difference may seem more one of emphasis than of substance, but putting income distribution at the center and relating it to different patterns of linkages, of payment streams, and of technological dependency between industries, sectors, and classes leads to an altogether different vision of how the economy works. Perhaps the best way to explain this is to list the principal differences.

The new vision can be called a "general equilibrium" approach, if one likes. But it departs from the orthodox meaning of that phase by emphasizing the *interdependence of production*, rather than of markets; technical and institutional "interlocks"—or their absence—rather than purely market relationships.

A second difference between the new approach and the old lies in the treatment of "substitution." In the old picture substitution is the law of life on both the supply and demand sides. In response to price changes, different patterns of goods and/or of factors will be chosen; when prices change, cheaper things will be substituted for more expensive in household budgets and industrial processes. Yet we all know this is unrealistic so far as industrial production is concerned; indeed, the availability of opportunities for substitution may itself be an index of development. Moreover, the conventional picture assumes that households and firms have *given* ends—the production of "utility" or output respectively. It does not deal with the more important questions of introducing altogether new products and processes, changes which often alter the parameters of the system or perhaps even the consciousness of the society. Even within the narrow focus of the Neoclassical lens, however, many alleged cases of substitution really involve something quite different—technical progress, changes in the nature of the product, external effects on parameters of the system, and so on. Widespread possibilities for Neoclassical substitution must be a *special* case, and that is how the matter is treated in the new vision.

Third, the old vision treats the consumer as sovereign, and the effects of his choices enter into the determination of all major variables. This, of course, does not render the old vision incapable of discussing market power, producer sovereignty, or the "new industrial state." But, inevitably, such phenomena appear as special cases, limitations on the *general* principle of consumer sovereignty. In the new vision the consumer is cut down to size from the start. His preferences have little or *no* effect on prices and income distribution.

Fourth, markets are not supposed naturally to be stable, or to engender optima (though, of course, in some cases they may). Prices are determined largely, and in simple models, wholly from the supply side. The choice of industrial techniques depends on prospective profits, which in turn depend largely on *aggregate* demand and the state of the labor market. Aggregate demand depends on business saving and investment plans, which in turn depend on a wide variety of factors, including the political climate, past growth rates, and "animal spirits," none of which find much of a welcome in Neoclassical models. But aggregate demand is also influenced by, and influences, the distribution of income; indeed, this relationship is central to the new picture, and provides a sharp contrast to the old.

A fundamental difference can be seen when we consider the *purposes* of the two visions. The basic constituents of the old vision are consumers and firms, agents whose optimizing behavior, individually or in the aggregate, the equations of the models describe. In particular, maximizing behavior is what the theory is all about, and the *object of the theory, by and large, is to predict such behavior and its consequences*. But the circumstances in which behavior takes place are taken for granted.

By contrast—and oversimplifying—the new vision is primarily interested in structure, in the patterns of dependency between established institutions, in how the system hangs together, and works or fails to work. The job of economic theory is to delineate the *blueprint* of the economic system, of the environment in which economic behavior takes place. The basic constituents of theory are industries, sectors, processes, or activities, defined in technological terms; so defined, the new vision's basic constituents normally will coincide with "decision-making" agencies. Neither the word "household" nor the word "firm," nor any synonym for either, appears in Sraffa's *Production of Commodities by Means of Commodities*, the basic work laying the foundation of the new paradigm. For decision making, the prediction of behavior of what *will* happen, is not the goal. The new vision is concerned to see how an economy keeps going, what is *supposed* to happen, and from that to discover what makes it break down, and what makes it develop into an economy of a different kind. These are seen as questions primarily addressed to the analysis of the system of production, and of the social relations surrounding production.

The central distinction between the two visions, then, lies in the treatment of production and distribution. For the traditional Neoclassical economist, production is a one-way street, running from primary "factors" to "final products." Among the primary factors are land, labor, and, above all, *capital*, each receiving in competition a reward proportional, in some sense (depending on market circumstances) to its "contribution."

Not so in the new paradigm. The notion that the three traditional factors are on the same footing is discarded altogether. The great achievement of the Marginalist Revolution, as seen by its nineteenth-century proponents, namely, the development of a unified theory applying to all three factors, is utterly dismissed. This can be seen nowhere so clearly as in the new conception of ''capital,'' in reality a revival of a point well understood before the Marginalists confused everything. ''Capital'' has two meanings. On the one hand, it is property in the means of production, enabling owners of equal amounts of claims in these means to receive equal returns (given competitive conditions). In this sense it is a homogenous fund of value, capable of being embodied in different forms.

On the other hand, ''capital'' also means produced means of production—that is, specific materials, tools, instruments, machines, plant, and equipment, on which, with which, and by means of which labor works. In this sense it is a set of heterogenous, disparate products. *Capital goods are not the same thing as capital.* ''Capital'' is relevant to the analysis of the division of income among the members of society, but a nonspecific fund has no bearing on production. ''Capital goods'' are relevant to the study of production, but have no bearing on the distribution of income, since profit is earned and interest paid on the *fund* (value) of capital invested, regardless of its specific form. ''Capital goods,'' specific instruments, can only be converted into a fund of ''capital'' on the basis of a given set of prices for these instruments; but to know these prices we must already know the general rate of profit (in a reasonably competitive capitalist economy).[1] Hence the amount of ''capital'' cannot be among the factors which set the level of the rate of profit. But in the orthodox or Neoclassical theory the ''contribution'' of ''capital'' to *production* supposedly determines the demand for capital, which together with the supply determines the rate of profit. This must be rejected. No sense can be given to the ''contribution'' to production of a *fund* of capital.

This is not to say that *saving and investment*, and their long-run consequences, are irrelevant to determining the rate of profits and relative shares. Quite the reverse; by eliminating the alleged ''contribution of capital'' in production as an influence or determinant of distribution, we open the way for a theory of distribution based on the relation between the growth of spending, of capacity, and of the labor force, on the one hand, and on the market power available to the various parties, on the other. Unequal rates of inflation of money wages and prices necessarily imply changes in the relative shares going to capital and labor, as Keynes pointed out in the *Treatise on Money*. Inflation is partly a consequence of the ratio of demand to supply, but it also reflects relative market power. And here is where the rules of the game—the rules of property—come in. For property confers advantages, though not absolute ones, in the setting of prices and in bargaining for money wages. Exactly what these advantages are, how they work, by what kinds of forces—are among the questions which a theory of distribution should be able to answer.

In short, the new vision adopts a picture of the relation between production and distribution altogether distinct from that which has ruled the economists' roost since the Marginal Revolution. This, in turn, entails rejecting some widely used techniques of empirical analysis, in favor with both radical and straight economists. In particular, "production function" studies, e.g., of technical progress, the contribution of education, the effects of discrimination, and of shares during growth, all involve a fatal flaw. For insofar as they proceed by assuming that a factor's *income share* indicates in any way its *productive power* at the margin, they are based on precisely the relationship which the new vision rejects.[2]

It thus seems that conventional theory, although it contains much of value and importance, contains a fatal flaw.[3] The Neoclassical theory of the general equilibrium of production, distribution, and exchange holds that the payments in the *factor markets* are *exchanges* in the same sense as payments in the *product markets*. "Distribution is the species of exchange," wrote Edgeworth, "by which produce is divided between the parties who have contributed to its production." Distribution, say the proponents of the new vision, is *not* a species of exchange; and capital *goods*, rather than capital, contribute to production. The ideological teeth begin to bite: an exchange, in equilibrium, means that *value equivalent is traded for value equivalent*. No exploitation there. But if distribution is *not* a form of exchange, then we must ask, Who Whom?

This catalogue of differences, and especially the last point, can be nicely illustrated by comparing two simple diagrams which visually summarize the two paradigms. The first, adapted from Samuelson and echoed in all major textbooks, is shown in figure 1 and presents what might be called a same-level division of society.

Business and the public (producers and consumers) confront each other more or less as equals in the markets for both products and factors. (The equality is an overall one; there are some large or allied firms, some collective consumers.) Households demand final goods and services and supply the services of productive factors, in both cases in accord with what economists rather pompously call "their given relative preference schedules," meaning what they like best. Businesses supply final goods and services according to their cost schedules in relation to the prices which consumers are prepared to pay, and demand the services of productive factors, according to their technical opportunities and needs in relation to consumer demand for products.

So goods and services flow counterclockwise, while money flows clockwise. In each set of markets, *equivalents are traded for equivalents*, the value of goods and services flowing in one direction being just matched by the stream of revenue in the other. No exploitation is possible in competitive equilibrium. The value of household factor supplies just matches aggregate household demand and the output of goods and services by business just matches the value of productive services which business demands. This may seem to ignore the fact that households save and businesses invest, meaning that some final demand flows not from the Public but from Business. But that is easily allowed for. To finance this demand, Business must borrow Household savings, by supplying bonds which

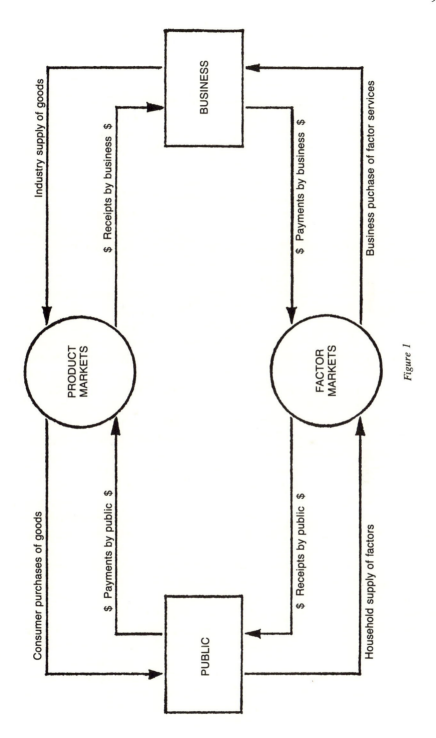

Figure 1

the public demands. Bonds are treated as a kind of good, flowing counterclockwise, while loans join the stream of money flowing clockwise. These points
enable the micro flow picture to be summed up as a macro flow picture, illustrat-
ing in the simplest way how macro rests on micro foundations.

Obvious objections to this economic schema can easily be raised. For instance,
not all "households" are on a par, since some *own* all the firms between them,
while the rest merely *work for* the firms. Also the distribution of profit and similar
income is not an exchange, since the only "service" which the owner of a
business in his capacity as owner need supply in return for its profits is that of
permitting it to be owned by him. (He does bear risks, of course, but so do the
employees who will be out of their jobs in the event of failure.) Other objections
were mentioned earlier in the charge that orthodox Neoclassicism ignores technological interdependences and institutional relationships, as the circular flow
picture makes evident. Nowhere in it can one find social classes or any specific
information about patterns of technical interdependence.

All these objections look at first like strong empirical problems which Neoclassicists should meet head on. In fact, however, the customary orthodox defense
is oblique and of dubious validity. To the charge that their model rests on
unrealistic assumptions, they reply that the *only* test of a model is the success of
its predictions. So there is no a priori error in making unrealistic assumptions.
Moreover "simplifying assumptions" and "theoretical constructs" are bound to
be, in some sense, "unrealistic," and there is no predicting without them.
Unrealistic assumptions may therefore be warranted, and the warrant is philosophical, positivism itself.

To these defenses we will return. But first consider quite a different picture of
capitalist society. Figure 2 epitomizes the new approach, which, if the old is
"Neoclassical," could be dubbed "Classical-Marxian." It cannot be claimed
that this is the only, or necessarily the best, distillation of an alternative picture
from that tradition, but it will certainly serve to illustrate the contrasts.

To keep the diagram comparable, we retain the circle for the final goods
market and the box standing for industry, though we shall interpret both quite
differently. "Households" and the "factor market" disappear altogether. Instead
we have a pyramid, representing the social hierarchy, divided into two parts: a
small upper class of owners and a large lower class of workers. Owners own
industry and receive profits; workers work for industry and receive wages.
Workers consume, but do not (in this simplified model) save; owners both
consume and (save in order to) invest.

Now consider the flows of goods and services and money payments. Labor is
the only "factor input"; other inputs are produced by industry itself, which is
assumed to have access to land, mines, etc. (We are lumping landlords and
capitalists together.) Hence we might expect to be able to value the total product in
terms of labor, and though the mathematics is complicated, this can indeed be
done, though not in all cases. The arrows running back and forth between

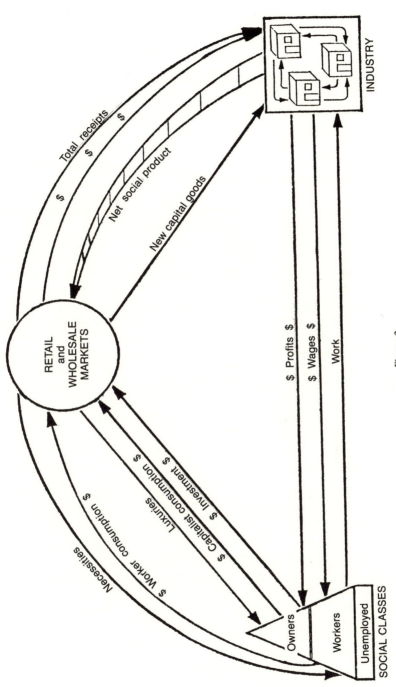

Figure 2

factories represent interindustry transactions, the exchanges between industries necessary to replace used-up means of production. The net social product is sold for total receipts, and consists of all goods over and above those needed for replacement. These can be divided (for convenience) into necessities, luxuries, and new capital goods.[4] Necessities go for worker consumption, luxuries for capitalist consumption, and new capital goods are installed in the factories in return for investment payments. Hence, the national accounts work out:

total receipts = net social product = wages + profit = wage consumption + capitalist consumption + investment demand = necessities + luxuries + new capital goods.

From the point of view of political economy, however, the most important fact is that while wages are paid for work, and one can (and in some circumstances should) think of the wage bill, equal here to worker consumption, as reproducing the power to work, *profits are not paid for anything at all*. The flow of profit income is not an exchange in any sense, metaphorical or otherwise. The Samuelson diagram is fundamentally misleading; there is no "flow" from "household supply" to the factor market for capital. The *only* flow is the flow of profit income in the other direction. And this, of course, leads straight to that hoary but substantial claim that the payment of wages is not an exchange, either, or, at any rate, not a fair one. For wages plus profits add up to the net social product, yet profits are not paid for anything, while wages are paid for work. Hence the work of labor (using the tools, equipment, etc., replacement and depreciation of which is already counted in) has produced the entire product. Is labor not therefore exploited? Does it not deserve the whole product?

The latter question opens Pandora's Box; as for the former, it all depends on what you mean. What does certainly follow, however, is that distribution is *not* an exchange, profits are not paid *for* anything, and they serve no essential economic function. This may not be exploitation but it shows clearly that no purely economic justification can be found for profits, interest, dividends, and the like.[5] Moreover, since the payment of profit is no exchange, there can be no equilibrium, in the usual sense. A century-old school of thought, holding that our troubles come from the *excessive* profits sucked in by giant monopolies, and idolizing small competitive enterprise earning "normal profits," is thereby undercut. There is no merit in "normal profit," indeed there is no such thing. The issue for political economy is the profit system itself, not its alleged abuse.

Figure 2 helps us to understand how the division of income comes about. Remember that the orthodox doctrine held that the distribution of income was determined in the factor market, by the marginal "contribution" of factors in conjunction with their relative scarcity. Figure 2 makes it clear that income distribution interacts with all aspects of the economy, not just with the "factor market." This point can be made quite simply, though its consequences are far-reaching. Labor's share is given by the real wage times the amount of work. But the *real* wage is the *money* wage divided by an index of consumer goods prices. The money wage is set in the labor market, but prices are set in the final goods market. Labor's share, then, depends on *both* markets. Moreover, as the diagram shows, consumer demand depends on labor's share; the system is strongly interdependent in ways not found in orthodox teaching.[6] [. . .]

We have now discussed the two paradigms. The Neoclassical one is far better known but we feel it is significantly misleading. The new paradigm, by contrast, is clearly more realistic, and more capable of handling questions such as property and social class.

These claims are widely resisted, for the reasons mentioned. Conventional economists often contend that a paradigm cannot be "misleading" in its representation of institutions *if it leads to models that predict well.* "Realism" is not important; abstraction must take place, and a model can abstract from anything, so long as it performs well.

Such a defense is a methodological claim based on a, today, rather questionable philosophy of science. One response might be that Neoclassical models have not done very well on their chosen ground. Prediction has not been the greatest success of modern economics. But a more fundamental response would be to challenge the methodology itself. There is an intuitive appeal to the idea that a model of social institutions must be a good representation of things as they are at a given moment regardless of how they work out over time. It may be too much to demand of economics that it predicts what will happen. In modern industrial societies the economic system is too closely interlocked with other aspects of society to be isolated enough for effective tests. But to add *ceteri paribus* clauses simply tends to reduce predictions to vacuity. Instead, we must examine the definitions and assumptions of our models for their realism, and for the extent to which they incorporate the essentials. If they are realistic, the working of the model should mirror that of the economic system in relatively simple and abstract form. It should be clear from this that our case can be defended from the methodological objections of the Positivists.

The new approach is a coherent picture of the economy capable of providing technical analysis of a sophisticated nature.[7] But it has not been developed for its own sake, or simply because it presents a better, more accurate picture of capitalism. It should be more fruitful, but the fruit should redden as it ripens. The new picture is intended precisely as *political economics*, as a guide to the criticism of the capitalist socioeconomic system, and the objection to orthodox thinking was that in treating the distribution of income as a form of exchange it misrepresented the way the system works.

Orthodox economics tries to show that markets allocate scarce resources according to relative efficiency; political economics tries to show that markets distribute income according to relative power. It is good to know about efficiency, but in our world, it tends to be subservient to power.[8] By failing to appreciate this, and consequently failing also to accord the distribution of income between labor and capital a properly central role, orthodox economics has become cut off from the central economic issues of our time, drifting further into ever more abstract and mathematically sophisticated reformulations of essentially the same propositions. The heart of the matter is the concept of "capital," and its relation to social class and economic power. When this is put right, as in the new paradigm, economic theory can once again speak to the critical issues of the day.

Notes

1. This is perhaps the central issue in the recent dispute over capital theory between the "two Cambridges," Cambridge, England, maintaining the view presented here, against Cambridge, Massachusetts, which argued that the essential Neoclassical story could be developed in a "heterogeneous-capital" model. Unfortunately, to do this, Cambridge, Mass. found that it had to assume conditions in which a simple Labor Theory of Value held! It is now widely agreed that Neoclassical capital theory is defective.

2. Put this baldly, of course, it seems an extraordinary assumption for anyone to take seriously. Given what we know about how our society works, if we read the newspapers (or the Valachi papers), we would never in our ordinary thinking expect to explain a change in the income of a group primarily by reference to a change in its marginal productivity. We would certainly think of demand and supply, and of income elasticity; these would provide the framework, within which bargaining, power plays, and politics would settle the final (or temporary) outcome. Marginal productivity might or might not come into it; just as it might or might not be measurable, but it would hardly be decisive. Is the shift in the income going to the top 5 percent since 1960 to be seriously taken as reflecting an increase in their marginal productivity? Is the relative rise in professional income 1900–1970 evidence of a long-term upward drift in their productivity at the margin? Yet, in spite of common sense and advanced theory, the production function studies, aggregate and individual, continue.

3. This should be distinguished from the commonplace (though correct) criticisms that opportunities for substitution are not legion, that changes in techniques of production and consumption are time-consuming and costly, that information is hard to come by (and perhaps should be treated as itself a product!), that mobility is sluggish, foresight myopic, and expectations an irregular compound of habit and hope. These points will be readily admitted, for they merely indicate how far the actual world falls short of its own ideal type. The point of the present criticism is that the Neoclassical ideal market economy is *not* a picture of how the economic system would work under ideal conditions, for it fundamentally misrepresents the relationship of distribution to exchange, whether conditions are "ideal" or not.

4. The traditional interest in classifying goods along lines such as these, largely abandoned in the face of positivist criticism—"these are just value judgments"—has been revived in the light of Sraffa's important and far-reaching distinction between basics, goods which enter directly or indirectly into the means of production of all goods, and nonbasics.

5. Surely under both capitalism and market socialism profits serve the essential function of indicating where investment can most advantageously be directed. The *rate* of profit, similarly, serves to allocate productive resources between producing for current consumption and expansion for the future. There are two things wrong with this very common claim. First (as sophisticated Neoclassical economists will quickly admit), the function of profits and the rate of profit as indicators requires merely that they be

calculated; hence, in no wise justifies *paying* profits.

Calculated profit indicators are compatible with many different incentive schemes (e.g., salary bonuses to managers of state-owned enterprises, moral incentives, etc.). Second, profit-based indicators are only one set among several. In a stationary economy, for example, the correct indicators to achieve maximum output would be based not on profits but on *labor values*! (Cf. Goodwin, ch. 4.) In general, profit indicators alone are likely to be misleading; the rate and pattern of growth must also be considered in trying to identify the best investment plans. Even so, from the strict economic point of view, forgetting social complications, the best choices for maximizing consumption may differ from the best choices for maximizing growth. Once we allow for quality, the effect on the environment, etc., the variety of possible indicators becomes considerable.

6. This diagram also illustrates a proposition first discovered in the 1930s by the great Polish Marxist economist, Michael Kalecki, who independently and at the same time set forth the main propositions of the *General Theory*. [. . .]

7. The picture can be very much improved as a representation of the modern economy by channeling profits, not directly to owners but to "Wall Street," where banks, boards of directors, and financial institutions decide how much to retain, how much to invest, and how much to pay out in dividends. Then capitalist consumption will come out of distributed profits and realized capital gains, and savings will flow back to Wall Street in the form of bond and share purchases. This properly separates ownership and control, and shows the separation of financial and production decisions, the former dominating the latter. The model can also be modified to take account of worker savings, which, however, are empirically inconsequential.

8. Power, of course, is usually enhanced by efficiency, but the two are nevertheless quite distinct. Economic power ultimately rests on the ability to inflict a loss—the stick. A subsidiary form is the ability to bribe—the carrot. If economists paid as much attention to bribery and extortion as they do to marginal utility, we should be able to develop rough quantitative indices, by means of which one could sensibly discuss (and plan strategy to alter) the distribution of economic power in society.

II

Post-Keynesian and Neo-Ricardian Political Economy

Introduction

The Post-Keynesian and Neo-Ricardian schools of political economy developed concurrently with the rise of new left Marxian analysis and with the abandonment of textbook Keynesian treatments by mainstream economists. Although distinct in their content and focus of analysis, the Post-Keynesians and Neo-Ricardians will be examined together in this anthology. Both schools are credited with originating in Cambridge, England, and are sometimes called the "Cambridge School." This in part has to do with the overlap among the original theorists in these two schools—particularly Joan Robinson and Piero Sraffa. Of the four schools of political economic thought explored here, Post-Keynesian and Neo-Ricardian are the most recent in their intellectual roots. Post-Keynesians are indebted to Keynes's work—particularly the *General Theory*—and Michal Kalecki, a lesser-known economist working at the same time who developed similar ideas. Neo-Ricardian analysis began with the resurrection of Ricardo's collected works by Piero Sraffa and Sraffa's own work, *Production of Commodities by Means of Commodities* (1960). Both of these theories of economic activity and production are currently undergoing significant theoretical development in which the boundaries and methodologies will be better defined. The relative newness of these two schools leaves much room for development and exploration.

From the onset it must be made clear that the Post-Keynesians and Neo-Ricardians have different projects, methods, and internal debates. It is their geographical and intellectual roots and newness that bind them together here. Post-Keynesians are rooted in a general equilibrium model and can best be understood in the context of their divergence from the Keynesian-Neoclassical synthesis. Neo-Ricardians, on the other hand, are firmly fixed to the debates and issues in Marxist theory. In fact, it is nearly impossible to understand the impact of Neo-Ricardian thought without understanding Marxist economic theory—particularly the use of the labor theory of value. The reader who is completely unfamiliar with Neo-Ricardian economics might be well advised to read the section on Marx in tandem.

Post-Keynesian theory has been developing since the publication of Keynes's and Kalecki's work in the 1930s and 1940s. Most of the earlier work in this area was done by Cambridge theorists, including Joan Robinson, Nicholas Kaldor, Luigi Pasinetti, and Roy Harrod. Contributions to understanding the mechanisms of change and disequilibrium in Keynesian systems were added by Robert Clower and Axel Leijonhufvud in the late 1960s and early 1970s. An article in the *Journal of Economic Literature* in 1975 entitled "An Essay on Post-Keynesian

Theory: A New Paradigm in Economics'' by Alfred Eichner and Jan Kregel exposed many mainstream economists, particularly in the United States, to developments in Post-Keynesian theory. Exciting new work is currently being done in this area, some of which can be found in *Challenge* magazine and *The Journal of Post Keynesian Economics*.

The object of analysis in Post-Keynesian economics focuses on the determinants of demand for investment and consumption goods and the corresponding levels of prices, output, and employment. It explicitly rejects the Neoclassical model of scarcity as a determinant in the allocation of goods and resources. Instead, the Post-Keynesian model examines the relation between the behavior of investors, entrepreneurs, and consumers, and the structure of markets to the corresponding levels of prices, interest rates, employment, and output. In doing this it calls into question many of the assumptions of economic orthodoxy. For example, Post-Keynesians pay close attention to the structure of financial markets in relation to the behavior of investors, as it is seen to be erratic and destabilizing to capitalist production; rather than assume that firms operate at a level of full capacity utilization, Post-Keynesians claim this is a function of the level of demand. Furthermore, since one cannot predetermine the level of capacity utilization, one cannot comfortably assume that firms operate at the point of diminishing marginal returns and in turn cannot assure cost minimization. An important economic outcome in the Post-Keynesian model is the distribution of income, a set of property relations assumed in the orthodox economic models.

Post-Keynesian economists have made their largest contributions to the critique of orthodox economics with three interrelated concepts: disequilibrium, uncertainty, and the use of historical time. The dynamic of change in the Post-Keynesian model is premised on the passage of historical time over any production period. This is in sharp contradistinction to the Neoclassical use of logical time or the Neoclassical-Keynesian orthodoxy reliance on static comparative analysis. The difference is that with any economic change (endogenous or exogenous), real time passes and nobody can predict what will occur during that time; that is, there will be uncertainty. Uncertainty in the Post-Keynesian model is much more than imperfect information as posed by orthodox theorists who are relaxing assumptions. The notion of uncertainty means never knowing the future because the information is impossible to determine. For example, no one knows what the price of silver will be in ten years. Uncertainty directly affects investment and consumption decisions in ways that cannot be mathematically modelled. Furthermore, the passage of historical (real) time ensures more uncertainty which further influences decisions. The interjection of uncertainty lays the foundation for disequilibrium theory. If economic actors cannot know the future, they cannot act "rationally" today, and investors, entrepreneurs, workers, and consumers might not always behave in such a way as to allow for the clearing of markets; prices of goods, interest rates, levels of production, and employment may never move toward economic equilibria as supposed by orthodox theorists.

This in turn generates more uncertainty and economic instability, resulting in economic crisis and chaos. The nature, direction, and causes of instability are at the heart of Post-Keynesian analysis and provide its lasting contribution to the development of political economy.

The range of debate in Post-Keynesian theory is rather wide, with the confines contested by the degree to which uncertainty, disequilibrium, and time determine economic activity, in particular investment and consumption demand. Post-Keynesian theorists have substantially advanced the frontiers of economic thought with the analysis of time and the consequent effect on economic behavior. They have also provided a powerful tool for exposing the fallacy of assumptions about information and decision making that are used to justify high unemployment rates (search theory) and blame workers and consumers for inflation (rational expectations) in Neoclassical theory.

Post-Keynesian theory has attracted a large number of economists, many of whom in recent years have rejected Neoclassical economics and the Keynesian-Neoclassical synthesis. In this book we provide a small sampling of work from Post-Keynesian theorists who have defined the critiques, boundaries, and directions of this school of thought. Although these three articles by no means exhaust either the major components or the diversity of Post-Keynesian theory, they can provide the reader with an introduction to some of the major confines and debates within this school of thought.

Whereas Post-Keynesian analysis develops out of a critique of general equilibrium analysis and generates discussion about the determinants of demand for production, Neo-Ricardian discourse represents a departure from Marxian class analysis and its use of the labor theory of value. Piero Sraffa edited David Ricardo's work and developed his own to understand better the determination of value of commodities and the accumulation process in ways not addressed by Marx's treatment of classical economics. Neo-Ricardian analysis uses and critiques many of the same terms and subjects of Marxian analysis such as class, the labor theory of value, unequal exchange, and the production and allocation of surplus in class societies.

The intellectual roots of Neo-Ricardian economics are to be found almost exclusively in Sraffa's lifelong work. In fact, some Neo-Ricardians would rather be called Post-Sraffa Marxists. Neo-Ricardians employ a class analysis but reject the labor theory of value—they argue that it impedes the generation of a class-based theory of production and reproduction of commodities because it misspecifies the relation between exchange values and prices. Neo-Ricardians define their sphere of discourse much more narrowly than any of the other three schools of political economy. For this reason, it is sometimes difficult to compare and contrast them in all areas.

The major contribution made by the Neo-Ricardians is the specification of the *standard commodity*, that special good that embodies the average factors of production. With this discovery the transformation problem, the relation between value and prices, is solved. Yet, because the standard commodity is the sum of many physical inputs, not just labor, the Neo-Ricardians have called into question the basis of Marxist value theory and with it much of Marxist analysis. The discussion over value theory has become much more than a technical question for Neo-Ricardians, rather it is the focus of a fierce debate over economic theories of capitalist production.

Once the value form is specified, Neo-Ricardians begin with the wage bill and the physical condition of products (which are socially and technically determined) to produce an analysis of production and reproduction that allows for the determination of profit rates, the effect of changes in wages and technology, relative prices, and consumption on the distribution of surplus product. Like the Marxist model, Neo-Ricardians show that wages and profits are inversely related and not dependent on changes in prices. Yet, the relative shares of capital and labor are determined outside the model and provide a mechanism for change. Nonetheless, the inverse relation between wages and profit provides the source of conflict within this model.

Markets and Institutions as Features of a Capitalistic Production System

JAN A. KREGEL

Jan Kregel provides a Post-Keynesian interpretation of Keynes in relation to Neoclassical theory. He rejects the idea that Keynes's theory is the Neoclassical model modified by the introduction of rigid wages and physical quantity adjustments. Instead Kregel shows how Keynes's understanding of uncertainty negates the self-adjusting mechanisms described by orthodox economists. Once Kregel establishes that the economy cannot restore equilibrium through price flexibility, he turns to the role of both real and monetary adjustments in accommodating economic disruption. To deal with the ever present uncertainty, financial markets and wage contracts develop, but even these cannot correct the instability generated by uncertainty.

Attempts by a number of theorists working within the tradition of general equilibrium (GE) analysis to reproduce the basic results of Keynes's *General Theory* have reawakened interest in the role of price and quantity adjustment in attaining economic equilibrium. Within a GE framework, Keynes's claim that the economic system is not self-adjusting implies either impediments to the perfect flexibility of prices in response to disequilibrium (rigid prices, rigid quantities, or market imperfections), or institutional factors that abrogate the implicit adjustment process. For the theoretical formulation of the GE process of adjustment, "it seemed reasonable to suppose . . . prices rose when there were unsatisfied buyers and fell when there were unsatisfied sellers" (Hahn 1977: 36).

Yet, analysts of real markets considered the abrogation of this process as commonplace,[1] even before Keynes attempted to provide a theoretical justification for the failure of the system to achieve full employment. As should now be well known, Keynes's approach could hardly have been considered novel had it consisted simply in pointing out the deleterious effect of expectations on the process of price adjustment (see Kregel 1977). [. . .]

Instead, Keynes isolated the cause of the system's failure to adjust in its response to the *fact* of the existence of uncertainty: the use of "money" as a store

Jan A. Kregel, "Markets and Institutions as Features of a Capitalistic Production System," *Journal of Post Keynesian Economics* 3, 1 (Fall 1980), pp. 32–48.

of value. From this point of view, it would have been inappropriate for Keynes to follow the path of orthodox economists by beginning his analysis with a Robinson Crusoe economy and then extending the results to industrial economies. Keynes realized that the real world he wanted to explain could be approached only "by never thinking, for simplicity's sake, in terms of a non-exchange economy and then transferring [the] conclusions to an economy of a different character" (Keynes 1973: 14, 369; quotation from the third proof of *The General Theory*).

In formulating his position, Keynes recognized the important role of money, not only in exchange, but also in production. Since the principle of effective demand is often presented as a "real" rather than a monetary concept, it may be helpful to investigate the way Keynes integrated the two concepts. This integration can be demonstrated most clearly by examining the evolution of Keynes's thought during the period from the predominately "monetary" *Treatise on Money* to the supposedly "real" *General Theory*.

Challenging Say's Law

In his lectures at Cambridge in the period following the publication of the *Treatise*, Keynes initiated his analysis of the level of output from the viewpoint of Say's law: the supply and demand for output as a whole. Keynes recognized the important contribution made by this approach in emphasizing the "dual" nature of aggregate economic variables (the circular flow discussed in textbooks): the costs of production of final outputs represent incomes that are expended to purchase that output.[2] The "real" flow of goods has its counterpart in the "money" flows of nominal incomes.

Yet, this recognition led Keynes to characterize a Say's law economy as a "neutral" (as opposed to a barter or monetary) economy where "expenditure = current output = current income." These equalities would hold, Keynes argued, when "the factors as a whole get the totality of the whole product and nothing else." That is, when "the factors were rewarded in the real goods they are producing—not money." Keynes christened such arrangements a "cooperative" or "real-wage" economy and noted that there could never be a "deficiency of demand" in such economies, for "whenever some people are set to work the income earned in respect to their product necessarily constitutes an increase in expenditure equal to the increase in output" (Joan Robinson's suggested phrasing, in Keynes 1973: 13, 639). The only limit to this process was full employment.

Since Keynes was interested primarily in demonstrating that the economy might move away from, and not toward, this limit, he felt he first needed to show that expenditures might fall short of income, since under such conditions the sales receipts of producers would not cover production costs and losses would be incurred that would induce producers to reduce output levels (or bankruptcies would reduce the number of producers).

The "Entrepreneur" Economy: Wages Paid in Money

Keynes noted that, in an economy where wages are paid in money, "some part of income [may not be] spent on current output [and] the factors of production will get total current output without spending their total earnings." In such an "entrepreneur" economy, as opposed to a real-wage economy, "fluctuations in income resulting from [fluctuations] in the ratio of expenditure to income [will cause] fluctuations in effective demand."[3] The impact on profits of changes in demand relative to costs would lead entrepreneurs to change their desired levels of output and employment.

This recognition that the payment of wages in money makes possible savings out of wages did not, however, assure that aggregate expenditure would differ from aggregate earnings. If savings were ultimately used to buy or finance the purchase of investment goods, then the overall equality of income and expenditure would be maintained. As Keynes noted, "For the individual [disbursement] does not equal his income. But for [the] community aggregate disbursement must equal income." "Savings and investment for individuals are distinct but must be equal for the community" (Bryce's lecture notes, November 13, 1933).

The question of how differences between expenditure and costs arise and produce fluctuations in "aggregate incentive," and thus "fluctuations in employment," cannot be answered simply by assuming an economy that pays wages in money. [. . .] In the terminology of *The General Theory*, the introduction of the psychological law of consumption is not by itself sufficient to disprove Say's law.

Expectation and the Variability of Income and Expenditure

Toward the end of 1933, Keynes introduced what he thought to be the key to this theoretical conundrum. In a Say's law economy, current expenditure is always determined by, and equal to, current income. The "entrepreneur" economy was an attempt to show how some of this "current" income might be withheld from the circular flow, thus causing shifts in the ratio of expenditure to income.

In his lecture of November 6, 1933, Keynes suggested that, while *current* income may be a perfectly adequate determinant of households' consumption decisions, for investment decisions made today to produce goods for future sales, the income the investment is *expected* to yield is more relevant. Instead of emphasizing the distinction between spending and not spending (investment and saving), Keynes introduced a distinction between decisions based on realized results and those based on expected results (consumption and investment). In an economy where the expenditure of current savings at a future date cannot be foreseen with certainty, entrepreneurs will have to make current decisions on investment expenditure on the basis of the profits they expect to earn during the expected life of the project. Entrepreneurs' current incomes then affect their current expenditure to the extent that their current incomes influence their expectation of future income.

The introduction of this new distinction implies that Keynes's entire analysis must be rewritten in terms of *expected* values. It is expectations that allow current expenditure to depart from current income, for current expenditure is now determined by *expected* income.[4]

Such a position concerning the determinants of investment expenditure could be justified only if entrepreneurs not only do not, *but cannot*, know what (and when) future demand, represented by current savings (the excess of income over expenditure), would be forthcoming over the life of their investments; in other words, if this information were not provided by any market signal. (This view also implies that, for consumers, future income and hence expenditures—or savings—are not predictable, indeed, cannot be predicted.)

The implications of such an assumption for the role of markets in equilibrating the level of output is clear. The decision to save, since it is a decision to reduce present consumption, produces a clear current market signal to producers by means of a reduction in receipts. But, if investment is completely (or partially) independent of current income, this does not affect expectations of future income. More important, however, no future market signal is given because there is nothing more to signal. In the absence of a knowledge of future incomes, households cannot enter into future expenditure commitments based solely on present savings. Their only action is thus to change current expenditure. Without a knowledge of consumers' future consumption plans, investors must make predictions in the absence of future market information. Indeed, Keynes criticizes "classical" theory for "fallaciously supposing that there is a nexus which unites decisions to abstain from present consumption with decisions to provide for future consumption" (1936: 21). The only possible link in the absence of concrete information is entrepreneurs' expectations, for the use of current market information would be mistaken (and definitely destabilizing).

The problem is that, when income is not given but variable, households' current consumption (and thus their savings, or demand for future consumption) cannot be known until current income is determined. But current income depends on the demand for households' services, which in turn is linked to aggregate household consumption and business expenditures on investment. The latter, however, is related to future household expenditure and thus to future incomes, and to the amount of present consumption that depends on current investment. The information required concerning current and future incomes, as well as future choices between consumption and saving, does not exist today. What must be known to decide today will be known only when the effects of those decisions take place. Under these conditions future markets, such as those postulated in modern GE analysis, would not be used to contract for future consumption streams because the objective constraints required in such markets do not exist.

The distinction between expected and realized values is crucial to Keynes's argument that decisions to save would not produce market signals of a type that would lead market agents to provide for the future consumption represented in current savings by making investments of a like amount. As a corollary to this argument, however, Keynes had to identify those factors of the real world that produced conditions under which there were no market signals because there was no information for the market to signal. Thus, Keynes claimed that saving "does not create demand for more future consumption" and investment of a similar amount to provide for it because "(a) They [the producers] don't know what you will want in the future; (b) [you] don't give data; (c) [you] can't give promise you ever will consume" (Bryce's lecture notes, November 11, 1933). In short, producers can't know what consumers will want to buy in the future because consumers themselves don't know. The absence of the very information that would allow income and expenditure always to be equal is due to uncertainty about future consumption expenditure on the part of households. This, Keynes pointed out, is in direct contrast to the orthodox position, in which "saving was considered . . . as a distribution of consumption through time."[5]

Uncertainty is then seen to apply in all economic decisions and must be taken into explicit account in economic analysis. By taking it into consideration, Keynes could show that there would be no systematic tendency to full employment because no known certain link exists between *current* income and expenditure on *current* production, as had been posited by Say's law. In an economy where *current* expenditures are determined by the expectation of *future* income, there will be no long-period "tendency to an optimum position, i.e., to destroy unemployment" (Bryce's lecture notes, November 14, 1932). Thus Keynes *defines* a monetary production economy (ME), in contrast to a neutral (Say's law) economy, as one in which there exists no natural market force tending to eliminate unemployment. The system fails, not because of operational *or* institutional malfunction, nor because uncertainty leads to perverse buyer behavior, but because there is *no market* capable of linking future consumption decisions to present expenditure decisions if the former do not exist when the latter must be undertaken.

In a "money-wage" or "entrepreneur" economy where incomes are not received in kind or in the output the worker produces, and the "psychological law" relating changes in consumption to changes in income allows positive saving out of wage incomes, expenditures may fall short of incomes. Further, since "an individual decision to save does not, in actual fact, induce the placing of any specific forward order for consumption, but merely the cancellation of a present order" (Keynes 1936: 211), current investment decisions must be made on the basis of entrepreneurs' best guesses as to what future demand, cost, and hence incomes will be. In a monetary economy current investment expenditures relate not to current income but to expected income. Therefore, it is possible for current expenditures to differ from current income for both consumers and investors (households and firms), while they are equal in the aggregate.

The Interest Rate as the Link to the Future

Yet, Keynes recognized that these perceptions of the operation of a real economy were not sufficient to support his conjecture about the nature of a monetary production economy. It still had to be shown that, in such an economy, it would not be true "that an increased desire to hold wealth (i.e., an increase in the divergence between household income and expenditure), being much the same thing as an increased desire to hold investments, must, by increasing the demand for investments, provide a stimulus to their production; so that current investment is promoted by individual saving to the same extent as present consumption is diminished" (p. 211). If Keynes could not show this, then any divergence between income and expenditure on current output would be offset by expenditure on investment goods in such a way that, even if income and expenditure were unequal for individuals, they would be equal in the aggregate *at full employment*; in other words, the interest rate would bring investment and saving into equality and thus reestablish Say's law. Therefore, if Keynes could not show that "an act of saving does nothing to improve prospective yield" and hence "does nothing to stimulate investment" because it does not produce a future market signal in the present, his attempt to show that the economic system was not self-regulating would fail (p. 212).

In analyzing this point, Keynes was led to identify the crucial feature of a monetary production economy that allowed consumers *not* to spend all of their income, *not* to know what they would consume in the future, and to forestall decision over the expenditure of their income: a store of value that preserves the purchasing power of current income.[6]

Keynes began his argument by assuming the existence of a durable store of value that can act as a "bottomless sink for purchasing power" in such a way that, when the demand for it rises, the demand for labor is unaffected, there is no signal in the labor market, even if the quantity supplied expands. Only after showing how the existence of such an asset produces the results implicit in his definition of a monetary production economy does Keynes deal with the properties such an asset would have to possess in order to yield such results. In Keynes's terminology, this means "tacitly assuming that the kind of money to which we are accustomed has some special characteristics" (p. 227) or "essential properties" that are presumed during the initial discussion and only later explained.

The Essential Properties of Interest

The importance of demonstrating the divergence of individual income and expenditure in disproving Say's law lies in the possibility that some part of current income (savings or hoarding) may not lead to an equivalent current market expenditure on goods currently produced by labor. If savings are to preserve purchasing power, they must be converted into a durable form. *Any* durable asset has the property of existing through time, of serving as a store of value, *by definition*. Thus, Keynes emphasized, the saver does not necessarily desire "a capital asset *as such*"; what "he really desires is its prospective yield" (p. 212). Therefore, *all* potential stores of value must be classified in terms of their prospective yields to determine which will be purchased by savers.

In determining this classification, Keynes identifies several different aspects of the "yield" of durable assets: the net yield (q) that may be earned from the holding or the use of the asset in production; the carrying cost (c) of holding and maintaining the asset through time; and the liquidity premium (l) as determined by the variability of the asset's value in terms of other goods and the ease and convenience with which it can be converted into the desired goods at *any* future date. All durable goods can thus be ranked in terms of this overall return $(q - c) + l$, which determines their suitability as stores of value.[7] This is simply what Keynes, following his earlier analysis of interest rate parity in financial markets and Sraffa's extension of the concept to real durable assets in terms of their "own rate of return," called the "marginal efficiency" of an asset. [. . .]

The analytical problem facing Keynes was thus to show why savers would choose, on the basis of this classification, durable goods *that would not require labor in their production*. Otherwise, an "individual act of saving is just as good for effective demand as an act of individual consumption" (p. 211). Put another way, Keynes had to show why "money" might be preferred by savers even though it has a very low or zero $(q - c)$.

Keynes first noted that the prospective yields of "nonmonetary" durables will not, in general, be independent of savers' demands for them. In the short period, the net yield of such assets (their marginal efficiency) will be inversely related to the demand for them (Keynes alluded to the same argument of declining returns invoked in explaining the declining MEC curve [p. 228]). Thus, savers will continue to demand the nonmonetary durable with the highest prospective yield as a store of value until the expansion in its supply has caused its yield to fall to equality with the prospective yield of the next highest ranked asset, and so on, until the $[(q - c) + l]$ of all potential stores of value have been driven to equality.

In an economy with no durable that possesses the "tacitly" assumed "special characteristics" of money, this process of equalization of net yields will continue until: (a) all assets have the same prospective yields; and (b) the quantity of all durables has been increased up to the point where the aggregate money demand for newly produced durables equals net current savings (net returns may, but need not, be driven to the point where demand price equals supply price). This result can be considered as the formal equivalent to Say's law, for current income is always spent on current output whether it is "consumed" or "saved" and used to purchase stores of value. An increase in output always produces demand sufficient to purchase it—the only problem may be temporary disproportions (mal-investments) between consumption and investment goods.

If, however, there is a durable in the system that possesses the "essential properties" of money, the process of equalization of net yields may be halted before full employment is reached because this durable good, called "money," offers an alternative store of value whose prospective yield is determined not by technical conditions of production which produce declining returns in response to an increase in demand, but by its liquidity premium. This premium, Keynes maintained, is set by the psychology of the public or "liquidity preference," which may be independent of changes in the supply of money.

When the liquidity premium of money is high enough, savers will prefer to store wealth in the form of "money," and the demand for newly produced nonmonetary durable stores of value will fall short of the value of savings by the amount of the demand for money as a store of value: current income will exceed current expenditure by the amount of money held as a store of value. In such a case, it is the "marginal efficiency of money"—the rate of interest—that will "rule the roost" because it stops (crowds out) the demand by savers for capital goods as stores of value before it reaches the level required to balance full employment savings. Thus Keynes was able to declare that in a "monetary production economy" there is nothing to guarantee that liquidity preference will be such that the rate of interest will be low enough to ensure the results of a "neutral economy," i.e., to ensure that the interest rate "stop" will not be operative.

The Essential Properties of Money[8]

Keynes's argument can proceed no further without a return to the deferred explanation of the "special characteristics" that make "money" a "bottomless sink for purchasing power." It is obvious that if a decision to hold money, rather than a nonmoney durable, leads to a market signal, for example, a rise in the "price" of money relative to costs, and hence to an expansion of the "production" of money, the demand for labor to produce money may be increased. Or, if money has a close substitute, the increase in demand may "spill over" to a durable that is produced by labor. In either case, the demand for money as a store of value would then be no different in its effect on the level of employment than the demand for a nonmonetary store of value, and there would be nothing to prevent the system from attaining the full employment equality of income and expenditure. If, however, the "special characteristics" of money are a low or zero elasticity of production and substitution, then saving which is translated into demand for money as a store of value is "not a substitution of future consumption demand for present consumption demand" (p. 210); it does not "involve the placing of any specific forward order for consumption, but thereby the cancellation of a present order. . . . since the expectation of consumption is the only *raison d'être* of employment, there should be nothing paradoxical in the conclusion that a diminished propensity to consume has *cet. par.* a depressing effect on employment" (p. 211).

It is thus possible for Keynes to conclude that in a monetary production economy (defined as one where "money" exhibits the above-mentioned "special characteristics"), when incomes are paid in terms of money, income will represent demand for either current output or stores of value. The use of income to demand "money" as a store of value, however, is not an *effective demand* (for labor), because it does not lead to the expectation of future sales of producible goods and thus does not create the *expectation* of income. In contrast to the classical theory of interest, there would be no "signal" to increase the demand for investment and thus for employment. Indeed, the only "signal" that results from an increased demand for money is a *decreased* demand for current output and thus a decrease in current income. To the extent that current income influences expected income, this will reduce rather than increase investment.

In such an economy, "money" is not neutral. In such an economy, the determination of "effective demand" is necessary to ascertain whether current expenditure will exceed or fall short of current output, whether expectations will be fulfilled or disappointed, and whether output and employment will be adjusted to suit new expectations. Thus, current demand must be based on expectation, for current income is not a good predictor of expenditure when some of current income may not be "effective," that is, may be used to demand existing durables (what Keynes called "swaps" in his lectures) or durables that do not require labor for their production.

In this way, Keynes may be said to have criticized his contemporaries' implicit assumptions about the properties of the competitive price system by noting that the demand for money as a store of value is a demand that produces effects in financial markets, but does not give signals to producers faced with the problem of predicting consumers' future expenditure decisions. Such demand is undefined (or ineffective) demand for a still to be determined product, at an as yet to be determined time. It gives no "information" upon which to base a rational decision on investment in productive capacity. Further, because saving and investment are brought into equality by the level of income, and not by the interest rate, this "signal" to the financial markets is prevented from influencing investment in a "decisive way" (p. 164).

Such criticism could not be termed as the identification of market failure; since there is no information to be transmitted, the market can hardly be said to have failed. Rather, it is an identification of the structural characteristics of a capitalist economy, or a criticism of misspecification of the demand used in traditional models. Current income is not relevant to the aggregate demand for current output; current saving is not relevant to the demand for future output. In this context, the "essential properties of interest and money" are crucial, for they define a monetary production economy in which the demand for money will be "ineffective" in eliciting signals that influence investment and the demand for labor. They also make necessary the formulation of the theory of effective demand in order to identify the determinants of the level of output and employment.

From this perspective, one can also appreciate the different emphasis Keynes gives to the role of money in economic analysis. It is not money as such that causes unemployment for, as Keynes noted in 1937, if the future can be accurately foreseen, "why should anyone outside a lunatic asylum wish to use money as a store of wealth?" (1973: 14, 115–16). But, although money is the least *un*certain link between the present and the unknown future, it does not follow that changes in the quantity of money or "money" variables will have a direct effect on savers' and investors' assessments of the future or their reactions to uncertainty. Behavioral reactions in the face of uncertainty are quite independent of the fact that money provides the most certain link between the present and the future and of the reasons why such a link is needed.

In a monetary production economy, "money" is representative of the fact that investment to create the capacity to produce output at any future date must be decided in the present, while the demand for future output can be held in a liquid store of value (a sink for purchasing power), thus postponing the "market signal" until the instant of decision of future purchase. In a capitalist production system, the information needed today for rational decision making does not *exist* today, it is only available tomorrow, while current income is determined by decisions to produce for future consumption. In such a world, it is an objective fact that the future is uncertain in a nonpredictable way, and it is natural that investment should be volatile. The management of money cannot make the future any less uncertain, though it surely can affect the stability of the system and the ability of any commodity to act as money.

From Keynes's point of view, the conditions necessary for the existence of a monetary production economy take precedence over the physical properties of the durable that plays the role of money in such an economy. The essential properties are less important as a classificatory aid in identifying what serves as money than as a definition of the conditions required of a monetary production economy, that is, the conditions under which Say's law will not hold. For this latter point they are crucial, and as such they are critical to Keynes's entire theory.[9]

At the same time, they demonstrate clearly why the key to Keynes's theory is to be found not in implicitly realistic assumptions about rigid prices, quantity-constrained adjustment, dual decision hypotheses, or relative speeds of price and quantity adjustment, but in the essential properties of interest and money.

Summary and Conclusions

As noted above, one of the crucial points in the development of Keynes's theory was the recognition that the profitability of investment in long-lived capital equipment would depend on information that would become available only after the decision to invest had already been taken. Current income could be no more than an imperfect indication of future profitability. Thus, expected income became the central force determining current investment expenditure (and thus current output and employment). Under such conditions, the information required for rational decision making does not exist; the market mechanism cannot provide it. But, just as nature abhors a vacuum, the economic system abhors uncertainty. The system reacts to the absence of the information the market cannot provide by creating uncertainty-reducing institutions: wage contracts, debt contracts, supply agreements, administered prices, trading agreements. Since all are meant to reduce uncertainty over time, it is natural that their value be denominated in the unit whose value is most stable over time—money—or, as seen above, in terms of the durable whose own rate of return declines least rapidly with an increase in demand. Institutions and markets also develop to deal in these contracts; they are, however, markets producing signals which are in no sense related to the information required to lead the system to a full employment level of investment. Yet, the proxies for this information and the signals generated by the markets trading them are often mistaken for the real thing: interest rates are believed to produce signals that act as a proxy for future demand.

What Keynes attempted to show was not only the error of identifying one type of information with another, but also the reasons why, in the case of the money market, the signals generated would be ineffective in their impact on investment and employment. Thus money, which seems to bridge the gap between the present and the future, between the need to know and knowledge, could do no more than that. It could not predict the future, nor could its price (the interest rate) lead to actions that would prove to be correct in the future. Moreover, intervention in the money market could not guarantee the right information, because it need not produce the "correct" signal to the labor market.

Keynes's policy recommendations thus contrasted sharply with those of his contemporaries (as well as with those of GE-type Keynesian models). Since money was a reflection of the capitalistic system that had produced growth and development, the two would be preserved together. Because its role in the system was to link value through time, it was of vital importance to keep its value stable; this implied that *other prices must be kept stable*, in particular the price of labor. Such stability would also reduce the risk of uncertainty-sharing contracts and the existence of the markets in which they were traded, upon which capitalist production depended. The system, in response to the lack of one automatic market mechanism to adjust investment to the full employment level, creates a framework that abhors such adjustment mechanisms in all other markets where they operate and attempts to dampen their operation at the same time that it makes it impossible for them to provide self-adjustment for the system as a whole.

It is precisely this aspect of the real world that theory must take into account. Once this is done, it is easy to see that automatic adjustment mechanisms such as freely adjusting wages and prices can only diminish the role of money as a store of value, thereby eliminating the framework of contracts and financial markets upon which capitalistic investment depends. Neither in theory nor in practice can the capitalist system be self-adjusting. This is not to deny that such a self-adjusting system can be conceived, but it would be a "real-wage" economy, not a capitalistic monetary production economy such as now exists in both East and West.

Notes

1. "One of the worst effects of a period of falling prices is that it breeds lack of confidence in prices themselves. . . . The one thing that tends to check buying, and therefore to prevent the recovery of prices, is [that]. . . . No one will buy because they are afraid that prices will go lower still, and just because no one is buying prices do fall further" (J. A. Todd, *The Fall of Prices* [1931], quoted in Withers 1939: 95–96).

2. "Double analysis of income $Y = C + I = E + Q$ is the significant theory" (Bryce's lecture notes, November 20, 1933); $E + Q$ is the *current* income of the community.

3. Lecture of October 15, 1933 (Bryce's notes). Note that even at this early stage effective demand is want plus the ability to finance expenditure, i.e., what Clower (1969: 209) defines as "effective demand."

4. Subject to the natural proviso that external financing sufficient to cover desired investment expenditure is available.

5. As well as in contrast to permanent income theory.

6. There are, in fact, two analytical points involved. We emphasize here the effects of the demand for money on the existence of a tendency toward full employment. The second, which has been the major preoccupation of commentators (e.g., Davidson 1978: 159; Minsky 1975: 77), concerns the reasons why people should choose to hold money, or the "demand for money" proper. Only by a full appreciation of the former, in which any durable may potentially serve as "money," is it possible to see the vital distinction between "liquidity preference" and the orthodox concept of the "demand for money."

7. Keynes treats these attributes as percentages: "own rates." Davidson (1978: 74) converts them to money sums per period to make q comparable with the demand price (present value) of an asset.

8. The "essential properties of money" as opposed to the "essential properties of interest" have been treated extensively in the Post-Keynesian literature. See the references cited in note 6 and Davidson (1980).

9. See the discussion between Davidson and Friedman in Gordon (1974: 99–101, 154).

References

Bryce, R. B., Notes of Keynes's lectures, 1932 and 1933, mimeo, Cambridge (reference by date of lecture). (Similar material has now been published in Keynes's notes on these lectures, *The Collected Writings of John Maynard Keynes* vol. 29, 1979.)

Clower, R. W. (1969) "A Reconsideration of the Microfoundations of Monetary Theory." In *Monetary Theory*, ed. R. W. Clower. Harmondsworth: Penguin.

Davidson, P. (1978) *Money and the Real World*. 2d ed. London: Macmillan.

————. (1980) "The Dual-Faceted Nature of the Keynesian Revolution: Money and Money Wages in Unemployment and Production Flow Prices." *Journal of Post Keynesian Economics* 2, 3 (Spring): 291–307.

Friedman, M. (1974) "A Theoretical Framework for Monetary Analysis and Comments on the Critics." In *Milton Friedman's Monetary Framework*, ed. R. J. Gordon. Chicago: University of Chicago Press.

Gordon, R. J., ed. (1974) *Milton Friedman's Monetary Framework: A Debate with His Critics*. Chicago: University of Chicago Press.

Hahn, F. H. (1977) "Keynesian Economics and General Equilibrium Theory: Reflections on Some Current Debates." In *Microfoundations of Macroeconomics*, ed. G. C. Harcourt. London: Macmillan.

Keynes, J. M. (1936) *The General Theory of Employment, Interest, and Money*. London: Macmillan.

————. (1973) *The Collected Writings of John Maynard Keynes*, ed. D. Moggridge. Vols. 13 and 14. London: Macmillan.

Kregel, J. A. (1977) "On the Existence of Expectations in English Neoclassical Economics." *Journal of Economic Literature* 15 (June).

Minsky, H. P. (1975) *John Maynard Keynes*. New York: Columbia University Press.

Sraffa, P. (1932) "Dr. Hayek on Money and Capital." *Economic Journal* (March).

Withers, H. (1939) *The Defeat of Poverty*. London: Jonathan Cape.

The Revolutionary Character of Post-Keynesian Economics

NINA SHAPIRO

Nina Shapiro argues that Post-Keynesians significantly diverge from Neoclassical econo-mists in both content and method. Although the object of Neoclassical economics is the allocation of scarce goods reduced to the expression of individual's "rational economic behavior," Shapiro claims that Post-Keynesians' understanding of the capitalist system represents a sharp break from the thinking that begins with Keynes's treatment of invest-ment.

Keynes believed that investment is determined by expected profitability rather than the marginal product of capital, making it a completely self-sustaining process. Likewise, savings (especially in Kalecki's model) is a function of profitability rather than indi-vidual's decisions to consume now or later. Once the motives and independence of invest-ment are established, the object of Post-Keynesian economics becomes understanding the expansion of investment or the process of accumulation.

The distribution of income is a focal point in Post-Keynesian analysis because it determines the relative shares of wages and profits and hence money available for invest-ment and growth. Prices are important not in their role as the allocator of scarce resources but because they are the way in which firms ensure the availability of money required for the expansion of production. Shapiro argues that the task at hand for Post-Keynesians is to model the process of accumulation in capitalist economies in the face of uncertainty.

The Post-Keynesian critique of the Neoclassical theory of capital has brought to the fore the question of the existence of Post-Keynesian economics as an alterna-tive to Neoclassical thought.[1] For this critique focused attention not only upon the characteristics of Neoclassical economics but also upon those of Post-Keynesian economics. Indeed, by pointing to the inadequacy of Neoclassical theory it pointed to the necessity of examining Post-Keynesianism, of discerning the extent to which it departs from Neoclassical economics.[2]

The following discussion takes up this question of the specificity of Post-Keynesian economics. It turns first to the historical origins of Post-Keynesian theory, the Keynesian theory of employment and income, and examines the nature of the latter's break with Neoclassical economics, that is, the "revolutionary character" of Keynes's *General Theory of Employment, Income, and Money*.

Nina Shapiro, "The Revolutionary Character of Post-Keynesian Economics," *Journal of Economic Issues* 11, 3 (September 1977), pp. 541–60.

The *General Theory* and Investment

The *General Theory*'s break with Neoclassical economics, and the specific character of this break, is clearly expressed in its treatment of investment. Although this theory formulates the problem of the determination of the level of investment in strictly Neoclassical terms, its actual treatment of this problem differs, in fundamental respects, from the Neoclassical. As we will see, in chapters 11 and 12 of the *General Theory* the level of investment is progressively separated from its Neoclassical determinants.

In chapter 11 the level of investment is tied to the relationship between the marginal efficiency of capital and the rate of interest.[3] This treatment of investment is formally equivalent to the Neoclassical connection of the level of investment to the relationship between the marginal product of capital and the rate of interest. The formal similarity between this treatment and that of Neoclassical economics, however, conceals the critical difference in their respective meanings. In particular, the Keynesian notion that investment decisions are governed by the marginal efficiency of capital is not the Neoclassical notion that they are governed by the *physical* productivity of capital goods. It is, instead, the idea that investment decisions are governed by the expected *profitability* of investment.[4]

Indeed, to the degree that this Keynesian notion involves the introduction of expectations into investment decisions, it only makes sense in terms of this departure from Neoclassical economics. As is clear in Keynes's own discussion of investment decisions, the uncertainty surrounding investment is not the uncertainty concerning its "physical product" but rather the uncertainty concerning the realization of the *value* of its products.[5] This realization is uncertain because the configuration of prices in the economy may change between the time of the installation of capital equipment and the time of the existence of its products. The speculative character of investment is, in this manner, bound up with the existence of its products as profits. The introduction of expectations into the treatment of investment therefore becomes necessary to the extent, and only to the extent, that the results of investment are treated as profits rather than material or physical goods.[6]

In chapter 12 of the *General Theory*, the treatment of investment loses even its formal resemblance to that of Neoclassical economics. Investment is no longer linked to the relationship between the marginal efficiency of capital and the rate of interest. Nor is it linked to any other given relationship, any other set of factors that are *given to* investment. Rather, investment is simply linked to "itself." What we find in this chapter is not an alternative to the Neoclassical investment function but the absence of this function itself, that is, the treatment of investment as an autonomous process. Entrepreneurs invest only in order to invest. The "aim" of their attempt to expand the value of their capital is not the "maximization of their profits" or the "maintenance of a capital-output ratio" but simply the expansion of its value. In Keynes's words, entrepreneurs invest because investment is their "way of life."[7]

Investment, viewed as an autonomous process, is not the means to a given end; in particular, it is not the means to the satisfaction of the given consumption needs of individuals. This Keynesian characterization of investment thus departs, in a fundamental manner, from that of Neoclassical economics.[8] Indeed, in the latter, investment is "nothing but" this provision of consumption, it is the act of refraining from present consumption for the purpose of expanding consumption in the future.

The other side of this Keynesian break with the treatment of investment as the provision of consumption is a break with the characteristic Neoclassical connection of investment to the intertemporal consumption decisions of individuals. Whereas investment, viewed as the means to the satisfaction of consumption needs, is necessarily tied to these decisions, when it is viewed as an autonomous process it is, in principle, indifferent to these decisions and, indeed, to "individual choice" as such. Since investment, viewed as an autonomous process, is not the means to a given end, it is not the result of choices made by individuals in the pursuit of the satisfaction of their ends. Thus, in chapter 12 of the *General Theory*, investment is neither the product of the consumption decisions of individuals nor is it the product of any other rational decision-making process. Investment here is, instead, the result of the "animal spirits" of entrepreneurs.[9]

Investment, viewed as an autonomous process, not only appears as a "self-justifying" process, as one that has no end outside of itself, but also as a "self-sustaining" one. Investment, viewed in this manner, appears as a process that produces or generates its necessary conditions rather than one which depends for its existence upon given conditions such as "the fertility of the soil" (as in classical economics) or, as in Neoclassical economics, the relation between the given "productivity of capital goods" and the given intertemporal consumption preferences of individuals. The Keynesian treatment of investment therefore involves a break with the Neoclassical specification of the conditions of investment as well as its specification of the "ends" of investment.[10]

This Keynesian break is expressed in one of the central propositions of the *General Theory*: the determination of the level of savings by the level of investment. This characteristic Keynesian view of investment as "self-financing" is, implicitly, the notion of investment as self-sustaining. It is the idea that investment *itself* generates the funds required for its existence. [. . .]

The separation of savings from investment rests upon the autonomy of the latter, that is, the independence of investment from the rate of interest and thus from the intertemporal consumption decisions of individuals. The possibility of a rupture between investment and the full employment level of desired savings therefore also rests upon this autonomy. Finally, and perhaps most important, the key role of investment in the Keynesian determination of the level of employment and income depends upon this autonomy or the "givenness" of the level of investment. Once this autonomy is eliminated, this key role of investment disappears along with the central propositions of the Keynesian argument. It was precisely through this elimination that the argument of the *General Theory* was integrated into Neoclassical economics.[11]

Savings and Investment

The autonomous character of investment in the Keynesian theory of employment is expressed, in the clearest manner, in Michal Kalecki's formulation.[12] The difference between this formulation and that of Keynes lies within its treatment of savings, the funds required for investment. Concretely, in Kalecki's theory the proportion of savings out of income is linked to the "degrees of monopoly," the ratio of aggregate proceeds realized by firms over their wage and raw material costs, rather than to the "propensity to consume." Although the degree of monopoly plays the same role in Kalecki's theory as the propensity to consume does in Keynes's and is (under certain conditions) the same formal expression as the propensity to consume, it nevertheless has a different meaning.[13] In particular, its existence in Kalecki's theory indicates a view of savings different from that of Keynes.

In the *General Theory*, the level of savings is tied to the level of income.[14] This treatment of savings expresses simultaneously Keynes's departure and "lack of departure" from the Neoclassical view of savings. On the one hand, to the extent that this connection ties the savings realized by individuals to the given level of investment, it removes savings from the intertemporal consumption decisions of individuals and thus constitutes an implicit departure from the Neoclassical treatment of savings. This departure is expressed by the absence of the rate of interest in Keynes's savings function.[15] On the other hand, however, to the degree that this connection characterizes savings as an element of the revenue received by individuals, it leaves savings within the realm of individual consumption decisions. Savings are subject to these decisions precisely to the degree that they are a part of the income of individuals. This Neoclassical aspect of Keynes's treatment of savings is expressed in its attribution of the proportion of savings out of income to the "propensity to consume."[16]

From the standpoint of the Keynesian treatment of investment, the importance of this Neoclassical characterization of savings is that it obscures and, to some extent, contradicts the autonomous character of the Keynesian investment process. Since this characterization brings the funds required for investment into the sphere of consumption decisions, it, at least implicitly, also brings investment into this sphere. To the degree that it ties the funds for investment to the consumption preferences of individuals, it makes investment dependent upon these decisions.

In contrast to Keynes's theory of employment, in Kalecki's theory savings are not a part of the revenue received by individuals. They are, instead, an element of the profits realized by firms through the sale of their commodities on the market.[17] This connection of savings to profits brings savings within the realm of the production or, more precisely, the expansion decisions of firms rather than the consumption decisions of individuals. It thus separates the funds required for investment from the consumption needs of individuals and ties these funds, instead, to the expansion needs of firms.[18]

Savings, viewed as an element of profits, are determined by the determinants of profits. Indeed, if one assumes a "classical" savings function, that is, that the role of firms or the "capitalist class" is to invest, then savings become identical with profits, and the problem of the determination of the level of savings becomes that of the level of profits. Similarly, the proportion of savings out of income becomes equal to the proportion of profits out of income. Thus, in Kalecki's theory, the problem of the specification of this proportion, the specification of the "consumption function," is *not* the problem of determining the consumption behavior of the population. Rather, it is one of determining the distribution of income between profits and wages, which problem is, in turn, that of determining the "degree of monopoly," the competitive structure of the economy.

Once the proportion of savings out of income is tied to the degree of monopoly, as it is in Kalecki's formulation of the Keynesian theory, then the level of income and employment no longer depends upon the investment decisions of firms *and* the consumption decisions of individuals (the "propensity to consume"). It instead depends upon the competitive relations among firms (the degree of monopoly) and their investment decisions. Thus, in Kalecki's formulation of the Keynesian theory of employment, there not only exists a rupture between investment and the consumption decisions of individuals but also one between the level of economic activity as a whole and these decisions. It is this rupture, or this separation of the operation of the economy from the consumption preferences of individuals, that constitutes the revolutionary character of the Keynesian theory.

Capital Accumulation

This Keynesian break with Neoclassical economics is developed in the course of the development of the Post-Keynesian theory of capital accumulation. As we will see, the Post-Keynesian project of tracing out the "long period" implications of the argument of the *General Theory* is, in effect, nothing other than that of developing its implicit treatment of investment as an autonomous, self-sustaining process.[19]

The initial step in this project, R. F. Harrod's theory of growth, is the first of its kind in modern economics which formulates the problem of growth as one of specifying the conditions within which growth can be sustained. This departure from the Neoclassical view of the growth problem is expressed in the central focus of Harrod's theory, the "knife-edge." The problem of the knife-edge is one of the divergence of the growth process from the conditions required for its continuation. In the terms of Harrod's theory, it is the problem of the divergence of the actual rate of growth from the "warranted rate," where the latter rate of growth is that rate which can reproduce itself.[20]

Harrod's departure from the Neoclassical view of growth is expressed in the central concept of his theory, the warranted rate of growth, as well as in its central problem. As implied in the above discussion, the warranted rate is a self-renewing growth rate. To the extent that the warranted rate defines such a growth rate, it constitutes an implicit treatment of growth as self-sustaining.[21]

Although Harrod's theory develops, in this manner, Keynes's break with the Neoclassical theory of investment, it still reproduces important aspects of the Neoclassical theory. In particular, it retains the Neoclassical characterization of savings. In Harrod's theory, savings are tied to the income received by individuals and thus to their intertemporal consumption decisions. This connection of the funds needed for investment to consumption decisions implies the dependence of growth itself upon these decisions. Harrod's self-reproducing growth rate is therefore that rate which is "warranted by" or consistent with the given propensity to save of individuals.

Thus, in Harrod's theory, growth is, on the one side, a process that generates its own conditions and, on the other, one which depends upon conditions "given to" or independent of the growth process itself. The result of this contradictory treatment is the "knife-edge." Since the self-sustaining growth rate in Harrod's theory is *simultaneously* that rate which is consistent with given conditions, growth (the "actual rate of growth") can only be self-sustaining if it "happens to be" consistent with these conditions.[22]

The knife-edge disappears in the Post-Keynesian development of Harrod's theory of growth precisely because the "Neoclassical" side of this theory disappears. The latter is removed through the replacement of Harrod's treatment of savings with that of Kalecki. More specifically, the Neoclassical side is eliminated in two distinct but related steps. The first is the connection of savings to profits, that is, the introduction of the "classical" savings function.[23] Savings is made an element of the profits realized by firms; consequently, the proportion of savings out of income, Harrod's "propensity to save," becomes tied to the distribution of income between profits and wages.

The next step is the connection of the profits realized by firms to the extent of their expansion activities taken as a whole.[24] Investment is made the determinant of profits so that profits become both the quantitative means for the expansion of capital and the product of that expansion itself. Concretely, investment is transformed into a self-financing process through tying the distribution of income between profits and wages to its requirements.[25]

In this manner, Post-Keynesian economics eliminates the dependence of Harrod's growth process upon the intertemporal consumption decisions of individuals. The result of this elimination is, in turn, the disappearance of the knife-edge. These steps, taken together, subordinate the proportion of savings out of income to the requirements of capital expansion and, in so doing, transform the latter into a process that is, in principle, self-sustaining. In Joan Robinson's words, the result of these steps is that "whatever I/Y [investment/income] may be, P/Y [profits/income] and therefore s [savings/income] is equal to it; . . . an equilibrium growth rate may be anything between zero and g^*, the upper limit set by the minimum level of the real wage."[26]

Thus, in the course of the Post-Keynesian development of Harrod's theory, growth becomes a process that necessarily renews itself rather than one which can only renew itself "by accident." The self-reproducing growth rate becomes that rate which is consistent with the expansion "desires" of firms rather than that rate which is consistent with the consumption desires of individuals.[27] The self-reproducing growth rate becomes Robinson's desired rate of growth rather than Harrod's warranted rate, and the knife-edge disappears.

The existence of growth or, more precisely, the accumulation of capital as an inherently self-sustaining process in the Post-Keynesian theory of accumulation is clearly expressed in its treatment of the rate of profit.[28] In this context, it is important to recognize that determining the rate of profit is essentially the problem of determining the rate of accumulation. [. . .]

This idea that the accumulation of capital determines itself is the idea that accumulation determines the degree to which its conditions are realized. It is therefore the idea that the conditions of accumulation are realized by and through this accumulation itself. The characteristic Post-Keynesian connection of the rate of profit to the accumulation of capital is thus the expression in the Post-Keynesian theory of profits of its treatment of accumulation as a self-sustaining process.[29]

This treatment of accumulation as self-sustaining underlies the argument of the Post-Keynesian theory of accumulation as a whole and gives to the latter its specificity vis-à-vis the Neoclassical theory. Indeed, the special contribution of Post-Keynesian economics to the theory of accumulation is precisely the analysis of the particular way in which the expansion of firms generates the markets and profits that it requires.

Distribution and Price

The above discussion implies that the treatment of accumulation as self-sustaining is bound up with a specific account of the distribution of income. In particular, this discussion indicates that this treatment is tied to an account of distribution that links distribution (the distribution of income between profits and wages and the rate of profit) to the extent of the expansion of capital rather than to the extent of its scarcity.[30] The Post-Keynesian break with the Neoclassical account of accumulation is thus simultaneously a break with its account of distribution. Indeed, the historical development of the Post-Keynesian theory of accumulation has been accompanied by the development of an alternative to (and critique of) the Neoclassical theory of distribution.[31]

This treatment of accumulation is also bound up with a specific account of price, one which also differs, in fundamental respects, from that of Neoclassical economics. This treatment is tied to or, more accurately, contains within it the conception of exchange as the process of the realization of the funds required for the expansion of capital rather than the process of the allocation of scarce resources. [. . .] To the extent that accumulation, in this treatment, finances itself through its effect upon the profits realized by firms, then the process which realizes these profits, that is, the series of exchanges between firms and firms and workers, is the realization of the funds needed for the expansion of capital. [. . .]

From the standpoint of the development of the price and accumulation connections, the significance of Kalecki's theory of price is that it ties the price of the firm's product to its gross profit margin. The latter is the major source of the firm's investment funds, so that Kalecki's connection of price to the extent of the firm's gross profit margin is, at least implicitly, the connection of price to the firm's ability to expand its capital.[32] Indeed, if the capital-output ratio of the firm is taken as given, then its gross profit margin determines the extent of its profitability (its rate of profit) and thus the extent to which it can expand its capital (its rate of capital accumulation).

The problem of price in Kalecki's theory is, then, not one of determining the scarcity of the firm's product. Rather, it is the problem of determining the growth potential of the firm. More specifically, price, in this theory, is determined by the firm's prime costs and the percentage mark-up on these costs.[33] If the prime costs of the firm are taken as given, then the problem of the determination of its price is that of the determination of this "mark-up," its gross profit margin.[34]

Once the price of the firm's product contains, as one of its components, the gross profit margin, then the sale of the firm's products becomes the realization of profits. In Kalecki's theory, then, this sale provides the firm with the funds it needs for its expansion and thus makes this expansion possible.

In turn, what makes this sale possible are the expansion activities of firms taken as a whole. The sale of the firm's products presupposes a demand for them, and in Kalecki's theory this demand presupposes the existence of a positive rate of capital accumulation. As implied in the discussion of Kalecki's theory of employment, the existence and extent of the demand for the products of Kalecki's firm depend upon that of the accumulation of capital in the economy. More specifically, given the market share of this firm, its sales depend upon the extent of the market as a whole (the level of "effective demand"), while the latter depends upon the level of investment along with the gross profit margins of firms.

The dependence of the firm's expansion funds upon the sale of its products is, then, dependence upon the accumulation of capital. This sale is, in effect, the link between the profits of individual firms and the accumulation of capital in the economy as a whole. The former is adjusted to the latter (accumulation finances itself) precisely through the effect of the latter upon the rate of sales of firms.[35] In

Kalecki's theory, exchange not only realizes the profits that firms need for expansion but also adjusts these profits to this expansion.

In this context, it should be emphasized that this adjustment of profits to capital accumulation presupposes the specific treatment of price found in Kalecki's theory. This adjustment presupposes, first, this theory's separation of price from demand. As long as price is linked to demand, then a change in the latter will have its major impact upon the price of the firm's product rather than upon its sales. Demand takes on its Keynesian role as "effective demand," as the determinant of output, only to the extent that it is separated from the movement of price.

Second, this adjustment presupposes the existence of a link between price and the gross profit margin. The sale of the firm's product can provide it with funds for expansion only if the product's price allows the firm to realize a surplus value, that is, a value in addition to its costs. The determination of sales can then only be the determination of the funds available for accumulation if the formation of price is simultaneously the formation of the gross profit margin. Thus, the adjustment of these funds to capital accumulation through the latter's determination of sales presupposes, as one of its necessary conditions, Kalecki's treatment of the pricing process of the individual firm.[36]

The connection of price to accumulation in Kalecki's theory is taken one step further in Joseph Steindl's theory of accumulation. In this theory, the gross profit margin is joined to the accumulation of capital.[37] Kalecki's connection of price to the source of firms' expansion funds thus becomes the connection of price to their expansion itself.

In particular, in Steindl's theory, price formation under competitive conditions becomes tied to accumulation. Under these conditions, the gross profit margins of firms within an industry are determined by their expansion.[38] Since this expansion, in turn, is tied (through its connection to the growth of the market) to the rate of capital accumulation in the economy as a whole, these profit margins are also tied to this rate.[39] Thus, under these conditions, the process of price formation in an individual industry becomes an expression of the accumulation of capital in the economy as a whole.[40]

Although price is joined to accumulation in the most concrete or systematic manner in Steindl's formulation of the Post-Keynesian theory of accumulation, it is also linked to accumulation, at least implicitly, in Robinson's formulation. In her formulation, this connection of price to accumulation is implicit in the adjustment of the distribution of income between profits and wages to the savings requirements of investment. Since this adjustment occurs through changes in the prices of the products of firms, this adjustment is simultaneously the adjustment of price to the requirements of investment.[41] Indeed, the determination of distribution by the rate of capital accumulation in this formulation is, in effect, the determination of the gross profit margins of firms.[42]

The Break with Neoclassical Theory

The preceding discussion suggests that the Post-Keynesian treatment of accumulation involves a break with all aspects of Neoclassical theory and contains within it an alternative to this theory as a whole. Indeed, as we have seen, the development of this treatment brought with it an alternative to the Neoclassical account of income and employment (Keynes and Kalecki), distribution (Nicholas Kaldor and Robinson), and price formation (Kalecki and Steindl).[43]

It is important here not to view this Post-Keynesian alternative as simply an alternative to the particular problems dealt with by Neoclassical economics. For the differences between Post-Keynesian and Neoclassical economics are not so much differences in their subject-matter as they are differences in their treatment of economic life. Where Post-Keynesian economics does depart from the specific concerns of Neoclassical economics, this is an expression of its break with the Neoclassical notion of economic life.

In particular, the absence of a treatment of "resource allocation" or, more precisely, of the problem of scarcity in Post-Keynesian economics is the result of the absence of this notion. The Neoclassicists' concern with this problem is an expression of their view of the economic process as the adjustment of resources to the given needs of individuals, that is, "the allocation of scarce factors among competing ends."[44] The problem of scarcity is absent in Post-Keynesian economics precisely because this view is absent.

Indeed, the Post-Keynesian treatment of accumulation breaks, in a fundamental manner, with this conception of the economic process. Accumulation, as a self-sustaining process, depends neither, on the one side, upon nature-given (scarce) resources nor, on the other, upon the preferences or needs of individuals. Since its conditions are its own products, it cannot, in principle, be limited by nature-given conditions. As Robinson has pointed out, where this process confronts a natural barrier such as the "scarcity" of fertile land or labor, this natural barrier must give way rather than accumulation.[45] Similarly, this process cannot be determined by the desires or needs of individuals for the same reason that it cannot be determined by natural conditions. Since these needs neither constitute its end nor determine the extent of the funds available for its existence, it cannot be governed by them.[46]

On one level, the significance of the Post-Keynesian treatment of accumulation is this break with the Neoclassical view of economic life and, in particular, with its connection of the economic process and thus accumulation to the given needs of individuals. For this connection of accumulation to these needs is its connection to factors which, by their very "givenness," are indeterminate, so that as long as accumulation is determined by these needs its characteristics cannot, in principle, be determined. Thus, by separating accumulation from the given needs of individuals the Post-Keynesian treatment brings accumulation within the reach of economic theory.[47]

Although Post-Keynesian economics opens up, in this manner, the possibility of a theory of accumulation in modern economics, it itself does not provide such a theory. The determinants of capital accumulation are not specified within Post-Keynesian economics, and thus the rate of capital accumulation is left undetermined. The possibility of a theory of accumulation in Post-Keynesian economics is therefore just that—a possibility.

This absence of a Post-Keynesian determination of accumulation is expressed in Robinson's theory by the multiplicity of possible "growth paths." The growth process, here, can take on a variety of forms, that is, the form of a "golden age," a "limping golden age," a "platinum age," and so forth, precisely because the rate of capital accumulation can take on a multiplicity of values.[48] Since there is no determination of the rate of accumulation, it is not possible to eliminate different forms (ages) of growth and, still less, determine the forms that growth assumes in the course of its development.

While this multiplicity of growth paths is peculiar to Robinson's formulation of the Post-Keynesian treatment of accumulation, the indeterminacy of accumulation that underlies this multiplicity is not. This indeterminacy exists, to one degree or another, in all formulations of the Post-Keynesian treatment of accumulation, even in the most developed or systematic of these, that is, Steindl's. Although the latter goes further than the others and, indeed, goes a considerable distance in developing a theory of accumulation, it does not bring this theory to fruition. In Steindl's formulation we find the beginnings, but only the beginnings, of an analysis of how the accumulation process "reacts back upon itself," determines its qualitative and quantitative dimensions.[49]

This element of indeterminacy is expressed in the sharpest manner in the Post-Keynesian connection of the rate of accumulation to the "animal spirits of entrepreneurs."[50] For the connection of this rate to "animal spirits" not only leaves this rate undetermined but also makes it dependent upon factors which are intrinsically indeterminate. Indeed, in this connection the Post-Keynesian treatment approaches that of Neoclassical economics. By making accumulation dependent upon animal spirits Post-Keynesian economics makes it dependent upon the whims or given desires of individuals, albeit their whims as entrepreneurs or capitalists rather than as consumers.[51] The characteristic Post-Keynesian ascription of accumulation to animal spirits thus not only signifies its break with Neoclassical economics but also the incomplete character of this break.

In this regard the Post-Keynesian notion of accumulation as a "game" is also instructive, for it, too, denotes the degree to which Post-Keynesian economics still remains within the confines of the Neoclassical treatment of accumulation.[52] This notion is, first, the idea of accumulation as a process that has no end outside of itself. It therefore expresses the Post-Keynesian view of accumulation as autonomous or self-sustaining and, in particular, its view that accumulation governs the ends and actions of economic agents rather than being governed by them, that is, the "rules" of the "accumulation game" regulate the actions of its "players." At the same time, however, this notion is, second or equally, the idea of accumulation as an indeterminate process. Accumulation, viewed as a game, has the same arbitrary character as a game. It may or may not be played (exist), and the extent to which it is played (the rate of accumulation) depends upon the whims of the players.

Thus, the Post-Keynesian notion of accumulation as a game indicates, as does its ascription of accumulation to animal spirits, the incomplete character of its break with Neoclassical economics. Most important, it indicates the retention within Post-Keynesian economics of that indeterminacy which characterizes the Neoclassical accumulation process.

The result of this retention is the absence of a "real" or developed Post-Keynesian alternative to Neoclassical theory. For this retention means that the Post-Keynesian treatment of accumulation as a self-sustaining process is not developed into a theory of accumulation, and therefore this treatment's break with Neoclassical economics is not developed into a concrete or systematic alternative to the latter. The existence of this alternative thus awaits the development of this treatment into a theory of accumulation. More precisely, it awaits the development of an analysis of the particular way in which the accumulation process determines itself in the course of sustaining itself.

Notes

1. The main representatives of Post-Keynesian economics are taken to be Nicholas Kaldor, Luigi Pasinetti, Piero Sraffa, Joan Robinson, and Joseph Steindl. What unites the work of these economists and what unites their work to Keynes will become clear in the course of this discussion.

2. This examination has recently been taken up by a number of economists. See Paul Davidson, *Money and the Real World* (New York: Halsted Press, 1972); Maurice Dobb, *Theories of Value and Distribution Since Adam Smith, Ideology and Economic Theory* (Cambridge: The University Press, 1973), ch. 8 and 9; Alfred Eichner and J. A. Kregel, "An Essay on Post-Keynesian Theory: A New Paradigm in Economics," *Journal of Economic Literature* 13 (December 1975): 1293–1314; J. A. Kregel, *The Reconstruction of Political Economy: An Introduction to Post-Keynesian Economics* (New York: Halsted Press, 1973); G. C. Harcourt, "The Cambridge Controversies: Old Ways and New Horizons—or Dead End?" *Oxford Economic Papers* 28 (March 1976): 25–65; and Edward J. Nell, "Economics: The Revival of Political Economy," in *Ideology in Social Science*, ed. Robin Blackburn (London: Fontana, 1972). For an interpretation of Post-Keynesian economics similar to the one presented here see David P. Levine, *Economic Theory* (London: Routledge and Kegan Paul, 1978), vol. 1, ch. 8.

3. John Maynard Keynes, *The General Theory of Employment, Income, and Money* (New York: Harcourt, Brace, 1965), pp. 135–37.

4. Ibid., pp. 137–41. Joan Robinson makes a similar point in "Keynes and Kalecki," *Collected Economic Papers*, (Oxford: Basil Blackwell, 1975), vol. 3, p. 96. Also see A. Asimakopulos, "The Determination of Investment in Keynes's Model," *Canadian Economic Journal* 4 (August 1971): 382–88.

5. Keynes, *General Theory*, pp. 141–46.

6. This aspect of Keynes's departure from Neoclassical economics (the break with its static equilibrium method and its corresponding analysis of the market economy in "real" terms) is what Keynes himself regarded as the revolutionary element of the *General Theory*. (See Keynes, "The General Theory of Employment," *Quarterly Journal of Economics* 51 [February 1937]: 209–25.) Paul Davidson and Sidney Weintraub (among others) have followed this view of Keynes's in placing uncertainty and monetary relations at the center of their development of his theory.

The macro theory developed by Davidson and Weintraub has important similarities with Post-Keynesian economics (such as its treatment of the money wage, the pricing process, and inflation) as well as critical differences (such as its treatment of money and the effect of the money supply on output and investment). For a detailed discussion of these similarities and differences and for references to the important works of the "Keynes school" of macroeconomics, see Davidson, *Money and the Real World*.

7. Keynes, *General Theory*, p. 150.

8. G. C. Harcourt has suggested (in private correspondence) that the treatment of investment found in this chapter not only departs from that of Neoclassical economics but also implicitly approaches that of Marxian economics. In particular, this treatment is similar to Marx's idea that the expansion of the firm has no rationale other than itself ("accumulate, accumulate, that is Moses and the prophets").

9. Keynes, *General Theory*, pp. 161–62.

10. Again, in its specification of the conditions of investment, the Keynesian treatment approaches that of Marxian economics. Indeed, the notion of investment as a self-sustaining process is one of the distinguishing characteristics of Marx's theory of capital accumulation. See Levine, *Economic Theory*, vol. 3, ch. 1.

11. For the Neoclassical reconstruction of the Keynesian theory of employment see J. R. Hicks, "Mr. Keynes and the Classics," *Econometrica* 5 (April 1937): 147–59, and Don Patinkin, *Money, Interest, and Prices* (New York: Harper and Row, 1965).

12. For Kalecki's formulation see *Essays in the Theory of Economic Fluctuations* (London: Allen and Unwin, 1939) or *The Theory of Economic Dynamics* (New York: Modern Reader Paperbacks, 1968).

13. The conditions required to make the degree of monopoly the same formal expression as the propensity to consume are: (1) The prime costs of firms taken as a whole are equal to the wages bill, and (2) the latter is equal to consumption, that is, the capitalists' propensity to save is equal to one, and the workers' propensity to save is equal to zero. Under these conditions, the degree of monopoly is the reciprocal of the marginal (and average) propensity to consume.

14. Keynes, *General Theory*, pp. 89–96.

15. Ibid., pp. 93–94.

16. It could be argued that Keynes's connection of the share of savings out of income to the propensity to consume does not, at least implicitly, express the same idea of savings as the Neoclassical. In particular, it appears that, for Keynes, the propensity to consume is as much a product of the customs and institutions of a nation as it is the result of the intertemporal consumption decisions of individuals. Thus, even in Keynes's reproduction of the Neoclassical notion of savings there exists an implicit break with this notion. See Keynes, *General Theory*, p. 109.

17. Kalecki, *Theory of Economic Dynamics*, ch. 3.

18. At certain points in Keynes's discussion of savings it appears that savings for Keynes (as for Kalecki) exists mainly in the form of profits. Keynes, however, unlike Kalecki, does not trace out the implications of this existence of savings as profits for the theory of employment and income. The fact that Keynes does not develop these implications is clearly expressed by the absence in the *General Theory* of a distinction between the propensity to save out of profits and the propensity to save out of wages. See Keynes, *General Theory*, pp. 96–106, 108.

19. J. A. Kregel makes a similar point in *Rates of Profit, Distribution, and Growth* (London: Macmillan, 1971), p. 6.

20. R. F. Harrod, "An Essay in Dynamic Theory," in R. F. Harrod, *Economic Essays* (New York: Harcourt, Brace, 1952), p. 256.

21. We do not mean to suggest here that Harrod's theory is similar, in all respects, to Keynes's. There are, of course, important differences (such as their respective treatments of expectations). For Harrod's views on the revolutionary character of Keynes's theory see Harrod, "Keynes and Traditional Theory," in *Economic Essays*, pp. 237–53, and Harrod, *The Life of John Maynard Keynes* (London: Macmillan, 1951), ch. 11.

22. Robinson makes this same point in *Essays in the Theory of Economic Growth* (New York: St. Martin's Press, 1964), p. 12, and in *Economic Heresies* (New York: Basic Books, 1971), p. 110.

23. Nicholas Kaldor, "Alternative Theories of Distribution," *Review of Economic Studies* 23 (1955–1956): 95; and Robinson, *Essays in the Theory of Economic Growth*, pp. 38–39.

24. Kaldor, "Alternative Theories," p. 96; and Robinson, *Essays in the Theory of Economic Growth*, pp. 40–41.

25. In Kalecki's treatment of profits (savings), the profits realized by firms are also a product of their expansion activities. The only difference between this treatment and Robinson's (and Kaldor's) is the way in which they link profits to investment. Instead of tying profits to investment through the effect of the latter upon the distribution of income between profits and wages (the degree of monopoly), Kalecki links profits to investment through the effect of the latter upon the rate of sales of firms (output).

26. Robinson, "Harrod After Twenty-One Years," *Economic Journal* 80 (September 1970): 733.

27. Robinson, *Essays in the Theory of Economic Growth*, pp. 47–51.

28. The reference point for this discussion is Robinson's formulation of the Post-Keynesian theory of accumulation. For her formulation see *The Accumulation of Capital* (New York: St. Martin's Press, 1966), books 1 and 2, and *Essays in the Theory of Economic Growth*, part 2.

29. Steindl's theory of accumulation contains the same treatment of the rate of profit as Robinson's and thus the same view of accumulation. Indeed, Steindl takes as the explicit task of his theory the development of an "endogenous" theory of investment, that is, the development of an analysis of the way in which the investment process determines itself. See Joseph Steindl, *Maturity and Stagnation in American Capitalism* (Oxford: Basil Blackwell, 1952), pp. v–ix.

30. This connection of distribution to the rate of capital accumulation is found in Pasinetti's theory of distribution as well as in Kaldor's, Kalecki's, Robinson's, and Steindl's. See Luigi Pasinetti, *Growth and Income Distribution, Essays in Economic Theory* (London: Cambridge University Press, 1974), ch. 5 and 6.

31. For the Post-Keynesian alternative to (and critique of) the Neoclassical theory of distribution see G. C. Harcourt, *Some Cambridge Controversies in the Theory of Capital* (London: Cambridge University Press, 1972), ch. 1–4, and appendix to ch. 4. A statement of Harcourt's current views on the significance of this Post-Keynesian critique can be found in "The Cambridge Controversies."

32. If investment by the firm is financed with its own funds, then its gross profit margin *is* the means of its expansion. Although the firm's profit margin ceases to be the only source of its expansion when the capital market is introduced, the extent of this margin will still affect the firm's ability to borrow. See R. J. Ball, *Inflation and the Theory of Money* (London: George Allen and Unwin, 1964), ch. 1 and 2; G. C. Harcourt, "A Two-Sector Model of the Distribution of Income and the Level of Employment in the Short-Run," *Economic Record* 41 (March 1965): 103–17; Harcourt, *Some Cambridge Contro-*

versies, pp. 210–14; Kalecki, *Theory of Economic Dynamics*, ch. 8; and Adrian Wood, *A Theory of Profits* (Cambridge: The University Press, 1975), ch. 1 and 2.

33. Kalecki, *Theory of Economic Dynamics*, ch. 1.

34. This "mark-up" treatment of the pricing process has important implications for the problem of inflation. It suggests that the key determinant of the price level in the short run (when the gross profit margin and output per worker are more or less given) is the level of money wages. Changes in aggregate demand would then have their primary impact on the price level through their effect on the money wage rate (as, for example, when a growing level of employment improves the bargaining position of workers and thus their ability to realize increases in their money wage rate). See Paul Davidson and Sidney Weintraub, "Money as Cause and Effect," *Economic Journal* 83 (December 1973): 1117–32; John Eatwell and Joan Robinson, *An Introduction to Modern Economics* (London: McGraw Hill, 1973), pp. 211–12; and Robinson, *Accumulation of Capital*, ch. 20.

35. Kalecki, *Theory of Economic Dynamics*, pp. 45–47.

36. This discussion suggests that Kalecki's treatment of price is the one that is required by the Keynesian theory of employment. This treatment not only allows demand to appear in its Keynesian role as effective demand but also allows investment "to finance itself," that is, it is compatible with and, indeed, required for the Keynesian adjustment of savings to investment through the latter's effect upon sales (income). For a detailed discussion of the relation between this treatment of price and the major propositions of the Keynesian theory of employment see Harcourt, "A Two-Sector Model"; Harcourt and Kenyon, "Pricing and the Investment Decision"; and Nina Shapiro, "Essays on the Theory of the Firm and Macroeconomics," Ph.D. diss., New School for Social Research, 1976, ch. 2.

37. For Steindl's determination of the gross profit margin see Steindl, *Maturity and Stagnation*, ch. 5–7.

38. Ibid., pp. 43–47.

39. Ibid., p. 122.

40. This Post-Keynesian departure from the Neoclassical theory of price is an aspect of a more general break with the "methodology" of Neoclassical economics, that is, the characteristic Neoclassical procedure of deducing the workings of the economy as a whole from those of its individual parts. Whereas in Neoclassical economics the economy is no more than "the sum of its parts" (macroeconomics is aggregate economics), in Post-Keynesian economics the economic system has laws of its own (the laws of capital accumulation), which laws, in turn, determine the activities of its individual parts. For the methodological differences between Neoclassical and Post-Keynesian economics see G. C. Harcourt, "Decline and Rise: The Revival of (Classical) Political Economy," *Economic Record* 51 (September 1975): 339–54; Harcourt, "The Cambridge Controversies"; Pasinetti, *Growth and Income Distribution*, pp. 42–45, 92–93; and Joan Robinson, "The Unimportance of Reswitching," *Quarterly Journal of Economics* 89 (February 1975): 32–39, and "History versus Equilibrium," *Thames Papers in Political Economy* (Autumn 1974).

41. Robinson, *Accumulation of Capital*, ch. 19, and *Essays in the Theory of Economic Growth*, pp. 70–74. A treatment of price formation which is similar to Kalecki's can also be found in Robinson's work. See A. Asimakopoulos, "A Robinsonian Growth Model in One-Sector Notation," *Australian Economic Papers* 8 (June 1969): 41–58; Harcourt, *Some Cambridge Controversies*, pp. 232–40; and Robinson and Eatwell, *An Introduction to Modern Economics*, pp. 153–55.

42. This determination of distribution is also the determination of the gross profit margins of firms in Kaldor's theory. See Kaldor, "Alternative Theories of Distribution."

43. This treatment is also bound up with or, more precisely, is based upon an alternative to the Neoclassical treatment of production, that is, the notion of production as reproduction, the idea of production as "the production of commodities by means of commodities." The Post-Keynesian notion of accumulation as self-renewing is the expres-

sion of this idea of production in the theory of growth ("expanded reproduction"). For this Post-Keynesian alternative to the Neoclassical theory of production see Piero Sraffa, *The Production of Commodities by Means of Commodities* (Cambridge: The University Press, 1963).

44. For an extended discussion and critique of this view see Levine, *Economic Theory*, vol. 1, ch. 1.

45. Robinson, *Essays in the Theory of Economic Growth*, p. 15.

46. The Post-Keynesian separation of accumulation from consumption needs opens up the possibility that these needs will not be satisfied by accumulation. It at least makes this satisfaction a by-product of accumulation rather than (as in Neoclassical economics) its "motor-force."

This absence of need-satisfaction in the Post-Keynesian accumulation process, however, should not be construed as a "misallocation of resources." The point is not that "resources" are inefficiently utilized. Rather, the principles for their efficient utilization are different in Post-Keynesian economics, that is, the principle is the expansion of capital rather than the "maximization of utility." Moreover, in Post-Keynesian economics, the needs whose satisfaction are in question have a fundamentally different character than those needs which form the starting point of Neoclassical economics. These needs (the "composition of demand") are determined by the requirements of production (or "expanded reproduction"). See Sraffa, *Production of Commodities*, ch. 1 and 2.

47. By bringing accumulation into the subject-matter of economics Post-Keynesianism brings the Marxian problem of analyzing "the laws of motion of capitalist production" back into economic analysis. Indeed, since for Post-Keynesian economics the economic process is the accumulation process, the economic problem for Post-Keynesian economics is nothing other than this "Marxian" problem.

48. Robinson, *Essays in the Theory of Economic Growth*, pp. 51–59.

49. See Steindl, *Maturity and Stagnation*, part 2.

50. Robinson, *Accumulation of Capital*, p. 84, and *Essays in the Theory of Economic Growth*, pp. 15–16.

51. The issue here is not whether accumulation occurs through the decisions and actions of individuals. Accumulation, of course, as any other social process, can only be realized in this manner. Rather, at issue is how these actions are themselves *treated*, whether they are reviewed as being open to explanation, subject to "law," or subject to "caprice" (animal spirits). If these actions are treated in the latter manner, then the very treatment of the actions through which accumulation is realized precludes an account of accumulation.

For modern economics, the economic system is populated with free individuals whose very freedom precludes an explanation of their actions. Modern economics would therefore view this element of indeterminacy in Post-Keynesian economics as the inevitable result of its subject matter rather than as a limitation in its *treatment* of that subject matter. Although a discussion of the issues raised here would take us out of the confines of this essay, we should make explicit what is already implicit in our discussion—we depart from the position of modern economics on the possibility of explaining the needs, decisions, and actions of individual economic agents. In so departing, we are returning to the classical (and Marxian) view of the economic system, to the idea that there exists an "invisible hand" which governs the independent decisions and actions of individuals, creates order out of "anarchy," and thus makes these actions subject to economic science. (See Ronald L. Meek, "The Rise and Fall of the Concept of the Economic Machine," inaugural lecture, University of Leicester [Leicester: University Press, 1965].)

52. This notion and the related idea of accumulation as originating in animal spirits have their historical origins in Keynes's treatment of investment. See Keynes, *General Theory*, pp. 161–63. For the clearest expression of this notion in the Post-Keynesian treatment see Robinson, *Accumulation of Capital*, ch. 1.

Alternative Analyses
of Short and Long Run
in Post-Keynesian Economics

FERNANDO CARVALHO

The following article gives the reader a sense of the diversity and wide range of economic analysis within the school of thought called Post-Keynesian economics. Carvalho discusses five different models of short-run vs. long-run equilibrium. They point to the influence of all the schools of thought discussed in this reader on the development of Post-Keynesian economics.

The first two models presume a somewhat systematic movement over time from a short-run situation to a long-run equilibrium. In this way they incorporate more "classical" features in their interpretation of economic activity. The first is derived from the Sraffian model and depicts a static long-run "center of gravity" to which the economy converges. The second is a growth model that predicts a dynamic long-run equilibrium. The following three models focus less on movement toward a stable point and concentrate on the process of decision making and uncertainty in modeling the passage of time. The Kaleckian alternative seeks to explain cyclical economic behavior, rather than an end point. In it institutional behavior is incorporated as a salient feature of a capitalist economy. The fourth model relies heavily on the concepts of uncertainty in investment decisions; the long run is open to the influences of short-run expectations. The last model is the least determinate of all. In this Post-Keynesian interpretation, even the notion of a long-run situation becomes problematic because of the difficulty in predicting future events.

It has been frequently noted that Post-Keynesian economics is distinguished "by a dislike of orthodox or Neoclassical economics" (Harcourt 1982) rather than by coherence or agreement of fundamentals by its contributors. Different subjects but also different methodologies and assumptions are characteristics of the present state of Post-Keynesian economics. This may be uncomfortable but not necessarily troublesome. As Joan Robinson once observed, "There is no simple theory to cover the multifarious evolution of a private enterprise economy" (1980: 14). This diversity is the strength of the Post-Keynesian view (Kregel 1976). Assumptions and concepts should be changed to fit in the nature of the questions that can be formulated (cf. Davidson's intervention in Harcourt 1977: 391–92). An excessively eclectic attitude, however, may conceal the inconsisten-

Fernando Carvalho, "Alternative Analyses of Short and Long Run in Post-Keynesian Economics," *Journal of Post Keynesian Economics* 7, 2 (Winter 1984–85), pp. 214–34.

cy of assumptions and methodologies which at some point may hinder the further development of a theoretical body.

There is no general a priori resolution to this problem. Different methods and assumptions can coexist in a given theoretical school without precluding efforts aimed at examining and classifying them. Diversity, then, is not a problem if it does not refer to the "vision" of the economy, that is, as long as it is possible to obtain a common view of what does and what does not constitute the fundamental subject of study for the "school" as a whole. In this paper I propose to adopt as a classifying criterion the treatment and manipulations of the concepts of short and long run. The treatment of time reflects fundamental choices made by each author as to which processes constitute the core of economic life (Carvalho 1983–84). The use of long- or short-run models is determined by those choices.

The classical (Smith-Ricardo) approach singled out gravitation processes around "natural" positions (Garegnani 1976: 27). This reflected very precise views about what is relevant in the operation of a capitalist economy. On the other hand, when Keynes says that in the long run we will all be dead (1924: 100), he is forcefully proposing a radically different choice of subjects (and not only of methodologies). Therefore, I believe that the use of the dichotomy "long run/short run" can be a significant criterion for classification of Post-Keynesian "branches" and thus to illuminate the coherence among them.

For most of the uses and purposes the distinction between long and short run is analytical rather than temporal. Actually, the extension of these distinctions to embrace a temporal meaning is almost always a source of logical contradictions for the schools that attempt to do it. Some authors clearly recognize this point. For instance, Koopmans warns that "while this designation [short run] suggests a time limitation, the common analytical characteristic of problems covered by this term appears to be the presence of certain fixed factors of production, not subject to change, or in any case not subject to increase, within the alternatives admitted in the problem" (1957: 16). In the long run we have "problems in which no fixed factors of production are recognized" (p. 24).[1] [. . .]

Samuelson (1979: 269–76) shows that certain conditions have to be met to obtain a movement that converges to equilibrium (either of the first or of the second kind), warning that these conditions may be difficult to meet. Nevertheless Samuelson's followers adopted a much more optimistic view of the problem. "Rational" behavior combined with the increased number of degrees of freedom given by the possibility of "long-run" adjustments led most authors to believe that convergence to equilibrium was a *fact* of economic life. This became a matter of "faith" regarding the self-adjusting dynamic properties of the capitalist system.[2] The role of the distinction between short and long run is, then, to make it possible to devise a process of "noise-removal" through which full equilibrium can be attained if "enough time" is allowed for the required changes to occur. The illusion of temporality is then fully integrated and becomes functional to validate that faith in the self-adjusting capacity of the economy.

There is no reason, however, for these ideas to be so readily accepted. As Samuelson suggested, there is no a priori reason to expect convergence to equilibrium. [. . .] Moreover, it is acknowledged that even the existence of equilibrium is threatened by the introduction of money and finance in the Keynesian sense (Arrow and Hahn 1971: 356–61; Minsky 1980: 21; Davidson 1978: ch. 16).

In sum, in Neoclassical economics the "long run" cannot be a temporal concept. It does not refer to any real world process of evolution or change. Even *notional* processes are shown to be difficult to conceive. "Long run," *by definition*, refers to a situation in which no mistakes are made and all the (theoretically expected) adjustments are achieved. It is not in time, it is not even a secular trend. It is just an aprioristic statement of what the world would look like should the theory be correct.

Post-Keynesian Models

Post-Keynesian theory was born of dissatisfaction with Neoclassical economics. It is rooted in the innovative efforts developed in Cambridge, England, from the 1930s to the 1950s to reconstruct economic theory by a group of economists led by Keynes which included P. Sraffa, R. Kahn, and J. Robinson. Economists of other origins, like Kalecki, Harrod, and Shackle, also joined this struggle against the ruling view of economics.

Being born as a refusal of orthodoxy, Post-Keynesian economics came to embrace a wide variety of models, employing methods of different nature, attacking an ample set of issues (Harcourt 1982; Davidson 1982: ch. 1; Kregel 1975). These models range from theories of long-run determinants of prices and growth to theories of decision making under uncertainty, usually (but somewhat incorrectly) seen as short-run models.

In these terms, we could identify a spectrum of Post-Keynesian models as follows: (1) the Garegnani/Eatwell approach, concerned exclusively with long-run equilibrium positions of prices and output, identified as static gravity centers; (2) the Kaldor/Pasinetti model of determination of long-run growth rates usually seen as dynamic (moving) gravity centers; (3) the Kaleckian alternative, which combines both long- and short-run models, displacing the emphasis, however, to cyclical movements as the major phenomenon to be explained; (4) the Davidson/Kregel/Minsky approach, where uncertainty undermines the usefulness of gravity center models and the necessity for historical models is posed; (5) the Shackle alternative, which concentrates attention in the study of expectations and the nature of imagination in the *moment* of decision making. Absent from this spectrum is Joan Robinson. The explanation for the omission is that her views seem to have changed substantially over time. For this reason she has crossed more than once the boundaries here proposed. For this reason I opted for discussing Joan Robinson's views separately.

In what follows I examine each of the alternative models.

The Static Gravity Centers Approach

The authors that constitute the group favoring the static gravity centers approach start from the Sraffian revival of Ricardian economics and its critique of the marginalist theory of distribution. The leading members of this school are P. Garegnani and J. Eatwell.[3] Their aim is to reconstruct economic theory via Smithian/Ricardian methods of theoretical investigation. This classical method consists of "the study of the permanent effects of change by means of comparisons between positions of the economic system characterized by a uniform rate of profits" (Garegnani 1976: 25; Eatwell 1983: 3). These positions are defined as "long-run" positions or "gravity centers" (Garegnani 1976: 25). The starting point is the Sraffian theory of prices of production, to which is sometimes added a long-run theory of employment.

The focus of this group is exclusively directed to "long-run" situations. The short run is the terrain of "accidental" influences, therefore of "noise." Scientific study has to be confined to the long run because systematic forces are operative *only* in the long run. The "short period," in which "historical processes" are developed, resembles "areas in which anecdote and description replace the derivation of general analytic principles" (Eatwell 1983: 24). Thus themes like actual market prices (or, for that matter, money) are nonissues for this school.

These authors are concerned with "determinacy" (Carvalho 1983–84: 276; Harcourt 1982: 14). Arguments that introduce uncertainty about the outcome of economic processes are, *for this very reason*, ruled out and assumed to be essentially irrelevant (Garegnani 1976: 39; 1979a: 72; 1979b: 182). In Eatwell's words: "Market prices were believed [in the classical tradition] to be influenced by a variety of forces—uncertainty, harvest failure, monopoly, and so on—and thus were not amenable to analysis in terms of systematic forces, as were natural prices" (Eatwell 1977: 64n).

It is crucial to note that the influence of that "variety of forces" that can make outcomes uncertain is asserted *to be confined* to the short run, by *postulating* that short-run influences are *only temporary* (Garegnani 1976: 28) and do not change the forces that determine the long-run equilibrium. Short-run factors can be ignored. Short-run events are not only temporary but they ultimately disappear *without leaving traces*.

Nevertheless, this assumption is still not sufficient to ensure convergence to the equilibrium position. As Samuelson pointed out, another condition is necessary, namely, "all motions approach [the stationary equilibrium] in the limit . . . *if [it] is stable*" (Samuelson 1979: 329, my emphasis).

The question of the importance of static gravity centers, therefore, becomes whether or not the long-run position is stable. This point is not formally addressed by any of the Post-Keynesian authors espousing the "center of gravity" view. Of course it is often suggested that the traverse or adjustment process involves the transference of resources from industries with lower rates of profit to sectors with higher profit rates. "Normal," "natural," or "production" prices are obtained when, through this adjustment process, an equal rate of profit is established for all industries. [. . .]

In Garegnani's view, deviations are temporary and, even more importantly, short-run changes are *qualityless* (Georgescu-Roegen 1971: intro.), that is, completely reversible. Garegnani's use of Adam Smith's approach indicates that the gravitation process is just a process of adjustment of quantities *produced*. Short-run movements are restricted to those that don't change the data of the model. But this requires that the operation of the gravitation process (in the short run) involves the realization of investments under very peculiar assumptions (Robinson 1980; Carvalho 1983–84). Investments must be determined by *current* differences in rates of profit while mistaken investments do not lead to the loss of the capital value invested.[4] Thus, firms are able to reorient their resources from less to more profitable sectors without significant capital loss.

To the extent to which expectations are involved in the investment decisions, these expectations should be "subjectivity-free." To obtain this result Eatwell connects directly the environmental conditions to investment decisions by defining the "state of long-term expectations" by "the role of the state, the relationship between finance and industry, the recent history of competitiveness and technological change, the state of industrial relations and so on" (Eatwell 1983: 30). In other words, instead of having "flimsy foundations . . . subject to sudden and violent changes" (Keynes 1973: 271), investments become solidly rooted in the structural features of the economy.

In sum, for Post-Keynesians such as Garegnani and Eatwell, the only objects of economic analysis are the "long-run positions" of the system. Short-run behaviors are not considered amenable to analysis and, therefore, are irrelevant. The result of this procedure is to solve the question of the relation between short and long run by eliminating the former. This forces the analysis to fall back upon vague references to competition when it is asked how long-run positions are reached.

The Moving Gravity Centers Approach

The moving gravity centers approach is the next alternative in the Post-Keynesian spectrum. It is close to the Garegnani/Eatwell approach because of its emphasis on long-run positions, although its subject is *growth paths* instead of given states. Moreover, even if prices of production are not a central concern to this approach, attempts to integrate the Sraffian analysis into the theory are carried out by some of its practitioners.

Leaders of this second group are Kaldor (1970) and Pasinetti (1970; 1983). Their theoretical constructions originate in Harrod's "knife-edge" models of growth (Harrod 1970). Like Solow, Kaldor considered Harrod's description of the determinants of growth too dependent on special assumptions. With less restrictive assumptions Kaldor suggests that the kind of instability expected by Harrod is unwarranted. In Kaldor's scheme it is changes in income distribution that adjust "warranted" and "natural" rates of growth to each other.

The warranted/natural growth path analysis is interpreted as referring to long-run paths (despite Harrod's [1970] hope that it would explain business cycles). It is not clear, however, whether the actual economy is supposed to gravitate around that growth path or if these paths are just statements of equilibrium conditions. Kaldor stresses that *if* some specified conditions are satisfied "there will be an inherent tendency to growth and an inherent tendency to full employment" (1970: 89). But the unanswered question remains: Are those conditions expected to be satisfied? The Kaldor model, however, does not depend *only* on full employment but also on demand-determined prices (p. 84). This condition shows that Kaldor's model contains a conception of long run as an aprioristically established equilibrium situation. The assumption of price flexibility, in the context of full employment, is intended to allow the treatment of short-run disequilibria as temporary maladjustments that do not prevent long-run trends to affirm themselves.[5] This allows the dissociation between short- and long-run problems. The possibility of studying short-run "cyclical" behavior is not denied. These questions, however, have nothing to do with the determination of long-run growth paths.

Pasinetti adopts similar procedures. Both in his aggregate model (1970) and in the disaggregated version (1983) he explicitly states that he is concerned with " 'permanent' causes moving an economic system, irrespective of any accidental or transitory deviation which may temporarily occur" (1983: 127). [. . .]

A common feature of all these gravity center theories is that one freely passes from definitions of abstract equilibrium conditions to descriptions of actual growth paths. The whole possible field of research regarding the relations between short and long run is completely ignored. This prevents the development of a complete theory of the gravitation process itself beyond the point of merely stating its *necessity*, which is especially obvious in the theory of investment.

Since Pasinetti is concerned with a theory of growth and income distribution, the question of his theory of investment is crucial. The volume and composition of investment is the first link in the causation chain of his model (1983: 146). Nevertheless, no theory of *actual* investment is offered; instead, only the necessary volume of investment to maintain the long-run growth path is specified. Thus Pasinetti avoids having to choose between a theory of investment similar to Garegnani's or else allowing short-run "noise" to be crystallized into the set of long-run determinants of the growth path. [. . .]

In sum, the approach of "gravity centers," whether static or dynamic, eliminates short-run considerations by definition, assuming them to be "temporary" (meaning by temporary qualityless and reversible).

The Cycle and the Trend

Kalecki (1943; 1954; 1971) represents a third Post-Keynesian alternative view. In his works the dichotomy between short run and long run exists but long-run states are no longer gravity centers. There are no forces that make the economy *converge* to those positions. In particular, long-run positions are not, in any sense, equilibrium states, characterized by equal rates of profit or full employment or any other such condition.

To analyze Kalecki's views on the subject requires first the acknowledgment that his works can be broadly divided into two groups. In the first, we find the development of mechanistic models of cyclical and trend movements, designed to allow statistical verification. These models present an essentially moneyless economy with a thermostat-type theory of investment. The second group (we may denote it as "literary" papers for comparison with his mechanistic models) comprises the papers in which Kalecki described the operation of the capitalist system liberated from the formalism of mechanical models. This differentiation of literary from mechanical models is important because the imperatives of the use of mathematical language forced Kalecki to adopt some procedures in the first set of essays that are ultimately uncomfortable to the author.

The handling of the dichotomy of short/long run strikingly illustrates the point. In his literary papers Kalecki avoids the problems mentioned with respect to the two gravity center approaches. Not only is there no contradiction between short- and long-run processes but they are presented in a very coherent manner in which long-run behaviors are developed *in the same world* as the short-run. In other words, long-run factors are present in the short run and, in fact, it is in the short run that they are invested with reality. Long-run factors are merely those that exercise a *durable* influence in the economy. This influence, however, is effective in the succession of short terms. Long- and short-run behaviors are interwoven in such a manner that it is not possible to separate them in the real world. Elements like class struggles, institutional features, technological aspects, and so on are present in the short run as determinants of "short-run" processes as well as "long-run" ones. Kalecki's markup price theory (1971: ch. 5) exemplifies the point by bridging "long-run" determinants (such as the degree of market concentration) with "short-run" factors (such as the cyclically changing relations of power between corporations and trade unions or between prime costs and overheads). This is particularly clear in the relations presented between investment, technology, and income distribution.[6]

In the mechanistic models this complexity and richness is lost (Castro 1979: ch. 5). The mathematical impossibility of using accelerator/multiplier models to show cycles and growth *at the same time* (Samuelson 1939) leads Kalecki to the same separation of arguments of which he was a critic. In one of his last papers (1971: ch. 15) Kalecki declared that his treatment of the relation of cycles with trends was made "in a manner which now I do not consider entirely satisfactory: I started from developing a theory of the 'pure business cycle' in a stationary economy, and at a later stage I modified the respective equations to get the trend into the picture. By this separation of short-period and long-period influences I missed certain repercussions of technical progress which affect the dynamic process as a whole'' (p. 166). Even in his last attempt to integrate the two dimensions in a simple model, however, Kalecki was not completely successful in overcoming the analytical separation of trend (long-run) from cycle (short-run) factors.

Kalecki's treatment of short/long-run processes in his literary papers points to the interaction and *joint* existence of both. Differently from gravity center theories, for Kalecki long-run positions are not equilibrium configurations that exist independently of short-run processes. In Kalecki's words: "In fact, the long-run trend is but a slowly changing component of a chain of short-run situations; *it has no independent entity*" (1971: 165, my emphasis). His literary framework allows the study of short-run phenomena in which there are also long-run factors in operation. Orderliness is not solely a privilege of the long run. Therefore, the short run is also intelligible. Unfortunately, most of the implications of those propositions were lost in Kalecki's mechanistic models in which short-run and long-run variables are independent, thereby sacrificing the complex patterns of interaction suggested in Kalecki's literary papers.

Unalterable Past, Perfidious Future

The next Post-Keynesian view, espoused by Davidson, Kregel, and Minsky, is inspired by Keynes's views of the operation of monetary production economies. The change in the concepts of long and short run, in favor of the latter, is carried one step further. This is mainly due to the stress laid by Keynes on the importance of uncertainty on the determination of the key variables of capitalist dynamics. The most remarkable feature of Keynes's behavioral functions (like the liquidity preference or the marginal efficiency of capital) is their dependence on given states of expectations, shifting when these states change. In Keynes, as opposed to Eatwell, the states of expectations can be highly volatile, causing the system to be subject to instability.

Keynes (and this Post-Keynesian group), therefore, could not recognize any role for long-run positions which could be established as gravity centers. The economy does not *tend* to anything over calendar time. The theory is open, in fact, even in the "long run," given the role attributed to expectations. This does not mean that anything is possible, but that the limitations emerge in the form of institutions and interrelations instead of gravitation forces.

This approach is essentially dynamic in the sense that motion, not states, is the subject. Moreover, it is historic because it refers to economies with past and future. The present inherits material conditions, in a specific shape, institutions, and contractual commitments from a past that cannot be undone. The future will inherit the results of decisions, actions, and commitments made in the present (Davidson 1978: 13; Minsky 1982: 17). It is this "unfolding" of relations that constitutes the subject of the theory. Each period contains in itself all that it is important to know, either as limitations or as possibilities. As a result, "long-run" factors are considered to the extent to which current decisions and actions are influenced by them: "The actual historical path of economic activity for real world monetary economies is not one which can be decomposed into separate and logically independent secular trend and short-run trade cycle aspects" (Davidson 1978: 18). For some, this view runs the risk of underestimating long-period influences because they are diluted in the small segments that are contained in each period. An evaluation of their global impact would depend on the possibility of studying a whole sequence of periods instead of concentrating on each one of them.

Long-run factors in Keynes's view, nevertheless, are operational only to the extent that they shape long-run expectations. In other words, technological developments, expansion of markets, and other factors that usually constitute the set of long-run forces act through the expectations that are formed about them. As Minsky stresses (1975: ch. 4), every decision in a capitalist economy is speculative in nature. The Keynesian concept of uncertainty causes the influence of those long-run factors to be operational only through the filter of expectations (Minsky 1982: 93–95; 1975: 64–68). In Keynes the future is *telescoped* into the present by entrepreneurs' expectations (cf. Shackle 1968). Once contractual and financial commitments are realized, they also become part of the long-run environment.

In sum, long-run expectations induce short-run behaviors (decisions and actions) like those of the investment process. This means that variables like those contained in the Kaleckian *trend* do not have much importance except as a description of past results.

The subject of analysis is radically changed, in this way, from long-run *positions* to long-run *expectations*. The corresponding variables now exist as inheritances from the past, like capital goods (Davidson and Minsky), financial claims and institutions (Minsky), supply contracts (Davidson), and as future values *anticipated* in the present.

The long run is open: it refers to values that are imagined by entrepreneurs.[7] It is no longer a state or trend in the traditional sense of these terms. The main dichotomy emerges as the one between long-run and short-run *expectations*: they are distinguished by the action each one induces (e.g., investment decisions result from long-run expectations and output decisions from short-run expectations—Keynes 1964: ch. 5). Moreover, long-run expectations by their nature "are not readily checked in short periods by observing realized results" (Davidson 1978: 23; Davidson and Kregel 1980: 140–42), compared to short-run expectations that Keynes supposed to be revised continuously.

Finally, two characteristics of this approach should be noted. First, short-run processes are no longer considered qualityless. Just the opposite. *Crucial experi-*

ments are being realized at every moment: actions carried out in the short run change irreversibly the general conditions within which the economy operates (Davidson 1978: 15–16). As a corollary, the concrete order in which things happen becomes important. Past and future, therefore, are not interchangeable anymore. As put by Minsky, ''An economic theory that is relevant to a capitalist economy cannot evade the issues involved in *unidirectional historical time*'' (1982: 81, my emphasis). Second, even if long-run ''positions'' are not logically impossible to conceive, their analytical usefulness is very uncertain (Davidson 1978: 8).

Decision Theory under Uncertain Expectations

The last approach in our spectrum is the one presented by Shackle (1969). It emphasizes the freedom of human imagination in the formation of expectations about uncertain futures. Its subject is decision making (Hicks 1979: 4–5, 88).[8] It is supposed that the cosmos is ordered enough to make decisions meaningful (Shackle 1969: 4) but History is not predestinate and, therefore, human decisions can make a difference (p. 3).

The most visible characteristic of Shackle's approach is its visceral antideterminism. In his view, the whole subject of decision making only makes sense if the history of the future is yet to be written. The continuous gain in knowledge brought about by the human intervention in the environment causes the world to *be* different at each instant. Each decision (or, better, each set of decisions/actions) represents, therefore, a ''cut between the past and future, an introduction of an essentially new strand into the emerging pattern of history'' (p. 3).[9]

For Shackle, the usual ''rational'' behavior results are inadequate to describe real world agents' behavior. ''Reason cannot attain demonstrative practical conclusions except it be supplied with sufficient data'' (1973: 518). If the future is to be created reason *cannot* be supplied with information about it. Expectations, ''figments of imagination,'' have to take the place of information. Choice and imagination are, then, *uncaused causes* (1983: 28). Uncertainty, nevertheless, makes expectation volatile. This (and its implications) is Keynes's subject in Shackle's view and it is the core of the Keynesian revolution. Put very simply, it is the acknowledgment that ''expectations do not rest on anything solid, determinable, demonstrable. 'We simply don't know''' (1973: 516).

Because actions are based on nonfirm expectations, temporal stability of behavior cannot be expected and hence it is fruitless to formulate mathematical functional behavioral relations in which parameters appear to be independent of time and history. Equilibrium becomes an artificial concept even if no more than a reference point. Yet, disequilibrium models are just as pointless. Disequilibrium is just a counterpart of equilibrium. It is the idea that human behavior can be modeled that is at stake.

Long-run positions are completely foreign to this approach. Even the notion of short run becomes problematic (see Carvalho 1983–84) when Shackle focuses his attention in the imagination of agents, in the solitary existential experience of "creating" the future. The absence of references to the social environment that surrounds each individual, his limits and interrelations with other individuals, makes it difficult to advance from the point of expectations formation to the examination of those sequels that are "partly the work of *many people's* choices to come" (Shackle 1983: 28) that constitute the short run itself.

In conclusion, Shackle is the polar opposite of the gravity center approach. Shackle represents a denial of the possibility of having a point fixed in space/time around which actions will gravitate. Long-run possibilities cannot be described independently of the hearts and minds of those who take the decisions that will shape those possibilities. The social system, and particularly the economy, is not tending anywhere and even the short run is fundamentally open. [. . .]

A Note on Professor Robinson

For many reasons it is very difficult to classify Joan Robinson's approach to my subject. She was, doubtless, one of the authors that most clearly realized what was involved in the use of concepts like long run and short run. This allowed her to use them without committing herself to only one approach. As a result, it is necessary to discuss her works as an approach by itself, drawing from many sources to create a remarkably original synthesis.

Joan Robinson used the dichotomy of short/long period to classify variables that are *acting in the present*. In this sense, they refer to processes that will exhaust their possibilities at different lengths of time. Everything actually happens in the present, which means that events happen in the "short run" (1971a: 180). The long run does not exist separately from the short run. As in Kalecki, but with a broader definition, long-run values result from the sequence of short periods. However, differently from Kalecki, and closer to Keynes, the influence of long-period factors is exercised by the expectations agents have about them (1971b: 22; 1980: 128).

The short run is defined by the "slowness" with which things like capital accumulation and technical change can happen. Although their rhythm of change is not fixed, varying with the trade cycle, "every week-long period changes, resulting from past decisions, are coming into being—stocks are changing slowly through time while flows may run rapidly to and fro" (1980: 140). The slowness of these changes is explained by the *inner limits* that the system poses to their operation (availability of finance, limits represented by the capacity of certain specialized capital-good industries, by balance of payments, etc.). It refers, therefore, to the *timing* of these changes (1971a: 50–53).

For Robinson (1980: 130), Keynes destroyed the basis of the Neoclassical notion of long-run equilibrium. The Post-Keynesian tradition is alternatively anchored in the notion of historical time (1980: 16; Eichner and Kregel 1975:

1294–96). This did not preclude the possibility of studying the *existence* of equilibrium growth paths (Robinson 1971b: 111). However, in Robinson's view the economy *does not tend* toward equilibrium growth paths in any sense.

What Garegnani (1976) calls the "classical" method, that is, the study of long-run positions, is not entirely rejected by Joan Robinson. In fact, her concept of *tranquility* is designed to allow the description of *potentialities* that are inscribed in factors like the level of capital accumulation and technical development at any period. But Robinson's method differs in two important ways from Garegnani's: (1) she introduces expectations and uncertainty into the definition of tranquility (1971a: 59; 1980: 128); and (2) as a consequence, the economy is no longer approaching a "gravity center." The concept of tranquility is made to refer only to *potentialities* instead of *actual tendencies*. There is nothing to *push* the economy in the direction of any long-run path of growth.

Like many others Joan Robinson reserves the concepts of long period and short period to classify variables according to the degrees of permanence of their effects. In Robinson's works, however, this criterion is used to classify variables in their *actual* existence, not in aprioristically established equilibrium relations. Thus, the analyses of long-run factors and of tranquility states do *not* constitute the same subject. This allows her to avoid logical contradictions between short- and long-period analyses without being forced to give up the study of factors that have durable effects. There are no *parallel* worlds in Joan Robinson's universe.

Conclusion

Why is this issue about the relation between short- and long-run theories so important? For one thing, this relationship indicates how "long-run" determinants are thought to be translated into perceptions, decisions, and actions of (and pressures on) economic agents. How authors treat the relation between short- and long-run factors sheds light on fundamental features of the *vision* entertained about the evolutionary processes of the system. It also reflects fundamental theoretical choices about what are conceived as the relevant economic processes and how they are to be described.

From the preceding discussion one can suggest that there are two alternative starting points. For the Garegnani/Eatwell and the Kaldor/Pasinetti groups the starting point of any analysis should be (static or dynamic) long-run positions of the system, for the short run lacks "determinacy." Only in the long run the transcendental and permanent forces of the economy dominate the accidental features that populate the short run. The alternative starting point states that life happens in some sort of "short run." The investment process, in particular, *freezes* expectations formed under uncertainty conditions into *long-run* data. This destroys the stability required by equilibrium situations to become gravity centers. Therefore, there is no separate space/time in which long-run forces assert themselves independently of short-run occurrences. Short-run acts permanently imprint their character in the long-run paths, making it impossible to develop a theory of the latter that is invariant to what happens in the former. In this sense the "determinacy" of gravity centers is just the result of a formalistic illusion. The economy has, therefore, to be approached in terms of historical time.[10]

For gravity center theorists, the historical time models are not satisfactory for two main reasons: (1) they allow indeterminacy to be all-pervasive in their theories; (2) they prevent the "derivation of general analytical principles" (Eatwell 1983: 24). Their first criticism, as I indicated, is relevant only to the extent that economic processes themselves are determinate. Determinacy is not a theoretical requirement in itself and can be judged only with reference to the real processes that the theory intends to describe (Keynes 1973b: 2). Moreover, *orderliness* is sometimes confused with the concept of *determinacy*. The requirements posed by the concept of orderliness, however, are far less restrictive than what is necessary for processes to have "determinate" solutions.

The second criticism is potentially more serious, because it refers to the very possibility of construction of theories. On a closer examination, however, we see that this point is raised against the historical time models of Keynesian origins more as a warning than as a serious criticism. For instance, Eatwell (1983: 24), after stating that "what is needed is the integration of historical and institutional factors *within* theoretical analysis" instead of historical time models, cites as an example of that integration Keynes's theory of liquidity preference!

Gravity center theories, on the other hand, are also subject to some important criticisms. These models rely on pseudo-time concepts, and short-run processes are taken to be qualityless and reversible. This last characteristic restricts possible short-run processes to a very narrow class that excludes, remarkably, investments. With even more important consequences, this approach does not discuss how different agents' behavior has to be when one passes from the discussion of long-run equilibrium positions to real world life. As Nell (1973: 198–200) has observed, in these models *necessities and possibilities* are shown without reference to the way those conditions are supposed to be satisfied.[11] But if mechanisms cannot be defined to show that those positions *must* be attained, only *possibilities* are left. If those long-run states are to be seen as *necessary* gravitation forces have to be clearly and unambiguously characterized. This point remains valid even if those equilibrium positions are to be understood as no more than "reference situations." The relevance of the idea of reference can only be established if it is possible to explain "disequilibria" by the failure of the forces that lead to equilibrium to operate. Otherwise, any characterization of reference states of any sort is equally valid, thereby radically reducing the theoretical usefulness of the concept of reference itself.[12]

In conclusion, major issues separate Post-Keynesian gravity center models from historical time theories. This difference seems to be rooted not only in the choice of subjects but, in fact, in the *vision* adopted by each group. Historical time models are not just "short-run" models. It is the dichotomy between short-

and long-run models itself that is rejected.[13] Gravity centers models, on the other hand, assume that it is possible to separate long-run forces from short-run occurrences, ignoring the latter. This involves assuming the ability to *postulate* results without being able to indicate the ways they can be attained.

Notes

1. Although this distinction is very conspicuous in the theory of the firm, few authors realize that concepts like the "long-run cost curves" relate costs to size of plants *at a given moment of time*. In the current usage, however, it becomes a *path* to be followed by firms in the search for the optimum position. Feijo (1980: 21) warns that this confusion is likely to lead to inadequate analyses of processes of industrial concentration.

2. Cf., e.g., Malinvaud (1980: 34); Solow (1970: 162). In the dogmatic language of textbooks: in the long run "by definition, all adjustments have taken place" (Dornbusch and Fisher 1981: 424).

3. See Garegnani (1976; 1978; 1979a; 1979b; 1980); Garegnani et al. (1979); and Eatwell (1977; 1983). An important work whose classification is less clear is Roncaglia (1978). [. . .]

4. This is, in fact, the classical method. Ricardo's analyses of the relationship between market and production prices follows the same premises: (1) all capital is circulant capital. This implies: (a) that the devaluation of the capital mistakenly invested in some sectors is smaller than would be the case with fixed capital; (b) the time to recover the value invested is also smaller than would be the case with fixed capital; (c) the adjustment of investments, in the absence of fixed capital, is equivalent to production adjustments (only the quantity of working capital changes). (2) It should also be noted that Ricardo keeps the same firms in their original sectors. Certainly, these conditions are very different from the ones we find in modern economies. (See Ricardo 1971: ch. 4.)

5. It is fair to note that Kaldor sometimes restricts the scope of his model to showing that Harrod's results were incorrect. Nevertheless, even in these passages, Kaldor's criticisms refer to Harrod's attempt to derive *both* a model of growth and a model of cyclical movements from the same argument rather than the gravitation process around an equilibrium rate of growth itself (1970: 86).

6. For a Kaleckian analysis of income distribution with these features, see Asimakopulos (1980–81).

7. It is important to note that the problem is *not* that the diffusion of information is deficient (as in Leijonhufvud 1968: 2, 3) but that the relevant information *cannot exist* if it refers to the future: "no future market signal is given *because there is nothing more to signal*" (Kregel 1980: 36, my emphasis).

8. Sir John Hicks (1979) seems to have moved toward Post-Keynesian views to such an extent that Davidson (1980: 581) asks "how much more Post-Keynesian can Sir John get?" This is not to say, however, that Hicks and Shackle share the same views. Actually, Shackle (1979: 55) considers the change in Hicks's views to have reached "limited extent." For our purposes, however, the points of contact between the two authors seem sufficient to justify the use of quotations from Hicks's work in support of Shackle's view.

9. That is why criticisms like Arrow's (1970: 46) may be misdirected. Arrow says that "the influence of experience on beliefs is of the utmost importance for a rational theory of behavior under uncertainty, and failure to account for it must be taken as a strong objection to theories such as Shackle's." This assumes that the act of learning does not affect the world itself. Therefore, the agent is *external* to the object of knowledge. Shackle, on the contrary, is concerned with the *internal* observer. For this agent the world is not the same after it is *known*. To know and to decide is to *shape* the world. For Arrow

learning is a passive activity. For Shackle, to learn is to create.

10. Eichner's works cross the proposed boundaries. His 1980 discussion about the behavior of oligopolies emphasizes the crucial role of investment *plans* of firms, in the way I suggested Keynes did. More recently, in his macrodynamic works, long-run forces are sharply distinguished from short-run variables and cycles are then defined as fluctuations around a given norm (1979: 13). The difficulty lies in how to combine the idea of investments being determined by firms' long-run *expectations* with the idea that they are the result of objective determinants of the system.

11. We do not refer only to the necessity of incorporating variables like money and credit. The point is that agents *behave* differently in each situation. Examples of the type of changes I am referring to are Parrinello's (1983) discussion of consumer's behavior and Davidson's (1978: ch. 3) pricing theory under uncertainty.

12. Why is one able to say that the production prices scheme is superior, as a "reference" to Walrasian models? Both are supposed to be obtained as a result of competition. But competition is a *process* and it is the characterization of the process that is the decisive criterion.

13. For Keynes, for instance, the long run of a monetary production economy is no more determinate than its short run. This type of economy is the one in which "the course of events cannot be predicted, either in the long period or in the short, without a knowledge of the behavior of money between the first state and the last" (1973b: 408–409). As shown by many authors the existence of money, as Keynes conceived it, is sufficient to undermine any kind of gravitation process. With expectations and uncertainty, "it is as though the fall of the apple to the ground depended on the apple's motives, on whether it is worth falling to the ground, and whether the ground wanted the apple to fall, and on mistaken calculation on the part of the apple as to how far it was from the center of the earth" (1973b: 300).

References

Arrow, Kenneth J. (1970) *Essays on the Theory of Risk-Bearing*. Chicago: Markham.

Arrow, K., and Hahn, F. (1971) *General Competitive Analysis*. San Francisco: Holden-Day.

Asimakopulos, A. (1980–81) "Themes in a Post-Keynesian Theory of Income Distribution." *Journal of Post Keynesian Economics* 3, 2 (Winter): 158–69.

Carvalho, Fernando (1983–84) "The Concept of Time in Shacklean and Sraffian Economics." *Journal of Post Keynesian Economics* 6, 2 (Winter): 265–80.

Castro, Antonio B. (1979) *O Capitalismo Ainda é Aquele*. Rio de Janeiro: Forense-Universitaria.

Davidson, Paul (1978) *Money and the Real World*, 2d ed. London: Macmillan.

———. "Causality in Economics: A Review." *Journal of Post Keynesian Economics* 2, 4 (Summer): 576–84.

———. (1982) *International Money and the Real World*. New York: Wiley.

Davidson, P., and Kregel, J. (1980) "Keynes's Paradigm: A Theoretical Framework for Monetary Analysis." In *Growth, Profits and Property*, ed. E. Nell. Cambridge: Cambridge University Press.

Dornbusch, R., and Fisher, S. (1981) *Macroeconomics*. New York: McGraw-Hill.

Eatwell, John (1977) "The Irrelevance of Returns to Scale in Sraffa's Analysis." *Journal of Economic Literature* (March).

———. (1983) "The Long-Period Theory of Employment," unpublished.

Eichner, Alfred S. (1979) "Introduction." In *A Guide to Post Keynesian Economics*, ed. A. Eichner. White Plains, N.Y.: M. E. Sharpe.

———. (1980) *The Megacorp and Oligopoly*. White Plains, N.Y.: M. E. Sharpe.

Eichner, Alfred S., and Kregel, J. (1975) "An Essay on Post-Keynesian Theory: A New

Paradigm in Economics.'' *Journal of Economic Literature* (December).

Feijo, Carmen A. V. C. (1980) ''Tecnologia e concentracao,'' Federal University of Rio de Janeiro, dissertation.

Garegnani, Piero (1976) ''On a Change in the Notion of Equilibrium in Recent Work on Value and Distribution.'' In *Essays in Modern Capital Theory*, ed. M. Brown et al. Amsterdam: North-Holland.

―――. (1978) ''Notes on Consumption, Investment and Effective Demand: I.'' *Cambridge Journal of Economics* 2: 335–53.

―――. (1979a) ''Notes on Consumption, Investment and Effective Demand: II.'' *Cambridge Journal of Economics* 3: 63–82.

―――. (1979b) ''Reply to Joan Robinson.'' *Cambridge Journal of Economics* 3: 181–87.

―――. (1980) *Le capital dans les theories de la repartition.* Paris: Maspero.

Garegnani, P., et al. (1979) *Debate sobre la Teoria Marxista del Valor.* Mexico City: Siglo XXI.

Georgescu-Roegen, N. (1971) *The Entropy Law and the Economic Process.* Cambridge: Harvard University Press.

Harcourt, G. C. (1977) *The Microeconomic Foundations of Macroeconomics*, ed. G. C. Harcourt. London: Macmillan.

―――. (1982) *Post Keynesianism: Quite Wrong and/or Nothing New.* London: Thames Papers in Political Economy.

Harrod, Roy F. (1970) ''Dynamic Theory.'' In *Growth Economics*, ed. A. K. Sen. Harmondsworth: Penguin.

Hicks, John R. (1979) *Causality in Economics.* New York: Basic Books.

Kaldor, Nicholas (1970) ''A Model of Distribution.'' In *Growth Economics*, ed. A. K. Sen. Harmondsworth: Penguin.

Kalecki, Michal (1943) *Studies in Economic Dynamics.* London: George Allen and Unwin.

―――. (1954) *Theory of Economic Dynamics.* London: George Allen and Unwin.

―――. (1971) *Selected Essays on the Dynamics of the Capitalist Economies.* Cambridge: Cambridge University Press.

Keynes, John M. (1924) *La Reforme Monetaire.* Paris: Sagittaire.

―――. (1964) *The General Theory of Employment, Interest and Money.* New York: Harbinger.

―――. (1973a) ''The General Theory.'' In *Monetary Theory*, ed. R. Clower. Harmondsworth: Penguin.

―――. (1973b) *The General Theory and After.* Part 2, *Collected Writings of John Maynard Keynes*, vol. 14. London: Macmillan.

Koopmans, Tjalling (1957) *Three Essays on the State of the Economic Science.* New York: McGraw-Hill.

Kregel, Jan A. (1975) *The Reconstruction of Political Economy.* 2d ed. London: Macmillan.

―――. (1976) ''Economic Methodology in the Face of Uncertainty.'' *Economic Journal* (June).

―――. (1980) ''Markets and Institutions as Features of a Capitalistic Production System.'' *Journal of Post Keynesian Economics* 3, 1 (Fall): 32–48.

Leijonhufvud, Axel (1968) *On Keynesian Economics and the Economics of Keynes.* New York: Oxford University Press.

Malinvaud, Edmond (1980) *The Theory of Unemployment Reconsidered.* Oxford: Basil Blackwell.

Minsky, Hyman P. (1975) *John Maynard Keynes.* New York: Columbia University Press.

―――. (1980) ''Money, Financial Markets, and the Coherence of a Market Economy." *Journal of Post Keynesian Economics* 3, 1 (Fall): 21–31.

————. (1982) *Can "It" Happen Again?* Armonk, N.Y.: M. E. Sharpe.

Nell, Edward J. (1973) "Theories of Growth and Theories of Value." In *Capital and Growth*, ed. G. Harcourt and N. Laing. Harmondsworth: Penguin.

Parrinello, Sergio (1983) "Flexibility of Choice, Adaptive Preferences and the Theory of Demand," unpublished.

Pasinetti, Luigi (1970) "Profit and Growth." In *Growth Economics*, ed. A. K. Sen. Harmondworth: Penguin.

————. (1983) *Structural Change and Economic Growth.* Cambridge: Cambridge University Press.

Ricardo, David (1971) *On the Principles of Political Economy and Taxation.* Harmondsworth: Penguin.

Robinson, Joan V. (1971a) *The Accumulation of Capital.* London: Macmillan.

————. (1971b) *Economic Heresies.* New York: Basic Books.

————. (1980) *What Are the Questions?* White Plains, N.Y.: M. E. Sharpe.

Roncaglia, Alessandro (1978) *Sraffa and the Theory of Prices.* New York: Wiley.

Samuelson, Paul A. (1939) "Interactions Between the Multiplier Analysis and the Principle of Acceleration." *Review of Economic Studies*.

————. (1979) *Foundation of Economic Analysis.* New York: Atheneum.

Shackle, George L. S. (1968) *A Scheme of Economic Theory.* Cambridge: Cambridge University Press.

————. (1969) *Decision, Order and Time.* Cambridge: Cambridge University Press.

————. (1973) "Keynes and Today's Establishment in Economic Theory." *Journal of Economic Literature* (June).

————. (1979) "On Hick's Causality in Economics: A Review Article." *Greek Economic Review* 1 (December): 43–55.

————. (1983) "The Bounds of Unknowledge." In *Beyond Positive Economics?* ed. J. Wiseman. London: Macmillan.

Solow, Robert (1970) "A Model of Growth." In *Growth Economics*, ed. A. K. Sen. Harmondsworth: Penguin.

Piero Sraffa and the Rehabilitation of Classical Political Economy

ROBERT PAUL WOLFF

Robert Paul Wolff argues that both David Ricardo's and Karl Marx's works suffered from a major theoretical flaw: the inability to articulate fully a labor theory of value that can be transformed into exchange values or prices. Wolff claims that this incomplete treatment of classical analysis as developed by Ricardo and Marx in part accounts for the predominance of marginalist economic theory in the nineteenth century. He then turns to how Piero Sraffa solved the dilemma of the transformation of values to prices.

Once the riddle of the "transformation problem" is solved, Wolff goes on to a discussion of how this has affected the development of political economy and in particular Marxist theory. In the final part of the article he provides a road map of contemporary Neo-Ricardian theories.

[. . .] Since the 1870s, our understanding of the workings of capitalism has been shaped and limited by the economic theories which constituted the "marginalist revolution." All of us, left, right, and center, think about economic matters—when we think about them at all—in terms of subjective utility, marginal products, and the efficient allocation of scarce resources. The elementary doctrines so elegantly expounded in the latest edition of Paul Samuelson's famous textbook (and in the countless imitations it has spawned) do not differ fundamentally from those set forth by Léon Walras almost 120 years ago. By an irony of history, the classical theory of Ricardo was eclipsed by marginalism just as it had reached its transformation and fulfillment in the work of Karl Marx. Driven from center stage were the classical themes of growth versus stagnation and the class conflict over the distribution of the social product. Instead, theoretical attention was focused on the static, conflict-free problems of allocating resources in a maximally efficient manner within a given, unquestioned, and uncriticized distribution of wealth and income.

It would be easy enough to explain the eclipse of the classical tradition in purely ideological terms. With the defeat of the landed interest in the earlier part of the nineteenth century, social as well as theoretical attention was coming to be focused on the central fact of capitalism: the irresolvable conflict of interest

Robert Paul Wolff, "Piero Sraffa and the Rehabilitation of Classical Political Economy," *Social Research* 49, 1 (Spring 1982), pp. 209–38.

between the working class and the capitalist class. Already in the decades after the publication of Ricardo's *Principles* in 1817, temporizers and popularizers (those whom Marx so effectively labeled "vulgar" economists) sought to soften the harsh implications of Ricardo's analysis, to show that perhaps the interests of labor were not so diametrically opposed to those of capital. The time was ripe, in the 1870s, for a new theory that represented capitalism as a cooperative undertaking in which objective, impartial, transtemporal and transsocial principles of instrumental rationality would suffice for the achievement of social order and economic efficiency. Marginalism, we might say, was needed by the now-dominant capitalist class as a rationalization for its interests and its behavior. [. . .]

Nevertheless, in this case ideological analysis is too quick, too easy an explanation for the failure of the classical approach. To give plausibility to the thesis that the economic theories of Ricardo and Marx got shunted aside for ideological reasons, one would have to establish three propositions: *first*, that those theories were a threat to the ruling class; *second*, that they were true, or at least as sound as any other theories available at the time; and *third*, that this theoretical soundness was so obvious that only the distorting prism of class interest could conceal the fact from supposedly objective scholars.

Now, it is not difficult to demonstrate that Marx's economic theories were a threat to the capitalist class. They were a deliberate, frontal assault on the very existence of capitalism. Nor is it impossible to demonstrate that Ricardo's theoretical perspective was inimical to the security and hegemony of the capitalist class, although at least a bit of argumentation might be needed to establish that. So the ideological explanation of the victory of marginalism passes the first test.

Alas, it utterly fails the second test and therefore, a fortiori, the third as well. For the classical tradition of Ricardo and Marx was beset by purely theoretical problems and failures of such magnitude that the most ardent proponent of the interests of the working class could be forgiven for forsaking it and searching elsewhere for a more adequate analysis of capitalist economy.

In the century and more since the publication of the first volume of *Capital*, there has been no shortage of champions ready to proclaim the relevance, the importance, the truth, indeed the historical necessity of Marx's revolutionary program. There have been legions willing to die for the labor theory of value, but no one who could demonstrate that the classical/Marxian approach to the analysis of capitalism was a plausible theoretical alternative to the ruling marginalist orthodoxy.

Piero Sraffa has provided that demonstration. For the first time in more than a century, it is possible to take Marx seriously as an economist, and there can now be serious intellectual debate between competing schools of economic theory. The first round in that debate took place in the 1960s, with the forces of Cambridge, Massachusetts, led by Paul Samuelson, arrayed against the forces of Cambridge, England, generaled by Joan Robinson. Victory went to the Neo-Ricardians of Cambridge, England, as Samuelson has acknowledged with becoming grace in subsequent editions of his textbook. The dispute was highly formal, and even the "popular" explanations of it tend to involve more mathematics than the general literate audience can stomach. But it would be a bad mistake to suppose, therefore, that such arcane battles are of little or no importance to the public at large. John Maynard Keynes's familiar words are still apposite: "The ideas of economists and political philosophers, both when they are right and when they are wrong, are more powerful than is commonly understood. Indeed the world is ruled by little else. Practical men, who believe themselves to be quite exempt from any intellectual influences, are usually the slaves of some defunct economist. Madmen in authority who hear voices in the air, are distilling their frenzy from some academic scribbler of a few years back."

[. . .] Marx was many things: a left-Hegelian philosopher of the human condition, a prolific journalist, a brilliant political analyst, and a pretty fair armchair historian. But if Marx has any claim at all to lasting fame, it is as an economist. He himself thought of his economic theory as the core of his mature work, to which he devoted his most productive middle years. The full-scale development and elaboration of his theories, taken together with the detailed criticisms of virtually all of the political economists who preceded him, occupies somewhere in the neighborhood of five *thousand* pages of printed text. And yet, in the capitalist West where Marx is widely regarded as perhaps the leading intellectual influence of the past century and a half, no major economist or school of economics took his theories seriously until twenty years ago.

To make clear the nature and magnitude of our debt to Sraffa, therefore, we must talk a little economic theory. What follows is an attempt to summarize a rather complex historical and theoretical development.

Value in Classical Economics

The central theoretical and practical topics for the classical economists were *distribution* and *growth*. How is the annual social product, the totality of corn, iron, shoes, linen, coats, and eggs, divided up among the three great classes of society? What determines whether that annual product will grow larger and, if it does, what its rate of growth will be? The answer to the question of growth seemed reasonably straightforward to Adam Smith and to David Ricardo as well. Growth results from the productive reinvestment of as much of the annual physical surplus as can be withheld from personal consumption and put to use employing more workers, clearing more fields, and building more factories. Since both Smith and Ricardo considered the landowning class to be self-indulgent and profligate, and the entrepreneurial class to be abstemious and prudent, they concluded that growth would proceed most rapidly when rents were held down and profits kept up.

The first question posed rather more complex problems. The central mechanism of allocation and distribution in a capitalist economy is the market. The market regulates distribution by determining, in the free play of competition, the wage paid to workers for their labor, the rent paid to landlords for the use of their land, and the profit paid to capitalists as a return on their investment. The market also determines the possibilities of growth, if Smith and Ricardo are correct, for high rents and low profits will mean little growth, while high profits and low rents will mean rapid growth.

It follows that a theory of growth and distribution must rest ultimately on a theory of the market. In a money economy, the quantitative measure of market exchange is price, and so a theory of the market will be, before all else, *a theory of price*—or, in the language of the eighteenth-century writers who created the discipline of economics, *a theory of value*. Then, as now, the theory of price is the foundation on which any systematic account of capitalist economy and society must be reared.

Classical political economists started from the intuition that all the "necessaries and conveniences" of life, in Smith's phrase, derive ultimately from the mixing of human labor with nature. For John Locke, this intuition served as the foundation for a *justification* of private property. But Smith and Ricardo were interested in *explaining* the distribution of wealth as well as in justifying (or criticizing) it. Abstracting a good deal from the particularities of their exposition, the argument runs as follows:

The goods we exchange in the market arise out of the application of human labor to nature. Since nature, in its abundance, is God's free gift to us, the only expenditure required of us is our labor. Hence, in what Smith called the "early and rude state of society," rational men and women will exchange what they have acquired through their labor in proportion to the amount of labor they have expended. If it takes me one day to catch a beaver, and it takes you two days to catch a deer, then you will be unwilling to give up your deer for anything less than two beaver, and I will be unwilling to give up more than two beaver for a deer. Since the *price* of anything is the ratio in which it exchanges for other things, and since a *theory of price* is simply a theory which explains (and predicts) the ratios in which goods exchange for one another, what we have here, in a very rudimentary form, is a *labor theory of price*.

Now two major problems arise, which Smith describes as "the appropriation of land and the accumulation of stock." First, nature's endless bounty turns out, at least in England, to be strictly limited, and after a while all the land is owned ("appropriated") by landlords, who are quite unwilling to allow laboring men and women free access to it. Second, in any but the very rudest state, production of necessaries and conveniences requires tools, seed, factories, and so forth as well as human labor. Even the hunters, after all, use something other than their bare hands to catch the deer and the beaver. So perhaps the simple labor theory of value will not suffice to explain relative prices, and with them wages, rents, and profits. Some way must be found to take account of privately owned land and accumulations of stock, or capital. (Notice, by the way, that the theoretical problem with capital is not that it is privately owned, but simply that it is required for production. Since something other than the expenditure of human labor is needed to produce goods, it is plausible to suppose that the amount of human labor required will not, *by itself*, explain the ratios in which goods exchange.)

Enter David Ricardo. Drawing on the work of his contemporaries Torrens, West, and Malthus, Ricardo demonstrated that, contrary to what one might imagine, the scarcity of land and the necessity of paying rents to landlords had no effect on the price of the food grown on the land. Instead, the appropriation of land simply shifted a portion of the capitalist's profits into the pockets of the landlords. This demonstration, which was perhaps the greatest analytical achievement of economic theory in the classical period, set to one side the first objection of the labor theory of value or price. To handle the second problem—the accumulation of stock, or capital—Ricardo conceived the brilliantly simple idea that tools, seed, factories, and so forth be thought of as just so much stored-up labor from past times. After all, any bit of capital, no matter how complex its nature and long its lineage, must be traceable ultimately to the product of human labor applied to nature. So Ricardo put forward the theory that, in a capitalist competitive market, goods exchange in proportion to the quantities of human labor that have been required directly (in the present production period) and indirectly (in past production periods) to produce them.

The labor theory of value, in Ricardo's formulation of it, focused our attention on the distinction between the technical, or technological, determinants of production, as represented by the quantities of labor directly or indirectly required, and the social determinants of distribution, as represented by the wage, the profit rate, and the rental per acre of land. What Ricardo thought was the case (or, more accurately, what he thought *ought* to be the case) was that the relative prices of goods would be determined entirely by the objective technology of production. Changes in distribution—in the wage, the profit rate, and the rental of land— would then be determined by an ongoing class struggle among workers, capitalists, and landlords. Improvements in technology, by reducing the amounts of labor directly or indirectly required for production, would open up the possibility of a larger total product to be distributed, but the distributive *shares* would still be determined quite independently by class struggle.

In Ricardo's theory, the independent distributional variable is the *wage*. First the wage is fixed, by population pressures or collective bargaining or state law or class struggle. Then the profit rate is determined as, in a manner of speaking, the "leavings" from wages. Finally, the fixing of the wage and the profit rate determines the rentals to be paid to land of varying qualities.[1]

The Ricardian theoretical perspective makes it natural to think of technology as independent of this or that particular pattern of ownership of productive resources and distribution of annual product. It makes it equally natural to think of the working class as the one objectively indispensable participant in the annual reproduction of society. For all Ricardo's championing of the interests of the capitalists against those of the landed aristocracy, his economic theory invites, indeed cries out for, a critique of the role of the capitalist class and of its share of the social product, namely, profits. Despite the elegance and power of Ricardo's analysis, his labor theory of price is not correct, a fact which he himself recognized almost as soon as he had formulated it. Save in a very special set of cases, the theory does not explain the ratios in which goods exchange in a capitalist market, and it cannot show that the exchange ratios, or prices, are determined independently of the distributional variables—the wage, the profit rate, and the land rents. To see just why the theory is wrong, let us work through an imaginary example. (Following the traditions of economic science, I have constructed the following example without the slightest concession to realism.)

Let us suppose that to grow 200 bushels of wheat, I must expend 100 hours of labor in year one to make tools and clear the land, and then an additional 100 hours of labor in year two to grow the wheat, weed it, and harvest it. Since it takes 200 hours of labor directly (in year two) and indirectly (in year one) to produce 200 bushels of wheat, it takes an average of one hour of labor directly and indirectly to produce one bushel. So the *labor value* of one bushel of wheat is one hour.[2]

Let us also suppose that to catch 20 deer, I must expend 50 hours of labor in year one making my bow and arrow (from scratch, as before), and 150 hours of labor in year two hunting and shooting the deer. Since it takes 200 hours of labor directly and indirectly to produce, or catch, 20 deer, it takes 10 hours to catch one deer. So the *labor value* of one deer is 10 hours.

Now, according to the labor theory of price, when capitalists invest in the growing of wheat and the catching of deer, and then exchange their products in a market which establishes a consistent economywide price system and a single rate of return on the value of capital invested, they ought to exchange wheat and deer in a ratio of 10 to 1, or 10 bushels of wheat for 1 deer, for that is the ratio of the labor value of wheat to the labor value of deer. Let us see whether the theory is right.

To make our calculations simple, let us assume that there is a single grade or quality of labor which sells for a wage of $1 per hour. We shall also assume that, in the economy as a whole, a profit rate of 10 percent prevails. A prudent capitalist who decides to invest in wheat production will hire 100 hours of labor, at $1 per hour, in year one, to make tools and clear the land. (Never mind, for the moment, how it comes about that he has money to invest and that there are men and women willing to sell their labor for wages. Capitalists, by the way, are almost always men, and hence will be referred to in the masculine.) In year two, he will hire 100 more hours of labor for an additional $1 per hour. How much must he sell his 200 bushels of wheat for at the end of year two in order to get back his $200 outlay and also earn the going rate of profit? Well, on the $100 invested in year one, he must earn 10 percent in the first year and 10 percent in the second year, for a total of ($100) × (1.10) × (1.10), or $121. In addition, on the $100 invested in the second year, he must earn 10 percent, for a total of $110. So, the total price that will cover his outlays and his profits is ($121 + $110) = $231, which works out to $1.15 1/2 per bushel of wheat.

An equally prudent capitalist who invests in deer production will have a somewhat different calculation to make. He must earn 10 percent in the first year and another compounded 10 percent in the second year on $50, plus 10 percent on the $150 invested in the second year. His total price, for his 20 deer, must therefore be [($50) × (1.10) × (1.10) + ($150) × (1.10)] = $225.50, which is $11.27 1/2 per deer.

So a deer will cost only 9.762 times as much as a bushel of wheat, even though the labor value of a deer is 10 times that of a bushel of wheat. Time, in the form of the compounding of interest, turns out to play a role in the determination of price, in addition to the amount of labor required for, or "embodied in," the goods being exchanged. What is more, a little reflection should make it obvious that as the profit rate rises or falls, its effect on the prices of commodities will not be at all regular. Goods whose labor inputs derives mostly from the present period will be relatively unaffected by variations in the profit rate, whereas goods whose production requires significant labor inputs from earlier periods—goods whose production is, in the phrase of Böhm-Bawerk, more "roundabout"—will be more heavily affected by a changing profit rate.

This may seem, at one and the same time, a trivial and extremely arcane problem, important to economists, no doubt, but scarcely worthy of note by the larger thinking public. In fact, however, as Ricardo himself saw, this difficulty strikes at the very heart of the entire classical attempt to understand capitalism. If prices are not proportional to labor values, then classical economic theory has no theory of price. Without a theory of price, it has no analysis of the distribution of the social product via wages, rents, and profits. If changes in the distributional variables (wages and profits) generate complex price shifts, then it becomes impossible to determine, for example, whether a rise in the money wage makes workers better off or worse off.

The Marxian Project

At this point, the project of classical political economy had come to a dead halt. In the half century after the publication of Ricardo's *Principles* in 1817, the discipline of economics moved backward, if at all. The clear-eyed, uncompromising recognition of inevitable class conflict that lent such power to the work of Ricardo gave way to eclecticism, confusion, and the sort of apologetics characterized by Nassau Senior's efforts to demonstrate that any reduction in the working day would cause profits entirely to disappear.

Marx comes onto the field now with an extremely complex, characteristically "dialectical" project. He proposes, at one and the same time, to complete and to transcend the theoretical task of the classical school. Even in its barest outline, the story becomes quite complex, but it is well worth following, for Marx offers us what is still, to this day, the most powerful theoretical alternative to the account of capitalism that has been built on the concepts of subjective utility and marginalist analysis.

Marx begins by taking a step backward in order to pose a question so fundamental that Ricardo and his followers had not thought to ask it. There *is* one special set of circumstances in which Ricardo's theory of natural price works. When the ratio of labor required directly in the present production period to labor stored up and carried over in the form of raw materials and tools from previous production periods is the same in each industry (a condition that could never be expected to happen save by the oddest sort of accident), then as a matter of fact commodities exchange precisely in proportion to their "labor values."[3] Now, this fact is of little theoretical interest by itself, for there is no real world social or economic state of affairs that corresponds even approximately to such an equality of ratio. Nevertheless, Marx chose to write all of volume 1 of *Capital* from the point of view of, or on the assumption of, precisely this equality of ratio. His reason is that he has something dramatic to say about the very foundations of capitalism, and he does not want it mucked up with complications about the deviation of commodity prices from their labor values. What is more, he wants to recreate the theoretical impasse that Ricardo has got himself into, in order to show that his—Marx's—theory provides a way out.

The problem is this: Even if all industries exhibit the same ratio of labor directly required to labor indirectly required so that prices are exactly proportional to labor values, how do capitalists make any profit at all? Think about it for a moment. Capitalists buy their inputs in the market (corn, iron, tools, labor, and so forth). These inputs are all bought *at their labor value*, by the hypothesis on which volume 1 of *Capital* is written. The capitalists combine the inputs (or, more precisely, command them to be combined) and sell the outputs, the finished commodities, *at their labor values*. They get back what they put in, to be sure, but how on earth do they make a profit?

Well, someone might say, the canny capitalists jack the prices up above the labor values and pocket the difference. But in that case, commodities don't sell at their labor values, for the inputs for capitalist A are the outputs for capitalist B. What is more, how can a capitalist in a competitive market get away with artificially putting up his prices? Surely his competitors will simply drive him to the wall.

So the challenge put by Marx to the classical economists is this: Before you trouble yourself to explain the subtle ins and outs of price fluctuations, the effects of taxation on rents, the causes of growth and stagnation, just explain the most fundamental and obvious fact of any capitalist economy—*profits*. How is it that at the end of each cycle of production, the workers are as poor as before, but the capitalists have augmented their holdings? Everybody recognizes that a physical surplus of goods is produced in each year—more corn, iron, linen than is needed to run the system for another year. But how does it come about that the capitalists own all of that surplus, while the workers merely have enough to feed and clothe themselves for another year? And, Marx adds, I want you to explain this to me in the theoretical case that is most favorable to your own theory of value, namely, the case in which commodities really do exchange in proportion to the quantities of labor directly and indirectly required for this production.

Ricardo and company have no answer to Marx's question, but Marx does. By means of the distinction between labor and labor power and the concept of surplus value, Marx believes that he can explain and demonstrate the exploitation of the working class by the capitalist class. [. . .] Marx argues that what the workers contract to sell in the marketplace is not labor but rather their labor power, their capacity to labor. Strictly speaking, they rent it out on a daily or weekly basis. Labor power is quite unlike any other commodity in the market, in two fundamental ways. First, it cannot be taken back to the factory without its owner going along. [. . .] The inseparability of the worker from her labor power is no "accident" at all. Rather, the central fact is that the workers have been separated from the means of production, and hence are forced to sell their own labor power as though it were a commodity.

The second peculiarity of labor power is that, when it is put to work in production, it does not merely transmit to the finished product as much value as was embodied within it. Rather, labor power put to work *creates new value*. For by the classical economists' own testimony, labor is the stuff, or substance, or essence of value. It is the quantity of labor embodied in—or, as Ricardo says, "bestowed upon"—a commodity that determines its value. Now the fact is that when a worker's labor power is put to work in the factory, a great deal more value is created thereby than is embodied in that labor power. [. . .] So in addition to reproducing his own means of existence or its equivalent, he will be creating as well some new value, some surplus value. And like the products of all the other inputs that the capitalist has purchased, this new value belongs not to the original owner of the labor power but to him who has rented it for the day. [. . .]

From each worker, a quantum of labor is extracted over and above what is required merely to reproduce that worker's capacity for labor for another time period. This *surplus labor* is the source of the surplus value which accrues to the capitalist. The total profit accumulated by the capitalist just equals the total surplus value extracted from the labor inputs into his production process. The total profits of the capitalist class as a whole exactly equal the total surplus value extracted from the working class. Thus profits arise because workers are forced to sell their labor power, as though it were a commodity, for a price equal to the cost of its reproduction, but far short of the total new value that it can create when it is put to work. The total value of the physical surplus churned out by the economy each year is exactly equal to the surplus value extracted from the workers and appropriated by the capitalists.

Or so the story goes in the special case to which all of volume 1 of *Capital* is devoted. But when the ratio of labor directly required to labor indirectly required is *not* the same in all lines of production, then in fact commodities do not exchange in proportion to their labor values. This was the problem that undermined Ricardo's economic theory, and thus far Marx has said nothing to advance our theoretical understanding.

At this point, Marx attempts a really brilliant *tour de force*. He proposes to treat the deviation of prices from labor values in the general case not as a weakness of the labor theory of value but as its greatest strength. He is going to explain exactly how this deviation takes place, and, in the process, he is going to unmask the mystifying device by which capitalism seeks to conceal the real exploitative origins of profit. In short, he is going to turn the refutation of Ricardo's theory into a demonstration of his own.

Briefly, Marx's idea is this: The total surplus value extracted from the entire working class is the real, underlying source of all the profits appropriated by the capitalist class. Hence, the aggregate quantity of surplus value generated in the economy in a single time period equals the aggregate profit appropriated by the capitalist class. In this or that individual industry, the profits appropriated may actually be greater or less than the surplus value extracted from the workers in that industry, due to the deviation of prices from labor values. In general, industries which are very labor-intensive will generate more surplus value than is reflected in the profits, while industries that are very capital-intensive will generate less. Since capitalists care about profits, not about surplus value, competition will move capital about from industry to industry until the profit rate is equal throughout the economy, even though the rate of surplus-value generation is different from one industry to the next. But no matter how competition moves surplus value about, the quantity remains unchanged and is equal to the total profits appropriated by all the capitalists put together.

As a consequence of this surface deviation of prices from values, and profits from surplus value, the real origin of profits is effectively concealed from view. The capitalist, after all, when taking his profit markup, computes his 10 percent on the total value of all the capital he invests—on the capital that goes for iron and coal as well as the capital that goes for wages. He earns his 10 percent on each bit of it, not merely on the part that has been paid to the workers. So if we tell him that his profits actually come out of the workers alone, he will immediately and confidently reject the suggestion as contrary to the evidence of his senses and his accounting procedures. On the surface, it appears that the profits come directly out of the capital that has been invested, regardless of what it is invested in, and so it makes perfectly good sense that the owner of that capital, the capitalist, should "earn" the profits that accrue to it.

At the level of the individual capitalist or worker, indeed even at the level of the individual industry, the real relationship between profits and surplus value is obscured. According to Marx, only when we recognize that capitalist society is a confrontation between two classes, the capitalists and the workers, can we for the first time see clearly, and with mathematical precision, that profits = surplus value = surplus labor time put in by workers.[4]

Well, it is a beautiful idea, but unfortunately it doesn't quite work either. Marx himself offers no proof of his conservation principle, nor does he provide us with a satisfactory theoretical analysis of the process by which labor values are transformed into prices by the processes of competition and the equilibration of the profit rate. Even the detailed numerical examples which he gives are incorrect (although some rather sophisticated modern reinterpretations of Marx have suggested that his examples can be construed as the first stages of an iterated procedure which, after summing some infinite series, actually give the correct results). Marx's inability to provide a mathematically consistent analysis of the determination of prices, profits, rents, and wages leaves him in the same situation as Ricardo, without a coherent account of the distribution of social product among the major classes of capitalist society.

It would be quite misleading to suggest that the mathematical inadequacies of Marx's theory explain its failure to win a place in the mainstream of academic economics. [. . .] Nevertheless, the inner weaknesses of Marx's theory *have* stood in the way of any attempts to put Marx forward as a serious alternative to the marginalist orthodoxy. Despite Marx's enormous erudition, his acute insight into the sociology of early capitalism, his extraordinarily prescient predictions of the direction in which capitalism would develop (ever greater concentration, more serious realization crises, the industrialization of agriculture, and so forth), even the most sympathetic economists could not extract from *Capital* a satisfactory theory of natural price on which could be based a theory of exploitation and a critique of capitalism. As philosophy, as sociology, as history, even as literature, religion, and astrology, Marx's great work was a resounding success. As science, however, as mathematics, as *theory*, it was a failure.

Sraffa's Achievement

At last, enter Sraffa. Not a likely candidate for the role of savior of Marxian economics. Indeed, not a "Marxist" at all despite his impeccable left-wing credentials. Sraffa was a theoretical economist who devoted his life to reconstructing the theoretical foundations of classical political economy, so that once again the great issues of distribution and class struggle could seize the theoretical center of economic theory.

The facts of Sraffa's life are quickly told.[5] Born in Turin, Italy, in 1898, Sraffa became a professor of political economy, first in Perugia and then in Cagliari. At odds politically with the regime of Mussolini, he took up an invitation from John Maynard Keynes to come to Cambridge, and in 1927 he emigrated. In the 1920s, and again in the early 1930s, he entered certain theoretical debates in economics and made significant contributions to them in half a dozen journal articles. During a forty-year period stretching from the early 1930s to 1973, Sraffa carried out a definitive editing of the works and correspondence of David Ricardo, with the assistance of Maurice Dobb. In the 1920s, Sraffa developed some ideas growing out of the classical tradition of Smith and Ricardo. He elaborated them slowly and painstakingly during the 1930s, '40s, and '50s, drawing at times for certain sophisticated formal insights on the expertise of the distinguished mathematician Besicovitch. Finally, in 1960 he published his one and only book, *Production of Commodities by Means of Commodities*, a slender volume which, taking account of appendices and index, runs to all of 99 pages.[6]

Appropriately enough, it was to Ricardo that Sraffa returned, not to Marx, for Ricardo defined the problem with which classical political economy wrestled. At a superficial level, the problem is to develop a theory of price determination which permits us to study the processes by which the social product is distributed among the major classes of society. At a deeper level, the problem is to distinguish, within the context of that theory, between the objective constraints of technology on the one hand and the social struggle among competing classes on the other, so that we can determine in the shifting patterns of the market what is due to the ongoing class conflict and what is due to changes in the "facility of producing" various goods.

The debates over the adequacy or failure of Marx's theories had bequeathed a third, subordinate problem to students of the classical tradition: how to understand the process by which, through the competition of the marketplace, the labor values of commodities are "transformed" into the natural prices which rule in equilibrium. As we have already seen, Marx sought to explain the process by arguing that a certain mass of surplus labor value gets redistributed about in the economy without altering its aggregate quantity. But this explanation will not do. Sraffa did not undertake directly to "solve the transformation problem," but it was clearly to be hoped that an adequate classical theory of natural price would, as a secondary benefit, provide a precise understanding of the relationship between labor values and natural prices. [. . .]

The mathematics used by Sraffa is all quite elementary, not even rising to the level of the linear algebra and differential calculus which are the standard tools of modern economic analysis. And yet, as a consequence of Sraffa's practice of omitting from his exposition virtually all of the intermediate steps of proof which even the sophisticated reader might wish to have as an aid to comprehension, the argument is extremely hard to follow. It is as though Sraffa had been contemplating his equations for so long, and with such perfect clarity of insight, that he had lost all sense of the steps by which the untutored might approach an understanding of them. Strange as it may seem to say about a book of economic theory, reading *Production of Commodities by Means of Commodities* is a deeply moving experience.

What, then, is the book about? Briefly, Sraffa picks up and elaborates a classical notion, first set forth by the leader of the Physiocrats, François Quésnay, in his *Tableau Economique* of 1758, according to which the entire economy is a circular flow of commodities which are both the outputs and the inputs of productive processes. Following Ricardo, Sraffa sets to one side any consideration of commodities whose value results from their inherent scarcity (rare paintings, old furniture, and the like). He assumes the economy to be engaged in the production of commodities, such as corn, iron, and coal, whose quantity can be increased by appropriate applications of additional labor and capital. Adopting the familiar classical assumption that competition will establish a single price for each type of commodity or service, including labor, and a single, economywide rate of profit, Sraffa proceeds to demonstrate that such an economy will be entirely determinate, save for an inverse functional relationship between the wage rate and the profit rate. Once the wage has been fixed by a process of bargaining or class struggle between capitalists and workers, there is a single, consistent set of prices and a single positive profit rate which solves the equations of the model. Thus, from the technical facts of production taken together with the externally given level of the wage, one can ascertain all the relevant value magnitudes in the economy—prices, profit rate—without any assumptions about subjective tastes and preferences, the balance of supply and demand, or the initial holdings of individual households and firms. What is more, it is easy to show that the wage rate and the profit rate vary inversely to one another, thus exhibiting the objective basis for the unending conflict between labor and capital.

There remains a major problem, inherited from Ricardo. As we saw in the little example of deer and wheat, under most circumstances the profit rate distorts prices away from labor values, in such a way that goods no longer exchange in proportion to the quantities of labor required for their production. One of the immediate implications of this fact is that, when the profit rate varies, relative prices may alter, even though there has been no change in the techniques of production. In the deer/wheat example, wheat producers use a more "roundabout" technique of production than deer hunters. That is to say, more of the labor required for the production of wheat is labor *indirectly* required in previous time periods. When the profit rate goes up, therefore, wheat will be more severely affected than deer, and the price of wheat will therefore rise relative to deer.[7] Now, the wage rate varies inversely with the profit rate. So, putting all this together, we find that changes in the wage rate, resulting perhaps from more strenuous bargaining, will have a complex side-effect on prices. Hence it will be extremely difficult even in an abstract model to study the distributional variables—wages, profits, rents—independently of the price variables. It will be hard, in short, to tell what in the system is a consequence of technical changes in the "facility of production" and what is a consequence of purely social changes in the distribution of the social product. This was the problem that led Ricardo to search, in the last years of his life, for an "invariable standard of value." Ricardo had the essentially correct, but mathematically too simple, idea that what he needed was an industry with "average" conditions of production. As relative prices fluctuated due to changes in the wage rate and the profit rate, Ricardo thought, the effects of these changes would "average out" in this pivotal industry so that any changes in the price of its product relative to other products could be counted on to be due to some peculiarities in the production of the other commodity, not to those of the standard itself.

Ricardo was unable to find such a standard commodity—although he boldly asserted that gold would serve as one—but, in what was perhaps his most significant theoretical innovation, Sraffa succeeded. His success consisted of two connected demonstrations. First, he showed how to construct a hypothetical "commodity" which had precisely the properties Ricardo had been looking for. Then he demonstrated that every economy of single-product industries, regardless of its particular shape or size, could be analyzed by means of its own "Standard Commodity."

Once the idea of a Standard Commodity was introduced, Sraffa could demonstrate that in every system the wage rate, expressed in terms of this standard, bore a simple, linear relationship to the profit rate, and that this relationship was unaffected by fluctuations in relative prices. We might note that Sraffa offers no explanation of how a system is made determinate through the specification of either the wage or profit rate. He thus makes the outcome of the class struggle a matter to be settled outside his model. This lack of classes is regarded by his partners as a great strength, by his opponents as a fatal weakness.

Having established the fundamental theorems of his system, Sraffa went on to reconstruct the Ricardian theory of rent in modern terms and to tackle what is perhaps the theoretically most complex and vexing problem, the role of fixed capital. Taking up certain ideas that appear in the writings of the classical political economists, from Smith through Ricardo and Torrens to Marx, Sraffa developed a successful analysis of fixed capital (machinery, etc.). In one of those striking convergences that so often mark important theoretical advances, Sraffa put forward the same analysis as that developed by the great mathematician John von Neumann in his classic 1937 paper, "A Model of General Equilibrium."

The Consequences

All of this may seem quite arcane, and indeed on the jacket of Sraffa's book, someone (Sraffa himself, perhaps?) has written, "This is a work of a specialist character, addressed to those interested in pure economic theory." And yet the consequences of Sraffa's "specialist" book have been simply enormous. The first thing that happened was that a host of mathematically sophisticated economists with an interest in the theories of Marx recast Sraffa's theorems in a simpler and more general form with the help of linear algebra. Then Marx's own theories were reconstructed along the same lines, and the deep structural filiations between Marx, on the one hand, and Ricardo, Sraffa, von Neumann, and Leontief, on the other, were explored and clarified. It became clear, for example, that Marx's analysis in volume 2 of *Capital* of the relationships between the sector of the economy producing capital goods and the sector producing consumer goods was in fact a brilliant early anticipation of the input-output theories of Wasily Leontief.

With the aid of linear algebra, the "transformation problem," strictly so-called, was solved. That is to say, a general mathematical transformation was discovered which maps the labor values of a linear model onto the natural prices. The theories of rent and of fixed capital were cast in a more mathematically rigorous form, and both were considerably elaborated. As these theoretical developments occurred, new problems were discovered and new technical and theoretical constructions were put forward to overcome them. In short, Marxian economics, almost overnight, went from being a semimoribund branch of secular theology to being a lively, developing, controversial, innovative branch of theoretical economics.

Needless to say, this rapid theoretical development has been anything but peaceful and conflict-free. A many-sided dispute has raged for the past two decades, with the bitterness of some of the reproaches matched only by the sophistication of the methodology. The correct classification and grouping of the antagonists in left-wing infighting is notoriously difficult, and it is a foregone conclusion that knowledgeable readers of this essay who have not yet taken umbrage will do so at this point. Nevertheless, the following is at least a first approximation to the present state of affairs.[8]

Holding the center against all enemies, foreign and domestic, is the school of Sraffa himself, situated at Cambridge University in England. For reasons both of theory and of tradition and piety, this group, with Sraffa and Joan Robinson at its head, claims that there is a connected theoretical lineage running from Adam Smith and David Ricardo through Karl Marx to John Maynard Keynes. Determinedly British empiricist in its skepticism about what it calls "metaphysics," this group *rejects* the labor theory of value. It takes Sraffa to have shown conclusively that the distinctively Ricardian/Marxian insights into the phenomena of distribution and growth can be given a sophisticated modern articulation without appeal either to the mysteries of labor values or to the ill-conceived theoretical detour of marginalism. The most forceful and imaginative exposition and elaboration of the Cambridge-Sraffa position is to be found in Ian Steedman's *Marx after Sraffa*, possibly the angriest bit of mathematical economics ever written.[9] The Cambridge school see themselves as fighting a war on two fronts. To their left (or, they might prefer to say, to their rear) are the orthodox British communists who cling to the old prayers and rituals of Marxian value theory with the dedication and simple faith of Methodists. Steedman and company heap scorn upon these benighted souls for their dogged fidelity to portions of Marx's writings that the Cambridge group believe simply to have been proven wrong or confused.

On their right, the Robinson forces battle Cambridge, Massachusetts, and the marginalist economic establishment. Here the warfare is fought with the latest, most sophisticated weapons, although not therefore in a less bloody fashion. As we have already seen, the first great battle was won by Pasinetti and the Cambridge (or, as it is sometimes called, the Italo-Cambridge) group. Among the most vigorous younger captains in Sraffa's army is John Eatwell.

A second group of theorists have sought to advance the formal analysis of linear reproduction models, with varying degrees of attention to the relationships among Marx, Ricardo, Keynes, Sraffa, and other theorists. B. Schefold in Germany, whose work on the analysis of fixed capital is taken by all sides as fundamental, Gilbert Abraham-Frois and Edmond Berrebi in France, John Roemer in the United States, and others around the world have carried the new theory forward with extraordinary speed. Contributing to this effort, of course, have been such partisans of the Cambridge group as Steedman and Luigi Pasinetti.[10]

A third group of economists, led by Michio Morishima of Japan, have attempted a rapprochement between the marginalist theories of the Neoclassical school and the central theses of Marx's economic theories of growth and distribution. In the introduction to *Marx's Economics*, possibly the best-known book in this new literature, Morishima writes: "Orthodox economists . . . are in the wrong, not only in segregating Marxists but also in undervaluing Marx, who should in my opinion be ranked as high as Walras in the history of mathematical economists."[11] This is a far cry indeed from Paul Samuelson's famous characterization of Marx as a "minor Post-Ricardian" and an "autodidact." Along the same line, it is instructive to compare the work of Gérard Maarek, with an introduction by one of the leading theorists of Neoclassical general equilibrium, Edmond Malinvaud.

Finally, one finds economists living in countries officially "socialist" who construe the newly reconstructed Marxian theories not as a critique of capitalism but rather as a tool for the more rational management of a planned economy. Most notable among these socialist economists is András Bródy of Hungary.[12] It is not clear what Marx would have thought of this use of his theories, which he himself conceived as a critique of bourgeois political economy and, by extension, of bourgeois society. But it is fitting that after so long Marx's own writings should be a source of constructive insight for socialist planners.

If we stand back a bit from this detail and survey the international scene of political economy, we can get some sense of the dramatic changes brought about in only two decades by Sraffa and his followers. In 1960, when *Production of Commodities by Means of Commodities* first appeared, the Neoclassical synthesis of marginalism and Keynes was, quite simply, *the* economics of the noncommunist world. Those of us who, on grounds of politics or instinct or sentiment, had doubts about the wisdom or soundness of the dogmas of liberal capitalism had nowhere to turn for a defensible, intellectually sound alternative. We could gather in the streets to protest an evil war, an insane arms race, a racist educational system, or a sexist job world but, when challenged to put forward an alternative to the world view of established economics and political science, we fell silent. Some of us called ourselves "socialist," more as an act of defiance or nostalgia than as a meaningful description, and if we read the works of Marx, it was the juvenilia, the 1844 manuscripts and the *German Ideology*, rather than the economic theory of his mature years.

Now, as we live the last decades of the twentieth century, all that has changed. The Neoclassical synthesis is in retreat, defeated by an unstable capitalism that it can neither explain nor manage. Crackpot theories from the fringe right become public policy, and in the United States the state goes union-busting as the first step in a deliberate effort to drive down the standard of living of what it may soon be permissible once more to identify as the working class, so that capital accumulation can proceed apace. And on the left, there are once again viable theories, sophisticated critiques of capitalism on which practical policies and political alliances may perhaps be built. Piero Sraffa's timeless plainsong, sung in the ancient halls of Trinity College, Cambridge, has breathed new life into Marx's great nineteenth-century critique of capitalist economy and society.

Notes

1. This functional relationship is implicit in Ricardo's analysis, but the explicit demonstration of it requires mathematical tools which were not available to him. For a simple exposition of the essential points, see my "The Analytics of the Labor Theory of Value in David Ricardo and Karl Marx," *Midwest Studies in Philosophy* (March 1982).

2. For those with keen analytical minds or prior training in this sort of scholasticism, let me stipulate that the tools made in year one were made from scratch, with bare hands, not from previously mined ore with the aid of previously produced tools. Furthermore, let us agree that the clearing of the land lasts for only one cycle of production; then it must be done all over again.

3. This condition is mathematically equivalent to what would, in Marx's terminology, be called "equal organic composition of capital in all lines of production."

4. The simplified account given here is not quite accurate to Marx's text. What Marx asserts is that total profits equal total surplus value, and total prices of all commodities sold equal total labor value of all commodities sold. Marx correctly intuits that both these assertions are necessary to keep the equality of profits and surplus value from being a mere truism growing out of a particular choice of measuring units. Even Marx's two principles are, as stated, incorrect, because of the fact that profits and surplus value, prices and values, are measured in different units. The correct statement of Marx's conservation principle, as we may label it, is that (total price/total profits) = (total values/total surplus value). For a clarification and explanation of the technical assertions contained in this discussion, see my "The Analytics of the Labor Theory of Value."

5. All of the biographical data are taken from an admirably clear and concise entry by Luigi Pasinetti in the *Biographical Supplement* of the *International Encyclopedia of the Social Sciences*. Pasinetti's own *Lectures on the Theory of Production* (New York: Columbia University Press, 1977) is the best introduction to the larger field of economic theory in which Sraffa worked. It was Pasinetti who struck the winning blow in the battles between Cambridge, England, and Cambridge, Massachusetts.

6. Piero Sraffa, *Production of Commodities by Means of Commodities* (Cambridge: Cambridge University Press, 1960).

7. I am sorry to say that even this statement, complicated though it may seem, is a simplification, but it captures the essential point Sraffa wished to make, so I shall let it stand.

8. What follows must be understood as *my opinion* in an even stronger sense than is usually assumed in essays of this sort. No two students of Marx, Sraffa, and economics will parse the current disputes in the same manner.

9. Ian Steedman, *Marx after Sraffa* (London: New Left Books, 1977).

10. Bertram Schefold, "Fixed Capital as a Joint Production and the Analysis of Accumulation with Different Forms of Technical Progress," in *Essays on the Theory of Joint Production*, ed. Luigi Pasinetti (New York: Columbia University Press, 1980); Gilbert Abraham-Frois and Edmond Berrebi, *Theory of Value, Price, and Accumulation*, trans. M. P. Kregel-Javaux (Cambridge: Cambridge University Press, 1979); John Roemer, *Analytical Foundations of Marxian Economic Theory* (Cambridge: Cambridge University Press, 1981); Luigi Pasinetti, *Structural Change and Economic Growth* (Cambridge: Cambridge University Press, 1981).

11. Michio Morishima, *Marx's Economics* (Cambridge: Cambridge University Press, 1973).

12. András Bródy, *Proportions, Prices, and Planning* (New York: Elsevier, 1970).

Value, Price, and Profit

IAN STEEDMAN

Ian Steedman, perhaps the most vociferous Neo-Ricardian, presents a model of value based on a physical quantities approach. He first demonstrates that the transformation of values into prices using Marxist imputed values based on embodied labor does not bring about the required results. Steedman then argues it is only in dropping the labor theory of value that one can achieve a result where value is proportionate to price. For Steedman, this result implies that Marx's theories are incorrect. He specifically addresses the impact on Marx's theory of the falling rate of profit and the labor theory of value.

In *Capital* volume 1 Marx set out his theory of value and exploitation and showed, through his concept of the value of labor power, how "freedom" of exchange is quite compatible with exploitation and the existence of surplus value. His argument was both strengthened and simplified by the assumption that commodities exchange at value. In volume 3 Marx turned to the more detailed question of how the profit rate and prices are determined when the organic composition of capital differs between industries and consequently commodities do not exchange at value. He was anxious to stress the idea that fundamentally profits and prices are just "transformed" value quantities, so that the essence of the volume 1 argument is unaffected by the volume 3 complications. Over the last fifteen years or so, academic economics has generated a considerable discussion of questions which bear directly on Marx's treatment of the relations between wages, profits, values, and prices: relations which are clearly of importance for Marxist analyses of many issues in political economy.[1] The purpose of this article is to set out, by means of a simple numerical example, some of the conclusions which can now be drawn concerning Marx's analysis of the connection between values, prices, and profits.[2] (On the basis of these conclusions we shall then make a number of points concerning the "law of the tendency of the rate of profit to fall," but the latter is not the main focus of our attention.)

The Methods of Production and the Real Wage

Marx normally described the economy in terms of value quantities, such as C (constant capital), V (variable capital), S (surplus value), and W (total value of

Ian Steedman, "Value, Price and Profit," *New Left Review* 90 (March-April 1975), pp. 71–80.

gross output). These value quantities, however, were determined by two different things which Marx assumed to be given, in a given capitalist economy at a given point in time. On the one hand they depended on the existing conditions of production, both technical and social, which defined the relations between inputs and outputs in the productive process. On the other hand they depended on the division of the net product between workers and capitalists in that society. We shall turn to the value quantity representation of the economy below but, for reasons which will emerge later, we start by describing the economy in physical terms.

Consider a very simple economy with three industries. One industry produces the means of production, let us call it iron, one produces gold, and the third produces a necessary consumption good, say corn. In each industry the production process uses only labor and iron as inputs; the amount of iron used per unit of labor varies between the industries, but whichever industry iron is used in it is completely used up in one year. Thus there is no *fixed* capital.

Table 1 shows the physical inputs to, and physical outputs from each industry, with inputs to the left of the arrows and outputs to the right. (The argument does not, of course, depend on the particular figures given here.) The final row shows the physical inputs and outputs for the economy as a whole.

Table 1

	Iron	Labor		Iron	Gold	Corn
Iron industry	28	56	→	56	—	—
Gold Industry	16	16	→	—	48	—
Corn industry	12	8	→	—	—	8
Total	56	80	→	56	48	8

Thus the first row shows that 56 units of labor, working with 28 units of iron, produce 56 units of iron; the second shows that 16 units of labor, working with 16 units of iron, produce 48 units of gold; while the third shows that 8 units of labor, working with 12 units of iron, produce 8 units of corn. (The physical units to which we refer might, for example, be thousands of tons in the case of iron and of corn and kilograms in the case of gold. Labor is naturally measured in time-units: for example, thousands of hours of homogeneous labor. The second row would then state that 16,000 hours of homogeneous labor, working with 16,000 tons of iron, produce 48 kilograms of gold.) The final row, being merely the sum of the first three rows, shows that, in the economy as a whole, 80 units of labor are being performed and 56 units of iron are being used up, while 56 units of iron, 48 units of gold, and 8 units of corn are being produced. Since the output of iron = 56 units = the amount of iron used up in production, it will be clear that our economy cannot expand (this is *not* important for the questions we wish to examine). *Net* output therefore consists of 48 units of gold and 8 units of corn. We shall assume that the total real wage bill paid to the 80 units of labor consists of 5 units of corn, this corn wage bill being paid at the beginning of the year, as assumed by Marx. The capitalists receive, at the end of each year, 48 units of gold and 3 units of corn. (Thus, of the 8 units of corn available at the end of a year, 3 units go to the capitalists as part of their profit for that year, while 5 go to the workers as wages for the *next* year.)

Value and Surplus Value

By the value of a commodity, Marx meant that quantity of labor socially necessary for the production of that commodity. This value, or quantity of labor, includes, of course, not only the labor directly used in the production of the commodity but also the labor used indirectly in its production or, in other words, the labor required to produce the means of production used up in the direct labor process. This latter labor, in turn, includes the labor directly used in the production of these means of production *and* the labor required to produce the means of production used in making them. Continuing this process backwards through time (always "resolving" the labor embodied in means of production into direct labor and further labor embodied in means of production), we then see the value of a commodity as made up of a sequence of expenditures of labor spread out through time. If we let the values of a unit of iron, gold, and corn be l_i, l_g, and l_c respectively, then we can determine these values from the data of table 1.

To determine l_i, consider the first row of table 1. The total value of output in the iron industry is clearly 56 l_i. This is made up of 56 units of direct labor time *plus* the indirect labor required to produce 28 units of iron. This latter quantity of labor can be found by simply *halving* all the quantities[3] in the first row of table 1; it will consist of 28 units of direct labor *plus* the labor required to produce 14 units of iron. This last quantity of labor can now be found, in the same way, by taking *one quarter* of the quantities in the first row of table 1; and so on. As we repeat this process without limit we find that

$$56l_i = 56 + 28 + 14 + 7 + 3\ 1/2 + \ldots\ldots,$$

where the successive terms on the righthand side are the quantities of labor done, further and further back in the past, for the production of 56 units of iron available in the present period. Since the terms on the right can be shown[4] to add up to 112, we have

$$56l_i = 112 \text{ or } l_i = 2.$$

For every unit of iron produced "now," 2 units of labor, direct or indirect, have had to be performed "now" or in the past.[5]

Now that l_i has been determined, l_g and l_c can be found directly. From the second row of table 1 we see that 48 l_g is equal to 16 (direct labor) *plus* the labor embodied in 16 units of iron, the latter simply being 16 l_i = 32. Hence

$$48 \, l_g = 16 + 32 = 48 \text{ or } l_g = 1.$$

In the same way, from the third row of table 1, we see that

$$8 \, l_c = 8 + 12 \, l_i$$

and thus

$$8 \, l_c = 8 + 24 = 32 \text{ or } l_c = 4.$$

It will be noted that the values of the commodities (l_i = 2, l_g = 1, l_c = 4) have been determined solely from the physical data given in table 1; they are quite independent of wages, profits, and prices.

While the physical data of table 1 are sufficient to determine the values of iron, gold, and corn, however, they do not suffice to determine the value of the commodity *labor power*. The value of labor power is, by definition, the value of the commodities required to maintain the working class, i.e., the commodities necessary to reproduce labor power. The value of labor power, therefore, depends on what quantities of commodities are obtained by the workers, as well as being dependent on the values of these latter commodities. In our example, since labor power is reproduced by the working class's consumption of 5 units of corn, the value of labor power, V, is given by

$$V = 5 \, l_c = 5 \times 4 = 20.$$

Total surplus value, S, follows immediately since $(V + S)$ = total live labor = 80; thus

$$S = 80 - V = 80 - 20 = 60.[6]$$

It should be noted that, given the total of living labor and the real wage paid, V and S depend only on l_c and that l_c, in turn, depends only on the production conditions in the iron and corn industries. Changes in the production conditions in the gold industry, that is, would have no effect on V or S. (This illustrates the point, often made by Marx, that increases in labor productivity in industries that are not involved, directly or indirectly, in the production of commodities consumed by the workers do not generate "increases in relative surplus value." It should also be noted, more generally, that by considering various possible changes in the physical data one can explain, simply and clearly, Marx's concepts of both absolute and relative surplus value.)

Hence from our knowledge of the physical conditions of production and the real wage, we can determine values, value of labor power, and surplus value. The *rate* of surplus value, S/V, is then also known (and equal to $60/20 = 300$ percent in our example). From the physical data, that is, we can deduce the value description of the economy, showing how workers are exploited by working part of the time (3/4 in our example) for the capitalists. Indeed we can easily convert our table 1 into table 2 which is the value schema, for our example, as used by Marx. Each entry in the first column of table 1 is multiplied by the value of iron ($= l_i = 2$) to give C, each entry in the second column is divided into V and S in the proportions 1:3, and, finally, the outputs are multiplied by $l_i = 2$, $l_g = 1$, and $l_c = 4$ respectively to give the W's.

Table 2

	C		V		S		W
Iron industry	56	+	14	+	42	=	112
Gold industry	32	+	4	+	12	=	48
Corn industry	24	+	2	+	6	=	32
Total	112	+	20	+	60	=	192

It may perhaps be objected, at this point, that we appear to have spent much effort merely to arrive at the point reached by Marx 110 years ago! While it may be of some interest to show how the value scheme can be derived from physical quantities, is it important to do so? it may be asked. One answer to this, and not a trivial one, is that it is always worthwhile to analyze concepts into underlying concepts. Physical conditions of production and real wages are subject to different forces and trends of change, so that it is much better to study them separately, even if one's final objective is to study changes in, say, V or S.

The Transformation of Value and Surplus Value

We wish to concentrate, however, on another reason for basing our analysis of fundamental relations in political economy on the physical data of production and real wages. This is the fact that, in general, it is not possible to explain the rate of profit and prices solely on the basis of the data set out in a value schema such as that of table 2.[7] As is well known, Marx, starting from such a schema, attempted to explain profits and prices in the following way. He asserted that the ratio of *total* surplus value to total constant and variable capital determined the rate of profit. He then determined a "price of production" for each commodity by multiplying the appropriate $(C + V)$ by $(1 +$ the rate of profit). Applying this procedure to our example, Marx would have obtained the following results:

Rate of profit $= \dfrac{60}{112 + 20} = \frac{5}{11} = 45\frac{5}{11}\%$

Iron price of production $= (56 + 14) \times (1 + \frac{5}{11}) = 101\frac{9}{11}$

Gold price of production $= (32 + 4) \times (1 + \frac{5}{11}) = 52\frac{4}{11}$,

Corn price of production $= (24 + 2) \times (1 + \frac{5}{11}) = 37\frac{9}{11}$.

On the basis of his argument Marx "showed," and this is naturally confirmed by our example, that the aggregate price of production equals the aggregate value and that total profit equals total surplus value.

Now Marx's argument cannot be regarded as acceptable. We may note first that while Marx "transformed" the values of outputs into prices of production he did not so transform either the value of iron used as input (the C terms are unchanged) or the value of corn advanced as wages (the V terms are unchanged). Thus both iron and corn appear to have different exchange values when sold as output from when they are purchased as inputs; but this is nonsensical since sale and purchase are two aspects of the same transaction. Hence inputs must be transformed as well as outputs. (Marx knew this and drew attention to it but does not appear ever to have modified his calculations accordingly.)

Merely allowing for the transformation of the inputs will not, however, suffice to produce a coherent theory of profits and prices.[8] The more fundamental flaw in Marx's argument lies at the beginning of it, when he equates the profit rate to $S/(C + V)$ for the economy as a whole. As Marx himself emphasized, the rate of profit is a concept which we use in analyzing a capitalist economy at the "level of prices," not at the "level of values," and the tendency to the uniformity of profit rates as between industries is enforced by the mobility of money capital. Thus the rate of profit is equal to the *price* of gross output minus the *price* of the inputs, divided by the *price* of those inputs. Now, when prices are not proportional to values, there is no reason at all why this ratio should equal the *value* of gross output minus the *value* of inputs, divided by the value of these inputs. (As will be seen below, the two ratios are very different in our economy.) In other words, $S/(C + V)$ is *not* the rate of profit in a capitalist economy.

If we are to explain profits and prices adequately we must leave the value schema and return to the physical quantities description of the economy. *This* is why we started with the latter. In the next section we show how the physical data suffice to determine profits and prices even though the data of the usual value schema do not (in general).

The Rate of Profit and Prices

Following Marx, we shall treat gold as the money commodity, so that the price of a commodity is the quantity of gold with which it exchanges.[9]

Denote the rate of profit by r and let w, p_i, and p_c be the money wage rate per unit of labor, the money price per unit of iron, and the money price per unit of corn respectively. (The money price of a unit of gold is, of course, unity by definition.) Now consider, together, the first row of table 1 and the following equation:

$$(1 + r) (28p_i + 56w) = 56p_i.$$

We see that this equation says that the price of the iron and labor inputs in the iron industry, multiplied by 1 plus the profit rate, equals the price of the iron industry output. The latter price, that is, covers the price of the capital advanced *plus* profits at the rate r on that capital. In the same manner we have, for the gold and corn industries respectively,

$$(1 + r) (16p_i + 16w) = 48$$

and

$$(1 + r) (12p_i + 8w) = 8p_c.$$

Furthermore, since the money wages paid to the workers must just enable them to purchase 5 units of corn, it must be true that

$$80w = 5p_c.$$

We thus have four equations to determine the four variables r, w, p_i, p_c. The (approximate) solutions are[10]

$$r = 52.08\%, w = 0.2685,$$
$$p_i = 1.7052, p_c = 4.2960.$$

It will be noted at once that the rate of profit, 52.08 percent, is very different from that given by Marx's formula $S/(C + V)$, i.e., 45 $^5/_{11}$ percent. In other words, $S/(C + V)$ does not even give a good approximation to the profit rate.

Some rather tedious calculations show that the aggregate price of output (approximately 178) is *not* equal to the aggregate value of output (192) and that total profit (approximately 61) is *not* equal to total surplus value (60). (Nor does either of the elements of capital have an aggregate price equal to aggregate value.) The idea that total profit equals total surplus value is just as false as the idea that $S/(C + V)$ is the rate of profit.

It is not difficult to see that the second of our four equations, that relating to gold production, is relevant to the determination of w, p_i, and p_c (which are all money quantities) but is irrelevant to the determination of r.[11] Other things being equal, a change in the production conditions for gold will have no effect on the profit rate. This gives us another way of seeing that $S/(C + V)$ is not the rate of profit; for while S and V depend only on the real corn wage and on the production conditions for iron and corn, total C depends on the production conditions for gold as well. Thus if the latter change, while all other physical conditions remain the same, $S/(C + V)$ will change but the profit rate, r, will not; clearly, then, the former can equal the latter only by a fluke.

Principal Conclusions

Starting from the physical conditions of production and the real wage, one can derive values and surplus value, showing how the values of commodities other than labor power depend only on the (technically and socially determined) physical conditions of production, while the value of labor power and surplus value depend, in addition, on the real wages of the workers. The nature of exploitation is thus revealed, as is the fact that V and S are independent of the conditions in industries irrelevant to the production of wage goods. One can also derive from the physical picture of the economy a coherent theory of profits and prices. In doing so, however, one finds that, in general,[12] profits and prices *cannot* be derived from the ordinary value schema, that $S/(C + V)$ is *not* the rate of profit, and that total profit is *not* equal to total surplus value. Thus not only can one build the theory of profits and prices around the physical schema, rather than the value schema, but one is forced to do so.

It may be helpful to represent our principal conclusions as in figure 1. The solid arrow labeled (a) shows that from the physical data all the value quantities may be explained (in our example, l_i, l_g, l_c, V, S, and the value schema set out in table 2). Arrow (b) shows that from the same data one can explain profits and prices, etc. (in our example, r, w, p_i, p_c, total profit, etc.). The dashed and "blocked off" arrow (c) represents the fact that one cannot, in general, explain profits and prices from value quantities as set out in the usual value schema, that $S/(C + V)$ is not the rate of profit, etc. We thus have to picture our theoretical structure as having a "fork-like" character, with a "value prong," arrow (a), and a "profit-price prong," arrow (b). There is no way from one prong to the other.[13] [. . .]

A Brief Remark on the Falling Rate of Profit

Marxist analysis of the long-run development of capitalism often makes reference to the "tendency of the rate of profit to fall," presented by Marx in *Capital*, volume 3, part 3. It is, therefore, of some importance that this aspect of Marx's theory be subject to constant scrutiny. As is well known, Marx, starting from his formula $S/(C + V)$ for the rate of profit, pointed out that a rise in C/V tended,

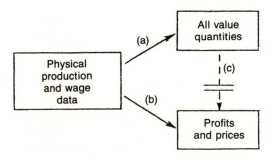

Figure 1

S/V remaining constant, to reduce $S/(C + V)$. He asserted, further, that C/V does rise through time under capitalism. Thus, while he drew attention to a number of counteracting tendencies, Marx does appear to have thought that $S/(C + V)$ would fall in the long run. As is also well known, this argument has always been subject to certain criticisms.[14] In the first place, there is no obvious reason why any tendency to fall should be regarded as "fundamental," while tendencies to rise should be dubbed "counteracting." The labels could just as well be reversed, and it is far from clear why the cheapening of the elements of constant and variable capital should not suffice to maintain or raise $S/(C + V)$. Second, while Marx *asserted* that C/V tends to rise under capitalism, he did not *know* that it rises. Indeed no one knows or ever has known the magnitude of C/V for a single economy even at one point of time, let alone known its trend over time. While C/V, the ratio of labor embodied in means of production to labor embodied in the wage goods, is calculable *in principle*, the fact is that it never has been calculated and that any attempt at such a calculation would be fraught with difficulty. Nor may the movement of C/V be inferred from published statistics, for the latter are always in price terms and value aggregates may move quite differently from the corresponding price aggregates.

We have seen above, however, that the above traditional criticisms are, in a sense, irrelevant. The rate of profit under capitalism *does not equal* $S/(C + V)$, so that if we want to discover whether the profit rate tends to fall, argument about whether $S/(C + V)$ will tend to fall or not is neither here nor there. There is no reason at all why the methods of production and the real wage should not change through time in such a way that $S/(C + V)$ falls while the profit rate rises, or vice versa!

If we look to our analytically sound theory of the profit rate, can we predict that the rate will fall (or rise)? It would seem not. Our analysis tells us, not surprisingly, that the rate of profit is inversely related to real wages but positively related to the efficiency of production methods. Since both real wages and productivity tend to rise in the long run, there is no basis for any a priori expectation about the long-run direction of movement of the profit rate.

There is, at present, no respectable Marxist theory of a long-run tendency for the rate of profit to fall. Thus any existing Marxist analyses of capitalist development which are based on the existence of such a tendency are, as yet, without theoretical foundation.

Appendix

1. To make our example as simple as possible, we felt obliged to assume only one produced means of production (iron). This has the disadvantage that in our example one can, in fact, derive profits and prices from our table 2 (provided, of course, that one follows the method of Bortkiewicz and not that of Marx)! Thus the need for simplicity has meant that our example does not *fully* illustrate the force of our argument and that some of our assertions go beyond that example. We felt, however, that this difficulty was worth facing in the interest of simplicity.

2. As soon as there is more than one produced means of production one cannot derive profits and prices from a value schema in which "c" is given as a single figure, essentially because the different means of production will have different price/value relations, so that one cannot "transform" the single figure "c" by a single price/value ratio. If, however, "c" is split up into a separate "c" for each means of production, then the resulting schema is really no different from a table of physical data. To see this, suppose that physical units of commodities have been so chosen that every commodity has a value of unity—the table of physical inputs and the table of disaggregated "c's" will then be numerically identical.

Notes

1. Much of this discussion was provoked by Piero Sraffa's *Production of Commodities by Means of Commodities* (Cambridge, 1960); for a nontechnical review see Joan Robinson, "Piero Sraffa and the Rate of Exploitation," *New Left Review* 31 (May/June 1965).

2. I should like to thank Pat Devine, Maurice Dobb, Norman Geras, Phil Leeson, David Purdy, and Bob Rowthorn for helpful comments.

3. There is an implicit assumption here that producing half the output involves using half as much of each input, hence that there are no "economies" or "diseconomies" of scale.

4. The righthand side $= 56 (1 + \frac{1}{2} + \frac{1}{4} + \frac{1}{8} \ldots)$ and it is a standard textbook result that the terms in the bracket sum to 2.

5. A quicker way to obtain this result is to see from the first row of table 1 that $56\, l_i = 56 + 28\, l_i$, whence $l_i = 2$. The derivation given in the text, while slower, brings out more clearly that value is made up of a series of expenditures of human labor power.

6. That our calculation is correct may be checked as follows. The capitalists obtain 48 units of gold plus 3 units of corn and the value of these commodities $= 48\, l_g + 3\, l_c = 48 \times 1 + 3 \times 4 = 48 + 12 = 60 = S$.

7. See appendix for a somewhat more detailed discussion.

8. To see this, let k_i be the price/value ratio for iron and k_c be that for corn and suppose that the profit rate is ($\frac{5}{11}$) as argued by Marx. If we now transform both inputs and outputs we obtain, from the first and third rows of table 2,

$(56 \, k_i + 14 \, k_c) \, (1 + \frac{5}{11}) = 112 \, k_i$

and

$(24 \, k_i + 2 \, k_c) \, (1 + \frac{5}{11}) = 32 \, k_c.$

These two relations simplify to

$2 \, k_c = 3 \, k_i$

and

$5 \, k_c = 6 \, k_i$

respectively. Now the latter equations are simply inconsistent; *there are no* positive price/value ratios, k_i and k_c, which satisfy both these relations. Hence the assertion in the text that the problem in Marx's approach lies deeper than his not having transformed input prices.

9. Since one unit of gold is produced by one unit of labor ($l_g = 1$), it follows that the price of a commodity is numerically equal to the labor embodied in the gold with which that commodity exchanges. This can be compared with the value of that commodity.

10. It may be of interest to note that in the limiting case of workers obtaining the whole net product (8 units of corn and 48 units of gold), the equation $80 \, w = 5 \, p_c$ would have to be replaced by $80 \, w = (8 \, p_c + 48)$; the solution would then be

$r = \text{zero}, \, w = 1,$
$p_i = 2 = l_i, \, p_c = 4 = l_c.$

11. To see this, ignore the second of our four equations and divide through each of the others by p_c. There are then three equations and only three unknowns, namely r and the *ratios* (w/p_c) and (p_i/p_c). Thus r can be determined, as can (w/p_c) and (p_i/p_c), quite independently of production conditions in the gold industry. The latter conditions merely determine, via our second equation, the absolute levels of w, p_i, and p_c. The point being made here has also been emphasized by Paul Sweezy (following Bortkiewicz) in chapter 7 of his *Theory of Capitalist Development* (London, 1962); see, in particular, pp. 123–25.

12. See appendix.

13. This conclusion, we should perhaps emphasize, is the conclusion of an argument in logic; if anyone wishes to challenge it, they must do so by showing a *logical flaw* in that argument. They cannot challenge this conclusion by, for example, merely reminding us that it appears to differ from Marx's conclusion or by asserting (whether rightly or wrongly) that the conclusion is politically or ideologically "dangerous."

14. For a recent exposition and development of these traditional criticisms, see Geoff Hodgson, "The Theory of the Falling Rate of Profit," *New Left Review* 84 (March/April 1974).

Value and Post-Sraffa Marxian Analysis

PRADEEP BANDYOPADHYAY

Pradeep Bandyopadhyay explores some distinctions and similarities between Marxist and Neo-Ricardian (or what he has termed Post-Sraffa Marxist) paradigms. Bandyopadhyay claims that Marx's theoretical dilemma (as outlined by Neo-Ricardians) concerns the level of analysis and depictions of the source of surplus value. He offers the Sraffian theory of value as the answer. But unlike Steedman, Bandyopadhyay suggests that the inclusion of Marx's understanding of capitalist production—especially the dynamics of the social relations of production—in the Post-Sraffa approach is not only possible but desirable. He argues for the Post-Sraffian's concern with the political struggle over distribution, not merely the technical aspects of the determination of prices, profit, and value.

In the years since the appearance of Steedman's *Marx after Sraffa*, there has developed an extensive literature in defense, elaboration, criticism, and rejection of some of the basic claims made in that work.[1] [. . .] The aim of this paper is neither to attempt a defense of the post-Sraffa claims by refutation or critical rejection of the various arguments of the critics, nor to present a comprehensive exposition of the positive results of the post-Sraffa work that is generally labeled "Neo-Ricardian."[2] More modestly, it aims to present some general grounds for accepting the post-Sraffa recommendation to reject the labor theory of value (LTV) and to proceed with the reconstruction of Marxist analysis without it. It is concerned entirely with the dispute over whether the labor theory of value is necessary to an understanding of some basic features of capitalist economies.

Some Marxists have maintained that the quantitative explanatory role and the qualitative aspects of property and production relations are not *dissociable*, and that to abandon the LTV will lead also to abandoning the social relational aspects of Marxist analysis.[3] This claim of Sweezy's may be compared with the contrary claim that the social relational aspects with which the LTV is associated are separable from the LTV as a specific theory of valuation, and that if the LTV is defective with regard to capitalist economies an alternative and appropriate theory of valuation will both be consistent with the social relational structures and provide them with a measure-space for quantitative calculations. [. . .]

The post-Sraffa Marxists have a quite different approach to valuation, prices,

Pradeep Bandyopadhyay, "Value and Post-Sraffa Marxian Analysis," *Science & Society* 48, 4 (Winter 1984–85), pp. 433–48.

and profits and provide a distinctive set of answers. These are: that the "law of value" in LTV terms does not regulate capitalist dynamics; and that exchange values are simultaneously determined for inputs and outputs when commodities are used to produce commodities. The orthodox LTV Marxist must demonstrate not that labor values can be calculated—for in the absence of certain complications such as joint production, that is *not* disputed—but that they are *required* to explain prices, profits, and accumulation in a capitalist economy. This general problem encompasses the frequent Marxist claim that the relation of values to prices is that of essence to appearance and that to reject the LTV is to regress to "vulgar economic" analysis in Marx's sense.

This paper will discuss these issues in an interrelated manner, avoiding formal technicalities. The first section states some of the most basic post-Sraffa Marxist claims. This is followed by a discussion of valuation in which the relation of value to representations of production in Marx and Sraffa is explored, and the question of the nature of exchange value in different economic systems is addressed.

The Post-Sraffa Marxist Claims

The most simple claims may be summarized as follows:

a) The value magnitudes of the LTV are derivable from the physical data of the sociotechnical conditions of production (STCP), including the amount of labor performed in units of time and the real wage rate.

b) The magnitudes of the prices of production of the commodities and the general rate of profit are also *directly* derivable from the same physical data as above, and therefore we do *not need to know* the value magnitudes in order to know the prices and profits magnitudes.

c) Given the social relations of property and production (the nonuniversal private ownership of the means of production with private owners hiring nonowning workers in an asymmetric relation of hiring or being hired; with the workers receiving wages and the private owners receiving profits on their productively used property, i.e., with the owners being capitalists; and the social separation of those who through ownership and control over the means of production decide where, how, and what production will take place and those who must adjust to such decisions as a condition of the wage payment, etc.), the capitalist exploitation of workers can be shown quantitatively in terms of the ratios of the proportion of the net product received by capitalists and workers respectively, and this can be expressed in labor time so that the distinction between "necessary labor" and "surplus labor" can be recognized and measured.

d) Quantitative variation of certain characteristics of the labor process possible within the social relations of property and production, such as the length of the working day, the intensity of work activity, and economy of material inputs, can be analyzed within this physical production data framework, at least as regards their influence on the rate of profits and/or the specified real wages.

e) The problem of heterogeneous labor (whether different in terms of concrete activities or levels of skill) can be taken account of, without requiring any
reduction to homogeneous simple labor, so long as the various types of labor are
indicated by different wage rates either in terms of the money commodity or as
commodity bundles which are physically specified. One can still show that
profits are associated with the performance of surplus labor, given labor inputs in
production.

f) Similarly, the pure costs of circulation, involving one type of unproductive
labor (i.e., not increasing the net product), can be incorporated into the analysis
revealing their effects on the rate of profit, the choice of technique being taken as
given. This shows that a distinction between productive and unproductive labor
can be warranted.

All these claims are sustained by a single mode of analysis, deriving from and
considerably extending Sraffa's work, which is thus shown to be capable of
further extension so as to take account of various complications without having to
abandon the method.[4]

One deliberate feature of the post-Sraffa Marxist claims (with the exception of
(d)) is that they are all about a capitalist economy at, as it were, one point in time
with all aspects simultaneous, the STCP given, and all markets cleared (i.e., all
the quantities produced of the various commodities are taken as socially necessary). The only processes of change in the above claims are those concerning the
quantitative variables within the labor process, which effect changes in the physical quantities involved and, depending on which elements change and in which
direction, variously affect the rate of profit, and the rate of surplus value as
measured by the ratio of surplus labor to necessary labor. That is to say, changes
in the labor process change the quantitative specification of the STCP data but can
be handled within it. The determinants of these changes are to be sought in the
social relations of property and production and the consequent strategic interaction, given differences in relevant resources and objectives, of workers and
capitalists. However, these labor-process changes concern only those variations
which are still possible *given* the choice of technology in an engineering sense and
the real wage as specified by the consumption commodity bundles of workers.
[. . .]

The Structure of Production and Surplus
Production: Marx and Sraffa Compared

To analyze these issues further, consider the contrast between Marx and Sraffa, in
Capital and *The Production of Commodities by Means of Commodities* respectively, as regards their starting points and initial claims. Marx begins with an
analysis of the commodity form and proceeds to develop the value form in a
dialectic of stages right up to the emergence of the universal equivalent or money
commodity and the expression of relative values as money exchange values; i.e.,

he explicates some properties of a structure of exchange relations without analyzing production by means of commodities. At the *start* of this development he has *already* claimed that the socially necessary labor time required to produce a commodity is the determinant of the value of that commodity and hence of exchange values.

Marx is looking for exchange values that express quantitatively some common property of commodities, a substance or substrate attached to commodities independently of their position in a *relational structure*, i.e., attached to them as *products* rather than as *commodities*. [. . .] Products become commodities only as elements of an exchange structure and thus acquire, given certain properties of the exchange structure as conditions, a common relational property which inheres in them qua commodities—an exchange value. Marx wants to know what determines the magnitude of these exchange values and asserts that whatever it is must also be inherent in commodities. This is the question of the substance or content of value: what is it that value measures? We know Marx's answer and his claim that under simple commodity production the exchange values of commodities will be their socially necessary labor values, and that under capitalist production prices will not be equal to labor values, owing both to exploitation and the differing organic compositions of capital, but instead will be modified values.

There are thus according to Marx *two* sources of deviation from exchange at labor values: (1) exploitation, with the deviation proportional to the rate of exploitation assuming a uniform rate of exploitation, and (2) the organic compositions of capital, with the deviation arising from the pro-rating of surplus value required to form the uniform or general rate of profit. He assumed that *both* sources of deviation were absent from simple commodity production and to be found only under capitalist conditions.

Now consider the early pages of Sraffa's work. We are given a description of an exchange economy in *simple reproduction*, which produces "just enough to maintain itself." There is no surplus product, and all the products are necessary inputs in production. We find that the exchange ratios of the commodities are determinate; any one commodity can be taken as the standard and the relative values of the others can be expressed in terms of it. This will give us the total value of production in terms of a single commodity and, assuming that all production processes require labor, and taking total social labor as unity, we can know what *fraction* of total social labor went into each line of production, and it will be obvious that the relative labor values of the commodities derived in this way are necessarily equal to their exchange ratios, and it cannot be otherwise because we postulate that the total social labor produced the total social product and the production data indicates that all products are used in production in specified quantities. But we can obtain the commodity exchange ratios in this case without knowing anything about labor at all. The ratios were determined by the *fixed* production requirements of a commodity economy with no surplus. There is no choice over distribution or allocation here, if simple reproduction is to be achieved.

Sraffa then considers the implications of a surplus product made possible, for instance, by more productive methods of production (a development of the forces of production). An immediate problem is that exchange ratios are no longer determinate without an allocation (or distribution) of the surplus product to the various lines of production. A further possibility is that the surplus can now be used to produce a new category of products which are not necessary as inputs into any of the production processes, termed by Sraffa "luxury" products. At any rate the existence of the surplus raises the problem of the *uses to which it may be put*. Before we can know the uses to which the surplus is put we must know who *decides* and that refers us to the relations of property and production. If capitalists and workers are distinct classes the *net surplus* is the residue after the consumption of workers, and will equal aggregate profits. Without a specification of this distribution of the surplus (in order to know the net surplus appropriated by capitalists) the exchange ratios remain indeterminate. The possibility of luxury products enables a distinction to be made between products which are required for production and products which are not, i.e., basic and nonbasic products. Here Sraffa mentions labor for the first time, pointing out that in the previous case the social labor was at a subsistence level, but now one possible use of the surplus product could be to improve workers' consumption beyond the essential.

It is at this point that Sraffa introduces the terms profits and wages, thus indicating that his subsequent discussion of the appropriation of the surplus will be against a background of the property and production relations, and the consequent classification of production interrelated persons, with which those terms are associated. He goes on to develop the concept of the "standard commodity" in order to show the inverse relation between profits and wages whatever the structure of production when both are expressed in terms of the "standard commodity." The important point is the significance of the surplus product, for it is this that forces an alteration of the exchange ratios given by the initial production conditions of the no-surplus case. Sraffa's almost exclusive attention is to the relation between profits, wages, and the surplus product (or net product or national income as he also terms it) in a *coherent and consistent commodity producing and exchanging economy* in which the profit-wage relation exists. The interest in relative prices (of production) is only so as to demonstrate that *coherence and consistency* while working out the relations between profits, wages, and national income. He mentions, but does not explore further, the situation where the entire surplus product goes to the workers and is *allocated by them to increased consumption*. He says that this reverts to the original equation system (without a surplus). A moment's reflection shows that now the consumptions of laborers, no longer at subsistence, are explicitly indicated as commodities. Here, as before, the exchange ratios (or exchange values) directly derived from the production structure equal the social labor content. In other words, here the problem generated by the surplus is resolved once we know how it is distributed and allocated for consumption.

One virtue of this analysis is that it suggests the importance of contrasting production and exchange without and with surplus products as an *analytically prior requirement* for the study of value and exchange value. Capitalist production necessarily requires as a precondition that there be surplus production. Yet in starting with the commodity form of the products of labor in which context the "law of value" is postulated, Marx nowhere raises the question of the valuation and exchange of commodities when total production includes a *surplus* production of heterogeneous products relative to the inputs used in production. Nor does he consider surplus production when he remarks on exchange at labor values under simple commodity production. It is possible that this is owing to the manner in which he discusses the dual aspect of the commodity: use value and exchange value. The two aspects are discussed without reference to *productive uses* of commodities. The illustrations given of use values are all, in effect, final consumption uses since the exchanged commodities are never considered from the viewpoint of reentering production in order to produce exchangeable products.

Had the problem been raised, Marx would have had to consider the various uses of the surplus product. Consideration of the productive uses of exchangeable products is begun by Marx only *after* the money commodity is developed and when the money form of capital is arrived at through accumulation of money in some hands and the separation of some workers from their means of production. At this stage Marx shows that increments to value (the M-C-M' circuit) cannot arise in circulation and must involve analysis of the productive uses of various commodities. There is now an explicit consideration of the surplus product: it is surplus value. This is because he already has postulated a theory of both the valuation and exchange valuation of commodities which only needs to be applied to the capitalist *relations of production*. At this point the surplus product is *identified* with surplus value by Marx. But one aspect of the relation of total production to the production process is not considered, viz., that there can be surplus production without the categories of capitalists and hired workers or any other social classes reciprocally related through exploitation, as in the case of Robinson Crusoe where one is considering production for useful effects without any distinction between laborers and nonlaborers. Surplus production is not *necessarily* exploitation, although it is a necessary condition for exploitation to be possible.

Marx is a little misleading in remarking that only the essential *elements of value* but, by implication, no form of valuation itself are involved in either Crusoe's, or the collectivist, economy. This is so only if the level or quantity of the useful effects sought, i.e., final consumption, is constant and fixed. With the possibility of surplus production there is a valuation problem, viz., how to distribute the potential for surplus production between more leisure and more consumption (or growth in production), and whatever our choice, there will be a consequent change of the initial production conditions.

We do not have exchange values here, but we do have a choice of alternatives, and some form of valuation is necessary in order to compare and choose nonarbitrarily. Given a level of consumption we would choose to *minimize* the amount of necessary labor required to produce the relevant set of useful products. So we would value alternative techniques in terms of the labor time associated with them, the optimal one being that which minimizes necessary productive labor.

In capitalist production and exchange the *relations of production* stamp a different modality of valuation than is the case with Crusoe, or indeed with the collectivist economy, because here the *relevant* surplus product from the capitalist viewpoint is the portion going to capital as a whole as against labor (this is a distributive relation exogenous to exchange between capitalists, and is the locus of the struggle over the level of the real wage rate and the amount of labor hired). [. . .] Equivalent exchange is realized when there is a uniform rate of profit and products exchange at exchange ratios that equalize the rate of profit. So, with separate and competing capitals producing and exchanging commodities, the value form is the price of production, which *is* the exchange value of commodities when all productive uses of separate capitals are equivalent. This equivalence is realized through the continuous movement of money capital flowing between different branches of production.

The point is that the relevant "law of value," from the capitalist viewpoint, regulating exchange values under capitalist production—while leaving active all the contradictory aspects of the relation between exchange values and market prices—is that the exchange ratios be such as to distribute the capitalists' surplus product as an equal, general rate of profit. It is now clear that the "prices of production" are exchange values and not merely the "price-form" in Marx's terminology. This way one is clear that if the production system is stamped with capitalist relations of production then the distribution of the surplus product between capitalists and noncapitalists (primarily workers) is a fundamental datum, as is the rule of equivalent exchange, in the formation of the exchange ratios in which the commodities produced will exchange. It also suggests that the dynamics of the system will depend on the forms of class struggle between capitalists *and* workers on the one hand and the forms of competitive struggle *among* capitalists on the other hand seeking to increase their individual appropriations of the net product. These two domains of struggle will bring about changes in the technology used, the commodity composition of production, the rate of expanded reproduction, the level of employment and relative prices, and consequently the levels of consumption of various subcategories of the population. These dynamic issues establish a definite scientific research program for post-Sraffa Marxian analysis.[5]

The post-Sraffa analysis is thus characterized by the location of exchange within, and subordinate to, production and production relations. A definite set of relations of production and production structure, and their momentary quantitative resolution, have to be given for exchange values to be determined as results.

In Marx, values and exchange values are determined by the socially necessary labor time expended; exchange values are transformed owing to differing organic compositions of capital into prices of production which are modified by contingent market conditions into market prices. Equivalent exchange is established with the exchange values, and the requirement of equal profit rates imposes a transformation of exchange values into prices of production.

The question that must be asked is: who are the parties to equivalent exchange at the level of Marx's exchange values? It cannot be the capitalists, since the condition for equivalent exchange for them is that exchange take place at prices of production. A plausible answer is workers and capitalists in the wage relation, since Marx argues that labor power is a commodity and exchanges at its value. But since only one commodity is involved in this transaction, this cannot be considered a satisfactory answer.

The post-Sraffa Marxists, on the other hand, have no difficulty with the analogous question. The parties to the exchange are capitalist producers of commodities, and the exchange values are prices of production determined by the STCP data and the real wage rate. The relevant exchange structure can be fully described, but workers and their wages are *not* considered an element in the exchange structure and are an exogenous condition for the determination of exchange value (i.e., prices of production). They are a condition to the extent that they are required for production and must be hired at a wage. Far from being a weakness this treatment of labor is a strength.

We have so far left hanging Marx's question: what determines the magnitude of value? Our answer is that it depends on the structure of the social relations of production. In our exchange economy with private property rights over the means of production, which is to say, with capital, it will depend on how the net surplus or the surplus product relevant to capitalists (i.e., the aggregate portion of Sraffa's net product that accrues to capitalists) is distributed.

With a different structure of the relations of property and production, e.g., in a collectivist economy with no private property relations, and given the *socially useful* product composition of output, the valuation of products will be in terms of the *socially necessary* labor expended. In other words, given a well-defined product composition of the output and the technology of production and the necessary allocation of labor to the branches of production, the values of the products will be equal to their labor values. This is tantamount to not having the problem of distributing Sraffa's surplus product. It is, perhaps, inappropriate to call such products commodities and such values exchange values. At any rate, this system differs from capitalist economies as regards the private appropriation of surplus product. In such a system the objective of the associated producers will be to *minimize* the socially necessary labor required to produce given bundles of products with their respective useful effects or use values. We thus obtain the traditional contrast between "production for use" and "production for profit"; production conditions will determine relative values of products in those social systems where production is directly subjected to socially useful effects. Labor-time relative values are relevant when minimizing socially necessary labor time required for the production of socially determined use values is the principle regulating productive activities.

Conclusion

We are thus led to the judgment that Marx's "law of value" has no *regulating* role in *capitalist* economies. It would appear that the source of the incessant disputes among those who share Marx's concerns and objectives arises from the fact that Marx rolled into one scheme two forms of valuation without due regard for the specific effects of distinctive social relations of property and production. The source of this problem appears to be his use of notions derived from a hypothetical simple commodity mode of production incorrectly or incompletely specified in terms of the relations of property and production and the structure of the production processes. This in turn relates back to his starting his analysis without a clear contrast between production with a surplus and production without, relative to the production structure itself.

Marx's theory of value provides us with a standard with which to judge the social efficiency of production from a collective viewpoint and in relation to the forces of production. This always relates socially necessary labor time to the products, given a socially determined use structure. Private property in the means of production vitiates this, and when commodities are produced for equivalent exchange revalues the products *relationally*: the intrinsic labor content of products thus becomes irrelevant to their exchange values. To make Marx's labor values relevant to production decisions we would have to alter the relations of production so that either there is no surplus (the inputs and outputs are in the aggregate equal) or the allocation of the surplus for expanded reproduction is collectively determined.

Notes

1. Ian Steedman, *Marx after Sraffa* (London, 1977).
2. The labels people attach have evaluative connotations. Critics of the claims made in *Marx after Sraffa* generally label the positions and the approach "Neo-Ricardian," suggesting thereby that it is both pre-Marxist and un-Marxist in its questions and results. In this paper we adopt a label with more positive connotations, "post-Sraffa Marxist," to name the same literature and mode of analysis. This highlights both the appreciation and sympathy for Marx's concerns and ideas, and the *forward*-looking nature of the work.
3. Paul Sweezy stated this in his *The Theory of Capitalist Development*, published in 1942, and reiterated the judgment in his contribution to Steedman et al., *The Value Controversy* (London, 1981), p. 21.
4. The classic reference is, of course, Piero Sraffa, *Production of Commodities by Means of Commodities* (London, 1960).
5. An early example of parts of such analysis is Luigi Pasinetti, *Structural Change and Economic Growth* (London, 1981).

Post-Keynesian and Neo-Ricardian Perspectives on Policy

The Post-Keynesian framework includes a broad range of analysis and analysts. It would be virtually impossible to outline a set of policy prescriptions with which most Post-Keynesians would agree. Most Post-Keynesians do not advocate a complete eradication of capitalist relations, but they do call for some major changes in the structure of economic institutions and decision making. This entails a call for more democratic and equitable economic outcomes.

Income distribution, investment, and international trade are crucial components in understanding the level of demand and with it output, employment, price, and interest levels. Post-Keynesian policy is directed toward ensuring appropriate levels of demand. This policy can include a large array of proposals which stem from knowledge of the structure and mechanisms of investment consumption and trade. Furthermore, the nature of participation, world economic activity, expectations, and economic stability will affect the type and role of policy. Given the nature of uncertainty and expectations, there will always be a need for a degree of latitude in policy decisions. What follows is a nonexclusive list of policy options that are consistent with some forms of Post-Keynesian analysis.

—The traditional tools of monetary and fiscal policy would probably be rejected by most Post-Keynesians because they cannot take into account the structure of capitalist economies (oligopoly and competitive sectors) and decision making within firms. At the same time, Post-Keynesians can offer some astute analyses on the likely effects of the types of monetary and fiscal policy currently used, and they might find some targeted government spending—particularly in the form of income redistribution—an important step toward increased demand and employment.

—Some forms of economic planning would certainly be supported by most Post-Keynesians. Indicative planning, rather than setting production targets, would be the most probable form. The recent debates on reindustrialization were proposed and supported by many Post-Keynesians. These policies provide ways to support certain industries and workers to continue production. Generally proponents of this type of planning (including the Trilateral Commission) support councils of government, industry, and unions making long-range investment, pricing, and wage-setting decisions. Planning, it is believed, generates stability leading to less uncertainty, which in turn aids increased demand and growth.

—Most Post-Keynesians would favor some form of financial restructuring. It is not clear how this might proceed, but it would entail reducing the current degree of financial leveraging and structure of extended credit. This, importantly, also would entail restructuring international financial structures and move toward solving the third world debt crisis. Some form of coordinate banking council would need to be established, and new and more stringent banking regulations would need to be set into place.

—A final policy possibility, one with which some Post-Keynesians might disagree, has to do with control over investment and investment decisions. Keynes outlined a way to stabilize investment at the end of the *General Theory*. He suggested that control over investment decisions be placed in more responsible hands (he suggested his own!) than the rentiers themselves. A more radical extension would displace control and ownership. In either case this policy prescribes that investment be part of the public domain and that workers and communities have a say in what is produced, how it is produced, and for whom. In this way, not only will investment be less subject to the vagaries of market fluctuations and individual looting, but through increased participation expectations would improve and uncertainty be minimized.

Neo-Ricardians are dedicated to understanding the production and allocation of surplus product. While a model of class struggle is often assumed from the onset of the analysis, it is an important component of the theory. Their analysis places primary importance on developing a theory of value that can inform the distribution of income and product within class societies. In this way Neo-Ricardian analysis can be used to understand the distributive impact on a change in technology and relative prices. As with Marxian theory, the Neo-Ricardian framework is premised upon conflict and the opposing interests of capitalists and workers.

The mechanical transformation of many of Marx's interpretations has served more important policy prescriptions than at first imagined. By "solving the transformation problem," Neo-Ricardians have added validity to Marx's economics. In turn, a translation of Sraffa's model into an input-output model has been (or could be) used by countries to understand the distribution of surplus product and possible alternatives of different planning schema. For countries with a mixture of private and public enterprises and with a government interested in planning major areas of output, the contributions of Neo-Ricardian economics become most apparent.

Neo-Ricardians are the first to acknowledge not only their intellectual and political debt to Marxian theory but also their "modest" contribution to political economy. Steedman claims that the Neo-Ricardian framework "is intended to be no more than one—important—part of an adequate theory of the working of capitalist economies. That it is not sufficient does not alter the fact that it is important."[1]

Note

1. Ian Steedman, "Ricardo, Marx, Sraffa" in Ian Steedman et al., *The Value Controversy* (London: New Left Books, 1981), p. 18.

Suggested Readings

Paul Davidson (1978) *Money and the Real World*. 2d ed. London: Macmillan.
John Eatwell and Murray Mulgate, eds. (1983) *Keynes, Economics and the Theory of Value and Distribution*. New York: Oxford University Press.
Alfred Eichner, ed. (1979) *A Guide to Post-Keynesian Economics*. Armonk, N.Y.: M. E. Sharpe.
————. (1980) *The Megacorp and Oligopoly*. Armonk, N.Y.: M. E. Sharpe.
G. C. Harcourt (1972) *Some Cambridge Controversies in Capital Theory*. Cambridge: Cambridge University Press.
Michio Morishima (1973) *Marx's Economics*. Cambridge: Cambridge University Press.
Luigi Pasinetti (1983) *A Structural Change and Economic Growth*. Cambridge: Cambridge University Press.
Alesandro Roncaglia (1978) *Sraffa and the Theory of Prices*. New York: Wiley.
Ian Steedman (1977) *Marx after Sraffa*. London: New Left Books.
Ian Steedman, Paul Sweezy, et al. (1981) *The Value Controversy*. London: New Left Books.

III

Institutional
Political Economy

Introduction

The Institutional school of political economy began with the work of Thorstein Veblen. The fact that every few years the American Economic Association or one of its stalwart members feels compelled to pronounce this school officially dead testifies to the continuity and persistence of this hearty band of heretics. After Veblen, the Institutionalists' contribution can be divided into three periods: pre-1945, post-1945, and the late 1960s to date. In the pre-1945 period Institutional analysis and activism was continued by economists such as John R. Commons, Wesley C. Mitchell, Walton Hamilton, J. M. Clark, Gardiner Means, Rexford Tugwell, and many others. The contributions of these economists are discussed in detail in Allan Gruchy's book *Modern Economic Thought: The American Contribution*. The post-1945 period is represented by the works of economists such as C. E. Ayres, J. K. Galbraith, and Gunnar Myrdal. Their contributions are discussed in another of Allan Gruchy's books, *Contemporary Economic Thought*. The third period, from the late 1960s to the present, coincides with the organization of the Association for Evolutionary Economics and its *Journal of Economic Issues*. This organization was greatly influenced by C. E. Ayres, who reemphasized the theoretical component of Institutional economics.

Institutionalists see the role of economic inquiry as a process of understanding the operation and evolution of the economy for the purpose of solving economic problems. As a result, Institutional economics is not "positive" in the orthodox sense; in fact, Institutionalists reject the positive-normative dualism as meaningless. This is an explicitly value-driven form of inquiry.

Institutionalists' concern with problem-solving leads them to careful inquiry about the actual, rather than ideal, operation of modern industrial economies. This concern caused early Institutionalists to spend much effort on careful empirical studies such as Wesley C. Mitchell's study of business cycles, which contributed to the dominant orthodox misconception of Institutional economics as purely descriptive and nontheoretical. Close study of the actual structure and operation of the economy is a necessary precondition for Institutional analysis, for the primary focus of concern is the interrelated character of economic, cultural, and political aspects of social behavior. The Institutionalists' concern with the interconnected character of the economy and their exploration of these interrelationships has led to their approach being described as holistic.

Central to understanding Institutional economics are three fundamental concepts: the concept of culture, the nature and causes of change, and instrumental value theory. Institutionalists treat economic behavior and all social behavior as cultural phenomena. As a result economic behavior requires explanation in cultural terms. This involves two important differences from orthodox economics. First is an explicit rejection of the notion that any economic behavior is the result of, or can be explained by, "human nature"—cultural behavior is learned and can be explained by the process of acculturation. This means that no human behavior is immutable. Second, using the concept of culture is an explicit rejection of the atomistic individualism of orthodoxy—all cultural behavior is social, so individual behavior is socially conditioned within cultural parameters. This makes the process of social conditioning, the social structure, groups within the social structure, the exercise of power by groups, and the location of individuals in particular groups of much greater relevance than explaining the peculiarities of a particular individual's behavior.

Institutionalists treat economies as evolving cultural systems. As a result they are very concerned with explaining how this evolutionary change takes place. To analyze change they use a tool of behavioral analysis referred to as the Veblenian dichotomy, which comprises instrumental (technological) aspects of behavior and ceremonial (institutional) aspects of behavior. Instrumental aspects of behavior are warranted by matter-of-fact, demonstrable knowledge. This instrumental behavior is responsible for our ability to develop and apply technology to solving problems, which results in progress. Instrumental behavior is inhibited by ceremonial aspects of behavior, warranted by appeal to tradition and myth. Ceremonial behaviors perpetuate themselves by the exercise of power through hierarchical social structures. This hierarchical power-relationship is required to maintain a social structure dominated by the ceremonial aspects of behavior because no matter-of-fact, demonstrable reason for this structure's perpetuation is possible. Ceremonial behavior's past orientation causes it to be inherently conservative and leads to resistance to change. The Institutionalist view of evolutionary change is one of the interaction of instrumental behavior's developing new technology for solving problems and ceremonial behavior's role in the resistance to this change through the arbitrary use of power.

The direction of change, whether progressive or degenerative, brings us to the Institutionalists' concept of value. Instrumentalist value theory assumes value is not intrinsic to a good or service, instead value is determined in a social context; that is, life is a problem-solving process, and things are valuable to the extent that they contribute to the continuity of and improvement in the quality of life. Goods, services, behaviors, attitudes, tools, and ideas are all evaluated by this same criterion. Goods and behaviors that help solve problems (progress) contribute to the continuity of the life process and as such are valuable. Instrumental aspects of behavior are those most consistent with and most likely to improve our ability to solve problems; ceremonial aspects of behavior inhibit effective problem solving. As a result, societies dominated by ceremonial behaviors decline because of the inability to solve problems. The nature of change is evolutionary and incremental. There are no preconceived equilibria and no guarantees that societies will progress.

This concept of value is intimately tied to the notion of change. Unlike orthodox economics, which employs static utility theory and price as a locus of value, instrumental value theory is dynamic in that it is concerned with the process of evolution.

All three fundamental concepts that have been discussed are interrelated and only analytically separable. Institutional economics is a method of analyzing economic processes for the purpose of solving problems. This requires the best understanding of complex social systems possible *and* the realization that the evolutionary character of social systems makes "complete knowledge" impossible, thus constant reassessment of what is already known is part of the process of inquiry.

Institutional economics offers no predetermined solutions contained in initial assumptions. Institutionalists are optimistic about the ability of science and technology to improve our capacity to solve major social and economic problems. This optimism is tempered by Veblen's observation, "But history records more frequent and more spectacular instances of the triumph of imbecile institutions over life and culture than of peoples who have by force of instinctive insight saved themselves alive out of a desperately precarious institutional situation" (Thorstein B. Veblen, *The Instinct of Workmanship* [New York: Augustus M. Kelley, 1964], p. 25).

The Institutional Approach
to Economic Theory

WALTON H. HAMILTON

Institutional economics got its name from this classic article by Walton Hamilton. In this article, Hamilton boldly denies microeconomics the status of theory. To defend this attack on the foundations of Neoclassical orthodoxy he sets out five criteria that any economic theory must meet, and he contends that the "institutional approach" meets these criteria.

Hamilton's article is simultaneously an attack on Neoclassical microeconomics, which he refers to as "value economics," and an argument for the general concerns of Institutional economics. The reader should note that Hamilton uses the term "institution" to mean both socially organized behavior and social structure. The dual usage of this term has led to consistent confusion in the Institutional literature.

An explanation of the "institutional approach" to economic theory is a plea for a particular kind of theory. It is possible to come upon the same object from different angles; but more often those who take different routes chance upon different things. The "institutional approach" doubtless has some importance because it is a happy way to acceptable truth, but its significance lies in its being the only way to the right sort of theory. An appeal for "institutional economics" implies no attack upon the truth or value of other bodies of economic thought, but it is a denial of the claims of other systems of thought to be "economic theory." This, however, is no pointless struggle in method to be carried on by breaking syllogisms over concepts and by engaging in polemics over niceties in statement. On the contrary, it involves the very nature of the problems which the theorist should set himself; its real issue is over what economic theory is all about.

The Nature of Economic Theory

The thesis here set forth is that "institutional economics" is "economic theory." This involves putting a particular meaning upon a word which has meant many things. From the first, economic inquiries have gone pell-mell across frontiers at which they should have stopped; they have halted where logic would have pushed them forward; and they have been dominated by vacillating and conflicting

Walton H. Hamilton, "The Institutional Approach to Economic Theory," *American Economic Review* 9 Supplement (1919), pp. 309–18.

purposes. To catalogue the subjects to which the term "economic" is applied is to belie the careful definitions of the science pent up in books; to find an economic theory consistent with this multiform expression is to dissipate that theory in polychromatic reality. In general, particular subjects such as money, transportation, and accounting have been set off from "general economics." From the latter two bodies of doctrine have developed which aspire to the dignity of "economic theory." One of these is primarily concerned with the origin and manifestations of value. It is represented by such treatises as Smart's *Theory of Value*, Boehm-Bawerk's *Positive Theory of Capital*, and Clark's *Distribution of Wealth*. The concern of the other is the customs and conventions, or, if you please, the arrangements, which determine the nature of our economic system. It is represented in classical economics by Smith's account of mercantilism, Whately's discussion of how competition organizes industrial activity, and Mill's exposition of the relation of the state to industry. Typical examples from modern economics are Cannan's account of the function of property in economic organization, Veblen's discussion of the dependence of wealth upon machine-technique, and Hobson's analysis of the relations under modern technical conditions of work to welfare. Between the two lies the issue of what is economic theory.

Institutional and value economics have many things in common. Both can claim a line of development running back to early classical economics. Both have emerged as by-products of the play of the human mind with the practical problems of social well-being. Both furnish materials that can be taken into account in passing upon questions of practical moment. The champions of each insist that its task is the positive one of garnering materials and formulating principles. Yet in actual use each has the taint of mixing judgments of goodness and badness into exposition. Only in recent years has value theory escaped a formal association with laissez faire and now even its most positive statements bear in such terms as "utility" and "productivity" and in the wording of principles implications about the worthwhileness of prevailing arrangements. Likewise institutional economics, in telling the elements which make up the economic system, passes judgments upon them. It is not in the legitimacy of their claims to stand in the line of succession, nor in their pretenses to unbiased scientific statement, nor in their dispositions to stray away after ethical judgments that the two differ. It is rather in their conceptions of the nature of the economic order.

The claim of value economics to the dignity of "economic theory" is not lightly to be put aside. In common speech it is recognized as "economic theory." This is not the place for the chapter in the history of economics which recounts how the two rival systems strove for the dominance of classical doctrine, nor for the equally interesting one which relates how at the passing of the older system institutional theory was dissipated and value theory passed into the inheritance. It is enough that it is built around "value," which is the most important concept in the science; it enjoys the prestige of the older body of doctrine; and that it is the most subtle, the most general, and the most articulate body of thought in economics. Yet its claim must be disallowed. Its merits are due to a failure to recognize the complexity of the relations which bind human welfare to industry. As our conception of the economic order has become larger and more intricate, value theory has hedged its problem about with greater limitations. At present its whole endeavor is an explanation of the nature of economic value and of the forms of income in which it expresses itself. The conclusions which it suggests about the kind of industrial society in which we live are indirect. They appear only because value theory is derived from the classical doctrine of the organization of industry upon the principle of free competition. Aside from such accidental statements, it is a specialized subject of inquiry with as little right to the dignity of "economic theory" as the theory of money or of accounting.

"Institutional economics" alone meets the demand for a generalized description of the economic order. Its claim is to explain the nature and extent of order amid economic phenomena, or those concerned with industry in relation to human well-being. In the words of Edwin Cannan, it attempts to tell "why all of us are as well off as we are" and "why some of us are better off than others." Such an explanation cannot properly be answered in formulas explaining the processes through which prices emerge in a market. Its quest must go beyond sale and purchase to the peculiarities of the economic system which allow these things to take place upon particular terms and not upon others. It cannot stop short of a study of the conventions, customs, habits of thinking, and modes of doing which make up the scheme of arrangements which we call "the economic order." It must set forth in their relations one to another the institutions which together comprise the organization of modern industrial society.

Characteristics of Institutional Economics

The case for institutional economics requires a reduction of the definition above to a catalogue of particulars. This, however, cannot be attempted here. Instead there will be presented for acceptance, for qualification, or for rejection a list of five tests which any body of doctrine which aspires to the name of economic theory must be able to meet. It is believed that institutional economics alone can meet these tests.

Economic Theory Should Unify Economic Science

The task of a general body of theory in any subject is to give unity to its investigations. At present economics is badly in need of such a unifying agent. Its sprawling frontiers reach from value theory across money, taxation, and transportation to salesmanship, insurance, and advertising. Each of these subjects has its own point of attack, its own method, and its own personnel. Those who seek truth in these remote fields of inquiry know little and care less for value theory. For all the constraints of Neoclassical theory, each of these subjects tends to develop an isolated body of thought. As a result economics today tends to break up into a large number of overlapping but unrelated inquiries and to lose the unity which in times past has been its source of strength. The mechanics of value determination possesses no magic which will draw together such divergent elements. Only institutional economics can perform that service. In describing in general terms economic organization it makes clear the kind of industrial world within which such particular things as money, insurance, and corporation finance have their being. It shows their nature by pointing out the parts they play in this larger whole. Its statements, always tentative, always enriched by inquiries in particular fields, are properly the point of departure for such specialized studies.

Economic Theory Should Be Relevant to the Modern Problem of Control

Students of economics should spend their efforts upon subjects worth investigation. If learning were a mere search for hypothetical truth, the principles governing the economic life of cave men, the inhabitants of Mars, or of a Crusoe-infested island might be worth formulating. But economists are few, time has scarcity value, and relevant subjects come faster than they can be seized. It is not the place of economics to pass judgments upon practical proposals. But, quite in keeping with its scientific character, it can impartially gather the facts and formulate the principles necessary to an intelligent handling of such problems. Such relevancy has always marked economics in the periods of its most fruitful development. Thus Adam Smith's point of departure was the relationship of economic organization to national wealth; thus Ricardo's principles are an outgrowth of his concern with the currency and bullion controversies; and thus the best work of the Austrian school grows out of a refutation of Marxian socialism.

If institutional economics has a relevancy which Neoclassical economics has not, it is because problems have changed. Early classical economics was formulated by men who sought to remove the artificial restrictions which had been imposed upon industry. Laissez faire was a formal and explicit part of its statement. It tended to show the beneficence of an industrial system automatically organized in response to the pecuniary self-interest of individuals. It made the scheme of arrangements wherein lay the real organization of society a part of the immutable world of nature. Since the Neoclassical doctrine has passed into the inheritance, the formal defense of laissez faire is gone, though it still lingers implicitly in terms and the statement of propositions. Formally it is concerned with the mechanical way in which the values of goods and of shares in distribution emerge in the market. But it has no concern with the organization of that market, the nature of the transactions which occur there, or the less immediate facts of the distribution of opportunity, property, and leisure upon which the size of these shares rest. Its explanatory terms are not matters subject to control.

A shift in problems and a general demand for control has made institutional economics relevant. This shift has been due partly to a discovery that institutions are social arrangements capable of change rather than obstinate natural phenomena, partly to a consciousness that activity, once apparently voluntary, is controlled by subtle conventions and habits of thought, and partly to the bad taste which laissez faire has left with us. But, however it has come about, there is a demand for an economics relevant to problems of control.

The Proper Subject-Matter of Economic Theory Is Institutions

The demand that economic theory relate to institutions is implicit in the plea for its relevancy. If it is to be germane to the problem of control it must relate to changeable elements of life and the agencies through which they are to be directed. Such elements of life and directive agencies are alike institutions. Control is exercised by modifying the arrangements which make up our scheme of economic life in such a way as better to satisfy our needs or our whims. Control is exercised through the peculiar agencies which we have at hand.

A control of particular aspects of economic life requires a knowledge of particular institutions. If one would deal intelligently with inflation, he must understand the organization of society in its financial aspects. This includes a knowledge of the price system, the level of prices, the places of credit in industry, and the relation of the unit for measuring pecuniary values to the maintenance of the economic order. If one would understand the corporation problem, he must learn the peculiar features of this form of business, the various devices which together make up its organization, and the place which it takes in industrial society. And if one would pass upon any of the many proposals for changing things in such a way as to enable some of us to make more and others less, he must know the relationship of the things he would change to the distribution of income. It is not enough to assert with the Neoclassicists that one receives the value of his services in the market; for, if matters subject to control are changed, he will still receive the value of his services, but he may pocket a different sum. He must understand, in addition, the conventions of competition, of contract, of property, of inheritance, of the distribution of opportunity which make incomes what they are.

In like manner a control of the development of industrial society is contingent upon a knowledge of the bundle of conventions and arrangements which make it up. The basis of material wealth in the machine technique, the scheme of natural rights which still inheres in the legal system, the resolution of all industry into a multitude of specialized and interdependent tasks, the rise of a complicated business mechanism which intervenes between wealth and welfare, the concentration of direction in the hands of an industrial hierarchy, the scheme of arrangements known as the wage-system, which is the means by which the laborer establishes a connection with industry—these and a hundred other things like them must be recognized by one who would direct, or, if he be an economic theorist, watch, industrial development.

Economic Theory Is Concerned with Matters of Process

If economic theory is to treat of institutions it must know both the kinds of things institutions are and the kinds of things they are not. Value theory deals with its phenomena as if they were physically complete, independent, unchangeable substances. The only variations which it admits are quantitative. At the beginning of one of its problems a certain situation exists; then a disturbing force makes its appearance; this is followed by a series of actions and reactions which continues until the normal is restored or an equilibrium is reestablished. By adding or subtracting units from a combination or by combining equations, formulas are found in terms of which economic values may be reduced to pecuniary terms. Such a method of procedure has, quite appropriately, been called "economic statics." Of late years a recognition of the limited number of problems upon which such an analysis throws light has led to a demand for an "economic dynamics." This, however, has served but to enlarge the older analysis by increasing the number of factors to be considered in attempting to understand problems. Both alike deal with physically distinct things; both alike reduce their problems to mechanical formulas; both alike find solutions in equilibria and quantities.

But the subject matter of economic theory cannot be handled in any such way. Competition, property, the price structure, the wage system, and like institutions refuse to retain a definite content. Not only are things happening to them, but changes are going on within them. A law, a court decision, a declaration of war, a change in popular habits of thought, and the content of property rights is affected. An increased demand for labor, a refusal of the nation to allow strikes, an enforced recognition of unionism, an establishment of wages upon living costs, and the wage system becomes different. Both by a change in its relation to other things and by subtle changes going on within, each of these institutions is in process of development. And, if this is true of particular institutions, it is likewise true of the complex of institutions which together make up the economic order. We need constantly to remember that in studying the organization of economic activity in general as well as in particular, we are dealing with a unified whole which is in process of development.

To this method the terms "historical" and "genetic" are frequently applied. The first, because of the associations which the word history brings up, is particularly unfortunate. It suggests an account of things which have happened to the subject of discussion during a definite period of time. Its emphasis is wrong because it is upon the accidental facts of past associations, not upon the essential nature of current reality. If it is rightly understood the term "genetic" is much better. But it must not be allowed to suggest a far-away, uninteresting, and irrelevant search for "origins." It must mean what the word so clearly implies that the thing is "becoming." Thus used the word "genetic" suggests, not a historical account, but a method of analysis. It goes to the past only with the end in view and so far as is necessary to explain what a thing is in terms of how it came to be. The economic system, which is so baffling and unintelligible to us, is not so much an interesting group of real things as a curious stream of tendencies. Many of these move slowly, some of them seem immutable. Yet the whole complicated affair which we call Modern Industrialism has existed for a very brief period in human history. If control is to be exercised, it is not to be by tinkering with this or that. It must be by changing the nature or functions of the institutions which make up our scheme of economic life. To insist upon treating such things genetically or as in process is nothing more than to insist that they are subject to conscious control.

Economic Theory Must Be Based upon an Acceptable Theory of Human Behavior

After all control and institutions and processes are immediate things. They can all be translated into terms of human conduct. The exercise of control involves human activity and leaves its mark in the changed activity of others. Institutions, seemingly such rigid and material things, are merely conventional methods of behavior on the part of various groups or of persons in various situations. The changes which processes reveal are merely changes in human actions. It is necessary, therefore, that economic theory should proceed from an acceptable theory of human conduct.

In the past economics has been fortunate in using a theory of conduct in harmony with the general thought of the age. It has been unfortunate in taking this unconsciously from the common sense of the times rather than arriving at it by careful observation and analysis. This has led to a disposition to preserve it as part of a traditional body of doctrine long after it had ceased to have meaning to those who had looked at it too critically. In no respect does Neoclassical economics more nearly resemble the body of doctrine from which it sprang than in its theory of the individual who knows the alternatives with which he is confronted and seeks his own greatest material good measured in pecuniary terms. The one touch which the economist has added to the theory as he took it from the ethicist is in making a pecuniary expression of self-interest a part of human nature. The extreme individualism, rationality, and utilitarianism which animated eighteenth century thought still finds expression in Neoclassical economics.

In its stead a theory of motives must be used which is in harmony with the conclusions of modern social psychology. At its best the older theory of conduct presented in self-interest nothing more than a blanket formula. One had to go behind it to find the concrete influences which animated the behavior of individuals. At its best it made all activity the result of conscious endeavor by individuals who knew thoroughly their own interests even in an environment as complex as ours and who ruthlessly set out to attain them. It falls short of explanation because self-interest is not a simple thing that can be easily discerned, but a huge bundle of conflicting values wherein the present and the future are at variance. It assumed that each judgment could be based upon the real facts of the situation and could be made in detachment. It failed to note that my life and yours is a continuous thing, and that what I do today constrains my acts of tomorrow. It overlooked the part that instinct and impulse play in impelling one along the path of his economic activity. And, most important of all, it neglected the influence exercised over conduct by the scheme of institutions under which one lives and must seek his good. Where it fails, institutional economics must strive for success. It must find the roots of activity in instinct, impulse, and other qualities of human nature; it must recognize that economy forbids the satisfaction of all instincts and yields a dignified place to reason; it must discern in the variety of institutional situations impinging upon individuals the chief source of differences in the content of their behavior; and it must take account of the limitations imposed by past activity upon the flexibility with which one can act in future.

Conclusion

The characteristics which have been discussed present a bare outline of the case for institutional theory. They all require explanation, elaboration, and illustration. Another champion would doubtless pick out other characteristics, such as the concept of society which underlies it, its freedom from utilitarian bias, its harmony with current tendencies in ethics, psychology, and politics, and the reliance which it places upon a scientific study of fact. But such things are implicit in the description given, which is typical rather than exhaustive.

It must be readily admitted that like the things with which it deals, institutional theory is in process. But it opposes the accomplishments of Neoclassical theory with something more than mere promises. Here and there is much that can be fitted into a theory of the institutional organization of industrial society. Smith, Mill, Whately, and other classicists have given us much which with restatement can be used. The writings of the Neoclassicists, even those of the type of Clark and von Wieser, are not without pertinent material. The English classicists, Marshall, Pigou, Chapman, have materials for us; for in England the older economics has never lost the general concern which the Austrian and the American utility theorists have taken from it. The writings of the socialists, particularly Marx and La Salle, stripped of their application to proposals for reform, contain many a bit of sound analysis. In recent years the English "welfare school," particularly Webb, Hobson, Cannan, Tawney, and Clay—if writers with problems and approached so differently may be grouped together because of their common departure from Neoclassical analysis—have made substantial contributions and have given the beginnings of a formal statement of a theory of economic order. American thought has lagged largely because efforts which in England have taken a constructive bent here have been spent in criticism of Neoclassical doctrine. Yet H. C. Adams, Cooley, Veblen, and Mitchell—to mention only the leaders—have made substantial contributions to an understanding of our system. Nor must we forget the lay economist. In a rapidly developing society such as ours the learning of the schools tends to become formal and scholastic. It requires fertilization from thought which grows out of a fresh attack upon a new problem. The contributions of Graham Wallas may be mentioned as a single example of what the nonprofessional economist has to offer.

Yet, when all these contributions are amassed, it is doubtful whether at this time a general description of the economic order can be given. It may require a decade or more for a process of trial and error to produce a relatively consistent body of thought. Even then it will lack the clear-cut, definite, and articulate character of Neoclassical theory. Its concern with reality, its inability to ground a scheme of thought upon a few premises, its necessity of reflecting a changing economic life, alike make its development slow and prevent it from becoming a formal system of laws and principles. It must find in relevancy and truth a substitute for formal precision in statement.

The future of institutional theory is uncertain. The history of economics suggests that survival has often depended upon the ability of doctrine to fit in with the habits of thought of the times. If the next decade demands formal value theory that avoids a discussion of what the economic order is like, institutional economics will fail. If it demands an understanding of our relationship to the world in which we live, it will survive. But survival will be assisted by the development of a theory of the economic order, vital, true, and relevant to the problems of the times.

The Evolution
of the Veblenian Dichotomy:
Veblen, Hamilton, Ayres, and Foster

WILLIAM T. WALLER, JR.

The Veblenian dichotomy, the distinction between ceremonial and instrumental aspects of behavior, is the primary tool of analysis of Institutional economists in the Veblen/Ayres tradition. Waller traces its development from the work of Veblen to the present, emphasizing the need for and possible direction of future change.

The article specifically addresses the dual usage of the term "institution" to mean both socially organized behavior and social structure. Waller also points out that a similar problem occurs with regard to the term "technology," which is used to refer to both tools (and their use) and the process of scientific and technological inquiry. The dual-usage problem has led to much misunderstanding of Institutionalist literature by those unfamiliar with how this school of thought uses these terms.

This article will reexamine the concept of "institution" and discuss its relationship to the concept of technology, in pursuit of a unified reevaluation and refinement of the Veblenian dichotomy. The article will first examine the historical development of the dichotomy by economists in the Veblen-Ayres tradition. Second, it will discuss refining the concept of institution's role in the evolution of the meaning of technology within the dichotomy, and some implications will be drawn.

The Veblenian dichotomy is the central analytical tool of institutional economists in the Veblen-Ayres tradition. In his work, Thorstein Veblen expressed the dichotomy in many particular forms.[1] The particular form of interest here, one of the most general, has thus come to be the representative expression: the distinction between what Veblen called "institutions" and "technology."[2]

The concept of technology has been a recent center of controversy among Institutional economists.[3] Institutionalists are refining the meaning of "technology," as well as reexamining its usefulness as a tool of analysis. The particulars of this debate will be discussed later. The fact that the debate is taking place may be more important than the issues involved, for the reason that the Institution-

William T. Waller, Jr., "The Evolution of the Veblenian Dichotomy: Veblen, Hamilton, Ayres, and Foster," *Journal of Economic Issues* 16, 3 (September 1982), pp. 757–71.

alists' concept of a technological process is an abstraction, a working hypothesis about human behavior. All hypotheses, and all elements of scientific knowledge for that matter, are tentative. The Institutionalists' concept of the technological process includes testing hypotheses to see if they have "linkages" with the rest of the hypotheses judged by the community of scholars to be warranted knowledge. Or, more simply, each hypothesis is compared and evaluated as to its consistency with those hypotheses currently judged to be most correct. Since this warranted knowledge is itself only tentative, the process of reevaluating hypotheses must be constant and ongoing.[4] The very meaning of the technological process calls for its own reevaluation.

The reevaluation of hypotheses of human behavior, for example, is one of the main differences between the Institutionalists and their orthodox counterparts. The Institutionalists view human behavior as a process of cumulative adaption to changing circumstances within the cultural context in which the behavior takes place. This view is acknowledged to be tentative and subject to change in the light of evidence to the contrary. Unlike the Institutionalists, the orthodox economists make an a priori assumption about the nature of human behavior, and do not subject it to any testing process. This assumption can be seen in the following statement from a widely used contemporary, intermediate micro-theory text:

> The postulate of rationality is the customary point of departure in the theory of the consumer's behavior. The consumer is assumed to choose among the alternatives available to him in such a manner that the satisfaction derived from consuming commodities (in the broadest sense) is as large as possible. This implies that he is aware of the alternatives facing him and is capable of evaluating them. All information pertaining to the satisfaction that the consumer derives from various quantities of commodities is contained in his *utility function*.[5]

It seems clear that in order to continue developing a scientific paradigm, the Institutional economists must use their analytical tools to evaluate their own concepts, as well as the usefulness of the conceptual constructs of their orthodox counterparts. The debate referred to above seems to indicate that this is in fact an ongoing reexamination of the concept of the technological process. Notably absent is a similar reevaluation of Veblen's concept of "institutions" or "institutional behavior." Reevaluation of technology without a similar reevaluation of the concept of institutions must be looked upon as truncated analysis. Veblen was analyzing behavior as being made up of technological aspects in association with institutional aspects in a social context. This implies that the concept of "technology" only has meaning when used in conjunction with the concept of "institution." To reevaluate one without reevaluating the other may lead to a distorted view of the Institutionalists' contribution.

In an effort to rectify what I see as a serious omission from the debate, this article will reexamine the concept of "institution" and its relationship to the outcomes of the current discussion of technology, in the hope that this will lead to a clarification and refinement of the dichotomy.

Early Development

We begin with an examination of the evolutionary development of the concept of "institution." The logical place to start is with Veblen.

Veblen

Veblen extended and elaborated his definition of "institution" throughout his work. In an early work he spoke of institutions as aggregates of spiritual attitudes:

> The institutions are, in substance, prevalent habits of thought with respect to particular relations and particular functions of the individual and of the community; and the scheme of life, which is made up of the aggregate of institutions in force at a given time or at a given point in the development of any society, may, on the psychological side, be broadly characterized as a prevalent spiritual attitude or a prevalent theory of life.[6]

He extended that definition in another article: "As a matter of course, men order their lives by these principles and, practically, entertain no question of their stability and finality. That is what is meant by calling them institutions; they are settled habits of thought common to the generality of men."[7] In one of his last works he defined an institution as "of the nature of a usage which has become axiomatic and indispensable by habituation and general acceptance."[8] Veblen used many variations of the dichotomy, each tailored to the particular aspect of society he was analyzing.[9] But his concept of "institution" remains substantially intact and consistent throughout his analysis.

An important aspect of this definition is that by "institution" Veblen is referring to behavior patterns or functions that exhibit the characteristics he attributes to them in his definitions. These institutional behavior patterns take place in a structural context. While the behavior patterns and structural context are two aspects of the same phenomena, it seems clear that Veblen was interested primarily in analyzing the behavior patterns.

Other authors have referred to these behavior patterns as "function," and to the structural context as "structure." It must be kept in mind that this distinction between "structure" and "function" is an analytical one. Although behavior patterns have been described as resulting from "conscious, deliberate choice making on the part of people holding and using power to establish structure," through repetition the "institutions" become habitual.[10] The original conscious decision-making processes which brought them into being are forgotten, and the "'institutions" appear and are thought to be "natural" and "eternal."[11]

The sense in which these behavior patterns are habitual is that they are used but not questioned. Their authenticity or appropriateness to the circumstance in which they are employed is generally explained by recourse to common sense or tradition. The appeal to tradition for verification is tantamount to religious justification of questioned beliefs or behaviors. [12]

A second important aspect of Veblen's concept of "institution" is that institutions are a nondynamic factor in cultural development:

> It is to be noted then, although it may be a tedious truism, that the institutions of to-day—the present accepted scheme of life—do not entirely fit the situation of to-day. At the same time, men's present habits of thought tend to persist indefinitely, except as circumstances enforce a change. These institutions which have so been handed down, these habits of thought, points of view, mental attitudes and aptitudes, or what not, are therefore themselves a conservative factor. This is the factor of social inertia, conservatism. [13]

That Veblen's concept of "institutions" is part of an analysis of behavior on the cultural level is evident:

> To any modern scientist interested in economic phenomena, the chain of cause and effect in which any given phase of human culture is involved, as well as the cumulative changes wrought in the fabric of human conduct itself by the habitual activity of mankind, are matters of more engrossing and more abiding interest than the method of inference by which an individual is presumed invariably to balance pleasure and pain under given conditions that are presumed to be normal and variable. [14]

Hamilton

The next major development in the evolution of the "institution" concept occurred in the 1930s and 40s, in the work of R. A. Dixon and Walton Hamilton. [15] The analysis will center on Hamilton for two reasons. First, he is generally credited with naming Institutional Economics, and second, he made an explicit, in-depth attempt to define "institution." [16] This attempt at definition was probably a result of the danger Hamilton recognized in naming a branch of economics with a term that had a meaning and usage in the vernacular that did not correspond to the specific meaning that these particular economists attributed to it. [17]

Hamilton's concept of an institution is very complex. To see the concept in a processual context, we will begin by comparing Hamilton's definition with Veblen's. We can then see how Hamilton expanded Veblen's view of "institution."

It can easily be seen that Hamilton includes in his definition those patterns of behavior that Veblen identified as "institutions." Both Veblen and Hamilton agree that institutions are cultural constructs; according to Hamilton, "our culture is a synthesis—or at least an aggregation—of institutions. . . . The function of each is to set a pattern of behavior and to fix a zone of tolerance for an activity or complement of activities."[18] Both point out the role of habit and custom in institutions. Hamilton believed that the concept of institution "connotes a way of thought or action of some prevalence or permanence, which is embedded in the habits of a group or the customs of a people."[19] They also agree that compliance with the requirements of the institution is usually unquestioned, that "as long as it remains vital, men accommodate their actions to its detailed arrangements with little bother about its inherent nature or cosmic purpose."[20]

A vital institution is a behavior pattern that is organizing activities still of technological importance to the community. An institution that interfered with technologically essential activities would in fact eventually be questioned. This reflects Hamilton's notion of evolving institutions, which is dealt with in the next section. Even while acknowledging this difference Hamilton clearly recognized the aspect of culture Veblen called institutions.

There are also, however, two crucial differences in the usage of the term "institution" by Veblen and Hamilton. The first concerns the role of institutions in cultural change. As stated earlier, Veblen saw institutions as a nondynamic factor in cultural development. More specifically, changing technological circumstances force institutions to change; institutions do not generate changes within a culture. Instead the source of the cultural change is outside the institution and "enforces" a change in the institutional patterns.[21] Hamilton does not specifically disagree with this description of institutional change.[22] In fact, his statement that "as an institution develops within a culture it responds to changes in prevailing sense and reason" shows an undeniable similarity to Veblen's thinking.[23]

But while Hamilton does state that institutions change in response to changes in outside circumstances, he also allows for the possibility that change in the institution is a cause of change in the outside circumstances: "In this continuous process of the adaption of usage and arrangement to intellectual environment an active role is assumed by that body of ideas taken for granted which is called common sense. Because it determines the climate of opinion within which all others must live it is the dominant institution in society."[24] Hamilton also saw an institution as "a folkway, always new yet ever old, *directive* and responsive, *a spur to* and a check upon *change*, a creature of means and a master of ends."[25] This concept of an institution as "a spur to change" seems fundamentally different from Veblen's concept of institutions as a drag on cultural change.

This is consistent with the second crucial difference between Hamilton's and Veblen's definition of an institution, illustrated by Hamilton's statement: "Moreover the way of knowledge is itself an institution."[26] Veblen, however, would place "the way of knowledge" in the realm of that behavior he describes as "technology." Veblen's theory treats technological behavior as the dynamic element of cultural change. Hamilton's definition is much broader than Veblen's since he includes both Veblen's ''institutional'' behavior and ''technological'' behavior in his definition of ''institution.'' Since he includes Veblen's ''technology'' in his definition of ''institution,'' it follows that he would see institutions as a dynamic force in cultural change. But Veblen is analyzing the institutional *and* technological aspects of cultural behavior, while Hamilton includes both aspects in his definition of institutions, so it is clear that their concepts of institution are fundamentally different. What makes this important is that both definitions are in the literature of Institutional economics and both definitions affected later scholars. While the similarities are often noted or assumed, the differences between the usages are not.[27]

Ayres

Historically and analytically the next major development of the concept of ''institution'' was to come in the work of C. E. Ayres. Ayres's concept clearly represents an extension of Veblen's.[28] Ayres is in agreement with Veblen in that he emphasizes the analysis of ''institutional'' behavior patterns rather than of social structures. While ''institutions'' are both functional and structural, Veblen and Ayres emphasize the functional rather than structural aspects. For Ayres, ''the term 'institution' is not a structural category. That is, it does not refer merely to the division of the total substance of society into its constituent parts. It is, rather, a functional category. As such it has reference to a certain type of social organization, or certain aspect of social behavior, which is qualitatively different from another aspect.''[29] Ayres also takes the Veblenian view of the role of institutions in social change: ''By virtue of its peculiar character, the institutional function is essentially static. In the process of social change, institutional function plays a negative part. It resists change.''[30]

Like Veblen, Ayres is trying to separate out and analyze a particular aspect of culture that is nondynamic and habit-oriented. Ayres also recognizes the danger of using the word ''institution'' to denote this aspect of culture.[31] He points out that ''no word is more frequently or more vaguely used in contemporary social science than 'institution,' ''[32] and that ''it is not necessary to be an accomplished scholar to realize that we use this term very loosely in common speech.''[33]

To rectify the confusion over the term ''institution,'' Ayres suggests a look back to Veblen. He does this by using the term ''ceremonial function'' to describe that aspect of culture that he and Veblen are trying to separate out, previously denoted by the term ''institution.''[34] A great many Institutionalists in the Veblenian tradition followed suit and the Veblenian dichotomy became the ceremonial-technological distinction.

This substitution of ''ceremonial function'' for ''institution'' had two major effects. It eliminated the vagueness associated with the term ''institution,'' because ''ceremonial'' does not have such common usage or a different vernacular meaning.[35] It also eliminated confusing associations with Walton Hamilton's wider conception of "institutions," also in use at this time.

Ayres also made a major contribution by way of making more explicit some aspects of the ceremonial function. He notes that "one peculiar feature which 'typical' institutions all seem to exhibit is that of determination of authorities. . . . Institutional authority is authority, defined and supported and limited by custom."[36] This authority organizes society into a hierarchical structure of privilege and subservience. The hierarchical structure persists because of habit and a ceremonial verification system: "Mores are always accompanied by legends; and these legends, of which every community has so rich a stock, invariably point to a moral. The mores are the morals to which the legends point; and the legends do not merely tell a story. The story which they tell is invariably a mythical explanation of the legendary reasons for the mores."[37]

These mythical explanations are believed as an act of faith and are beyond question, since they occurred in the ancient past, and were unique events. Ayres spent a large portion of his prolific career expanding the ceremonial-technological distinction.[38] Further examination of this distinction is unfortunately outside the scope of this article.

Foster

The next important contribution grows out of the work of a student of C. E. Ayres, J. Fagg Foster. Foster is associated with the so-called oral tradition in Institutional economics. Since Foster has published very little, we must look at definitions of "institution" attributed to him by his students.

In his recent book *The Discretionary Economy*, Marc Tool attributes the following definition to Foster: "The term institution means any prescribed or proscribed pattern of correlated behavior or attitude widely agreed upon among a group of persons organized to carry on some particular purpose."[39] Another student of Foster's, Paul D. Bush, defines institution in a recent paper as "a set of socially prescribed patterns of correlated behavior."[40] A third student of Foster's, Louis Junker, in an unpublished manuscript quoted Foster defining institution as "prescribed patterns of correlated human behavior with (a) instrumental aspects and (b) ceremonial aspects."[41]

This definition by Foster is, or at least allows, a more expansive view of institutions, permitting the definition in some ways to recover some of the flavor of the usage we have associated with Walton Hamilton. This expansion of the definition was mentioned by Junker in an earlier work:

> Clarification of this issue must be ascribed to Professor J. Fagg Foster of the University of Denver, who has broken down institutional structures into their instrumental aspects (after John Dewey) and their ceremonial aspects. This broadens Veblen's viewpoint considerably because he did not *concentrate* on this

point but seemed to be always contrasting obstructionary institutions against dynamic technology only. Thus Foster is making amends to Veblen's analysis by accounting for social behavior patterns that are in rapport with modern technology, and thus are efficient organizational structures. Veblen merely hints around the issue at times.[42]

Foster's ceremonial-instrumental dichotomy is such a significant refinement of the institution-technology dichotomy that it can be considered qualitatively different. This "new" version of the Veblenian dichotomy eliminated problems that arose consistently in the use of the institution-technology dichotomy. It also allows for the application of the dichotomy to new areas of inquiry about social behavior, as well as allowing us to be more precise about our reevaluation of past analysis. For example, it totally eliminates the structure-function problem. If someone uses "institution" in the structural sense, the ceremonial functions of this particular institutional structure can still be analyzed without the semantic difficulty encountered previously.

The new version also eliminates a similar difficulty on the "technology" side of the dichotomy. Technological behavior has been described by one prominent Institutionalist as "organized intelligence in action."[43] This process is considerably more than simply tools and tool skills, but Institutionalists have at times allowed themselves to slip back and forth from the "organized-intelligence" definition to the "technology-as-tools" definition. By substituting "instrumental behavior" for "technology," this slipperiness can be avoided.

Possibly the most significant aspect of Foster's refinement is that he isolated that aspect of culture that Veblen wished to analyze and called it ceremonial behavior, in addition to isolating those behaviors that oppose ceremonial behavior and calling them instrumental behavior. This allowed the dichotomy to be used as a tool of analysis not only to evaluate human behavior and identify its instrumental and ceremonial qualities, but also to evaluate their earlier version of the dichotomy itself. [. . .]

Bush and Junker, both students of Foster, have been simultaneously developing the notion of ceremonial encapsulation of technology using the "new" dichotomy.[44] Junker describes this phenomena:

> Spurious "technological" developments, on the other hand, are those which are encapsulated by a ceremonial power system whose main concern is to control the use, direction, and consequences of that development while simultaneously serving as the institutional vehicle for defining the limits and boundaries upon that technology through special domination efforts of the legal system, the property system, and the information system. These limits and boundaries are generally set to best serve the institutions seeking such control. . . . This is the way the ruling and dominant institutions of society maintain and try to extend their hegemony over the lives of people.[45]

Junker goes on to point out that this is not consistent with promoting the continuity of the life process but instead "it serves to shackle mankind."[46] Bush's development of this concept is essentially the same, while using slightly different terminology.

It is significant that the concept of ceremonial encapsulation of technology is being developed by Institutionalists using the "new" dichotomy. Using the "old" dichotomy the concept of "ceremonial" technology has no meaning. Using the "new" dichotomy it can be analyzed in the manner of Junker and Bush. This illustrates the fact that the "new" dichotomy leads to innovative social analysis in areas previously neglected, though not ignored, by Institutionalists. [. . .]

The meaning of "technology" in the vernacular is associated with implements and their application. The Institutionalists' conception of the "scientific-technological process" is larger and more encompassing. Even if Institutionalists focus on the correct version for their analysis, the term "technology" has a tendency to shift the focus of the analysis to techniques.

One problem resulting from this is difficulty in correctly identifying the problem or in asking the correct question. The scientific-technological process is a problem-solving process. If we focus on tools, scientific apparatus, and techniques, as we are apt to do in our complex society, we sometimes define the problems in terms of the techniques we use to solve them. An example of this in economics is when economists discuss at great length in the literature the use of sophisticated mathematical techniques to solve problems of choice involving risk by maximizing expected utility, while ignoring the issue of the meaningfulness of the concept of maximizing expected utility. We have concentrated on the use of a sophisticated tool while ignoring whether the application we have chosen is appropriate.

This emphasis on technique is like two individuals arguing over whether an ocean liner or a rowboat is more appropriate for crossing a lake, without ever considering walking around it. They have missed the point that the real question is how to get from one point to the other; emphasizing the techniques leads to misidentifying the question. Since we evaluate solutions to problems on the basis of all their consequences, we cannot properly evaluate all the consequences without examining all the alternatives.

A similar misidentification of the correct question can be found on the "institution" side of the "old" dichotomy. This occurs when "institution" in the structural sense is confused with institutional behavior. For example, if we identify the nuclear family or the Catholic Church as institutions, we have a tendency to overlook the fact that these structures are made up of technological (instrumental) behaviors as well as institutional (ceremonial) behaviors.

The dual usage problem may also lead to evaluating behaviors out of context. The best solution to a problem cannot be found if the social milieu in which the problem occurs is not considered completely. This is not a relativist position; the social milieu does not determine the correct or better solution to a problem. But all the consequences of proposed solutions cannot be evaluated without considering the environment in which this proposed action is to take place. This has not been a significant problem among Institutionalists; in fact their explicit consideration of the social milieu is one of the main things that differentiates them from their orthodox counterparts. But the "new" dichotomy, particularly through the concept of ceremonial encapsulation, makes this difference more pronounced and more explicit.

Implications

These problems, present in the old dichotomy *to whatever degree*, have achieved a crucial level of importance in recent years. The Institutional economist in the Veblen-Ayres tradition evaluates actions on the basis of all the effects of that action on the continuity of the life process. This evaluation process obviously requires the best information possible about potential consequences. That methodology which best makes us aware and anticipates consequences has always been the most desirable. We have recently been reminded that it is crucial.

The revelation in the last few years of the extent of the consequences of dumping toxic waste into the environment in general, and our water supply in particular, has served to remind us of the importance of unanticipated or ignored consequences. It has also served to illustrate the even greater importance of anticipating these consequences, because some have the quality of being irreversible. The irreversibility of some consequences is not new, but the scale of these consequences is unprecedented. Their destructive capacity has expanded to encompass the entire planet. [. . .] We discovered these consequences and the process of solving these problems is underway.

Discovering these consequences was crucial to the continuity of the life process. The improvement and refinement of our analytical tools to better anticipate consequences of this type, and to discover ways of solving problems resulting from our actions, is the most important task before the human race.[47]

The current discussion among Institutionalists on the methodological questions characterized in this paper as a conflict between the "old" and "new" dichotomy is in fact an attempt to refine their tools of analysis. The purpose of this paper has been to reemphasize that the dichotomy is an evolving tool of analysis and that it is necessary to frame current controversies among Institutionalists in terms of the meaning of the evolving dichotomy for future analysis. If what I have described as the "new" dichotomy is a superior tool of analysis, it should be used. This can only be determined if the controversy over the meaning of the dichotomy is addressed as a crucial methodological question, rather than on an issue-by-issue basis.

Notes

1. For a rather extensive listing see Marc R. Tool, "Philosophy of Neo-Institutionalism: Veblen, Dewey, and Ayres," Ph.D. diss., University of Colorado, 1954.

2. The generality of this particular formulation is attested to by the fact that later Institutionalists have seen fit to spend a great deal of time defining these particular terms, rather than other formulations, when writing economics texts. See, for example, C. E. Ayres, *The Industrial Economy* (Cambridge, Mass.: Riverside Press, 1952), p. 42; W. Nelson Peach, *Principles of Economics* (Homewood, Ill.: Richard D. Irwin, 1960), p. 10; Marc R. Tool, *The Discretionary Economy* (Santa Monica: Goodyear, 1979), p. 73.

3. For a representative sample of this discussion see the exchange between Hayden and DeGregori in *Journal of Economic Issues* 14 (1980).

4. This discussion is drawn from Jacob Bronowski's discussion of genuine knowledge in his book *The Origins of Knowledge and Imagination* (New Haven: Yale University Press, 1978).

5. J. Henderson and R. Quandt, *Micro Economic Theory: A Mathematical Approach* (New York: McGraw-Hill, 1971), p. 6 (emphasis in original).

6. Thorstein Veblen, *The Theory of the Leisure Class* (New York: Modern Library, 1934), p. 190.

7. Thorstein Veblen, *The Place of Science in Modern Civilization and Other Essays* (New York: Viking, 1919), p. 239.

8. Thorstein Veblen, *Absentee Ownership and Business Enterprise in Recent Times* (Boston: Beacon, 1967), p. 101.

9. Tool, *Philosophy of Neo-Institutionalism*.

10. Tool, *The Discretionary Economy*, p. 75.

11. This discussion is drawn from Tool's *The Discretionary Economy*, pp. 73–78. What we are concerned with in this context is Veblen's interest in the habitual nature of behavior patterns. I find Tool's discussion to be consistent with Veblen's views, but it should be recognized that Tool's analysis expands and extends Veblen's analysis significantly.

12. An excellent analysis of the religious character of explanations based on "tradition" is provided in Lord Raglan's *The Hero: A Study in Tradition, Myth, and Drama* (New York: Vintage, 1956), particularly part 1.

13. Veblen, *The Leisure Class*, p. 191.

14. Veblen, *The Place of Science*, p. 191.

15. Russell A. Dixon, *Economic Institutions and Cultural Change* (New York and London: McGraw-Hill, 1941), pp. 3–30; Walton Hamilton, "Institutions," *Encyclopedia of the Social Sciences*, vol. 7 (New York: Macmillan, 1932), pp. 84–89.

16. Walton Hamilton, "The Institutional Approach to Economic Theory," *American Economic Review* 9 (1919); Hamilton, "Institutions."

17. Hamilton, "The Institutional Approach."

18. Hamilton, "Institutions," p. 84.

19. Ibid.

20. Ibid., p. 87.

21. Veblen, *The Leisure Class*, pp. 190–98.

22. In fact R. A. Dixon, in his *Economic Institutions and Cultural Change*, uses Hamilton's definition of institutions, but quotes Veblen (see note 21) on institutional change, and sees the two as completely compatible.

23. Hamilton, "Institutions," p. 85.

24. Ibid.

25. Ibid., p. 89 (emphasis added).

26. Ibid., p. 88.

27. See, for example, John R. Commons, *The Economics of Collective Action* (New York: Macmillan, 1950), p. 21; Peach, *Principles of Economics*, p. 76, for definitions that incorporate both Veblen's and Hamilton's usage; also Dixon, *Economic Institutions*, ch. 1. The differences in the definitions are noted in D. Hamilton, *Evolutionary Economics* (Albuquerque: University of New Mexico Press, 1974), pp. 76–79.

28. C. E. Ayres, *Science: The False Messiah and Holier than Thou* (Clifton, N.J.: Augustus M. Kelley, 1973). See particularly the introduction, "Prolegomenon to Institutionalism."

29. C. E. Ayres, *The Industrial Economy* (Cambridge, Mass.: Houghton Mifflin; The Riverside Press, 1952), pp. 42–43.

30. Ibid., p. 49.

31. This is characteristic of Ayres's early work. A shift has been noted by some writers. See Marc Tool, "A Social Value Theory in Neo-institutional Economics," *Journal of Economic Issues* 11 (1977): 823. See particularly note 75 on p. 845. This shift is to a view similar to J. Fagg Foster's. I would like to acknowledge my debt to one of the referees for pointing this out in a review of an earlier draft.

32. C. E. Ayres, *The Theory of Economic Progress* (Kalamazoo: New Issues Press, Western Michigan University, 1978), p. 178.

33. Ayres, *The Industrial Economy*, p. 42.

34. The innovation by Ayres was not in the use of the term "ceremonial." Veblen used this term in *Imperial Germany and the Industrial Revolution* (New York: Viking, 1939). The innovative aspect is his consistent use of "ceremonial" in place of "institution" in the Veblenian dichotomy.

35. This type of problem was not completely eliminated, but appears to be reduced. See Ayres, *The Theory of Economic Progress*, p. 156.

36. Ayres, *The Industrial Economy*, p. 43.

37. "Mores" is William Graham Summers's term; Ayres sees it as similar, but not identical, to "institution." See also Ayres, *The Industrial Economy*, p. 44.

38. For an excellent discussion of C. E. Ayres's contribution see Louis Junker, *The Social and Economic Thought of Clarence Edwin Ayres* (Ann Arbor: University Microfilms, 1962).

39. Tool, *The Discretionary Economy*, p. 74.

40. Paul D. Bush, "The Ceremonial Incapsulation of Capital Formation in the American Economy," paper read before the Economics Section at the Annual Meeting of the Western Social Sciences Association, Lake Tahoe, Nevada, April 27, 1979), p. 2.

41. Louis J. Junker, "Institutionalism and the Criteria of Development," mimeographed (Kalamazoo: Western Michigan University, ca. 1969), p. 10.

42. Junker, *Social and Economic Thought of Ayres*, p. 46.

43. This definition of technology is from the lectures of Professor David Hamilton of the University of New Mexico.

44. Bush, "Ceremonial Encapsulation," p. 6; Louis J. Junker, "Markings on the Nature, Scope, and Radical Implications of the Ceremonial-Instrumental Dichotomy in Institutional Analysis," paper read before the Economics Section at the Annual Meeting of the Western Social Sciences Association, April 24, 1980.

45. Ibid., pp. 3–4.

46. Ibid., p. 4. I would contend that what I have called the "new" dichotomy is in fact the "radical" implications of the dichotomy to which Junker's paper refers.

47. Anne Mayhew provides an excellent analysis of these types of problems and their implications on the Ayresian view of technology in her article "Ayresian Technology, Technological Reasoning, and Doomsday," *Journal of Economic Issues* 15 (1981): 513–20.

Value and Its Corollaries

MARC TOOL

This selection is an excerpt from Tool's book, The Discretionary Economy. *It is a comprehensive statement of instrumental value theory as applied by Institutional economists. Institutional economics is explicitly value laden, in contrast to Neoclassical orthodoxy which claims to be value free. Tool explains the value principle underlying Institutional inquiry and explores several related corollaries that Institutionalists see as necessary conditions for progress and problem solving.*

It is important to note that Institutionalists totally reject the positive/normative dualism. Institutionalists are not arguing that economics should be a normative science rather than a positive science; they are arguing that all *science is a value-laden process.*

Social Value Identified

[. . .] Throughout the foregoing, we have repeatedly asked "which direction is forward" in a societal setting in which protracted problems seem not to yield to ism-ideology answers. We posed therewith the problem of choice and inevitably the problem of criteria of choice. We have now arrived at a point at which we can (1) provisionally advance a nonideological principle of social value, (2) offer some account of its explicit and implicit elements and referential content, and (3) draw distinctions and contrasts with other value principles. We then suggest in the following part of the chapter some corollary concepts of the instrumental value principle and representative applications to areas of contemporary revolutionary unrest.

(1) We now affirm that that direction is forward which provides for *the continuity of human life and the noninvidious re-creation of community through the instrumental use of knowledge.*[1] We consider the foregoing to be a criterion of judgment, a social-value principle, which is general in its relevance to the universe of the social process, to the functional components of that process (economy, polity), and to choices among institutional forms which organize that process. We suggest further that the resolution of political and economic problems in particular (in the sense in which "resolution" can be held to have rational meaning) probably requires the use of this criterion in lieu of other proffered theories of value. We remind ourselves that the only serious grounds on which

Marc Tool, "Value and Its Corollaries," chapter 15 of *The Discretionary Economy* (Santa Monica: Goodyear Press, 1979), pp. 291–314.

political economists for centuries have claimed significance for their work have been its alleged relevance to the resolution of real problems facing real people in real political economies. We respectfully acknowledge and join that tradition.

(2) Consider now some explicit and implicit elements of this instrumental principle of social (economic and political) value. *Explicit* aspects include the following:

Continuity: The whole of the human experience is with process, the social process. There is no human history except of evolutionary movement of human organisms and of the culture such persons create and preserve. "Continuity" in the value premise is grounded in this fact and asserts the obvious as an "ought"— that the continuance of human life is a precondition for the pursuit of all earthly concerns including the creation and use of all social and value theory. As Sidney S. Alexander has observed, "effectiveness is the first virtue [of social institutions]. The social system must work, it must permit at least the physical survival of the society. The evolutionary, if not the moral, priority of effectiveness . . . is illustrated in the history of mankind."[2]

Providing for continuity implies, beyond the obvious, an awareness of conditions which positively foster human life, indeed which reflect a this-worldly reverence for human life. Included is a deference to human potential and developmental capabilities. The social process is the locus of value[3]; it does not define social value. Asserting continuity of the social process is nevertheless critical, if commonplace. [. . .]

Re-creation of community: Here the intent is to make very clear that human life is feasible only in the context of culture. "We are members one of another" in a community in which institutions pattern (prescribe and proscribe) our lives. Re-creating community means reconstituting the structural fabric of that social order to provide for continuity by utilizing effectively the stock of human wit and wisdom. Since all people already reside in community, the task is to *re*-create. No human starts from ground zero socially or culturally; individuals are born into communities which are going concerns with language, custom, and order already affirmed in some definitive form.

Implied also is that this criterion is intended for use in choosing among and between institutional forms. Which prescriptions are now understood to be obsolete in view of current knowledge? Which patterns of correlated behavior have abandoned their original instrumental functions and have become vehicles for the retention of status or the exercise of power? Does not the negative connotation of *bureaucracy* derive from this circumstance?

Thus, "re-creation of community" delimits the universe of applicability of this instrumental value principle to the realm (mainly) of *social* choice. Under review here is a principle of social value. We are concerned with the character of the community and the impact it makes upon the lives of its constituent members. The principle may be found also to have relevance as a criterion in judging personal or individual conduct, but that is not our central concern at this point.

Noninvidious: This term speaks to the character of community just mentioned. Recall, Veblen used the term *invidious* to refer to "a comparison of persons with a view to rating and grading them in respect of relative worth or value. . . . An invidious comparison is a process of valuation of persons in respect of worth."[4] We at various points have remarked about the invidious use of race, sex, ethnicity, color, wealth, ownership, rank, age, power, etc., in one or another of yesterday's isms. Here we are saying that the invidious use of any distinction is to be avoided in the application of reliable knowledge to the re-creation of community to assure continuity. Here the inherent potential and worth of every human being is affirmed. We are confirming the fact of human reason and the fact of the historic concern for continuity and community as elements in an alternative value principle. [. . .]

Noninvidiousness permits qualitative judgments. Does a proposed structural change enhance dignity and sense of self-worth of individuals[5] or does it erode or destroy by denigration and discrimination? Where the latter occurs, the opportunities for instrumental involvement of such persons are seriously curtailed or eliminated. Their capacity to help re-create community is impaired. We return to this point below.

The instrumental use of knowledge: This phrase is intended to incorporate the idea that knowledge which is reliable is instrumental to an understanding of social reality and ought to be employed efficiently to relevant areas of human problems and experience.[6]

Reliable knowledge, recall, is a product of rational inquiry. Through recourse to factual subject matter and the imaginative and guiding use of hypotheses, causal relations in phenomena are explained when "conjugate correspondence"[7] is established between theory and fact, between concept and evidence. Such correspondence yields tentative truth.

Reliable knowledge includes the whole fund or stock of evidentially grounded, logically consistent recognitions of means-consequence connections evolving incrementally as a knowledge continuum. It includes warrantable knowledge of the natural and social sciences, of such folk wisdom as reason and evidence confirm, of cognitive recognitions in and out of libraries. It is the aggregative, cumulative product of tool and idea contributions running back beyond written records. Recognized is the fact that new knowledge represents recast and/or reconstituted old knowledge to which a modest additional fragment of demonstrable fact or insight has been added.[8] Such knowledge is reliable not because it is unchanging or absolute, but because it is credible in the sense that it is logically cohesive and evidentially warranted.

The reference to "instrumental use" of reliable knowledge in the value principle affirms the relevance of such knowledge in the identification and resolution of human problems. We call on the reliable knowledge of the medical doctor when bodily pain appears. We seek the reliable knowledge of economists when price levels vault up at rates of 2 to 5 percent per month. We request the reliable knowledge and council of political scientists and jurists when Constitutional crises confront the community and threaten the basic acceptance of the specified structure and function of governmental institutions. However, there is no implication from this use of knowledge that something ought to be done simply because it can be done, scientifically and technologically. We do not intend the intrusion of any kind of technological determinism. We would disallow all such inferences. The fact that an H-bomb could be built does not necessarily infer that it should have been built.

Reference to "instrumental use" conditions and constrains the use of reliable knowledge to that which is pertinent and compatible with the remainder of the principle. At issue is the fittedness or appropriateness of means chosen to serve ends-in-view, recognizing that means determine ends-in-view. [. . .] There is no presumption, moreover, of perfect knowledge or foreknowledge. Rather, the principle embodies an insistence that economic and political problems be identified and approached as a matter of a difference between what our reliable knowledge indicates is possible and desirable and what current practice shows is going on instead. Having been expelled from the front door, no positivism is to be permitted to sneak back in through an unguarded rear door. We suggest that reliable knowledge can and does include material usually characterized as normative. Again we reject the fact-value dichotomy.

Implicit in the principle of social value identified as "the continuity of human life and the noninvidious re-creation of community through the instrumental use of knowledge" are two additional elements:

First, it must be evident that this instrumental value principle assumes that human beings in the social dimensions of their lives do indeed have genuine problems of choice to which a social value principle is pertinent. We dissent from the view that people are wholly conditioned organisms for whom real choice is an illusion.[9] People do think and choose, and their choices make a difference. Their judgments are not wholly preconditioned or predetermined. No great defense is needed for the proposition that every legislative body in (say) the United States is in fact engaged in rewriting the rules with which people's lives are ordered. The judgments of legislators, governors, and presidents do make a substantive difference. The rules enacted may or may not be blatantly invidious, but they are the result of decisions overtly made. Volition is assumed to exist. Men and women demonstrably are discretionary agent-actors.

Second, it must also be evident that this principle of social value draws upon and is designedly relevant only to the realm of existential fact and experience. No recourse is made anywhere to special kinds of intuitive knowledge, to divine presence or revelation, to ideal and unknowable essences and powers.

This instrumental value principle purports to be the formulation of a criterion which in fact has been used historically since time out of mind. As a minute-long exercise, think back over the normative terms used to characterize leaders and led, and countries and communities. What has been meant by labels of "wise," "able," or "just," applied to leaders? What has been meant by captions of "reform," of "progress," or of "development"? Did not the "reforms" of the New Deal, the "progress" of the New Frontier, and the "development" of emerging nations in recent decades refer at bottom to the quest for continuity and instrumental effectiveness of policies to cope with real problems in ways to restore community and enhance human dignity? It would seem so.

In one sense, then, what is being proposed here is scarcely novel at all; it may in the minds of some be regarded as commonplace or even as conservative. In any case, it is to be reviewed and tested in the bright sunlight of stated assumptions, of open analysis, and of testable conclusions. It draws not at all on nonpublic realms of knowing or nonreasoned patterns of defense. It has little to suggest to those seeking psychic trips, introspective revelations, or "getting one's head on straight." There is no recourse to anyone's guru. We seek a principle drawn from existential fact about human experience. We submit that a revision and replacement (when it is necessary) will have to be drawn from the same universe of reason grounded in hard evidence.

(3) Consider next some contrasts and distinctions between social value as "the continuity of human life and the noninvidious re-creation of community through the instrumental use of knowledge" and other approaches and formulations. Our intent is to characterize and distinguish, and to stimulate and provoke.

First, of great importance is the recognition that this instrumental value principle, unlike the normative ideologies of capitalism, socialism, communism, or fascism, contains no particular institutional structure. It neither directs nor implies movement in the *direction* of a preconceived set of institutional forms. The oft used expression here of Walton Hamilton's—"Which direction is forward"[10]—refers to the need for making and remaking institutional choices. As he makes very clear, the expression does not suggest change to approximate an ism; exactly the contrary is intended. The social-value principle differentiates an approvable *condition* from one that is not.[11] It does not specify nor imply the structural changes that will be required to resolve problems and re-create community. This principle permits analysis of what has gone "wrong" with existing prescriptive or proscriptive arrangements; it does not impose an ism-defined adjustment as the solution. In consequence, this value principle is fundamentally different from those grounded in yesterday's isms; it is intended for use in lieu of ism criteria.

As a corollary, the "constants" which are implied in this alternative value principle have to do with procedures—open inquiry, honest reporting, public testing, empirical checks, tentative status of truth seeking, etc.—not with the elevation of favored institutional forms into the role of criteria. For example, this principle of value, as such, neither supports (as do the capitalists) nor attacks (as do the Marxists) the institution of private ownership of productive plant and equipment. The "ought" is not perceived as the fuller achievement of a free-enterprise capitalism nor of a public-ownership socialism. We can stand outside all of yesterday's isms and begin to make judgments of *condition* looking to functional performance or its lack instead of *direction* toward or away from somebody's ism.

Second, this social-value principle neither defers to nor depends upon wants, tastes, preferences. It enshrines none; it permits judgments among and between them by permitting examination of their character and of the consequences when they are satisfied—a blockage classical or Neoclassical theorists or ideologists seem not to have been able to surmount. There is no elevation here of given wants, whatever they are, into a value referent. There is no ethical relativism of "about tastes there is no disputin'," nor indifference to what it is that "makes people happy" (harassing blacks, putting women down, community organization, listening to Beethoven's Seventh Symphony).

Third, although the matter is arguable, this value principle is designed to be general and inclusive in the universe of its intended use—problem solving in political economy. Although the principle obviously does assume an achievement motivation and human concern about problems, it is not meant to be provincial or ethnocentric. It would seem to cater to no particular nation or people or subgroup. [. . .] The social-value principle here recommended is not the product of a singular national group. The United States has no monopoly on "virtue" so conceived. The principle raises the power and status of no group at the expense of another group.

Fourth, social value as "the continuity of human life and the noninvidious recreation of community through the instrumental use of knowledge" will not serve, we think, as a mask or screen concealing the desires of a few to rule the many. We intend to offer no glib apologia for an elitist economic and/or political power system. On the contrary, the reverse is intended, that is, to provide a criterion of appraisal which will assist with the unmasking and unmaking of power centers which remain unaccountable to those touched significantly by such power.

Fifth, clearly this instrumental value principle offers no utopian solution; it is no panacea. It is no magic elixir which if taken in prescribed doses will clear up economic and political aches and ills without inquiry and vigorous social action. There is no End in sight and none that can be brought into view. There are no ultimate "goods" implied and no "once-and-for-all" ideal solutions recommended. Indeed, one of the several purposes of this work is to argue the irrelevance of any such effort. Economic and political analysis which employs this non-ism value principle will be very mundane, not necessarily ordinary, but decidedly impure in the ritualistic academic sense. Practitioners will chew their pencils, risk ulcers, experience anguish and despair, get sore feet, and probably get their hands dirty. They may also experience the exhilaration that results from purposeful work that makes a difference.

Sixth, and finally, this value principle offers no escape from hard, arduous inquiry; it compels intellectual tool creation, theory building, and evidence compiling and evaluating. It offers no shortcuts, easy answers, or simple solutions. It is no recipe of ingredients which can be combined to produce the perfect product. It has no answer page at the end of the book. This criterion of judgment is a principle to use as a tool of inquiry; it is fashioned to perform the function of serving as a vehicle which allows choices to be rationally and evidentially made. Its universe of application is the social process; it is of central significance in economic and political analysis.

As with all conceptual tools, the test of the principle's adequacy is not a matter of the status or standing of its proposers, nor of its longevity, nor of its ism-ideological correspondence or lack thereof. The test, rather, is one of determining whether or not this value principle will function to identify problems which are instances of breakdown in the instrumental functioning of existing institutions—blockages, disjunctions, obsolescences, disruptions, terminations, violent outbreaks, and the like. Further, will this principle suggest avenues of inquiry which will enable creative minds to recommend revisions to reestablish some measure of functional effectiveness in ways which restore community and enhance the discretionary dignity of those affected? Treating people noninvidiously enhances discretionary dignity. The proof of the pudding is in the eating, 'tis said. The significance of this social-value principle will be determined in the context of its use.

Value Corollaries and Applications

Consider now some extensions and applications of the social-value theory herein proposed:

Understanding of our alternative value principle, the continuity of human life and the noninvidious re-creation of community through the instrumental use of knowledge, will be enhanced if we explore some derivative and corollary criteria which, we believe, are pertinent to the making of choices in the several areas generating revolutionary unrest—poverty and the economic revolution, elitism and the political revolution, discrimination and the racial and sexual revolutions, and environmental degradation and the ecological crisis.

(1) A corollary ethical concept for the economic revolution is the criterion of *instrumental efficiency.*

The term *efficiency* may immediately come under some heavy criticism by persons who see in it a shorthand caption for an amoral, computerized, dehumanizing, technological economy that is indifferent to human interests and compassion. Such an inference is not unreasonable as one reflects on the character of some recent use of nuclear technology, military technology, and computer technology which may appear intimidative and threatening. But *efficiency* can be recast and salvaged in a way which, we think, need not engender the bitterness and blanching its use has sometimes evoked. With the introduction below of certain constraints and clarifications, the term can be salvaged and its use as a derivative criterion delineated.

Interest here focuses especially upon the relevance of instrumental efficiency as a criterion in determining the level, character, and distribution of production. Whatever and wherever the economy, ideological characteristics notwithstanding, the economic function of producing and distributing real income must be performed tolerably well. "Tolerably" means acceptable or endurable to the people involved; "well" means effective use of resources as the latter are defined by currently available knowledge and its application as technology.

In determining the *level* of output of real income and the technological manner of its creation, *instrumental efficiency* utilizes, but harnesses and constrains, technical efficiency and directs its use to the service of inclusive human and humane purposes including problem solving through structural change in the economy. The harnessing and constraining of technical efficiency is accomplished by the override role of continuity, community re-creation, and noninvidiousness in the general criterion of social value described above. Technical efficiency is sought *provided* it is compatible with, nonsubversive of, these components of instrumental value theory.

Technical efficiency denotes extracting maximum output from resource inputs (physical, financial, institutional, technological). Recourse to technically efficient means of making steel via the oxygen process; technically efficient means of extracting maximum BTUs from coal; technically efficient means of macromanagement of the economy for full utilization of the available labor force; technically efficient means of organizing workers in productive teams; technically efficient means of distributing incomes, taxing incomes, or providing continuity in receipt of incomes illustrate the point. Economies ought to operate efficiently in this sense so long as the overriding criteria are not violated.

The concern here is with the appropriateness of means or tools used in achieving ends or results. What is the "right" tool (physical or conceptual), the instrumentally efficient tool, to accomplish the task at hand? At issue is the matter of pertinence. Is a hand saw useful in repairing a pocket computer? Is Say's Law (supply creates its own demand) an admissible conceptual tool in explaining determinants of aggregate income and employment? Is the positive-normative dichotomy mandated as a philosophical tool in addressing the normative problems of choice? The instrumental efficiency of the tool is determined in the context of its use by answering two questions: Were anticipated consequences in fact realized? Are the consequences approvable with reference to instrumental value theory?

In determining the level of output, then, the instrumental efficiency criterion calls for the most skillful use of appropriate conceptual tools in defining problems (e.g., of structural unemployment and/or administered inflation) and of formulating options as institutional change to correct for such problems.

However, this concept of instrumental efficiency does not, for example, validate the "growth of output at any cost" position. It is not exempt from judging the environmental consequences. To be so would violate the continuity principle as an overriding constraint. The efficient mining of the soil's fertility, efficient clear-cutting of timber, efficient exhaustion of fossil fuels, although feasible in a technical sense, may not in a larger context be tolerable at all. One must judge the *consequences* of such efficient use of knowledge and technology not on a short-term particularistic and/or pecuniary basis, but on a longer-term, cultural continuity, general community basis.

Similarly, the instrumentally efficient use of human resources does *not* connote the "scientific management" of people as developed by Frederick W. Taylor and his more recent devotees.[12] To do so would violate the continuity and noninvidiousness principles as overriding constraints. Treating people as machines, fragmenting work into simple chores and defining jobs thereon, making and insensitively applying time-and-motion studies of work requirements, denying workers' participation in determining rules governing work, psychologically manipulating workers into conformist roles, and the like tend to dehumanize work and alienate workers.

Instrumentally efficient use of labor means, in contrast, a catering to and encouragement of the fullest development of thinking skills, manipulative abilities, self-directing inclinations, and other distinctively human potentialities in the production process.[13] The human being is the premier resource. Creativity, imagination, motivation, and sense of achievement and of communal commitment ought to be enhanced by the work experience, not suppressed by it.

The instrumental efficiency criterion applies also to judgments in the realm of the *character* of production. What goods and services will be produced? What is to be the composition of the output mix? What array of occupations shall constitute the labor force?

Most are familiar with the conventionial version of this problem: determining the civilian-military product mix and the consumer-producer good mix. Even these conventional judgments, of course, compel the application of normative principles. When, if ever, is it instrumentally efficient to produce war goods? What pattern of capital-goods formation is optimum? What kinds of consumer goods should be made available? The answers will not necessarily come easily.

When, for instance, communities are compelled to set priorities in the character of production because of substantial interruptions in the flow of real income occasioned by natural disasters, warfare, political upheavals, and the like, the application of the instrumental-efficiency criterion would suggest that, for example:

a. basic foods be provided before goods for ceremonial display or invidious emulation

b. auto factories be rebuilt before gambling casinos and race tracks

c. skilled medical technicians be trained before bond salespeople

d. military production be confined to literally defensive operations only

e. houses and apartments be rebuilt before luxury second homes

f. social overhead capital expenditures (transport, communication and educational facilities, for example) be given a higher priority than display edifices for political elites.[14]

The extent to which the foregoing sounds approvingly commonplace is an indication of the degree to which the instrumental-efficiency criterion is already a part of judgmental habits. [. . .]

Finally, the subsidiary criterion of instrumental efficiency applies also to the *distribution* of production. This criterion will not sustain or defend marked inequality of income distribution. As most are aware, in any exchange economy, money-income receipt largely determines the extent and character of individual economic choices. Deprivation of income means deprivation of genuine economic choices. Since effective choice is essential for effective economic participation, the nonavailability of adequate flows of money income to significant portions of the community dramatically impairs their instrumental efficiency. Their capacity to secure minimally adequate housing, sustenance, education, health care, and recreation to permit their most effective productive involvement on a job and the fullest development of their latent physical, mental, and motivational capacities will be obstructed.[16] It is instrumentally *in*efficient to cripple any fragment of the community by deprivation, discrimination, or alienation. As Clarence E. Ayres often remarked, to cripple a part is to cripple the whole of a community.[17] The crippling results from the fact of pervasive interdependency. One person's injury is another person's burden. Consequences of individual and group behavior impinge on and extend or constrain other persons' behavior. Community means interdependency.

Few need to be reminded that income distribution in the United States *is* markedly unequal. For a generation and more the bottom fifth of family income recipients has received some 4 to 6 percent of total money income; the top fifth has received around 41 to 45 percent of such income.[18]

To illustrate further: In the United States in the mid–1970s almost 26 million people, or 12.3 percent of the total population, were living in poverty according to official Census Bureau definitions of poverty.[19] In 1969, when the poverty component evidently was roughly comparable, some 14.4 million Americans were facing outright hunger and malnutrition in the absence of food grants or assistance, and only 44 percent of those later *did* actually receive any food assistance.[20] Finally, if one may assume that the level of real income specified by the Bureau of Labor Statistics (BLS) as an "intermediate level of living" (a modest but not luxurious level)[21] is the minimum level necessary for continuing instrumentally efficient productive work, somewhere between one-third and one-half of the population falls below this threshold. For example, for an urban family of four, the median income in 1976 was $16,336; the BLS intermediate income in 1977 was $17,106.

Not only is the larger community deprived of the economic contribution which this eighth, or third, or half might otherwise be able to make (a concern shared presumably with the orthodox capitalists) but, more importantly, to reiterate, a paucity of income shrivels life's choices generally to the point where intellect, creativity, compassion, and commitment are stunted or destroyed for those denied. We then live in a layered or tiered community suffering from elitism and privation alike.[23] This would appear to be inefficiency of really monumental proportions.

Finally, a qualification (or disclaimer) needed in reflecting on the adequacy of instrumental efficiency as an economic criterion involves the recognition that all ism-ideology economies claim to be efficient—especially so perhaps with the capitalists, who have insisted for a century that an unfettered free-market system is the most efficient economic order conceivable. That such insistence is no longer credible should now be apparent to the most casual observer of the economies of self-proclaiming capitalist countries. [. . .]

Competitive market economies are not instrumentally efficient for a number of reasons:

a. They provide no way, ideologically or institutionally, for wants and preferences to be appraised in the market. The question of the character of wants is excluded from consideration. This is an abandonment of a normative responsibility which the community in some other way must cover. In the United States, often producers themselves make the judgment on the character of product and then, through media advertising, condition the public to concur.[24]

b. Competitive market economies do not address the fact of inequality of income distribution as a problem. The combination of functional distribution through competitive factor markets and personal distribution through nonmarket mechanisms is thought to suffice. Inequality allegedly generates the monetary savings which many of the orthodox still regard as determinant of investment and growth.

c. Competitive market economies do not provide for the introduction of nonpecuniary criteria in economic decision making. Prices are surrogates for real, utility values. Adjustment of prices or output to maximize profit is a sufficient indicator of the adequacy of judgments. Profits are the primary success indicator. The irony of some such expression as "Oh, the factory was destroyed? No matter; it was insured" is a reflection of our unease with the illusion that pecuniary values "stand in" for social value. Profits are not an indicator of instrumental efficiency.

(2) A corollary ethical concept for the political revolution is the criterion of *democracy*.

At an earlier point we suggested that in deciding the extent and character of political obligation, one might ask whether or not a particular government was worthy of support. We may now affirm that to the degree that the political process is organized to provide for participatory democracy, a government is worthy. That is, the idea of democracy itself may be used as a criterion, a standard in terms of which to make choices among institutional and candidate options. Does what is contemplated as structural change increase or decrease the ability and the opportunity of people to determine the rules governing their own lives? Does the candidate favor or oppose participatory involvement in determining policy? Democracy, recall, means self-imposed restraints. If a system does provide for self-rule, it is worthy; if a system does not, it is without legitimacy.

Democracy as a term does not define a given, rigid, and substantive set of political institutions as such (e.g., tripartite government, multiple-party system); it identifies the locus of responsibility for political decision making and suggests procedural conditions (e.g., free speech, due process, majority rule) through which it may be exercised. Thus, democracy is not an "ism" on a par with, say, capitalism or socialism; it offers no final institutional package or recipe; it is a continuing means, not a structurally defined End. Democracy defines a set of conditions for bringing reasoned judgment to bear on public problems; it does not specify a priori the institutional forms which ultimately may constitute the proposed solution.

Democracy is a necessary, but not a sufficient, criterion in choosing among alternatives, however. The fact that an institutional choice (e.g., to establish a national medical-insurance program, to reimpose the death penalty, to expand nuclear-fission energy installations) is made by a majority vote, directly or indirectly, does not necessarily mean that the "continuity of human life and the noninvidious re-creation of community through the instrumental use of knowledge" is therewith being served. Majorities may be "wrong," as we are often reminded by the elitists. Factually, such may well be the case. But the "rightness" or "wrongness" of majorities is not to be decided by elitist criteria nor, for that matter, by majoritarian criteria. The democratic contention is that the greater the degree of popular participatory involvement in the making of public judgments, the greater will be the interest in determining whether or not a decision is or will be "right."

In a democratic order, when a judgment is "mistaken," when in an instrumental sense the action taken does not resolve the problem, those who bear the incidence of the mistake are the ones typically who will be most interested and vigorous in seeking a correction. Those who most directly bear the human costs and dislocations of breakdowns—disruptions or distortions in the operation of existing institutions—are, in an open society, most likely to take a lively interest in the use of reliable knowledge to modify structure and resolve the problem. Even so, the reactions of some to a shortfall may be reasoned or irrational, instrumental or ceremonial, deliberative or violent, insight seeking or scapegoat hunting, but so long as the incidence of the problem remains unresolved, there will be a continuing stimulus to define mistakes and to formulate corrections.

There is, in democratic orders, an inherent tendency to subject public decisions to scrutiny and revision leading to real, if not final, solutions for problems. It is this process of deliberation and appraisal which warrants the contention that democratic orders are efficient. They are efficient in achieving needed institutional change to restore instrumental effectiveness to important areas of human endeavor.

Democracy, then, as an addendum criterion assists with the pursuit of that ancient political "Holy Grail"—the public interest. Every politician defends his or her votes and actions on grounds of "serving the public interest"; that is a part of the rhetoric of legitimacy. Why? Because obviously he or she seeks support (consent) from those he or she allegedly represents. The instrumental value theory advanced above does indeed identify the public interest, and democracy is the most efficient process thus far conceived through which to achieve some approximation thereof.

(3) A corollary ethical concept for the racial and sexual revolutions is the criterion of *noninvidiousness* itself.

Readers are well aware that much use has already been made of this criterion at several points in the presentation this far. Some additional explication of the idea in this context should help remove remaining obscurities.

We begin with an affirmation of some comfortable and generally settled conclusions about men and women as social beings. Evidently it is everywhere the case that people wish to be well thought of; they seek the recognition and esteem of others for the fact of their being and for the fruits of their labors and activities. Cultures and customs pattern the ways and means of seeking and exhibiting such recognition and esteem. Physical prowess, control over others' behavior, creation of art objects, reflective capacities, decoration of the human body, engaging in sports, acquisition of material possessions, demonstrated skills with tools, ordering and coordinating capacities, to mention but a few, are all areas in which and by which recognition and esteem have been and are being sought. The "psychology of ego involvement"[25] affirms this quest for identity, for notice, for recognition, for acceptance by others.

In addition, there is the obvious fact that everywhere human beings are different—frequently observably different—from one another on literally scores of divergent indexes. As we remarked above, such categories of difference include, among others, race, creed, national origin, sex, ethnicity, age, rank, parentage, wealth, income, religious belief, attained education level, stature, height and weight, intellect, sibling order, skin color, facial configuration, hair texture, color and styles of attire, power over others, temperament, aggressiveness, blood type, etc., etc. So much is a recitation of the obvious, but there is a reason for the reminder.

Invidiousness means the use of one or several of these distinctions among persons to challenge or assault the basic worth of human beings; it means to denigrate and demean people; it means to deny dignity *because* of the observed or assumed presence of such differences without regard to a context in which the distinction might or might not be significant or make an instrumental difference. To judge invidiously, then, is to denigrate the worth of particular individuals or classes of individuals.

Given recognition manifested in the way, as individuals, we do differ from one another, we seek, when we judge invidiously, to enhance our own egos, our own importance, our own conception of self-worth by demeaning those without our own traits simply because they are without such traits. Invidious judgments are unfairly discriminatory.

In the case of racial and sexual discrimination, no extensive catalog of examples is required.[26] Although gains have been made in eroding discrimination in recent decades, it still appears that politicians will sometimes use overt or covert appeals to racism in their campaigns; that women continue to have more difficulty than men in gaining access to loans and credit (credit cards, mortgage loans, etc.); that busing school children to achieve racial balance remains a source of intense domestic conflict; that differential pay for women for work identical to that done by men may still be found on occasion in education, business, and government. [. . .] Federal Affirmative Action programs were deemed necessary to interdict racism and sexism in hiring and promotion policies of universities receiving federal assistance. The Equal Rights Amendment to seek an end to sexism through Constitutional mandate has been blocked.[27]

Not quite so evident, however, is the fact that the invidious use of distinctions as a criterion directly conflicts with the more inclusive principle of social value set off above. Invidious judgments, by fostering interpersonal and intergroup conflict, directly threaten continuity of instrumental economic, political, and social functions. Race riots, religious conflict, terrorist tactics by aggrieved minorities, overt discrimination, political intimidation of ethnics, and other major and visible manifestations of invidiousness are ugly and dislocative; frequently they promote physical violence. When such conflicts become consuming and/or violent, the instrumental effectiveness of people to think and to act in a reasonable and rational manner is markedly impaired. Such conflict-engendered enmity makes the task of "re-creating community" virtually impossible. And, there is an instrumental-value rationale for the use of force to prevent violence and terrorism. A democratic noninvidious community does enforce the law and maintain civil peace. But the character of law and the nature of civil peace remain open as areas of discussion and discretionary action.

Community building means cooperative exploration of problems and the formulation of agreed-upon responses to such problems. Community building provides a vehicle for people to express and act on their commitments to each other, to children, families and friends, and to the physical environs which are familiar. Racism and sexism, for example, preclude community creation because they disintegrate conceptions of common purpose, or forestall the creation of common purposes, and convert resolvable differences of opinion into challenges of the right to life, to income, to have identity, to make a difference, to be "somebody" in one's own eyes as well as those of others, to be worthy and to be recognized by one's peers as such! But invidious judgments make such discretionary involvement difficult if not impossible, thus stripping people of their dignity. Where such conditions exist, there can be no real community.

(4) A corollary ethical concept for the ecological crisis is the criterion of *environmental compatibility*.

As most students are aware, social inquiry is concerned with person-person relations; person-thing relations are significant but are normally the purview of scholars in disciplines other than the social sciences (e.g., natural sciences). While person-thing relations are not the object of social inquiry, obviously they often set the terms or conditions within which social inquiry occurs. Similarly, a social community differs from a biotic community; the latter sets conditions in which the former occurs and operates.

A biotic community is composed of the interdependencies (mainly, energy-exchange and food-chain relations) of life forms with each other and of life forms with the physical environment.[28] The biotic community of interdependencies is a reflection of no doctrine of design. What environmental conditions do not favor, they prohibit. "Nature selects nothing; it simply eliminates or absolves."[29] A biotic community simply *is*. If there are momentary or enduring balances, that is a matter of fact, not of purpose. Such a community is neither pro nor con of life forms specifically or generally, including human life; it is neither virtuous nor insidious; it exhibits "neither grace nor right, but only displacement."[30] As such, it is amoral or nonmoral; it merely and profoundly is. "Nature flows carelessly, according to its monstrous insensate habit, impassive and undisturbed, whether or not men institute political relations among themselves."[31]

A social community must exist and seek continuity within the ecological limits of the biotic community. People are dependent upon and interdependent with other life forms. The biotic community sets conditions, but it provides no judgments. People alone make judgments. People as actor-agents define social community, affirm its purposes, delineate its relations, and live out its constraints and obligations. A social community can exist only when individuals perceive themselves as mutually committed to one another. As we have seen, democratic communities accept the obligation to observe rules which have been introduced by popular consent. A biotic community knows nothing of obligation or commitment, or consent.

The environmental ethical principle, then, is the criterion of compatibility—compatibility between the social and biotic communities. The social community, through its political judgments, must assure that it continues to function within constraints of the biotic community. The principle of compatibility corresponds with the more inclusive criterion introduced above—the continuity of human life and the noninvidious re-creation of community through the instrumental use of knowledge.

Logical and ethical implications of the foregoing would include the following:

(a) Preserve the biotic community *and* preserve the social community. The continuity component of the general criterion above cannot otherwise be met.

(b) Conserve life forms and the physical environs which sustain them. A principal reason is that knowledge of the complexities and interdependencies of life forms is not, and probably never will be, sufficiently complete to foresee the consequences of the extinction of any life form. For many, the esthetic reasons are equally compelling, of course.

(c) Conserve technologically defined resources; avoid pollution of air, water, and soil; forestall despoilation of forest, stream, and ocean—not because nonhuman life generally takes precedence over human life, but because the continuity of the social community is dependent on the continuity of biotic life.

Environmental compatibility of the social with the biotic community is, then, an applicable principle of judgment. There are implications and applications of this principle.

Perhaps nowhere in our quest for warrantable normative precepts in political economy is the ethical dilemma for an individual more sharply drawn nor easier to see. To an individual pursuing his or her private interests, following capitalist traditions, the land, including the flora and fauna, is an exploitable resource to turn to one's own economic (pecuniary) advantage. One "mixes his labor with the soil" and thereby gains a right to the fruits of that labor. To an individual as a member of a community, however, such pursuits by oneself and others similarly engaged may well seriously impair or destroy the biotic community, including now oneself. Accordingly, much of the literature on the ecological crisis affirms the need for the supremacy of public obligation to community (social and biotic) over private economic advantage.[32] It now appears that the creation of a viable social community, including the jettisonning of ideologically grounded beliefs, may well be a precondition, or at least a concurrent condition, for preserving a biotic community.

Economists of the traditional, Establishment, Neoclassical kind have sometimes had difficulty relating their explanations of pricing phenomena to the crises of environmental degradation. Committed to utility-value theory, the efficacy of free markets, and private enterprise, they have suggested that air and stream pollution, land-form emasculation, plant and timber eradication, and the like be viewed as "externalities"[33]—consequences outside the normal operations of supply-and-demand market processes. Such theorists and ideologists have attempted to apply their analytical models through efforts to "internalize externalities," that is, to bring the community's peripheral ecological costs (resulting from pollution and the like) within the market process by, for example, taxing firms that pollute for the full costs of repairing the damage their activity creates.[34] In this way the full costs (including costs to the environment) would be paid for by product users, and the market mentality would continue to reign supreme. A difficulty, of course, is that the pollution itself may very well continue even where policy is based on these premises.

A variant from the same general theoretical and ideological source would seek "the proper balance between the utility of resource-using activities to the individual and the disutility they impose, via the environment, on others."[35] Recourse is also made to Pareto optimality[36] and other utility-based criteria in attempts to find analyses to permit the identification of such balances.

But the problem of social value in the ecology crisis is not a matter of full-cost charges to private enterprise or of finding a balance of utilities and disutilities. The problem concerns the refinement and use of a criterion of ecological judgment which affirms the necessity of interdependent compatibility of the social and the biotic communities. This criterion would serve as an alternate principle to benefit-cost equivalencies, internalized externalities, utility-disutility balances, and the like. Our roles as public citizens seeking such compatibility must supplant, in this area, our pursuits as private citizens as necessary—especially, the "conquering of nature" for personal pecuniary gain.[37] [. . .]

It is important to note that there may well be times when conflict will occur between the economic criterion of instrumental efficiency and the ecological criterion of biotic and social community compatibility.[38] The application of the economic criterion, it should be understood, is generally to be conditioned by and subject to the constraints of the ecological criterion. Economically productive and equitably distributed real income probably can continue in most areas without extensive environmental degradation. There is no economic law which compels the production of nonbiodegradable materials, for example, or the production of plastic containers and their disposal at sea or by noxious burning. [. . .] There is no economic law that precludes the massive diversion of scientific and technical research personnel from military weaponry to the development of more environmentally compatible production methods and output. Even though rhetoric on the subject of environmental protection may be faddish, it cannot be dismissed; the "opaque facts" of the problem and its potentially disastrous consequences remain. [. . .]

Notes

1. Adapted from J. Fagg Foster, "The Relation Between the Theory of Value and Economic Analysis" (mimeo), University of Denver (no date), and "Current Structure and Future Prospects of Institutional Economics" (mimeo), University of Denver, 1975. Modified versions of the next few pages appear in my article, "A Social Value Theory in Neoinstitutional Economics," *Journal of Economic Issues* 11, 4 (December 1977): 823–46, and in my article, "Constructs of Value, Freedom and Equity in Institutional Economics," *The Social Science Journal* 15, 1 (January 1978): 27–38.

2. Sidney S. Alexander, "Social Evaluation through Notional Choice," *Quarterly Journal of Economics* 88, 4 (November 1974): 605.

3. See Clarence E. Ayres, *The Theory of Economic Progress* (Chapel Hill: University of North Carolina Press, 1944), ch. 10.

4. Veblen, *Theory of the Leisure Class*, p. 34.

5. *Dignity* and *a sense of self-worth* are difficult terms to extricate from their sometimes invidious use. We often tend to associate dignity with royalty and "breeding." And we remember that the Nazi SS troops had *a* sense of dignity and self-worth. Some effort to provide referential content or meaning is required in this context.

We intend a noninvidious meaning to include all of the following: growing knowledge of and trust in self, including capacities, sensitivities, commitments, and limitations; integrity as a willingness to adhere to principles rationally held and to honesty in their revision and application; decision capacity as indicated by an assertive claim to the right to decide in personal matters and to participate with others in social and public choices; self-confidence which derives from the approving feedback of others prompted by one's own confidence in others; reflective capacity as willingness to seek truth and to expose fruits of one's reflection; ungraded view of others which recognizes that one's own dignity is not diminished by another's, that dignity is not a scarce or finite good, and that it is not a product of status, rank, position, class, power, or income.

6. C. E. Ayres, *Theory of Economic Progress*, ch. 10.

7. John Dewey, *Theory of Valuation* (Chicago: University of Chicago Press, 1939), pp. 40–50.

8. C. E. Ayres, *Theory of Economic Progress*, ch. 6.

9. Consider human beings as represented in B. F. Skinner, *Walden Two* (New York: Macmillan, 1962).

10. Walton Hamilton, *The Politics of Industry* (New York: Alfred A. Knopf, 1957), pp. 165ff.

11. Adapted from J. Fagg Foster, "Notes on the Character of the Process and the Specific Identification of the Theory of Value," University of Denver, 1948.

12. See, for example, David Jenkins, *Job Power: Blue and White Collar Democracy* (New York: Penguin, 1974), pp. 25–35.

13. Ibid., pp. 282ff and passim.

14. Readers of Veblen will recognize adaptations here of the fundamental Veblenian dichotomy. See the author's "A Social Value Theory in Neoinstitutional Economics," *Journal of Economic Issues* 11, 4 (December 1977), p. 827.

15. For example, Food and Nutrition Board, National Research Council, *Recommended Dietary Allowances* (Washington, D.C.: National Academy of Sciences, 1974).

16. On this and related matters, see, for example, Oscar Lewis, "The Culture of Poverty," in *On Understanding Poverty*, ed. Daniel P. Moynihan (New York: Basic Books, 1968–69), pp. 187–200; also, Winifred Bell, Robert Lekachman, and Alvin Schorr, *Public Policy and Income Distribution* (New York: Center for Studies in Income Maintenance, School of Social Work, New York University, 1974).

17. Ayres, *Theory of Economic Progress*, p. 233, and *The Industrial Economy* (Boston: Houghton Mifflin, 1952), pp. 268–69.

18. Jonathan H. Turner and Charles E. Starnes, *Inequality: Privilege and Poverty in America* (Pacific Palisades, Calif.: Goodyear, 1976), p. 51. See also Morton Paglin, "The Measurement and Trend of Inequality: A Basic Revision," *American Economic Review* 65, 4 (September 1975): 598–609.

19. *New York Times*, September 26, 1975, pp. 1, 36. See also U.S. Department of Commerce, Bureau of Census, *Money Income and Poverty Status of Families and Persons in the United States, 1974–1975* (Washington, D.C.: U.S. Government Printing Office, 1976); Michael Harrington, "Hiding the Other America," *The New Republic*, February 26, 1977, pp. 15–17; and "Big Increase in 'Officially' Poor," *San Francisco Chronicle*, July 14, 1977, p. 9.

20. U.S. Congress, Senate Select Committee on Nutrition and Human Needs, *The Food Gap: Poverty and Malnutrition in the United States* (Washington, D.C.: U.S. Government Printing Office, 1969), pp. 20–21.

21. We do not intend to imply that BLS estimates of city worker budgets are necessarily ideal or that they are necessarily sufficient measures or standards with which to judge the adequacy, on instrumental-efficiency grounds, of various levels of money and real income. They are rough approximations, indicative but not definitive.

22. U.S. Department of Commerce, Bureau of the Census, *Consumer Income Re-*

ports, series P-60, no. 110 (Washington, D.C.: U.S. Government Printing Office, March 1978). U.S. Department of Labor, Bureau of Labor Statistics, *Autumn 1976 Urban Family Budgets and Comparative Indexes for Selected Urban Areas* (Washington, D.C.: U.S. Government Printing Office, 1978).

23. See also Ben B. Seligman, *Permanent Poverty: An American Syndrome* (Chicago: Quadrangle, 1968), ch. 2; and David Hamilton, "The Political Economy of Poverty: Institutional and Technological Dimensions," *Journal of Economic Issues* 1, 4 (December 1967): 309-20.

24. This is John K. Galbraith's "revised sequence," as we noted above.

25. Muzafer Sherif and Hadly Cantril, *The Psychology of Ego-Involvement* (New York: Wiley, 1947).

26. See Edythe S. Miller, "Veblen and Women's Lib: A Parallel," *Journal of Economic Issues* 6, 2-3 (September 1972): 75-86.

27. A general assessment appears in Kenneth B. Clark, "The Costs of Discrimination," *Challenge* 20, 2 (May-June 1977): 33-39.

28. One version is that of Aldo Leopold, *A Sand County Almanac* (New York: Sierra Club/Ballantine, 1970), pp. 251ff.

29. John F. A. Taylor, "Politics and the Human Covenant," *The Centennial Review*, (East Lansing: Michigan State University, 1962), p. 3.

30. Ibid.

31. Ibid., p. 5.

32. Leopold, *A Sand County Almanac*, pp. 258-61. Also, Barry Commoner, *The Closing Circle* (New York: Bantam Books, 1972), pp. 249ff; and Harold Wolozin, "Environmental Control at the Crossroads," *Journal of Economic Issues* 5, 1 (March 1971): 26-41.

33. Discussed in Robert Staaf and Francis Tannian, *Externalities: Theoretical Dimensions of Political Economy* (Port Washington, N.Y.: Kennikat Press/Dunellen, 1973).

34. See, for example, Commoner, *The Closing Circle*, pp. 249-91.

35. Robert Dorfman and Nancy S. Dorfman, *Economics of the Environment* (New York: Norton, 1972), p. xix.

36. For example, new condition A is better than new condition B, if in A at least one person would be "better off" without making anyone "worse off."

37. Regarding control of externalities, see Ralph C. d'Arge & James E. Wilen, "Governmental Control of Externalities, or the Prey Eats the Predator," *Journal of Economic Issues* 8, 2 (June 1974): 353-72.

38. In this connection, see K. William Kapp, "Development and Environment: Towards a New Approach to Socioeconomic and Environmental Development," in *Economics in Institutional Perspective*, ed. R. Steppacher, B. Zogg-Walz, and H. Hatzfeldt (Lexington, Mass.: Lexington Books, 1977), pp. 205-18.

A Theory of the Social Origin
of Factors of Production

DAVID HAMILTON

The so-called factors of production are infamous among Institutional economists and have played a prominent role in their critique of Neoclassical economics. Veblen argued that these taxonomic categories were concerned with distribution rather than production. David Hamilton extends this line of criticism using Durkheim's concept of collective representation. Hamilton argues that Neoclassical microeconomic theory is the religion of modern industrial capitalism. The factors of production are used to legitimate incomes received and have no relationship to actual productive activity. Moreover the categories used refer to the social hierarchy and status relationships in society and not the techniques or structure of production.

Within recent times the contributions of Emile Durkheim to an understanding of social structure have become increasingly apparent.[1] Yet his service to a clearer understanding of the origin of current economic conceptualizations remains to be appreciated. Outside of his *Division of Labor* little attention has been paid by the student of economic thought to the contribution of Durkheim to an understanding of social phenomena. The student of standard economic theory has not been one to wander far afield into what to him appear to be the byways of social inquiry. As a result economic inquiry in its underlying social preconceptions remains essentially where Adam Smith delivered it. Unfortunately the vast progress in the other social sciences, especially anthropology and sociology, has had little influence on the speculative peregrinations of the economic theorist.[2] Yet by turning to the work of the ethnologist and the sociologist a better understanding may be gained of the background of economic thought. In short it is to that area of inquiry now designated the "sociology of knowledge" that the modern student of economic thought must turn for a full appreciation and understanding of the background of economic thought. Durkheim is of extreme value as a contributor of new vistas in this area of inquiry.

I

One of Durkheim's major contributions was his demonstration that the idea of class arises from society itself.[3] Members of societies are arranged and graded on

David Hamilton, "A Theory of the Social Origin of Factors of Production," *American Journal of Economics and Sociology* 15, 1 (October 1955), pp. 73–82.

a basis peculiar to that particular society. The system of grades and ratings may have its authentication in kinship, feudal fealty, contract, force and fraud, sex, or what have you. Nevertheless, all societies with which the ethnologist is familiar have been found to be so graded. The character and intensity of the system varies, but it is just as much a status system whether among the Trobriand Islanders, the Coorgs of India, the Maori, or feudal society of Medieval Europe.

Durkheim also noted that these societies project this social stratification into a classification of the universe. All things of experience are so classified. Items of the universe take on the same complexion of grades and ratings that are peculiar to the social organization.[4] According to Durkheim there is nothing in the universe itself to suggest such a system of classification. In the case of the Australian totemic society he demonstrated that the scheme of classification of the universe was a projection of the totemic classification. It was because society itself was divided into clans, phratries, and tribes that the overall schemes of classification were derived. Although Durkheim seemed to err in attributing the origin of the concept class to a common totemic origin of all societies, he did have a concept that was useful to an understanding of classification systems in all cultures. Frequently those schemes of classification, which are resorted to whether in a totemically divided society or not, are themselves reflections of a system of social grades and ratings, of a myth-authenticated system of invidious distinctions. Although the abstract concept of classification as resorted to in many areas of inquiry, such as the biological sciences, is now reasonably free of immediate social origin, it is by no means true that all schemes of classification are so freed or uninfluenced by current social organization. There is reason to believe that classifications ostensibly drawn on a matter-of-fact basis in some areas of social inquiry are in fact projections of a preexisting social order. Precisely this can be shown in the case of what are called, in economic thought, the factors of production.

Within the realm of established economic discourse the factors of production have a long and honored place.[5] In fact both traditional production and distribution theory work from a basic classification of things into land, labor, and capital and sometimes management. (The latter is an addition recently made as a result of a cleavage in the cultural matrix that goes by the name of "the separation of ownership from control.") Within the main stream of economic thought, these factors have been looked upon as agents of production. They have been in prior existence to theory and in fact can be found in all cultures. It remains only for someone to claim them for there to be landlords, laborers, and capitalists. At least that would appear to be the gist of the following statement from John Stuart Mill, a position from which latter-day economists have not been known to dissent.

> The three requisites of production, as has been so often repeated, are labour, capital, and land: understanding by capital, the means and appliances which are the accumulated results of previous labour, and by land, the materials and

instruments supplied by nature, whether contained in the interior of the earth, or constituting its surface. Since each of these elements of production may be separately appropriated the industrial community may be considered as divided into landowners, capitalists, and productive labourers.[6]

Among economists of the present day it is fair to say that the factors of production are conceptualizations which to them seem to have a substantive meaning. The factors have a real existence and it is because they may be "separately appropriated" that there are landlords, laborers, and capitalists. In fact, so fixed is this concept in the habits of thought of Western man that frequently even the affairs of primitive cultures obviously far remote from such a state of organization as is Western culture, are viewed as ventures in the combination of land, labor, and capital.[7] As Veblen stated the case in regard to distribution, "e.g., a gang of Aleutian Islanders slushing about in the wrack and surf with rakes and magical incantations for the capture of shellfish are held, in point of taxonomic reality, to be engaged on a feat of hedonistic equilibration in rent, wages, and interest. And that is all there is to it. Indeed, for economic theory of this kind, that is all there is to any economic situation."[8] In short, the productive factors are held to be universal social constructs. But such is not the case.

The origin of the factors of production is to be found in those cataclysmic industrial events that long ago were dubbed "the industrial revolution" by an earlier Arnold Toynbee.[9] To analyze medieval handicraft or manorial agriculture in terms of land, labor, and capital, if not seeming absurd today, would have seemed so at the time. Medieval culture was one characterized by a social organization composed of lords of the land, knights, freemen, serfs, and slaves. The system of status as to categories was quite remote from that of present-day Western culture. There is to be found nowhere in medieval economic thought an allusion to the factors of production.[10] To describe the economic affairs of a manorial unit in terms of varying dosages of land, labor, and capital would be to miss the mark by a wide margin.

As the manorial organization disintegrated in the face of a rising industrialism so did that status system demarcated by land-lord, knight, freeman, serf and slave. In its place arose the business enterprise, the corporate form of which has come to predominate in more recent times. Although the status system of the medieval culture disintegrated, status as a differential ordering of mankind did not disappear. Under the suzerain of business enterprise, society came to be demarcated by the status groups which had come to the front in the business unit. In short, the industrial revolution broke down the feudal relations of social reciprocity which had been the core of the feudal status system. But relations of social reciprocity were not foregone. New ones were established in the way of landlord-capitalist and capitalist-laborer.[11]

It is a piece of popular conceit that status in contemporary Western culture is of no significance and that Western culture differs from its feudal predecessor by the substitution of contract for status.[12] This, however, fails to see that status exists in contemporary Western culture just as it did in medieval culture. What has changed is the basis of the status system and the status categories. Fealty was the basis of the feudal status system whereas contract is the basis of the business status system. The capitalist-laborer relationship can be defined in terms of rights and duties just as the lord-virgator relationship could be defined. In the latter case, the rights and duties were defined by long established use and wont reinforced by ecclesiastical fiat. In the former case, these relationships are defined by contract reinforced by the use and wont defined by the common law. But in either case the end product is a well-defined system of status.

What is of significance to the present discussion is the fact that as the last vestige of manorialism disappeared this newer status system came to pervade the entire society. Men were graded and rated in an overall status system bounded by landlord, capitalist, and laborer. The whole of Western culture came to be so divided. It is true that individuals might have relationships that placed them in more than one category. But it can be said without too much stretching of a point that the major source of one's income, in most cases, did define rather clearly the major category into which one would fall. On this issue of division into landlords, laborers, and capitalists the Marxian theorists would appear to be on safer ground than the fuzzy popular division into upper, middle, and lower class. Although this latter, at least at one time, corresponded to the landlord-capitalist-laborer division, it has come to mean very little except as a statistical division based on the place of one's income in an array of all incomes by size. As an interpretation of the normal distribution of income it has more to recommend it than as a description of status. Division on an income basis means very little so far as status is concerned. A laborer may earn more than a capitalist if the latter be an entrepreneur of some small affair, yet the latter position would fall higher on the social scale. Members of trade unions who in their workday affairs wear the traditional garb of the laboring man are not good material for the private country club no matter how financially solvent they are. Yet the creditor-harried proprietor of a shaky business enterprise is usually an acceptable candidate for membership.

In short, Western culture has come to be divided into landlords, capitalists, and laborers to an extent which the society itself is reluctant to recognize. There have been and are variations in this set of arrangements. It is truer of Western European peoples to include landlords as a division than it would be of those areas to which the economic arrangements of Western Europe were carried. In these latter areas such as North America, Australia, and New Zealand the vestiges of the feudal hierarchy are carried along only in some of the more archaic habits of thought which diffused with the social arrangements. But feudalism never had an opportunity in these new areas, not because of the free land available, but because such an organization of things was already on the wane in Western culture. Likewise in more recent times it would be more correct to include management as a category to the extent that this group has been successfully demarcated from that of capitalist and from that of labor. Such a separation has taken place in the modern corporation.

Such variations in the pattern are evidence for the major thesis of the present paper. These changes have been reflected in changes in what was held to compose the factors of production. At one time little question was raised on the inclusion of land as a factor of production. However, in recent times land has been more frequently subsumed under capital.[13] This is nothing to cause any great amount of surprise for except in a few limited areas in England and in that area until recently presided over by the Junkers in Germany, the landlord has become a vestigial appendage from an older order of things. In the newer areas of European settlement the ownership of land distinct from the capital appurtenances is not a common arrangement. Under these circumstances it has become common practice for capital to engross land in a factorial merger. The rise of a new social group distinct from both capital and labor in the form of business management has also given rise to a change in what are recognized as factors of production. As a result of management usurping the traditional rights, prerogatives, and appurtenances of capital in corporate direction and control a new factor has been found on the economic horizon.[14]

II

At this point the question of Durkheim's contribution is in order. It is all well and good to point out that the factors of production are derived from society itself. After all, it may be contended, economics is a social science and the productive factors are nothing more than a part of that social organization to which the inquiry is directed. They are the agents out of which flow goods and services and such would be apparent to any impartial observer. But such is not the case. As one critic has put it recently:

> What are the factors that affect production most decisively? If we could imagine ourselves attacking such a question today for the first time, there can be no doubt that our attention would be directed to such matters as the state of our knowledge, the prevalence of essential skills, the physical availability of essential equipment, the state of public order and social conditions generally, and all that sort of thing. As everyone knows today, these are the decisive conditions. . . .
>
> But according to the classical tradition of economics the factors of production are very different. They are: land, labor, capital and management. It may be true that these rubrics can be conceived in such a way as to include considerations of science and technology, and even those of social institutions. But in that case the difference of expression is still very striking. "Land, labor, capital, and management" is an odd way to summarize the blessings of civilization.[15]

This "odd way" of summarizing "the blessings of civilization" is a product of the conceptualizing process to an explanation of which Durkheim contributed so much. Economics in its classical form, just as systems of religion, is a conceptualization of the universe. The early formulators of economic thought did precisely what man has done time out of hand. To the explanation of this view of the universe they projected the status structure of the Western European business culture. Everything to which ownership could be extended, and there is little remaining to which some enterprising free-booter has not extended ownership, fell under one of these categories. Each of the multitude of items which make up the universe as experienced by Western man was subsumed under some one of the factorial heads.

It might well be argued that all scientific endeavor is taxonomic to some extent and that chemists and biologists have systems of classification which cover the universe similar in nature to those of the economist. There is, however, a significant difference between the taxonomic schemes of the chemist and biologist and that of the economist. The former classify on the grounds of some matter-of-fact demonstrable identity,- i.e., on distinctions that can be readily recognized by people of diverse cultures. The classifications of economic belief are based on some feeling of spiritual unity and participation. [16]

The multiplicity of things included under each of the factors of production should make this clear. Land includes a diversity of items under what is euphoniously referred to, at least since Ricardo, as the "indestructible powers of the soil." Herein are such diverse things as mere space itself, soil, flora and fauna established and domiciled by nature, coal, iron ore, oil, copper, lead, gravel, water, and a multitude of other things. To the untrained eye there is no seeming identity among these items. Yet they have a spiritual identity in the sense that they participate in those mysterious powers that beget classification as the "indestructible powers of the soil." [17]

Capital items are of the same diverse nature. Included under this head are such things as "factories clustered here and there over the country," "farms, retail and wholesale stores, barbershops, mines, office buildings, banks," "highways, postoffices, school houses, and power dams," "tractors and barber chairs, blast furnaces and display windows, derricks and typewriters, generators and electric motors," "stocks of raw materials, . . . goods on the assembly line, and . . . finished goods waiting to be shipped," "canned peas, soap, radio tubes, tires, tin cans, and baby bottles," "shoes and shirts and food and toothpaste. These items of equipment . . . and these stocks of goods in the possession of business firms, are known collectively as 'capital goods.'" [18] Other more inclusive classifications have been known to include techniques and ideas of manufacture (patented) under this head as well. Furthermore, bonds, stocks of gold, stock certificates, and good will are capital items of some sort and participate in some manner in the mystic force that ties together the items listed above under capital goods. All are of the essence of capital.

Labor is no better. Labor is held not to be the person of the laborer. Labor is an abstract thing called labor power or rather a multitude of identifiable skills acknowledged as manifestations of labor power. Included in this category are such diverse skills as medical, machinist, printing, janitoring, scavenging, horse bookmaking, gambling, lawyering, teaching, sciencing, and all the rest of the multitude of complex skills found in a modern industrial culture. Again the only identity would appear to be a spiritual participation in what is called "labor power."

The absurdities of such a scheme of classification have frequently been pointed out. In fact it is this basic factorial analysis that led Veblen to call traditional economic thought "taxonomy." The results of such taxonomic endeavor are fraught with absurdities and difficulties. A slave, for instance, engaged in the production of cotton is a capital item while the freeman beside him engaged in the same activity is classified as labor. A housewife, although performing the same tasks as an innkeeper and dietitian, remains a housewife outside the charmed circle of productive labor. Difficulties multiply. A croupier in Nevada is a productive laborer; a croupier in New York is a fugitive from free room and board at state expense. Capital can only be defined as something which yields a pecuniary return called interest, which is that type of pecuniary return received by the owner of capital, who in turn is differentiated as one who receives a pecuniary return from just such a source. The absurdities of applying such a tautological definition become apparent in practice. Automobiles become either capital or consumer goods. If they serve as the basis for an imputation of pecuniary return in the form of interest they are capital goods. If no such return can be imputed they are not. If owned by a capitalist or a capital-possessing enterprise, they will have some pecuniary return in the form of interest imputed to them, for a capital item is one to which can be imputed a pecuniary return called interest. Items to which such an imputation has been made take on all of the trappings of capital by common usage.[19]

But this "odd way" of viewing things is revealed for what it is by these absurdities and difficulties. Although factors make no sense in an analysis of production, they do have a meaning as establishing claims in distribution, based on an imputation of productive efficacy. There are people receiving wages who are labor, those receiving profits who represent owners of capital, and those receiving rents who represent owners of land. All members of Western culture fall roughly into such income categories, each of which is defined by custom-prescribed rights and duties or reciprocal obligations. All are related through the culturally defined practices of business enterprise as the larger caste groups of India are tied together by relations of reciprocity.[20]

In summary, there arose out of the Industrial Revolution new social relationships. An all-inclusive social hierarchy was established which graded and rated all income receivers into one of the various productive categories in accordance with the type of income to which it was entitled—rent, wages, interest or profits. In analyzing the economy, the early formulators of classical political economy projected these social classes into a view of the entire economic universe. All items of economic significance were fitted into one of these categories even if violence was done to reason.

Durkheim is significant, for he demonstrated the existence of such a conceptualizing process. It also appears, once this process as it worked itself out in Western economic thought becomes clear, that the analysis of production in terms of productive factors served some larger social purpose. By elaborate schemes of reasoning such as that of marginal productivity, the returns or rights of each one of these status groups was made to seem equivalent to the obligation or duties of each.[21] In this way a status system was rationalized and a "scientific" legend has been provided as attestation of the authenticity of the status system.

Notes

1. Claude Levi-Strauss, "French Sociology" in *Twentieth Century Sociology*, ed. Georges Gurvitch and Wilbert E. Moore (New York, Philosophical Library, 1945), p. 503ff.

2. An exception has been the Institutional school in America and some continental scholars. See for instance, W. Stark, *The Ideal Foundations of Economic Thought* (New York: Oxford University Press, 1944).

3. Emile Durkheim, *The Elementary Forms of the Religious Life* (Glencoe: Free Press, 1947), book II, ch. 3.

4. Ibid., pp. 141–44; see also Sir Baldwin Spencer and F. J. Gillen, *The Arunta*, vol. 1 (London: Macmillan, 1927), ch. 5.

5. See Edwin Cannan, *Theories of Production and Distribution* (London: King, 1924), ch. 2.

6. John Stuart Mill, *Principles of Political Economy* (London: Longmans Green, 1909), Ashley ed., p. 238.

7. See J. B. Clark, *Essentials of Economic Theory*, pp. 4–5. Some ethnologists have attempted to utilize these standardized conceptualizations in analyses of other cultures with rather indifferent results. See for example Melville J. Herskovits, *Economic Anthropology* (New York: Knopf, 1952); Raymond Firth, *Primitive Economics of the New Zealand Maori* (New York: Dutton, 1929); also *Malay Fishermen: Their Peasant Economy* (London: Kegan Paul, Trench, Trubner, 1946).

8. Thorstein Veblen, "Professor Clark's Economics," reprinted in *The Place of Science in Modern Civilization* (New York: Viking, 1942), p. 193.

9. Arnold Toynbee, *The Industrial Revolution of the Eighteenth Century in England* (London: Longmans Green, 1908), esp. chs. 2–8; see also J. L. and B. Hammond, *The Rise of Modern Industry* (London: Methuen, 1925), esp. parts 1 and 2. See also Edward Heimann, *History of Economic Doctrines* (New York: Oxford University Press, 1945), ch. 2, for an excellent presentation of the influence of the social background on the theories of the "predecessors of Adam Smith."

10. Certainly there were earlier formulations of what were considered to be "factors" of production. But these too were reflections of a social structure. What is referred to in the above statement is the latter day conceptual scheme of land, labor, and capital. See Edwin Cannan, *Theories of Production and Distribution*. "This triad of productive requisites did not very early become an integral part of English political economy. Its origin is apparently to be found in Adam Smith's division of the component parts of prices into wages, profit and rent" (p. 40). Also Max Beer, *Early British Economics*, p. 112.

11. For a general discussion of reciprocity as a function of social organization see Bronislow Malinowski, *Crime and Custom in Savage Society* (New York: Harcourt Brace, 1926).

12. For the classic presentation of this argument see Henry Maine, *Ancient Law* (London: Routledge, 1905), ch. 5.

13. For the standard treatment of this see Bruce Knight and Earl Hines, *Economics* (New York: Knopf, 1952), ch. 2.

14. See James Burnham's *The Managerial Revolution*, which says in a popular and somewhat superficial manner what Berle and Means, *The Modern Corporation and Private Property*, lead up to in a meticulous and scholarly manner.

15. C. E. Ayres, *The Industrial Economy* (Boston: Houghton Mifflin, 1952), p. 354.

16. For a discussion of this subject see Lucien Levy-Bruhl, *How Natives Think* (London: Allen & Unwin, 1926). Levy-Bruhl assumed that the principle of association by participation gave way in contemporary society to the law of contradiction. This difference in logic divides the prelogical from the contemporary logical period. This aspect of Levy-Bruhl's analysis is faulty, for no such clear cut distinction between man in "earlier" and "later" societies can be made. The fact of the matter is that the "law of participation" and the law of contradiction are characteristic of thought in all societies. But we owe to Levy-Bruhl a debt of gratitude for having pointed out these phenomena of the thought process.

17. In observing the actual universe in which production takes place George Geiger in *The Theory of the Land Question* (New York: Macmillan, 1935), demonstrates quite clearly that in fact there is not too much to distinguish capital from land except the secondary position of capital in the general production process. This argument seems to point further in the direction of the social origin of the three factors of production. See especially chapter 3, "Land and Capital."

18. Lorie Tarshis, *The Elements of Economics* (Boston: Houghton Mifflin, 1947), pp. 11-12.

19. W. W. Carlile, "The Language of Economics," *Journal of Political Economy* 17, pp. 434-47.

20. M. N. Srinivas, *Religion and Society Among the Coorgs of South India* (London: Oxford, 1952), ch. 2.

Power: An Institutional Framework of Analysis

WILLIAM M. DUGGER

The rise of the corporation as the dominant institution in our culture is the subject of Dugger's article. His argument makes the following points. Corporate culture is hegemonic and has subverted other social institutions (meaning social structures) to its goals. This is the source of the continued growth of corporate power, a power exercised by social institutions, not individuals. When individuals exercise power, they are able to do so because of their position within a social hierarchy and not because of any personal efficacy. Dugger notes the loss of independence by other social institutions and the decline of institutional pluralism. Dugger has extended his analysis in more recent writings (see suggested readings at the end of this section) which point to the consequences of this process.

The problems of power and of individuality are intertwined in such a complex fashion that one cannot be understood without understanding the other. Each is rooted in the institutional structure of a going society. Let me preview my approach to the problem of power by asking several questions. Where does one start an analysis of power? An institutional analysis cannot start with power itself. Rather, the place to begin is with the question of why individuals, often physically and mentally stronger than their rulers or leaders, willingly obey orders or instructions. That question leads to another: How do individuals acquire motives, goals, ideals, and means? The answer to this takes us down to bedrock, the institutional structure in which the individual is embedded. Institutional structure is the source of power, for individuals learn motives, goals, ideals, *and means* from their participation in society's institutions. In the family, church, school, military, corporation, and government, we learn what is expected of us, and we learn how to do it. *Some* of us also learn how to exercise power, and how to back it up if need arises.

The following is an attempt to construct a holistic (institutional) framework for analyzing power. Footnotes are minimized, and useful works appear in an annotated bibliography.

Any discussion of power should first define it. Here, *power shall refer to the*

William M. Dugger, "Power: An Institutional Framework of Analysis," *Journal of Economic Issues* 14, 4 (December 1980), pp. 897–907.

ability to tell other people what to do with some degree of certainty that they will do it. When power wielders must coerce others, power is tenuous and obvious. When coercion is unnecessary, power is secure and unnoticed. In twentieth-century America, coercion is minimal. This is because power is relatively secure, except during times of overt crisis and war. Twentieth-century Americans, usually, submit to power voluntarily. Individuals often do not even consider their behavior as submissive. Rather, they "choose" to do what is expected of them. They do not even notice power. Instead, they consider themselves as free, exercising individual initiative.

These illusions of individual choice and autonomy make it very difficult to see, let alone analyze, power. The following framework will place great emphasis upon the institutional structure and the individuals it produces. Only after grasping the relation between institutional structure and individuality can power itself be analyzed.

Institutional Structure

A society is a network of institutions, each linked more or less tightly to others. An institution is two things. First, it is an organized pattern of roles, often enforced with positive and negative sanctions. Second, it is the patterned habits of thought learned by individuals performing those roles. Institutions, as both these patterns, are clustered around general functions. Each functional cluster is linked to the dominant cluster. In the American case, economic institutions dominate, for ours is a pecuniary civilization. The corporation and the labor union are the primary institutions within the economic cluster. But as organized labor has come to represent an increasingly smaller percentage of the work force, the corporation has become paramount. It increasingly gives order to the American institutional structure by linking other clusters of institutions to itself.

Institutional hegemony

American society contains six clusters of institutions: (1) Economic institutions produce and distribute commodities; (2) educational institutions produce and distribute knowledge; (3) military institutions prepare for and conduct war; (4) kinship institutions produce children; (5) political institutions make and enforce laws, with recourse to the ultimate sanction—violence; and (6) religious institutions instill faith in a system of supernatural doctrines [contrast with Gerth and Mills 1953: 26–29].

Each of the noneconomic clusters is linked to the dominant economic institution, the corporation, in a kind of means-end continuum. That is, the corporation uses other institutions as means for its own ends. This is important, because it provides the first glimpse at the true source of power.

Educational institutions, particularly public schools and state universities, produce an ample supply of trained and disciplined specialists for corporate employment. In addition to serving their ''educational'' function, high schools, junior colleges, and universities are extensions of the corporate personnel office, grading the human capital for easier processing. [. . .] Educational institutions produce the means for pursuit of corporate ends. Of course, some elite (adequately endowed) educational institutions can exercise a degree of autonomy and pursue their own ends. Nevertheless, the main thrust of education is not education, but the production of suitable graded employees with suitable knowledge. Educational institutions can ignore this corporate imperative, but only at their own risk *and expense*.

The military occupies a unique position within our institutional structure. During a cold war, it protects corporate interests at home and abroad, by underwriting corporate research and development and by buying corporate commodities. During a hot war, military institutions become dominant. Instead of being means for corporate ends, they become the ends, and corporations temporarily become the means. Yet, hot wars are infrequent and are the occasional price paid for the more useful periods of cold war.

The major kinship institution in twentieth-century America is the family. It serves two major functions for the corporation. First, as a household, it is the major outlet for corporate commodities. It is the terminal point in the Galbraithian revised sequence. If that sequence breaks down, as it occasionally does, the fault often lies within the household for failing to follow the corporate imperative: ''Thou Shalt Consume.'' Because it is the weak link in the revised sequence, tremendous corporate pressure (in the form of advertising) and corporate investigation (in the form of market research) is directed at the household. Second, as a family, the major kinship institution produces the semiprocessed materials used as inputs into educational institutions. Children must be instilled with respect for authority lest school officials find them unduly active and irreverent. Children whose ultimate destination is corporate management (future technocrats) must also be instilled with a desire to succeed. If families fail in this general child-molding function, resort is often made to psychotherapy (drug abuse, either professionally applied or self-administered), corporal punishment, or incarceration.

Political institutions—parties, state and federal legislatures, executive and judiciary branches—are, in a sense, the most unruly of all twentieth-century American institutions. This is because they sometimes pursue ends that are not corporate means. The roles of persons in political institutions are of very ancient origin. They evolved long before the corporation. The people performing these roles often acquire motives, goals, ideals, and means that took concrete form in the Age of Enlightenment rather than in the Age of Corporate Capital. Some judges seek justice; some legislators seek equality, liberty, and fraternity; some presidents seek basic social reforms. The institutional roles they perform not only teach them these noncorporate habits of thought, but also provide them with the *means* to follow them. Such individuals possess power, that is, they can tell others what to do with some degree of certainty that they will do it, but most political officials exercise their power in the service of corporate ends. After all, corporations usually fund the higher educational institutions they attend, employ their fathers, give them their first jobs, finance their campaigns, provide them with the information they need to perform their public duties, and hire them when they tire of "public" service. In short, the habits of thought of most political officials are those learned in performing, or in preparing to perform, corporate roles. These political officials are *not corrupt*. They are *not conspirators*. They do not have to be. They simply follow the motives, goals, and ideals they have learned, and in doing so they also use the means they have learned.

The last major cluster of American institutions are those that pursue religious ends. But they employ economic means, and there is the rub. Most American religious denominations employ various functionaries and officials. These employees must be paid, or at least fed, clothed, and sheltered. Most denominations also use various and assorted houses of worship. These must be of a substantial nature, for they serve a substantial purpose. In short, religious institutions must be financed, and without the power to tax, financing comes from voluntary contributions. If a religious institution pushes too hard against the sensibilities of its financiers, it loses their support. Sad, perhaps, but the bottom line is brutally clear. Most religious institutions cannot aggressively attempt to change the habits of thought of their lay supporters for fear of losing their support. By and large, this means that most religious institutions have little autonomy. Even if religious leaders want to instill certain habits of thought in their lay supporters, the best they can do is legitimate or reinforce those habits of thought already held. If they preach against them, they may lose the means necessary to do so. Ours is a secular society.

In summary, at the close of the twentieth century, a structure of institutional hegemony clearly can be discerned in the United States. With a few exceptions, noneconomic institutions are either ineffective (religious) or perform functions linked to the corporation, the dominant economic institution. Most institutions are means to corporate ends. People performing roles in these subordinate institutions may possess power, but it is usually exercised in such a way that it serves corporate ends. Their power, such as it is, is not autonomous. Rather, it is literally and figuratively incorporated into an institutional structure of corporate hegemony.

Instruments of Hegemony

This corporate hegemony is not held together by a conspiracy. Several social mechanisms simply operate in such a way that they become instruments of hegemony, means of corporate domination, and, ultimately, the social cement holding the edifice together. These social mechanisms may be termed the superstructure, but the name is unimportant. Four of them are important to an understanding of power: subreption, contamination, emulation, and mystification.

In legal terms, subreption is unfair or unlawful representation through suppression or fraudulent concealment of facts. In this article it refers to the process whereby the function performed by one cluster of institutions becomes the means of another cluster of institutions. Thorstein Veblen's *Higher Learning in America* is perhaps the best study of subreption ever written. According to Veblen, higher learning has its own means and ends: the increase and dissemination of knowledge. The major institution performing this function is the university, but American universities are not autonomous. They are run by and for businessmen. As a result, the end of higher learning has become subrepted into a business means. Universities became "practical" and began producing practical knowledge (how to get something for nothing) and practical men. Knowledge for knowledge's sake faded into the background.

It is through subreption that the allegedly autonomous clusters of American institutions have become linked to one dominant institution, the corporation. Subreption is one of the least studied social phenomena of the twentieth century. The reason is simple. Subreption destroys the foundation of a pluralistic society. That is, subreption replaces institutional autonomy, a half-truth so near and dear to the hearts of mainstream liberals, with institutional hegemony, the foundation of corporate power and the reality of twentieth-century America. It is through subreption that the functions (ends) of our major institutions have become *incorporated* as the means of one dominant institution. In the process, the power of the subrepted institutions has either declined or has become an extension of corporate power. [. . .]

Contamination occurs when the motives appropriate for the roles of one institution spread to the roles of others. Religious institutions in the United States are contaminated with corporate (pecuniary) motives to the extent that the acquisition and display of wealth (conspicuous consumption) has become *the* motive of many religious officials. To the extent that they are judged by and judge themselves by their moral and theological stature, they are free of contamination. To the extent that they judge themselves and are judged by the stature of their real estate, they are contaminated. That is, their motives are those of business.

The same applies to people in other institutional roles. "Vote for John Doe and put sound business practices to work in city government." "This university should be run according to sound business principles." "What this family needs is a business manager!" Although obvious, it seldom consciously occurs to people in their roles as political official, university administrator, or parent that governments, universities, and families are not business corporations. As a result, motives appropriate for corporate roles have contaminated the roles performed in other institutions, giving corporate roles and those performing them far more weight than noncorporate ones.

Contamination is akin to emulation. Emulation, as used here, occurs when one institution or cluster successfully denies the prestige claims of other institutions and successfully realizes its own claims, becoming the fountainhead of social value. That is, emulation occurs when one institution becomes *the* source of status. Acquisition of status then comes from performing the top roles of the dominant institution and from displaying that successful performance. In our society, one must earn and then spend big money.

One earns it performing a top corporate role of one form or another. One spends it, not just in conspicuous consumption, which is a bit gauche, but also in "public service." A choice ambassadorial post is an excellent way to turn corporate cash to public account (acclaim). Philanthropy is also a suitable activity, for educational and religious institutions are always in need of the businessman's pocket *and the businessman's animus.* [. . .]

Through emulation, two things happen. First, corporate leaders cash in their corporate status by becoming leaders of other institutions. Second, and more important, people performing roles in other institutions do *not* object to the usurpers. Instead, they wish to be like their corporate benefactors. Through emulation, strong and proud men *willingly* accept the status claims of others and *willingly* denigrate their own.

Mystification is the emulation and distortion of symbols. It occurs when one institution produces the most important or the most valued symbols of a society and other institutions attempt to emulate or support them. Such symbols as "free (corporate) enterprise," "private (corporate) property," and "individual initiative" are examples of two things. First, they are very important symbols to most Americans. These symbols all originate in the corporate sphere of life and are actively disseminated by that sphere and by its outlyers. They represent or purport to represent things of great value to Americans in all walks of life. Second, these symbols are mystifications, distortions. In the twentieth century, free enterprise, private property, and individual initiative no longer mean what they purport to mean. Instead, they are mysteries or talismans of immense ceremonial potency. These symbols are used as weapons, both offensive and defensive. When used defensively, they rally public support for free enterprise (that is, corporate power to administer prices) in the oil industry, for example. When used offensively, they rally support for individual initiative (that is, union busting and right-to-work laws) in the southern textile mills, for example. Of course, the symbol "private property" is so powerful that its potency even protects *corporate* property from abuse at the hands of the profane (socialists and national planners).

In short, corporate hegemony is maintained, not through a conspiracy, but through four social mechanisms. Subreption ties all institutions together so that noncorporate institutions are used as means to corporate ends. Contamination puts corporate role motives into noncorporate roles. Emulation allows corporate leaders to gain acceptance, even respect, in noncorporate leadership roles. And mystification covers the corporate hegemony with a protective (magic) cloak of the most valued American symbols.

Individuality and Power

Individuality

The source or foundation of power should now be clear. It is institutional position, not individual strength, will, or cunning. But this statement may simply beg the question, for do not strong, willful, and cunning individuals rise to high positions and then use those positions for their own ends? The answer is no, because the question contains a false premise. The question assumes, incorrectly, that powerful individuals acquire their ends *independently* of the institutional roles they performed on their way to the top. This is not true. Prefabricated individuals are not simply selected to perform certain roles. Instead, as individuals perform certain roles, they are shaped by the roles they play.

An institution is an organized set of roles *and* the habits of thought people learn as they perform them. Furthermore, our current institutional structure is one of corporate hegemony, which means that in the family, the school, and then in the corporation proper, individuals are shaped by the roles they play in each institution, and each institution is itself linked to the corporation. For the individual who passes through the family and school on his or her way to the corporation, this institutional shaping produces the motives, goals, ideals, and means of the individual.

Veblen surely would have called the shaping process habituation to the corporate way of life, for that is exactly what it is. Individuals who pass through this habituation process and find themselves chief executives for the largest corporations are very powerful men. But they do not exercise *individual* power.

Power

The power of corporate executives is not individual but institutional, in both its source and in its direction. In other words, both the ends and the means of their power are institutionally determined. The ends of power are institutionally determined because the motives, goals, and ideals of the powerful have been learned in their role-by-role climb to the top. From the role of father's little man, through teacher's star pupil, to chief executive's protégé, the powerful executive learns how and why to act, how and why to think.

Furthermore, if he is religious, then God provides him with the ultimate sanction. If he has been in the military, then as chief executive of XYZ corporation, he performs his patriotic duty. If he has served in government, then political doors and regulatory rules are open to him. Such access helps him prevent unfair competition and unbusinesslike principles in government. In short, other institutions are his means. But his ends are corporate, not religious, not military, not political.

The means of power are also institutionally determined because, as a corporate executive, religious, military (outside of hot war), educational, and political ends are all available to him as means. The leaders and followers of the other institutions depend upon him for material and immaterial support. He is not depended upon as an individual, but as head of an institution. His power, and the willing obedience to it, are institutionally determined. Another can easily fill his shoes. This is because both individual power and what individuals do with it are determined by the institutional roles performed. Institutional roles, then, and the "superstructure" supporting them, are the ultimate source of power.

Conclusion

The top roles in the top institutions of any institutional structure (society) are supported by certain social mechanisms, by a substructure. This is what reinforces the power of a top role, whether that role be in second-century Rome or twentieth-century America. But in the former case, power is easy to see and to analyze because it was tenuous and based on coercion. In the latter case, power is difficult to see and to analyze because it is secure and based on voluntary compliance. Institutional analysis is the key to understanding power based on obedience or compliance. It is from institutionally organized roles that we, in twentieth-century America, learn the habits of thought conducive to getting along in the institutional structure into which we are born.

Getting along means adjusting to our position in life. We are aided in this adjustment process (Veblen's habituation) by four social mechanisms. These not only support and reinforce the top roles in our top institutions, but also help all of us, including the performers of the top roles, accept the situation, perhaps even enjoy it. Through subreption, the ends of teachers and students, parents and children, military officers and enlisted men, elected officials and bureaucratic staff, nicely mesh into a means-ends continuum. They provide the means, the corporation the ends. And he who serves best is happiest. Through contamination, a churchman can work for a huge building fund and feel good about it; a student and her teacher can work for a good job offer and feel the same. In short, people in all walks of life can acquire and follow a pecuniary animus, even though in doing so they are borrowing corporate motives and applying them to noncorporate activities. Nevertheless, they do so willingly. They individually and freely want to, therefore it is right and good; or so they think.

Being contaminated with the motives of corporate business, very few people notice that the values and prestige claims of corporate life are emulated in *all* walks of life, allowing successful performers of top corporate roles to cash in their claims by becoming leaders of noncorporate institutions. All this is done, not in the name of the corporation, but in the name of free enterprise, or private property, or individual initiative. Mystification allows (some of) us to think that individual initiative is served by union busting, to believe that private property is protected by fighting land use planning, and to believe that free enterprise is served by dismantling government regulation of corporate power.

These processes and the structure of power that they support (corporate institutional hegemony) are laid bare through an *institutional* not an individual framework of analysis. If we are to change that structure, and surely we must, because it is inconsistent with democracy, with liberty, equality, and fraternity, then we must first change the institutions and social processes that create and support it. Simply calling for a revival or a renewal of the individual human "spirit" will not suffice. That spirit is a pattern of learned habits of thought, and through institutional analysis, we know where those habits of thought are learned.

Annotated Bibliography

Arnold, Thurman W. *The Folklore of Capitalism*. New Haven: Yale University Press, 1937. Excellent work on mystification.

Berle, Adolph A., and Gardiner C. Means. *The Modern Corporation and Private Property*. Rev. ed. New York: Harcourt, Brace and World, 1968. Authoritative work on separation of ownership from control.

Coleman, James S. *Power and the Structure of Society*. New York: W. W. Norton, 1974. Discussion of the power of a new creature, the corporation.

Commons, John R. *Institutional Economics*. Madison: University of Wisconsin Press, 1961. Going concerns, working rules, and foundations of institutional analysis.

Dahl, Robert A. *Who Governs?* New Haven: Yale University Press, 1961. Pluralist social theory and empirical support.

Dowd, Douglas F. *The Twisted Dream*. 2d ed. Cambridge, Mass.: Winthrop Publishers, 1977. Institutional analysis from an evolutionary and radical perspective, focused on the United States.

Galbraith, John Kenneth. *The New Industrial State*. Boston: Houghton Mifflin, 1967.

————. *The Affluent Society*. 2d ed. Boston: Houghton Mifflin, 1969.

————. *Economics and the Public Purpose*. Boston: Houghton Mifflin, 1973. A grand summary of Galbraithian economics.

Gerth, Hans, and C. Wright Mills. *Character and Social Structure*. New York: Harcourt, Brace and World, 1953. Superb discussion of institutional roles and their shaping of individuals.

Kanter, Rosabeth Moss. *Men and Women of the Corporation*. New York: Basic Books, 1977. Excellent case study of corporate behavior.

Maccoby, Michael. *The Gamesman*. New York: Simon and Schuster, 1976. Psychological study of character types in the corporate world.

Melman, Seymour. *The Permanent War Economy*. New York: Simon and Schuster, 1974.

Mills, C. Wright. *White Collar*. New York: Oxford University Press, 1951. The social life of the middle class.

————. *The Power Elite*. New York: Oxford University Press, 1956. Classic study of power in the higher circles.

————. *The Sociological Imagination*. New York: Oxford University Press, 1959. Exploration of the relations between personal biographies and social forces.

Pirsig, Robert M. *Zen and the Art of Motorcycle Maintenance: An Inquiry into Values*. New York: Bantam Books, 1974.

Tool, Marc R. *The Discretionary Economy*. Santa Monica: Goodyear, 1979.

Veblen, Thorstein. *The Theory of the Leisure Class*. New York: Macmillan, 1899. Discussion of emulation.

————. *The Theory of Business Enterprise*. New York: Charles Scribners Sons, 1904. The means and ends of business.

————. *The Instinct of Workmanship.* New York: Macmillan, 1914. Discussion of the Veblenian dichotomy, pecuniary versus industrial.

————. *The Higher Learning in America: A Memorandum on the Conduct of Universities by Business Men.* New York: B. W. Huebsch, 1918. The subtitle is explanatory.

————. *The Place of Science in Modern Civilization and Other Essays.* New York: B. W. Huebsch, 1919. Collection of classic essays.

Whyte, William H., Jr. *The Organization Man.* Garden City: Doubleday, 1957.

Institutionalist Perspectives
on Policy

Institutionalists, like Marxists, are committed to progressive social change. Their view of the economic life process of a community is such that progressive social change is the successful application of organized human intelligence to social and economic problems. There is no preconceived end or goal to be attained. The objective is progress in the sense of solving today's problems and improving on our ability to solve tomorrow's problems. Moreover, there is no inevitability built into the Institutionalists' view of the economy. A society may progress or decline, a policy may succeed or fail, the life process is just one problem after another, the goal is to "keep the machines (and the community) running" (Ayres, *The Theory of Economic Progress*, p. 233).

In general terms, Institutionalist policy begins with the identification of a problem. The cause of the problem must be carefully analyzed. Of particular interest to the Institutionalists are the social structures in which problems occur. This is because the technical solution to a problem is often straightforward—the solution to the problem of hunger is the provision of food. However, rigid hierarchical social structure and other types of institutional attitudes and behaviors often inhibit the ability of a particular social structure to respond to a problem in an appropriate way. This has led Institutionalists to emphasize the process of institutional adjustment as an important part of their applied research.

No serious social or economic problem has escaped the attention of the Institutionalists. Three areas in particular where Institutional research has made important and unique contributions deserve special attention: the evolution, concentration, and exercise of corporate power have been areas of persistent interest to Institutionalists. Institutionalists have studied the development of the modern corporation from its beginnings as a small productive unit to its current status as the hegemonic cultural institution in the U.S. and world economy. The problems created by this institution are legion. There have been some discernible general characteristics of various policy prescriptions formulated by Institutionalists to cope with the growing power of large corporations. One characteristic is to formulate policies to strengthen democratic institutions in our society such as labor unions and consumer groups to offset the growing power of corporations. Along with this are policies that attempt to limit the penetration of other institutions, such as higher education and government, by the corporate structure.

Another characteristic of Institutional policy prescriptions designed to deal with growing corporate power is policies that propose using the powers of government to limit corporate activity. Policies of this type range from simple regulation to national corporate chartering to nationalization of some industries.

Economic development has also been an area of interest for many Institutional economists. The core of Institutional theory concerns itself with social change, particularly with the impacts of technological change on progress and the resistance of social institutions to progress. Institutionalists have always defined progress in terms of both qualitative and quantitative improvement, rather than increases in per capita income. As a result policy recommendations have centered around such issues as technology transfers, reducing institutional blockages to change, preventing the exploitation of developing countries by multinational corporations and their allies in developed countries, and encouraging production for domestic use rather than export. Development is the process of a society becoming better able to meet its own needs and to provide individuals in that society with the opportunity to lead fulfilling lives. This results in a strong emphasis in the area of development policy on education, health care, infrastructure, and agricultural self-sufficiency rather than industrialization and integration into world markets.

Institutional economists have also addressed systematically and persistently the problem of unemployment and underemployment. As with all problematic situations, much effort has gone into finding the causes of unemployment and carefully analyzing its impacts and the resulting poverty on people in society. Policy proposals cover a range of suggested solutions from training programs to public works projects to guaranteed employment in the public sector. In recent years interest has risen in so-called Institutional labor market theories. These fledgling theories take careful note of how jobs are allocated within firms. Moreover, they use the notions of status and invidious comparisons as criteria for employment, thereby reintroducing a cultural component into the analysis. In addition, these theories make no attempt to be value neutral; they are directed at problem solving. Even though the authors of these works often do not identify their ideas or themselves as Institutionalist, the above-mentioned characteristics seem to indicate the label is appropriate.

Institutional policy prescriptions are not intended to bring about a particular, preconceived societal structure. Institutional policy is directed at making any existing structure better able to solve its problems. Ideological adherence and allegiance to a particular type of social structure, whether market capitalism or socialism, are seen as institutional encumbrances that limit the range of human discretion. The goal of Institutionalists is to explore and expand our options.

Suggested Reading

The vast majority of the work of the early Institutionalists is available from Augustus M. Kelley Publishers, Inc. in their Reprints of Economics Classics series.

C. E. Ayres. *The Theory of Economic Progress*. 3d ed. Kalamazoo: New Issues Press, 1978.

—————. *Towards a Reasonable Society*. Austin: University of Texas Press, 1961.

W. Dugger. *An Alternative to Economic Retrenchment*. New York: Petrocelli Books, 1984.

J. K. Galbraith. *Economics and the Public Purpose*. Boston: Houghton Mifflin, 1973.

W. Gordon. *Institutional Economics*. Austin: University of Texas Press, 1980.

J. Munkirs. *The Transformation of American Capitalism*. Armonk, N.Y.: M. E. Sharpe, Inc., 1985.

M. Tool. *The Discretionary Economy*. Encore ed. Boulder: Westview Press, 1985.

M. Tool, ed. *An Institutionalist Guide to Economics and Policy*. Armonk, N.Y.: M. E. Sharpe, Inc., 1985.

IV
Marxist Political Economy

Introduction

Marxist analysis was in eclipse in many Western countries during the 1950s. In the United States, the cold war and its intensified domestic reflection in the McCarthy era meant that use of Marxist analysis could be dangerous to one's professional or physical life—it could cause social ostracism, loss of a job, incarceration. One or a combination of those sanctions befell authors, labor leaders, teachers, actors, and other citizens. In the United States renewed interest in and resurgent use of Marxist analysis date largely from the 1960s. A searching critical attitude toward Western societies and a domestic thaw in the cold war set the stage for exploration and renewed development of an approach to economics that had a long history.

Those who turned to Marxist analysis in the 1960s were often surprised to find a rich tradition. Paul Sweezy had published *The Theory of Capitalist Development* in 1942, prior to the cold war. He was also instrumental in establishing the popularly written journal *Monthly Review* in 1949, and keeping it alive through the McCarthy era. Paul Baran, an economist at Stanford University, published *The Political Economy of Growth* in 1957. By 1967 all three volumes of Marx's *Capital* were available in inexpensive English-language editions by International Publishers. Equally important, they could actually be found in bookstores, along with the work of Rosa Luxemburg, V. I. Lenin, Mao Zedong, Antonio Gramsci, and others who make up the Marxist tradition. In Europe Ernest Mandel's two-volume *Marxist Economic Theory* met with critical acclaim. It was translated into English and published in the United States in 1968. Baran and Sweezy together used a reformulation of Marxist analysis in *Monopoly Capital*, an analysis of modern capitalism, written in 1966. Mandel's analysis of contemporary capitalism appeared under the English title of *Late Capitalism* in 1975. The list quickly becomes overwhelming. The point is that a resurgence of more than twenty years' duration has included both scrutiny of original texts, some of which have only become readily available during that time, and a rich legacy of new work in this field.

Separating Marxist analysis from what has been done in the name of Marxism (or capitalism) has never been easy. World opinion about a particular political regime, Western attempts to forestall critical analysis of capitalism, the linkages between theory and practice—all of these factors impinge on attempts to separate the analysis from forms of political activity that bear the same name. The subject of this section of the anthology is Marxist analysis, understood as a methodology, a form of inquiry, a set of tools by which the world can be comprehended. A brief essay at the end of this section provides examples of policy prescription that could follow from this analysis.

Our introduction to this volume identified a number of defining characteristics of Marxist political economy. Some are shared with other schools of thought presented in the volume—for instance the historical and relatively broad scope of the analysis—and some, such as dialectical materialism, are unique to Marxist political economy. Despite debates within Marxist analysis, the following characteristics can generally be considered as essential to it. Each will be described briefly.

A Marxist analysis is fundamentally materialist and dialectical. Marx and Engels worked from a materialist understanding of history. That meant that they focused attention on the conditions under which production and material reproduction of life were carried out, and they understood those conditions to be centrally important in shaping a society. History consists of the development of the forces of production—those skills, tools, and methods by which people sustain themselves materially. In Marxist analysis these factors play a central role in shaping the way in which people, individually and as members of certain groups, relate to one another. They are also fundamental to shaping the governing institutions and even the ideas held in common by members of that society.

Change is taken to be constant in life, and the theoretical explanation of how change takes place lies in dialectics. This dialectical understanding of change is based in human activity. Marx's dialectics locates the origin of change within a particular social system as the result of the interplay of opposite, contradictory forces. Change involves transformations: the overcoming of contradictions, the creation of new ones. Fundamental contradictions can ultimately be resolved only through practical human action that is informed by theoretical understanding and critical insight. These historical and philosophical foundations call primary attention to production rather than exchange, and to analysis of the changing ways in which production takes place.

During the most recent few centuries capitalism has constituted the social and economic system of production and reproduction for much of the world's population. It has demonstrated an ability to produce an unprecedented social surplus for the core societies that are most adept at making it work in their interest. That social surplus—the material wealth over and above what is necessary for reproduction—reflects both the glory of and a basic contradiction within capitalism. Relative to previous ways of producing, its magnitude marks a major advance. Yet it is a limited advance in that most of it belongs not to society as a whole, but to a relatively small and privileged group in the society—those who own and control the means of production.

Marxist analysis is thus also a class analysis. Classes are groups in society defined in terms of their relationship to the means of production. Most fundamental to an analysis of capitalism are owners—the capitalists or bourgeoisie—and those people who work for them—the workers or proletariat. The relationship between these two classes is antagonistic; their interests are in conflict. The primary reason for this antagonistic relationship is the power that capitalists have to control the production process and its product, and ultimately to appropriate social surplus. Workers are exploited in that they receive far less than the value of what they have produced in a day. Those who own capital reap much of the surplus, and maintain control over production and other aspects of society in ways that assure that they can go on accumulating more surplus. The majority of society lives in poverty and insecurity relative to them.

Accumulation marks the logic of capitalism. Threats to profitability are threats to accumulation, and thus to the system itself. The constant quest for profit shapes battles and skirmishes in an unending, sometimes overt and sometimes more subtle, war between the two major opposing classes. It is that conflict that plays a major role in shaping the direction of change *within* capitalism, as changes in organization, technology, incentive systems, and state regulations are formulated in the interest, ultimately, of maintaining or increasing profitability. Similarly contests over work rules, hours worked and levels of pay, and benefits provided both at work and for those without work reflect labor's quest for a greater share of the social product. Labor, perhaps in conjunction with other groups in society, can work for changes within the system to ameliorate its most negative effects. However, Marxist analysis has traditionally recognized the working class as the group with the reason, the numbers, and the skills to transform the system fundamentally. Most basically that change would be to a more egalitarian, and ultimately classless, society.

The capitalist system grows geographically, it grows by turning more and more aspects of life into commodities that can be sold for profit, and it takes growing amounts of the world's resources to make those commodities. Contradictions abound, and the system is prone to crisis. In the quest for profit, the ever-increasing substitution of capital for labor in the production process can threaten profitability. It is, after all, human labor that creates the surplus from which profit is derived. In addition, people thrown out of work cannot afford to purchase the products of an ever more prolific productive apparatus. Growth is a necessity, but it requires confidence in the stability of the system and its ability to deliver profit, and that confidence often proves elusive. These forms of crisis coexist with an everyday reality of capitalism: that people within the system resist exploitation, as do people in regions or nations who are being newly subjected to it.

Marxist political economy is better known, more fully developed, and more regularly used than it was just two decades ago. It is put to use in orthodox forms that emphasize the economic laws of motion of capitalism, and in various Neo-Marxist formulations that emphasize political and cultural issues, or that integrate categories of gender or race on an equal footing with class in their analysis. Marxist political economy is both a means of understanding the world and more.

Karl Marx stressed the unity of theory and practice. Most who work in this school of thought accept Marx's argument that the point is not simply to interpret the world, but to change it.

Articles by John Gurley and Paul Sweezy provide good entry points to this analysis. Those by Anwar Shaikh and Nancy Folbre represent conceptually more complex work in this school of thought. The article by Herbert Gintis in part 1 could also be counted as part of this section. In addition to its critical component it presents a Marxist analysis of labor markets and the labor process.

Marx and the Critique
of Capitalism

JOHN G. GURLEY

John Gurley provides a summary of the basic principles of Marxist economic theory—one that emphasizes Marx's understanding of the ways in which capitalism works while not ignoring the broader historical themes of his analysis. His summary grounds much of what follows in this section by defining basic concepts—exploitation, surplus value, accumulation of capital, appearances and reality in capitalist society, crisis and transition—in an integrated, highly readable essay.

Marx and Engels generally addressed postcapitalist society in broad terms, purposely avoiding any attempt to sketch the future in detail. Professor Gurley distills some of their thinking on socialism and communism in concluding this article.

Few Americans seem to be acquainted with what lies at the very heart of Marx's thought: his economic analysis of the capitalist mode of production. It is not possible to appreciate the Marxian critique of capitalist society without some knowledge of his theories: how this mode of production actually works (which includes the theory of exploitation), how it is consciously or unconsciously distorted by its apologists, and how it will eventually be replaced by socialism. This article contains explanations of these theories and with them an understanding of why Marx's ideas continue to live throughout much of the world.

How Capitalism Works

Marx defined capitalism as a particular, historically determined mode of production. He analyzed this mode dialectically in terms of a growing contradiction between the productive forces and the social relations of production that would reveal itself in increasingly severe crises and ever more intense struggles between the bourgeoisie and the proletariat. Inasmuch as Marxian theory reflected the rise of the industrial working class, and served that class, it was highly critical of both the capitalist mode and its ideologists. It was also revolutionary in that it was at the same time an analysis, a prediction, and a catalyst of the coming overthrow of the bourgeoisie by the proletariat—and, hence, of bourgeois theory by Marxian theory.

John G. Gurley, ''Marx and the Critique of Capitalism,'' chapter 3 of *Challengers to Capitalism: Marx, Lenin, Stalin, and Mao*, 2d ed. (New York: W. W. Norton, 1980), pp. 31–61.

Marx insisted that "capital" is not a thing but a definite social relation which belonged to a specific historical formation of society. "The means of production become capital," Marx wrote, "only insofar as they have become separated from the laborer and confront labor as an independent power." Means of production are capital when they have become monopolized by a certain sector of society and used by that class to produce surplus value—that is, the income of the capitalist class (generally profits, interest, and rent) that comes from the exploitation of another class. Consequently, capital, for Marx, is not only part of the forces of production but it is also a particular employment of those forces, a social relation.

Capital appears in four major forms: (1) industrial, (2) trading, (3) lending, and (4) renting. Industrial capital *produces* and *realizes* surplus value—the former in the production sphere and the latter in the circulation sphere—while the other forms *redistribute* it among the various claimants of capitalists. Capital, in the social forms of instruments of labor, raw materials, and labor power, produces surplus value in the production sphere. Capital, in the social forms of commodities and money, realizes surplus value for the capitalist class in the sphere of circulation. Capital, in the social forms of merchants' (trading) capital, interest-bearing (lending) capital, and landed (renting) capital, distributes the surplus value among industrial, commercial, financial, and landed capitalists. Surplus value appears mainly as industrial profits, commercial profits, interest, and rent. (Major forms are shown in figure 1.)

The Production and Realization of Surplus Value

Marx demonstrated that surplus value is created in the production sphere. However, its realization (the sale of the commodities at their "value"—a term defined below) occurs in the sphere of circulation. Surplus value arises when a capitalist purchases labor power (the capacity for labor) at its value, employs the labor power in a work process that he controls, and then appropriates the commodities produced. Surplus value is the difference between the net value of these commodities and the value of labor power itself.

The *value* of labor power is the cost of maintaining and reproducing the worker and his family at a socially accepted standard of living. This level, in some poor countries, may include only the bare necessities, but in others it will also include a "moral element"—what "society," in its real development, has determined to be an average standard of living for a laborer and his family.

A worker sells his labor power—his mental and physical capabilities—to a capitalist for its value, and the capitalist uses the labor power to obtain commodities which have a value higher than that of the labor power purchased. Thus, the secret of surplus value is that labor power is a source of more value than it has itself. The capitalist is able to capture the surplus value through his ownership of the means of production and his historically established right to purchase labor power as a commodity, to control the work process, and to claim the product as

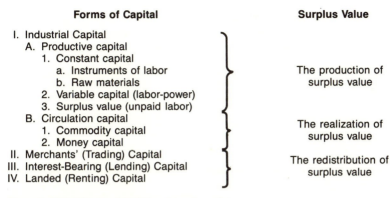

Forms of Capital	Surplus Value

I. Industrial Capital
  A. Productive capital
    1. Constant capital
      a. Instruments of labor
      b. Raw materials
    2. Variable capital (labor-power)
    3. Surplus value (unpaid labor)
  B. Circulation capital
    1. Commodity capital
    2. Money capital
II. Merchants' (Trading) Capital
III. Interest-Bearing (Lending) Capital
IV. Landed (Renting) Capital

The production of surplus value

The realization of surplus value

The redistribution of surplus value

Figure 1. Major forms of capital and surplus value

his property. This surplus value, according to Marx, is the measure of capital's exploitation of labor.

Marx used a simple model of the firm to illustrate his concept of exploitation. The gross value of a commodity produced by a firm is the socially necessary labor time which is embodied in that commodity at all stages of its production. ("Socially necessary" means that the commodity is produced under the normal conditions of production with the average degree of skill and intensity prevalent at the time—and that there is a demand for it.) Marx divided the *gross value* of a commodity into three parts.

The first portion of gross value is *constant capital* (*c*), which is the value—the socially necessary labor time—of capital goods and raw materials used up in the production of a commodity. For instance, machinery is used up in the sense that it depreciates when used to produce commodities. Such items are called "constant" because they add no more value to the final product than they themselves lose in the production process. That is, workers may have been exploited when they previously produced the machines and raw materials, but the machines and raw materials themselves cannot be exploited by the capitalist when they are used to produce other commodities, for they do not produce more than their own value; only labor does that.

The second part of a commodity's gross value is *variable capital* (*v*). This is the value of the direct labor which is used in the production process (along with the machinery and the raw materials) *and* which is paid for. It is the value of labor power. This is equal to the wages paid for the socially necessary labor time required to maintain and reproduce the worker and his family at a socially accepted level of living. Thus, if a worker, in a 10-hour day, is able to produce enough in 6 hours to maintain and reproduce himself, this is equal to his wage and is Marx's variable capital. It is called "variable" because the use of laborpower by the capitalist results in the worker producing more value than it costs to reproduce him.

Surplus value (*s*), the third portion of gross value, is the unpaid amount of the direct labor—a part of the value of the commodity produced by the worker in the remaining 4 hours of the workday, which is appropriated by the capitalist in the form of surplus value. Thus, if constant capital is 1 hour, the gross value is 11 hours. The gross value less constant capital and variable capital equals the surplus value of 4. The worker produces but does not receive 4 hours of commodities, which become, in money form, profits, interest, and rent.

The three components together make up the gross value of the product. That is, let

$$C' = \text{gross value of the product}$$
$$c = \text{constant capital}$$
$$v = \text{variable capital}$$
$$s = \text{surplus value}$$

then

$$C' = c + v + s.$$

The *net value* of the product omits the using up of the capital goods and raw materials and so is equal to $v + s$. Labor creates the full value of the net product ($v + s$) but receives only v. The capitalist, by virtue of his ownership of the means of production, is enabled to appropriate s, the surplus value.

The *rate of surplus value* (s'), or the degree of exploitation, is defined as S/V, the ratio of surplus value to variable capital. Marx also called this the ratio of surplus labor time to necessary labor time, the former being that portion of the working day during which the worker creates surplus value, the latter being that portion of the working day during which the worker produces enough to maintain and reproduce himself. Labor is exploited to the extent that a capitalist class appropriates privately what in fact labor produced.

Does that mean that machines and raw materials are not productive? No, they are productive: they transfer their value to the product. But they are not the creators of surplus value. Machines cannot be exploited by the capitalist. The labor that produced the machines has already been exploited by the previous capitalist who received the surplus value. The machine was then sold at its value (including the surplus value) and so cannot be exploited again at the next stage of production. At this later stage of production, the machine transfers its value, and nothing more, to the commodities. But do not machines raise the productivity of labor and so enable a capitalist to obtain larger surplus value? Machines do raise labor productivity. But, while machines enable the worker to produce more, it is only the labor that produces the surplus value. Only the workers themselves produce value for the capitalist that exceeds the value of their own labor power. A commodity is produced by direct labor and indirect labor (machines and raw materials); direct labor creates the surplus value, and indirect labor (embodied in c) aids direct labor in so doing.

Surplus value, then, arises in the depths of the production process, not on the surface of circulation, not by capitalists buying cheap and selling dear, not by their cheating. Marx illustrated this in the following way:

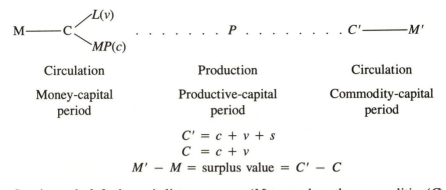

Circulation	Production	Circulation
Money-capital period	Productive-capital period	Commodity-capital period

$$C' = c + v + s$$
$$C = c + v$$
$$M' - M = \text{surplus value} = C' - C$$

Starting at the left, the capitalist uses money (M) to purchase the commodities (C) needed in the production process—that is, labor power (L) and the means of production (MP). These purchases occur in the circulation sphere, where equal values are exchanged, in this case money capital for two "inputs" in the production process. Thus, Marx termed this part of the circulation sphere (where commodities are bought with money and sold for money) the "money-capital period." The result of the production process (. . . P . . .) is the creation of a final commodity (C'), the value of which exceeds that of C by the amount of surplus value incorporated in it. This commodity is then sold for money (C'—— M'), a transaction carried out in the other part of the circulation sphere, where once again equal values are exchanged—initiated this time by commodity capital, the money used to buy commodities and thus to complete the circuit. C' minus C represents surplus value, as does M' minus M. The former, however, reflects the *production* of surplus value; the latter, the *realization* of surplus value. After realizing surplus value, the capitalist repeats the process on an enlarged scale with the larger sum of money capital. This means, for instance, that he enlarges the size of his plant and produces a larger volume of commodities.

The Redistribution of Surplus Value

Surplus value includes not only the profits of the industrial capitalists whom we have just considered, but also the profits of commercial capitalists, interest of money lenders or finance capitalists, and ground rent of landowning capitalists. Marx also noted that directors of business firms and others took shares of the surplus, too. We should further note that the state maintains its bureaucracy and protects the social relations of production with some of the surplus, in the form of taxes.

The rate of surplus value (s'), as we have seen, is equal to s/v. To measure the *rate of profit* (p'), Marx used $p' = s/(c + v)$ on the assumptions (1) that all machinery and raw materials were used up entirely, and labor power paid for, in the one production period, (2) that capitalists advanced wages to laborers, and (3) that all surplus value was retained by industrial capitalists. Thus, $C = c + v$ is the total capital advanced, and the rate of profit is the percentage that the retained surplus value bears to it. Since the rate of profit ($s/(c + v)$) is computed on a wider base than that used for the rate of surplus value (s/v), the rate of surplus value will be greater than the rate of profit if c is positive—that is, if machinery and raw materials are utilized in production.

A third ratio defined by Marx was that of the *organic composition of capital* (g), equal to $c/(c + v)$, which is a measure for the degree of capital intensity in production. This rate shows the extent to which a capitalist uses constant capital (c) relative to total capital ($c + v$). The organic composition of capital tends to be high when the value of machinery and raw materials is large relative to that of direct labor. This is the case, for example, in highly automated enterprises.

The three ratios—showing the rate of exploitation or suplus value (s'), the rate of profit (p'), and the organic composition of capital (g)—can be combined in one equation: $p' = s'(1 - g)$. This indicates that if g were zero—that is, if only direct labor were used by the capitalist—then the rate of profit would be equal to the rate of exploitation. As the capitalist uses more and more machinery and raw materials relative to direct labor, g rises and the rate of profit falls relative to the rate of exploitation. That is, the rate of profit then tends to understate the extent to which capitalists are exploiting labor. Thus, even though the rate of exploitation were 40 percent, the rate of profit might be only 10 percent, if the capitalist used a lot of machinery and raw materials relative to labor (enough to make $g = 3/4$).

By focusing on the rate of profit, businessmen and their supporters not only understate the rate of exploitation but in fact hide its true source. While surplus value results from the exploitation of direct labor, it appears as though this surplus value comes from total capital ($c + v$), from machinery and raw materials as well as from direct labor.

Furthermore, industrial capitalists do not retain all of the surplus value. Some of it is channeled to commercial capitalists (merchants), who, using commercial or money capital, buy and sell commodities within the circulation sphere. The activities of these commercial capitalists do not directly produce surplus value—it is produced entirely in the production sphere—but indirectly they contribute to its generation by shortening the time of circulation and by expanding markets. These contributions enable industrial capitalists to produce more surplus value with the employment of less capital. Since all capital, industrial and commercial, in perfectly competitive markets earns the same rate of profit, the industrial capitalists must transfer sufficient surplus value to the commercial capitalists to permit this equality to be achieved. This transfer takes place when the industrial capitalists sell their commodities to merchants at prices below their values, while the merchants resell the commodities to consumers at their values (plus the constant and variable capital employed by the merchants, which they must recover).

In addition to this drain from industrial capitalists' surplus value, the moneylending capitalists also get a slice. These capitalists give up the use value of money, which is its ability to produce surplus value, in return for a portion of that surplus value. The moneylending capitalists loan money to industrial capitalists (and others) at certain interest rates, which are the market prices that serve to redistribute surplus value to them. The portion of the surplus value going to moneylending capitalists is interest, while the portion remaining with industrial capitalists Marx called "profits of enterprise." Clearly, the higher the rates of interest, the higher is financial capital's share of surplus value relative to that of industrial capital. Interest rates are established by competition in the loanable funds markets, and their levels may be high or low depending on the market forces of demand and supply. As Marx saw it, there is room for much conflict between financial and industrial capitalists over relative shares of surplus value.

Finally, the agricultural capitalists, in the same way as the industrial ones, exploit labor and so obtain surplus value. In this respect, there is no distinction between these two productive sectors of the economy. This surplus value is shared with the landowning capitalists, the latter receiving it in ground rent. The total income of this landowning class includes absolute rent, which reflects monopoly gains from the private ownership of a nonreproducible resource; differential rent, which is based on two equal quantities of capital and labor employed on equal areas of land with unequal results; and an element of interest, which comprises charges for land improvements.

Consequently, productive (industrial and agricultural) capitalists do not retain all of the surplus value generated within their spheres. Some of it goes to commercial capitalists, some to financial capitalists, and some to landowning capitalists. Additionally, Marx claimed, other shares are plundered by private bureaucrats, hangers-on, and just plain swindlers. In any event, the industrial capitalists' profits (after taxes) are only a modest fraction of the total fruits of exploitation. Thus, when these profits are paraded as total income of the capitalist class, they divert attention from the other shares. Further, when these profits are related to total capital ($c + v$) to obtain a profit rate, both the rate of exploitation (surplus value) and its source are hidden. Finally, when these industrial profits are displayed after taxes have been taken out, the role of the state in supporting the capitalist class is concealed. That is, surplus value includes much of the state's receipts and expenditures, the latter intended to strengthen the class structure and its property relations.

Marxists maintain that the rate of industrial profits after taxes, therefore, is a gross understatement of the extent to which capital exploits labor. In 1974 in the United States, for example, industrial corporate profits after taxes were about $50 billion, but total surplus value (all corporate profits, interest, and rent before taxes) approached $200 billion, or about a quarter of employee compensation (wages and salaries) before taxes. Thus, the rate of exploitation, as Marx would figure it (if prices are used instead of values), was around 25 percent, while the rate of industrial profits on stockholders' equity was only a little over 10 percent.

Values and Prices

The value of a commodity, we have seen, is the socially necessary labor time required to produce it. The price of a commodity, on the other hand, is this labor time valued in terms of money—say, for example, that 100 hours of labor equal $250. This $250 is divided among constant capital (c), variable capital (v), and surplus value (s). If $c = \$150$, and the rate of exploitation is 100 percent, then $v = \$50$ and $s = \$50$ ($s/v = 100$ percent). In this case, the rate of profit is 25 percent—$s/(c + v) = 50/200$. If workers are free to move from one job to another to find their best advantage, wage rates for equal work will tend to be the same in each industry. Similarly, if capital is free to move, competition will tend to equalize the profit rates. Thus, following our numerical example, each sphere of production, when competition prevails, should have a profit rate of 25 percent. This would make prices proportional to values when commodities are traded one for another, provided that the organic composition of capital, $c/(c + v)$, is the same in each sphere of production—equal to 150/200, as in our numerical example.

Now, competition *will* tend to equalize rates of profit, but there is no reason to expect organic compositions of capital (the degrees of capital intensity) to be the same from one industry to the next. Suppose that our commodity has a higher organic composition than others on the average. In that event, the profit rate for our commodity would initially be lower than the average, because, while the exploitation rates, s/v, might be the same, the profit rate, $s/(c + v)$, is lower as c rises relative to v. The price of our commodity, therefore, would have to rise above $250 in order to equalize profit rates. This is accomplished by some capital moving out of this sphere, thereby reducing the supply of the commodity and raising its price. At the other end of the scale, if some commodities are produced with especially low organic compositions of capital, their profit rates will be above average. Consequently, their prices will fall below levels suggested by their values as capital moves into these spheres to take advantage of initially higher profit rates.

Thus, when the organic composition of capital differs among industries, prices will not be proportional to values, though the two will be systematically related to each other in accordance with the structure of the organic compositions of capital. The function of prices, in this case, is to redistribute surplus value among industrial capitalists so as to equalize rates of profit. Those capitalists with low organic compositions of capital, and hence initially with excess amounts of surplus value, lose portions of their surplus to other capitalists who are in the opposite position.

Surplus value is generated in the sphere of production, but it is generated differentially, in excess here and in deficiency there, depending on the organic composition of capital. To redistribute the surplus value so as to equalize profit rates requires that prices differ from values. Marx saw this process not as a weakness but as a decided strength of his analysis: the value-analysis revealed exploitation and its manifestation in surplus value; the price-analysis revealed how the total surplus value was shared within the class of industrial capitalists, in accordance with the laws of competition. At the same time, the price system also redistributed the surplus value among the various classes of capitalists—industrial, commercial, financial, and landed—as we have already seen.

Capital Accumulation

It was Marx's contention that the production of surplus value is "the absolute law" of the capitalist mode of production, that most of this surplus value is continually reconverted into capital—called capital accumulation—and that the system reproduces the capitalist relation: "on the one side the capitalist, on the other the wage-laborer." Capitalism is inherently an expanding system, for capitalists must constantly accumulate and extend their capital in order to preserve it; they must continually expand in order to remain capitalists, for if they did not they would be destroyed by competitors; they would be consumers and not capitalists. This expansion eventually occurs on a worldwide basis, for capitalists must push their mode of production into every nook and cranny of the globe. Nevertheless, capitalists also have an urge to enjoy the consumption of their capital. The overcoming of this urge is supposed to be "abstinence," which is a bourgeois justification, according to Marx, for the private appropriation of surplus value.

Marx asserted that the general law of capitalist accumulation is that it creates *both* wealth and poverty. That is to say, capitalist accumulation has an antagonistic character in that it produces and contains a unity of opposites. "The same causes which develop the expansive power of capital," Marx wrote, "develop also the labor power at its disposal," including the reserve army of labor (a relative surplus population), whose misery and pauperism grow in step with wealth at the other pole. Furthermore, Marx continued, capital accumulation transforms the workplace into a despotic, degrading, alienating environment, one which mutilates the laborer "into a fragment of a man" and destroys "every remnant of charm in his work." Capital accumulation produces an accumulation of wealth at one pole and an "accumulation of misery, agony of toil, slavery, ignorance, brutality, mental degradation, at the opposite pole." Poverty and misery are not capitalism's negligence but its imperative, its inevitable progenies. This is Marx's principal message about the process of capitalist accumulation.

That message today may sound "wild," and indeed in some respects Marx can now be seen as having incorrectly extrapolated conditions prevalent in his time. However, before the reader plunges in to judge the message too harshly, he should be aware of its depth. For Marx, wealth could not exist by itself, just as a capitalist class could not exist in isolation. Wealth in capitalism has no other meaning than a concentration of much of society's production (its means and its products) in relatively few hands, and there is no way for that to occur without the simultaneous creation of its opposite—poverty, the material deprivation of the many, at least in relative terms. But poverty and misery, Marx contended, must be understood not only as exploitation but as alienation as well—not only materially but also "spiritually."

The Marxian theory of alienation seeks to explain how individuals in capitalist society have lost their understanding and control of the world around them and have, in the process, been stunted and perverted into something less than full human beings. For Marx, the source of all alienation lies in the work process. Alienation means that individuals no longer have an immediate and intimate relationship to the environment; they have been specialized and sorted, made into "the most wretched of commodities," divorced from the products they produce, split into mental workers and manual workers, into town people and rural people, divided into dominant and subordinate classes, thrown into selfish competition with one another. The result of alienation is the loss of personal identity—a transference of an individual's essential powers to others and to "things," even to commodities. Alienation is the negation of productivity, the diminution of one's powers.

Marx saw human beings in capitalistic society as alienated not only from the products they create and from their own labor, but also from others and from themselves. That is, workers under capitalism lose control of their products, produce as cogs in a process they do not understand, are separated from and pitted against their fellow workers, and are deprived of their essential powers. They believe that power resides outside of themselves, in the products they have actually fashioned, and they humble, demean, and almost destroy themselves before the commodity world. In the same way, a religious person might fashion a wooden idol with his own hands, kneel before it, transfer his own powers to it, and thus reduce himself to something less than a full human being. In their manifold alienated states, people lose their inner selves and become passive; they allow themselves to be directed by outside powers that they do not control and do not want to control; they subject themselves willingly to manipulation; they have a sense of powerlessness; they cannot act effectively. Marx did not believe that capitalism was the original cause of alienation—for it existed before that—but under capitalism alienation in all of its forms is maximized.

The proletariat shares with the bourgeoisie every aspect of this commodity-dominated world. But, Marx stated, the latter experiences it as "a sign of its own power," while the former "feels destroyed in this alienation." The bourgeoisie, for Marx, sees no need for piercing the surface of phenomena; indeed it has a special interest in not revealing what is below, and even in deceiving itself on this score. On the other hand, the proletariat, while equally baffled, has a special interest in discovering the true relations and thus in developing a revolutionary consciousness. Productive activity is the catalyst of this transformation.

The capitalist mode of production extracts surplus value from wage-labor for the class of capitalists. The surplus value is used to expand capital, a process which is inherent to this social formation, and which is reinforced by competition. The accumulation process tends to generate increasing demands for labor to work cooperatively with the expanding means of production. However, accumulation leads to *concentration* of capital, which places greater magnitudes of capital in fewer hands and at the same time raises the organic composition of capital—the capital intensity of production—thereby moderating the growing demand for labor. Accumulation is also accompanied by the *centralization* of capital, by the larger capitalists gaining what smaller capitalists lose, by the expropriation of capitalist by capitalist.

The centralization of capital is the dynamic element in the accumulation process. It is furthered by the development of the credit system, which draws together scattered money resources for the use of larger capitalists; by competition, which destroys the weak and bolsters the strong; and by economies of scale (falling average costs), which give increasing cost advantages to the already-large capitals over the smaller ones, enabling the larger capitals to beat the smaller.

If capitalist accumulation is to persist, it requires above all else an ample supply of wage-labor that is continually replenished and available for work at wage levels that ensure the further production of surplus value for the class of capitalists. It is for this reason that Marx considered the reserve army of labor to be an essential ingredient of capitalism, a relatively redundant population of laborers that would expand and contract according to the requirements of the system. As soon as the accumulation process diminishes this surplus population to the point of endangering the further production of adequate amounts of surplus value (by raising wages and other advantages of labor), a reaction sets in: accumulation lags, the introduction of labor-saving machinery is quickened, the reserve army is replenished, and the rise in wages is halted. In these ways, Marx maintained, the foundations of the capitalist system are protected from the dangers of lessened exploitation. "The law of capitalist accumulation . . . excludes every diminution in the degree of exploitation of labor, and every rise in the price of labor, which could seriously imperil the continual reproduction, on an ever-enlarging scale, of the capitalistic relation." According to Marx, the laborer exists to satisfy the needs of capital; material wealth does not exist to satisfy the need of the laborer to develop into a complete human being.

Consequently, capitalist accumulation demands the replenishment of poverty and misery, through the reserve army, to serve its requirements. But, Marx continued, there are other ways that degradation is created by the process of accumulation. First, accumulation and capitalists' pursuit of ever-larger surplus value lead to the geographical concentration of the means of production in industrial urban centers. As Marx and Engels observed, this causes a "heaping together of the laborers, within a given space . . . therefore the swifter capitalistic accumulation, the more miserable are the dwellings of the working-people." Second, accumulation of capital tears apart the fabric protecting individual proprietors, craftsmen, and self-sufficient producers, transforming them into a surplus of dependent wage-laborers. Third, it draws wealth and talent from outlying areas into industrial and urban centers, converting the former into backward, stagnant subeconomies; or it reduces these outlying areas to specialized suppliers of raw materials for industrial capital, thereby increasing their vulnerability to adverse developments; and it transfers wealth from these areas via the price-market mechanism. Fourth, on an international scale, the capitalist mode has augmented its capital through forceful, market control of weaker areas and has drained surpluses from them into the industrial regions. By these means, wealth and poverty are created together, a unity of conflicting opposites.

How Capitalism Is Mystified

Marx alleged that capitalism presents itself on the surface of life in distorted forms—that what it is really like, within its deep recesses, is quite different from what its facial expressions suggest. These surface distortions, Marx contended, lead to illusions about the capitalist mode of production, and the illusions in turn are used by bourgeois ideologists to mystify the workings of the system. Thus, a web of mystification is spun around this mode of production, hindering a clear understanding of its true nature. We are all fooled, Marx said, by capitalism's distortions.

The Distortions of Capitalism

The capitalist mode of production turns labor power into a commodity, in a world of commodities, to be purchased and exploited by a capital-owning class that appropriates surplus value and is compelled to extend its capital and its mode of production to all corners of the globe. Capitalist relations comprise these two classes existing as a unity of opposites: the capitalist class, owning the means of production, buying the labor power of a dispossessed proletariat, controlling the work process, possessing the products of labor; and the proletariat, selling its labor power as wage-labor, working in an environment of alienation, receiving only part of its product, existing to facilitate capital's self-expansion. This, Marx affirmed, is the true substratum of capitalism, its bedrock.

The surface phenomena of capitalism, on the other hand, appear in forms that often distort and falsify the true relationships of this mode of production. Indeed, it was Marx's contention that capitalism, because of its perverted forms, maximizes illusion and mystification, that its essence is more heavily covered by layers of misleading superficial phenomena than that of any previous mode of production, including slavery and feudalism. The outward appearances of capitalism diverge fantastically from its inner laws, which are thereby largely hidden from view. Direct experience, within the capitalist mode, therefore, leads to illusions in the minds of those captivated by its surface data. These illusions can be dispelled only by scientific analysis of the capitalist mode, an analysis that is made possible by the rise of the industrial proletariat (and so of its ideologists) and serves the interest of that class. Thus, both the need for and the possibility of scientific analysis arise together as capitalism develops. Such insights into the workings of the system, however, are strongly resisted by the bourgeoisie and its apologists; furthermore, capitalism makes these insights extremely difficult to comprehend. This explains the continuing coexistence of illusions and their explanation.

In a precapitalist, rural patriarchal mode of production, social labor is revealed directly in the social products produced for the family. The work is divided according to age, sex, abilities, and other natural conditions. The different kinds of labor are direct social functions because they are functions of the family—spinning, weaving, growing food, gathering wood, and so forth. The articles produced are family products, not commodities seeking markets, and so they are directly social products. The social relations among the family members appear to them as mutual personal relations, because the labor of each is consciously applied as part of the combined labor of the family. The total products of these labors are social products to be used by the family in ways decided by the members.

Now consider a mode of production that breaks up such families into individual producers, each producing independently of the others, and each producing, not products for the family, but commodities for exchange—a mode that Marx termed "the most embryonic form of bourgeois production." This mode turns social relations between persons into material relations and material relations between things into social relations. In this mode, the social character of private labor, which was obvious and direct in the family situation, is now revealed only indirectly when private products are exchanged—that is, when equal values or labor times are exchanged. Individual producers now appear to have no relations with one another, but only with their material commodities: "Individuals exist for one another only insofar as their commodities exist." Marx means that individuals, in this mode, make contact with one another only through the exchange of their commodities. For this reason, exchange value appears to be a relation between commodities—this commodity is worth so much of that commodity—but in fact it is a relation between people, between labor times of workers. As Marx explained: "A social relation of production appears as something existing apart from individual human beings, and the distinctive relations into which they enter in the course of production in society appear as the specific properties of a thing—it is this perverted appearance, this prosaically real, and by no means imaginary, mystification that is characteristic of all social forms of labor positing exchange-value." Thus, the social relations of individuals appear in the inverted form of a social relation between things. This is an actual representation of this mode of production, albeit a representation which distorts the true relation between human beings.

This distorted form is carried over to the fully developed capitalist mode of production. In addition to it, however, the capitalist mode widens the gap further between its phenomenal appearances and its essence. Labor and the means of production, for example, are forces (factors) of production. But, in the capitalist mode, labor becomes wage-labor, a commodity, a material thing; means of production become capital, incarnated in the capitalist. Thus, living labor becomes a thing, and capital, which is dead (embodied) labor, becomes alive in the capitalist; an inversion of subject and object is accomplished.

The capitalist mode especially presents itself in ways that hide the fact that surplus value comes from the exploitation of labor within the sphere of production. Surplus value, in capitalism's fantastic forms, appears to arise in the circulation sphere or from inherent powers of capital in its various forms; its very existence is shielded by market expressions of the capitalist mode that misrepresent the real relations of production.

If these distortions of fundamental bourgeois relations are not recognized as such, but are instead believed to be the true manifestations of capitalism's inner laws, then illusions are created in the minds of those deceived. Marx believed that the surface distortions of the bourgeois mode are so forceful that most people are unable to discover capitalism's underlying mechanism and so remain confused. In fact, the capitalist mode, in its inverted phenomenal forms, generates false consciousness in both capitalists and workers. It produces both the actual surface distortions and the mental illusions about what lies beneath the surface. It is on the basis of these illusions that the mystification of capitalism arises.

The acceptance, as the real thing, of the distortion that transfers social relations from people to their products, leads to a series of illusions and fantasies. Commodities become fetishes in the same way that gods, the creation of humans, take on lives of their own, fashioning social relations among themselves and with the human world. In the "religion of everyday life," objects are endowed with life, taking on the powers relinquished by their producers, who, as a consequence, diminish and deceive themselves; the objects come to rule over man. Since "the god among commodities" is gold-money, the possession of money becomes an insatiable desire, the greed of all. This social form of wealth is transformed, under capitalism, into the private power of private persons, who are able, through the power of money, to transform their own personal incapacities into their opposites. According to Marx, "Money is the supreme good, therefore its possessor is good. . . . I am *stupid*, but money is the *real mind* of all things and how then should its possessor be stupid? Besides, he can buy talented people for himself, and is he who has power over the talented not more talented than the talented?" Money, Marx claimed, "is the common whore, the common pimp of people and nations."

The Illusions of Capitalism

If the faces of capitalism are distorted, they are powerful and convincing ones which give rise to numerous illusions about this mode of production. The perverted forms of the actual world produce conceptions in the minds of people that diverge drastically from the underlying realities.

The most important of these illusions concerns surplus value—its production, its transformation as profits among industrial capitalists via the price mechanism, its realization in the circulation sphere, and its distribution among industrial, commercial, financial, and landed capitalists.

The origin of surplus value is concealed in many ways. The wage-form, especially when workers are paid by the number of the item produced, extinguishes every trace of the division of the working day into necessary labor and surplus labor, and it therefore creates the illusion that all labor is paid labor. To add to this, wage-labor appears to be "free" labor, even though actually bound to the class of capitalists. This freedom to choose to work for any capitalist reinforces the illusion that labor is not being exploited, that the production sphere cannot be the source of surplus value. Further, industrial profits of enterprise appear to be wages of management, so that both workers and industrial capitalists appear to be rewarded for different kinds of labor, some menial and some managerial. Marx commented that this makes "the labor of exploiting and the exploited labor both appear identical as labor." He added: "Now, the wage-laborer, like the slave, must have a master who puts him to work and rules over him. And assuming the existence of this relationship of lordship and servitude, it is quite proper to compel the wage-laborer to produce his own wages and also the wages of supervision, as compensation for the labor of ruling and supervising him." The greater the antagonism between the producers and the owners, the greater the role of supervision. This reaches its peak in the slave system. This tenuous claim by "rulers and supervisors" to part of the surplus value is therefore a claim that arises from the antithesis between the laborers and the capitalists, one producing and the other owning the means of production; its antagonistic nature would vanish with the disappearance of classes. Therefore, while in one sense wages of managers are part of variable capital, not surplus value, Marx saw them as largely the latter because they reflected a class relation that would disappear in a "cooperative society of associated labor," Marx's phrase for a classless society.

The source of surplus value is further concealed when values are transformed into prices, thereby redistributing surplus value among the industrial capitalists, some of whom lose a portion of the surplus generated in their production sphere and others of whom gain some—in amounts which in competition equalize rates of profit on total capital. Thus, the average profit of any capital differs from the surplus value which that capital extracted from the laborers employed by it. This transformation process, Marx wrote, "completely conceals the true nature and origin of profit not only from the capitalist, who has a special interest in deceiving himself on this score, but also from the laborer . . . [it] serves to obscure the basis for determining value itself." Each capitalist is therefore under the illusion that his profit comes as much from prices and markets as from his own process of production, and the fact is obscured that all profits are due to the aggregate exploitation of labor by total social capital within the production sphere.

The realization of surplus value in the sphere of circulation creates the illusion that this is its source. Commodities, pregnant with surplus value, are exchanged for more money than the capitalist paid for the constant and variable capital to produce them, the difference being the surplus value itself. Such transactions produce the illusion that the mode of exchange is the dominant sphere and so the basis of the mode of production. The process of production, Marx stated, "appears merely as an unavoidable intermediate link, as a necessary evil for the sake of money-making." Money seems to be made in circulation, in buying commodities below their values and selling them above their values. Surplus value appears to originate from the acumen of capitalists, from their sharp business wits, from their abilities to cut costs, to outguess the market and beat the competition, and from their shrewdness in dealing with money, stocks and bonds, bills of exchange, and the other financial accouterments of capitalism. Marx believed that the entire process by which surplus value is produced is made especially incomprehensible in financial centers, such as London, where "the paper world" distorted everything.

Finally, the origin of surplus value is obscured by the glitter of illusions which emanate from each of its several elements. Interest, a part of surplus value, appears to arise from the inherent powers of money to increase itself, powers that are completely divorced from the production process. The illusion that money-capital has automatic self-expansion powers, occult properties, money generating money, Marx called "the mystification of capital in its most flagrant form." Interest is part of surplus value—unpaid, exploited labor—but it pretends to disavow this source in favor of the innate powers of a thing, of a thing come alive. Similarly, commercial profits appear clearly to come from clever buying and selling within the circulation sphere, and thus to be severed altogether from the productive activities of industrial capitalists. Also, rent seems to arise from the powers of the earth itself, not from social relations of production; from the land or from the presence of that personification of the land, the landlord. The landlord demands his share of the total product that land helped to create. "Just as products confront the producer as an independent force in capital and capitalists— who actually are but the personification of capital—so land becomes personified in the landlord and likewise gets on its hind legs to demand, as an independent force, its share of the product created with its help."

Land is productive but, while it adds to output, it does not "naturally" produce the social form called rent. Similarly, capital is productive but it does not "naturally" produce profit or interest. By the same reasoning, labor is productive but it does not "naturally" produce wages. Interest (profit), rent, and wages are all social forms of the class structure of society that have deep historical roots. They are all components of a total product created by work, and yet each seems to arise from a separate "thing": profit from capital goods, rent from land, and wages from labor. This illusion is played out fully when the capitalist, the owner of capital goods, claims the profit; the landlord, the owner of land, claims the rent; and the worker, the owner of labor power, claims the wages. Each appears to receive what each is entitled to. Marx called this "the trinity formula," which is "the complete mystification of the capitalist mode of production. . . . It is an enchanted, perverted, topsy-turvy world, in which Monsieur le Capital and Madame la Terre do their ghost-walking as social characters and at the same time directly as mere things."

The Mystification of Capitalism

Marx's analysis that labor is exploited to provide surplus value to a class of capitalists bent on expanding capital was a danger to the ruling classes, especially after the industrial proletariat, responding to the development of capitalism's productive forces, began to gain consciousness of itself as a class. This growing challenge, consciously perceived, stimulated bourgeois theorists to fashion analyses of capitalism that would absolve it of sin. These analyses, Marx stated, were mystifications to the extent that they were based on the perverted surface forms thrown up by capitalism's underlying movements, with the effect of making it doubly difficult for others to understand what was actually going on within the bourgeois mode of production.

The task of the bourgeois theorists was to raise profits to the same moral plane as wages. This could be done if it could be shown that these returns were explainable by some type of real cost or sacrifice incurred by the capitalists or by some special productivity of the capital that they owned. Marx had little respect for these efforts which comprised what he called "vulgar economy." He wrote that vulgar economy "is no more than a didactic, more or less dogmatic, translation of everyday conceptions of the actual agents of production . . . which arranges them in a certain rational order. . . [to] correspond to the interests of the ruling classes." In another place, Marx pointed out that "the vulgar economist does practically no more than translate the singular concepts of the capitalists, who are in the thrall of competition, into a seemingly more theoretical and generalized language, and attempt to substantiate the justice of those conceptions." The bourgeois economists who are engaged in this "dirty work for the knights of the moneybag" Marx called "pettifogging ideologists" and other names as well.

One theory in defense of profits is that they are the reward for abstinence—the abstention of the capitalist from present consumption in order to save. This sacrifice—this special pain of the capitalist—it is argued, must be rewarded if it is to be borne. Marx countered that there is no way to relate the abstinence of the capitalist to his profit. But, if there were such a relation, it would probably be an inverse one. As Maurice Dobb has explained: "He [Marx] had only to contrast the profit and the 'abstinence' of a Rothschild to feel that the so-called 'explanation' required no further refutation." The *ability* to save largely determines the volume of saving, which is therefore strongly related to relative affluence and only weakly related, if at all, to some "pain." As both Dobb and English economist Joan Robinson have pointed out, the sacrifice associated with current saving by the wealthy is more truly a burden or "pain" of the poor whose very poverty allows such wealth, from which most of the saving comes, to continue to exist. If it is true that saving is increased by such an unequal distribution of income, "then it would seem," Dobb says, "that the final incidence of this cost of saving must lie, not upon the rich, but upon the restricted consumption of the poor, which alone permits those high incomes to be earned from which the bulk of the investment is drawn.'' It is not the abstinence and waiting of the rich that should be rewarded but rather the general deprivation of the poor. ''To assert the contrary,'' Dobb concludes, ''is, surely, to be guilty of the circular reasoning of assuming the income of the capitalist to be in some sense 'natural' or 'inevitable' in order to show that what he invests of this income is the unique product of his individual abstinence in refraining from doing what he likes with his own.'' Joan Robinson has added that, since what the capitalist likes is often a luxurious standard of living, an unequal income distribution is an unnecessarily wasteful way of accomplishing the saving.

Marx's main point about this theory, however, was that capitalists are a historically determined class, which stands antagonistically against the proletariat, and which, in order to maintain itself as a class, *must* accumulate. Thus ''abstinence from present consumption as a sacrifice'' struck Marx as a most superficial depiction of a historical process that deeply involved class struggles and that largely determined the scope and direction of people's actions. Capitalists accumulated because they had to. Nevertheless, Marx declared, even at the superficial level, vulgar economists never seem to realize that every human action may be viewed as abstinence from its opposite. ''Eating is abstinence from fasting, walking, abstinence from standing still, working, abstinence from idling, idling, abstinence from working.'' It is true that capitalists, despite the compulsion driving them on to further extensions of their capitals, do develop in their breasts ''a Faustian conflict between the passion for accumulation and the desire for enjoyment.'' But this simply means that the abstention from either may be painful. Why not argue that capitalists deserve a reward for luxurious living, since they have such a passion for accumulation?

Marx also noted, in another connection, that original (primitive) accumulation was hardly a sacrifice for some capitalists in that it came from plunder and theft. The story of capital accumulation, said Marx, is written in blood and fire, and the sacrifices it involved were made by millions of poor and oppressed people the world over, assuredly not by the capitalist class. So whether one considers current accumulation or the fiery background of these fortunes, it is vulgar to suppose that the capitalist class should be rewarded for such advantages.

Marx believed that interest payments to financial capitalists were simply a portion of the surplus value, a portion which was set by the market forces determining rates of interest. Since Marx, a theory has been developed purporting to explain interest, not in terms of labor exploitation, but in terms of the notion of ''discounting the future''—that consumption now is worth more to people than an equal amount of consumption in the future. Therefore, since people feel this way, they must be rewarded for not consuming now, postponing it to the future. Joan Robinson has argued that such a notion is not based on direct observation, ''but arises from the desire to represent owning wealth as a 'sacrifice.' '' It is true that some people consider it a sacrifice not to consume now, but many others consider it a sacrifice *to* consume now—because they expect a lower income in the future, or their need for consuming power in the future is expected to be very large (as to finance the education of their children), or because they wish to leave an estate for their heirs. The rate of interest is positive, and thus financial capitalists receive interest returns, not because of a subjective rate of discount of the future, but because capitalists are in a position to exploit labor and thereby obtain surplus value—profit. When the rate of profit is expected to be positive, the rate of interest will be positive, because capitalists are willing to pay something for finance capital. Interest payments are based on exploitation, not on a myopic vision of the future.

Another theory in defense of profits is that labor that is aided by machinery can produce a larger total product than it could working without this aid. The difference in the two outputs should therefore be attributed to the productivity of capital. The owner of the capital, it is said, is rightly the recipient of these returns. This was later formulated more elegantly as the marginal productivity theory of capital. Marx's view was that capital goods make labor more productive, a relation that has nothing to do with the production of surplus value. Capitalists exploit both unproductive and productive labor. Joan Robinson has noted that, while capital goods are certainly productive, there is no justification for assigning their productivity to private owners; the bourgeois argument, as Dobb expressed it, "included the illicit link of imputing to the owner the 'productivity' of the things he owned. 'A social relation between men assumes the fantastic form of a relation between things': and the behaviour of things is not only represented animistically as due to some innate property in them, but imputed to the influence of those individuals who exercise rights of ownership over them." Granted that capital goods are "productive," their private owners are not. It was labor that produced the capital goods, and current labor that uses its own past labor (embodied in the capital goods) to produce more goods. If capitalists actually work, Dobb implied, they can receive a wage like everyone else.

How Capitalism Is Transcended

Marx worked out a theory as to how capitalism would be dialectically superseded by socialism. Lenin extended the theory to include the imperialist proclivities of monopoly capitalism and the revolts by colonial peoples against this imperialism.

Capitalist Crises

Marx did not develop anything approaching a complete theory of capitalist crises that would lead eventually to the overthrow of this mode of production. However, figure 2 presents the principal elements of Marx's analysis and of Lenin's extension of it. Figure 2 will serve as a guide to our discussion.

We have previously noted that Marx saw capitalist accumulation as producing

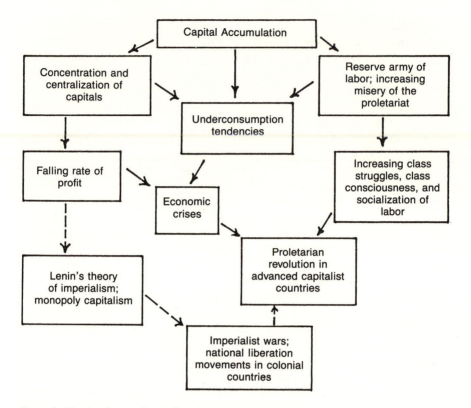

Figure 2. Marxian theory of capitalist crises

the opposites of wealth and poverty, each dependent on the other for its existence: on the one hand, the concentration and centralization of capital in the hands of the bourgeoisie; on the other, the increasing misery of the proletariat. Marx reasoned that the accumulation process would tend to increase the demand for labor and thus to raise wages. This would induce capitalists to substitute constant for variable capital in the attempt to restore the previous level of surplus value. However, this increase in the organic composition of capital, even when accompanied by a rising rate of exploitation, would ordinarily lower the rate of profit. This, in turn, would compel capitalists to reduce the pace of accumulation, which would bring on a crisis, swell the ranks of the reserve army of labor, destroy some of the value of capital, and so tend to reestablish conditions for a later expansion of production.

At the other pole of capitalist accumulation, poverty and deprivation are created. The process of exploitation leaves purchasing power in the hands of the proletariat that enables it to purchase only an inadequate portion of the total products turned out. The large remainder of the output must be fashioned and purchased by capitalists as part of the accumulation process. There is a continual threat, therefore, of too heavy a burden being placed on capitalist accumulation, a "burden" that stems from the exploitation of labor. The underconsumptionist tendencies of the capitalist mode, therefore, refer not solely to the relative poverty of the proletariat but also to the resultant "burden" placed on capitalists to produce and purchase ever-increasing absolute amounts of products if the accumulation process is to continue. "Underconsumption" does not indicate that during phases of rapid accumulation and prosperity wages are depressed. Instead, we have already seen that the opposite occurs. But, while workers in these exhilaration phases are thus enabled to raise their consumption levels somewhat, it is never enough to lighten significantly the "burden" on the capitalist class, which is soon made intolerable by a falling rate of profit. Thus, accumulation slows down until the previously favorable conditions for capitalists have been restored; and this involves principally the destruction of capital values and the replenishment of the reserve army of labor. The former reduces the organic composition of capital (g), while the latter raises the rate of exploitation $(s' = s/v)$, both factors tending to increase the rate of profit $(p' = s'(1 - g))$.

Marx contended that, in time, as a result of the above processes, the relations of production would become fetters on the further development of society's productive forces. "This will mark," as economist Paul Sweezy, editor of the socialist journal *Monthly Review*, has written, "the beginning of a revolutionary period during which the working class, at once oppressed and disciplined by its special position in society, will overturn the existing relations of production and establish in their stead higher, socialist, relations of production." The proletariat would be able to carry out this revolution because its prolonged class struggles would awaken it to its task and because the continued development of productive forces would socialize the production process while leaving its ownership in private hands. That is, socialization in the production sphere would increasingly come into conflict with the concentration of private ownership in the relations of production. This growing contradiction would be resolved by the proletarian revolution. The revolution, according to Marx, would occur in the most advanced capitalist countries because it is there that the industrial proletariat and capital centralization would be most developed.

Lenin, while clinging to this analysis for most of his life, nevertheless modified it in several ways, one of which is pictured in the chart. Monopoly capitalism in its highest, imperialist stage, Lenin thought, would be first breached at its weakest links, in the colonial areas. The superprofits of imperialist activity, according to Lenin, would buy off the top layers of labor in the advanced capitalist countries and so delay the revolution there. However, capitalist nations' own wars with each other plus successful national liberation movements on the periphery of international capitalism, Lenin believed, would gravely weaken the imperialist powers in their home bases. Eventually, the worldwide revolution against capitalism would sweep from capitalism's weak edges back to the industrial centers.

Postcapitalist Society

Marx had much to say in general outline about the higher mode of production which he predicted would succeed capitalism, but he gave few details about how it would operate—for instance, about how the planning mechanism would be organized. He anticipated that society would go through a transition period, after the revolution and overthrow of capitalism, in which the state would take the form of the dictatorship of the proletariat, the means of production would be held in common, but many features of the old society—such as classes, the distribution of income to workers on the basis of their productive contributions, and social differences (mental vs. manual labor, town vs. country, etc.)—would persist for some time. Marx called this transition period "the lower phase of communism." Today this is often referred to as socialism, the higher stage being communism itself, when, with ample productive forces, classes, and social differences, as well as the state as an oppressive force, vanish, and, as Marx put it, communism inscribes on its banner: "From each according to his ability, to each according to his needs."

Looking ahead to communism, Marx called postcapitalist society the "cooperative society" or the "associated mode of production," which would be one of freely associated individuals working with means of production held in common and having a definite social plan; it would be "a society in which the full and free development of every individual forms the ruling principle." Earlier, in the *Communist Manifesto*, Marx and Engels had declared postcapitalist society to be "an association, in which the free development of each is the condition for the free development of all." These pronouncements mean that the ruling principle will no longer be profit making but rather fulfilling the needs of individuals, and such fulfillment for any individual will not demand denial to others, as it does in a class society. Individuals are so associated that either they fulfill their needs together or they do not fulfill them at all.

In the associated mode, the workers own the means of production and thus are not under the discipline of capitalists or their representatives. Rather, they work for their own account and pay their own managers. The antagonistic nature of the labor of supervision thus disappears. The length of the working day would also change, but which way depends on particular circumstances. On the one hand, it would no longer be necessary to produce surplus value for the capitalist class. But, on the other, "means of subsistence" would expand its meaning and a part of what is now surplus value would become necessary labor for accumulation to benefit the working class. Furthermore, the fact that society regulates general production makes it possible for workers to move occasionally from one task to another, thus reducing job specialization and boredom.

In the associated mode, producers do not exchange their products, just as members of a family do not engage in market exchanges, such as "making a bed" for a meal. Hence, "commodities" disappear, and so does labor as the value of these products. Instead, the associated workers determine the amount of time devoted to different products by the products' social utility, and these products are used by society in accordance with its social plan. And, according to Marx, if "commodities" do not exist, neither does money as a particular social form, as a social relation. What exists are products of a classless society and the means of distributing the products.

Marx believed that in postcapitalist society the "general costs of administration not belonging to production" would decline, while expenditures on schools, health services, and other worker welfare programs would rise. Moreover, for the first time, human relationships would be direct and not perverted by money and market relations. As Marx expressed this, there would be "the complete emancipation of all human senses and qualities." Power would not come from the possession of money, as in bourgeois society, but would instead emanate from specific expressions of an individual's life: love becomes potent "if through a living expression of yourself as a loving person" you make yourself a loved person. No longer will love be bought.

As a reminder that a still higher stage lay beyond the associated mode of production, Marx declared that this mode still represents "the realm of necessity," and beyond it lies "the true realm of freedom." Marx concluded:

> In fact, the realm of freedom actually begins only where labor which is determined by necessity and mundane considerations ceases; thus in the very nature of things it lies beyond the sphere of actual material production. Just as the savage must wrestle with Nature to satisfy his wants, to maintain and reproduce life, so must civilized man, and he must do so in all social formations and under all possible modes of production. With his development this realm of physical necessity expands as a result of his wants; but, at the same time, the forces of production which satisfy these wants also increase. Freedom in this field can only consist in socialized man, the associated producers, rationally regulating their interchange with Nature, bringing it under their common control, instead of being ruled by it as by the blind forces of Nature; and achieving this with the least expenditure of energy and under conditions most favorable to, and worthy of, their human nature. But it nonetheless still remains a realm of necessity. Beyond it begins that development of human energy which is an end in itself, the true realm of freedom, which, however, can blossom forth only with this realm of necessity as its basis. The shortening of the working-day is its basic prerequisite.

The principal aim of society, as Marx saw it, is the full development of human beings—the free unfolding of their human powers, the full realization of their potentials in all their dimensions, the achievement of the rational regulation of their natural and social environment, the overcoming of alienation. The aim is the emancipation of man, the development of a truly human person who *is* much, as contrasted to one who *has* much. This emphasis on human beings was expressed by Marx in many ways, including the following: "A critique of religion leads to the doctrine that the highest being for man is man himself, hence to the categorical imperative to overthrow all relationships in which man is humbled, enslaved, abandoned, despised." Or, as Engels saw man in the new society: "Man, at last the master of his own form of social organization, becomes at the same time the lord over nature, his own master—free." Marx looked forward to the day when each person would become "the fully developed individual, fit for a variety of labors, ready to face any change of production, and to whom the different social functions he performs are but so many modes of giving free scope to his own natural and acquired powers."

The denial of this free scope for human development under capitalist society, Marx asserted in a variety of ways, is one of its most damning failures. That was Marx's most penetrating critique of a society that he came, more and more, to despise.

The Poverty of Algebra

ANWAR SHAIKH

The introduction to this section suggested some of the distinctions between orthodox as opposed to Neo-Marxist developments of Marxist political economy. Anwar Shaikh's article falls into the former of these very general categories. Shaikh's argument emphasizes the centrality of Marx's concept of value—the labor theory of value most fully developed by Marx in his theoretical analysis in Capital*—as the cornerstone for contemporary development of Marxist political economy.*

Part 2 of Shaikh's article serves as a sophisticated extension of material introduced by John Gurley. Shaikh's argument is presented here in the context of his critique of Neo-Ricardian economic thought, which attempts to dismiss much of the theoretical core of the Marxist approach. Part 3 can thus be read as a direct rebuttal to both the Neo-Ricardian critique of Marxist economics, and the general approach to economic theory typified in the article by Ian Steedman in this volume.

1. Introduction

Not long ago, it was fashionable in orthodox social science to proclaim that the millennium had begun: the end of poverty; the end of alienation; the end of ideology.

But this was all in theory, of course. Capitalist reality, on the other hand, has continued to develop in its own brutal and crisis-prone manner, in blatant disregard of the tender sensibilities of its ideologues. Nowhere has this had a more devastating effect than in orthodox economics, whose standing has plunged as it has suffered from what Marx once called the "practical criticism" of the real. At the same time, this justly deserved decline in the status of orthodox economics has been attended by a correspondingly rapid revival of interest in Marx and Marxian economics. We are all Marxists now, after a fashion.

But the trouble is that there is quite a difference between Marx and Marxian economics. Marx labored over the great body of work in *Capital* for more than twenty-five years, and he never quite finished even this core of his planned greater work.[1] Moreover, the systematic completion of this plan, which he had hoped would be carried out by his successors, was never really undertaken. Instead, in the more than 100 years since his death, Marxian economics has developed

Anwar Shaikh, "The Poverty of Algebra," in *The Value Controversy*, ed. I. Steedman, P. Sweezy, et al. (London: Verso Editions and New Left Books, 1981), pp. 266–300.

erratically and unevenly, with only sporadic connection to Marx's own work[2]: an equation here, a scheme of reproduction there, and a dialectical class struggle everywhere—with the intervening holes filled in with whatever material was already at hand. *And this material, by and large, has been appropriated from orthodox economics*. As a consequence, the original relationship between Marxist theory and capitalist reality has been "subtly but steadily substituted by a new relationship between Marxist and bourgeois theory."[3] We are all Keynesians now, after a fashion.

Given this history, it was inevitable that the revival of interest in Marx, especially in *Capital*, would pose a tremendous difficulty for Marxian economics: how to absorb Marx's conceptual structure, and particularly his theory of value, into a pre-existing "Marxian" economics in which the great bulk of the analysis is founded precisely on the *absence* of such concepts. How does one absorb the concept of value, for instance, into the dominant analyses of the labor process, price theory, effective demand, accumulation, imperialism, etc., when as currently constructed none of these really "use" this concept in the first place?

The predicament is unavoidable. If the structure of *Capital* is indeed scientific, then it is based on a *system* of concepts, interlocked and interdependent, and one cannot simply sample individual concepts as one might recipes in a cookbook. Moreover, each concept not only has its place in relation to others, but also has its own particular effects: it influences the facts one uncovers and the conclusions one draws. *It makes its presence felt*. From which it follows that its absence will be felt just as much. It is not possible, for instance, simply to absorb the concept of value into pre-existing analyses that are in fact predicated on its absence: *one or the other must give way*.

There are really only two basic ways out of this quandary. Either one must demonstrate that the system of concepts in *Capital* can indeed be extended and concretized to deal with existing arguments and historical evidence, or one must show that the dominant formulations in what is currently defined as Marxian economics are in fact based on a superior structure, and Marx's concepts, where "appropriate," must be reformulated to fit this. In the former case, it is Marxian economics that will inevitably be altered, perhaps decisively, as it is critically appropriated into Marx's conceptual structure. In the latter case, this conceptual structure itself will be modified, and perhaps even rejected in good part, as being inconsistent with currently accepted theories.

The Neo-Ricardians, of course, adopt the latter position. Their framework, they argue, is vastly more rigorous than that of Marx, and within it they are easily able to treat a host of issues involving prices of production without any reference whatsoever to value analysis. It follows from this, they insist, that the very notion of value is redundant. What is worse, it is inconsistent with price analysis, since magnitudes in terms of values generally differ from those in terms of price. Operating on this basis, they then conclude that the concept of value must be abandoned, as must a panoply of other arguments of Marx, such as those involving productive and unproductive labor, the falling rate of profit, etc. The remainder, that portion which fits into their framework, is then defined to be the "essence" of Marx's analysis, and this of course can easily be integrated into a modern framework in the Ricardo-Marx-Sraffa-Keynes-Kalecki tradition.[4]

I wish to argue exactly the opposite position. The analysis of Marx is, I claim, vastly superior in its overall structure to anything imaginable within the flat conceptual space of the Neo-Ricardians. Indeed, it is their vaunted algebra, on which they base so many of their claims to rigor, that is in fact their greatest weakness. This is so, as we shall see, precisely because their algebra goes hand in hand with a series of concepts taken directly from what Marx calls vulgar economy: equilibrium, profit as a *cost*, and worst of all, perfect competition and all that it entails. It is not the algebra but rather these concepts, whose apologetic and ideological roots are well known, that generate their basic conclusions. This will become immediately apparent when it is shown that exactly the same algebra generates very different answers and hence very different conclusions, once it is "asked" different questions. And these questions, in turn, are different exactly because the method and the system of concepts in Marx, his scientific analysis of the law of value, is so unlike that of vulgar economy.

It should be emphasized that I am *not* claiming that Neo-Ricardian analysis should be dismissed. On the contrary, I wish to argue that its real contributions can be fully utilized only when they are divested of the vulgar concepts smuggled in with them. This is what the term critique always means: a critical appropriation of knowledge.

In what follows I will therefore briefly outline the structure of Marx's argument in order to highlight the reason why labor time appears as the regulating principle of exchange relations and the way this regulation occurs. This will be done in section 2.

In section 3 I will present and critically examine the principal arguments of the Neo-Ricardians, as represented by the work of Ian Steedman. Here, the argument will proceed along the lines outlined earlier. Section 4 will then contain concluding remarks. [. . .]

2. The Basic Structure of Marx's Argument

1. *The Role of Labor in the Reproduction of Society*

In all societies, the objects required to satisfy human needs and wants imply a certain allocation of society's productive activities, of its labor time, in specific proportions and quantities. Otherwise reproduction of the society itself is impossible: the relation of people to nature must be reproduced if society is to be reproduced. Moreover, the relation of people to nature exists only in and through definite relations of people to people; these are therefore two aspects of the same set of relations that define the mode of (re)production of social life. The production of material wealth goes hand in hand with the reproduction of social relations.

None of this suggests that labor acts unaided. On the contrary, labor is a relation between people and nature, in which people actively and consciously utilize nature to their own ends. The important point here is that *the production process is a labor process, a basic human activity, without which the reproduction of society would be impossible.* By the same token, while it is true that use-values may occasionally arise as the spontaneous fruits of nature (wild grapes, for example), it is obvious that no society could long exist without the *production* of use-values, that is, without labor itself.

In all class societies, labor acquires yet another aspect, since under these circumstances it is the extraction of surplus labor and the creation of the resulting surplus product that forms the material basis for the reproduction of the class relation.

It is therefore Marx's contention that *labor time is fundamental to the regulation of the reproduction of society*: the performance of labor produces both use-values and social relations; the performance of surplus labor reproduces both the surplus product and the class relation; and a particular distribution of the "social labor in definite proportions" results in the production of "the (specific) masses of products corresponding to the different needs" of society.[5]

2. The Role of Labor in the Regulation of Capitalist Society

Capitalist production, like that in every other class society, is also subject to the same fundamental regulation through labor time. But capitalist production has the peculiarity that is based on generalized commodity production, in which the vast bulk of the products that constitute the material basis of social reproduction are produced without any direct connection to social needs. They are produced instead by private independent labor processes, each one dominated by the profit motive. Neither the connection of a given labor process to the social division of labor, nor indeed the actual usefulness of the product itself, is of any immediate interest to the capitalist involved: only profit matters, in the final analysis.

And so Marx points to the fundamental contradiction that exists here. On the one hand, each labor process is privately undertaken *as if* it was independent of all others, with exchange-for-profit as the goal. On the other hand, this undertaking assumes in advance that other similar labor processes will also intervene at the right time and in the right proportions. Buyers of this product, sellers of the means of production for this process, and sellers of the means of consumption for these capitalists and workers, must all be presupposed if this endeavor is to succeed, and even more important, if it is to be repeated (reproduced).

Each apparently private and independent labor must therefore *presuppose* a social division of labor. Moreover, in order for this presupposition to be realized in practice, the private and apparently anarchic labors must somehow in fact end up being integrated into a social division of labor.

It is in exchange that the apparent independence of each private labor process *collides* with the true interdependence inherent in a social division of labor. Exchange is the sphere, as Marx puts it, where the contradictions of commodity production are "both exposed and resolved."[6] It is the sphere where the private independent labors are *forcibly articulated into a social division of labor*.[7]

Notice what is being said here. Exchange is the sphere in which the contradiction *internal to production itself*, the contradiction between private labor and the social division of labor, is made visible. It is here that each capitalist first gets the good or bad news, through the medium of prices and profits. But at the same time, because this contradiction is internal to the social division of labor itself, its resolution implies the *domination* of the outcome of exchange, of prices and profits, by social labor time. The outcomes of exchange are "the form in which this proportional distribution of labor asserts itself."[8]

And so we have a double relation: prices and profits as the immediate regulators of reproduction, and social labor time as the intrinsic regulator of prices and profits and hence of reproduction. The operation of this double relation is what Marx calls the law of value, and it is precisely because of his analysis of the role of labor time in social reproduction that the law of value rests on a labor theory of value: "in the midst of the accidental and ever fluctuating exchange relations between the products, the labor time socially necessary to produce them asserts itself as a regulative law of nature."

3. Abstract Labor and Value

We have seen why labor time enters in a fundamental way into the regulation of exchange-value. Now we need to specify exactly how this regulation takes place.

In all form of societies, concrete (i.e., specific) types of labors produce specific types of products: a weaver produces cloth, a baker produces bread. The concrete qualities of their labors result in the concrete forms of their use-values.

However, commodity production is production for exchange, and in exchange the distinct qualities that give various commodities their concreteness are abstracted from by the process of exchange itself. When cloth is exchanged for bread, a certain quantity of the former is socially equated with a certain quantity of the latter. Their concrete differences are therefore subordinated to a common social property, that of having "quantitative worth"—what Marx calls exchange-value. So, by becoming a commodity, a use-value acquires an additional aspect, that of possessing exchange-value.

As a product, a use-value is the result of concrete labor. This means that the social process of equating different use-values and hence abstracting from their concrete qualities is at the same time a social process of abstracting from the concrete qualities of the labors whose results are these use-values. It follows that the very same set of social relations that endows use-values with the common quantitative property of exchange-value also endows the labor that produces this concrete use-value with the capacity to produce a common abstract quantity. Thus labor too acquires an additional aspect when it is aimed at producing commodities: it acquires the aspect of abstract labor, and from this point of view all commodity-producing labor becomes qualitatively alike and quantitatively comparable.

Because it is only labor actually engaged in the production of commodities that acquires the property of abstract labor, it is only the labor time of this commodity-producing labor that regulates the exchange-values of commodities. Moreover, since from a social point of view the total labor time required for the production of a commodity consists of direct and indirect labor time, it is this total that Marx calls the *intrinsic measure* of a commodity's exchange-value, the labor value of the commodity.[9]

It is important to stress here that the abstraction process described above is a real social process. Abstract labor is the property acquired by human labor when it is directed toward the production of commodities, and as such, it exists *only* in commodity production. The concept of abstract labor is not a mental generalization that we somehow choose to make, but rather the reflection in thought of a real social process. This in turn means that *abstract labor, and hence value, are also real*[10]: commodity-producing labor creates value, which is objectified (materialized) in the form of a commodity. We will see shortly how important this point is in relation to the Neo-Ricardians.

There is one further issue here. We have seen that abstract labor has its origin in the process whereby a use-value becomes a commodity. But this process in turn has two possible forms, with quite different implications for abstract labor.

Consider the case of a type of product produced not for exchange but for direct use, say by precapitalist peasant labor. Suppose now that a portion of this product happens to find its way into exchange. Then, in this case these use-values become commodities only in the *act* of exchange—which in turn means that the concrete labor that produced them is abstracted from, also acquiring the additional property of abstract labor, only in the moment of exchange itself. Noncommodity *production* therefore involves concrete labor and use-values only, and a portion of these are *realized* as abstract labor and commodities, respectively, only in exchange itself.

The matter is very different in the case of *commodity production*. Here the use-value is produced as a commodity, and indeed the whole nature of the production process is dominated by the fact that it is the exchange-value of this commodity that is central to the producer. In this case the use-value acquires its character as a commodity by virtue of the fact that this labor process exists within and through commodity relations, and not merely at the moment of exchange. This use-value is a commodity from its very conception, and the labor is both concrete and abstract from the very outset. *Thus labor involved in the production of commodities produces value, while exchange merely realizes it in money-form.* It is only because of this that Marx can distinguish between the amounts of value and surplus-value created in commodity production, and the generally different amounts realized through exchange. I will return to this point later on, for it is the defenders of Marx themselves who stumble over this issue.

4. Money and Price

The preceding analysis also implies that money is an absolutely necessary aspect of developed commodity production. Exchange is the process in which people equate different use-values to another, and money is the necessary medium in which this equation is expressed, and through which the articulation of the private labors is accomplished. Money is the medium of abstraction, and the means of forcible articulation.

The price of each commodity is therefore always a money-price, the golden measure of its quantitative worth. It is what Marx calls the *external measure* of exchange-value, and hence the *form* taken by value in exchange. [11]

Because price is the monetary expression of value in the sphere of exchange, it is always more complexly determined than value. Even in the simplest case, when prices are proportional to values, the money-price of a commodity is still a quantity of money (say gold) determined by the value of the commodity *relative* to the standard of price (say one ounce of gold), *and is therefore already a (trans)formation of the commodity's value.* As such, the movement of prices need not parallel those of commodity values. For instance, prices may rise even when commodity values are falling, if the value of gold falls even faster. [12]

We know, of course, that as Marx develops his argument in *Capital*, the relative complexity of the price-form becomes greater. In volume 1 price is generally treated as a simple money-form of value, but wages, as time-wages and piece-wages, are already more complex forms of the value of labor-power. In volume 2 costs of circulation and turnover add fresh determination to the price-form. Lastly, in volume 3, the development of prices of production and of the division of surplus-value into profits, rents, and interest further concretizes the price-form, while the distinction between individual and average value concretizes the determination of value magnitudes, and through them, those of price magnitudes (individual, average, and regulating prices of production; differential profitability; and rent, absolute and differential). It must be noted here that the increasing complexity of the price-value relationship is no defect. Since price magnitudes are the immediate regulators of reproduction, the law of value must contain within it a theory of the structure of price phenomena—right down to their most concrete determination. Otherwise the law remains abstract, unable to grasp the real movements of the system.

On the other hand, because the price magnitudes are themselves regulated by the socially necessary distribution of labor, the various forms of price categories must be developed in relation to the quantities of socially necessary labor time whose magnitudes and movements dominate and regulate these price phenomena. We must be able to conceive not only of the relative autonomy of price magnitudes, as expressed in their variability (complexity) relative to values, *but also of the limits to these variations, and of the connection of these limits to social labor time*. It is significant that in his own development of the increasingly complex categories of price phenomena, Marx never loses sight of the domination of these phenomena by the law of value:

> No matter how the prices are regulated, we arrive at the following:
>
> 1) The law of value dominates price movements with reduction or increases in required labor time making prices of production fall or rise. . . .
>
> 2) The average profit determining the prices of production must always be approximately equal to that quantity of surplus-value which falls to the share of individual capital in its capacity of an aliquot part of the total social capital. . . . Since the total value of the commodities regulates the total surplus-value, and this in turn regulates the level of average profit and thereby the general rate of profit—as a general law or a law governing fluctuations—it follows that the law of value regulates prices of production. [13]

In a highly modern vein, Marx goes on to note how meaningless—but how very convenient—it is to treat the difference between price and value (i.e., the *relation* between the two) as a mere separation:

> The price of production includes the average profit. . . . It is really what Adam Smith calls *natural price*, Ricardo calls *price of production*, or *cost of production* . . . because in the long run it is a prerequisite of supply, of the reproduction of commodities in every individual sphere. But none of them has revealed the difference between price of production and value. We can well understand why the same economists who oppose determining the value of commodities by labor time, i.e., by the quantity of labor contained in them, why they always speak of prices of production as centers around which market-prices fluctuate. They can afford to do it because the price of production is an utterly external and *prima facie* meaningless form of the value of commodities, a form as it appears in competition, therefore in the mind of the vulgar capitalist, and consequently in that of the vulgar economist. [14]

I remind the reader that Marx is speaking here of economists of his time who claim to ground themselves in "classical" economics—minus the labor theory of value, of course!

5. Two Aspects of Socially Necessary Labor Time

In any society, the necessary distribution of social labor time has two distinct aspects, and these in turn give rise to two different senses of socially necessary labor time.

On the one hand, under given conditions of production a certain type of use-value will require a definite quantity of social labor time for its production. Let us suppose, for instance, that 100,000 hours of social labor time are required (directly and indirectly) for the production of 50,000 yards of linen. Then 2 hours of labor time are socially necessary on average to produce *one* yard of linen.

But suppose the expressed social need for linen is actually 40,000 yards. Then the total amount of social labor time that needs to be directly and indirectly allocated toward the production of linen would be 80,000 hours, other things being equal.

We can thus see that these are two senses of socially necessary labor time. The first sense represents the actual total labor time (100,000 hours) expended under given conditions of production. In conjunction with the actual total product (50,000 yards), this defines the average labor time required per *unit* of product (2 hours per yard).

The second sense, however, refers to the total labor time that would be required in this branch in order to satisfy expressed social need (80,000 hours).

In commodity production, these two aspects of socially necessary labor time have further implications.

To begin with, the first aspect defines the total value of the product (100,000 hours) and the unit *social* value of the commodity. The latter is the average amount of abstract labor time socially necessary for the production of one unit of the commodity.

This unit social value is in turn the basis of the regulating price, a term by which Marx means that price which acts as the center of gravity of the commodity's market price. In volumes 1 and 2 this regulating price is supposed to be the commodity's *direct price* (price proportional to unit social value). In volume 3, after the form of value has been further developed, the price of production takes the place of the direct price as the center of gravity of market price. For ease in exposition, let us stick to direct price as the regulating price, and let us further assume that $1 represents 1 hour of abstract labor time. Then since the unit social value of a yard of linen is 2 hours, its direct price will be $2.

The second aspect of socially necessary labor time then specifies the relation between the regulating price and the market.

The actual production of linen is 50,000 yards, which represents 100,000 hours of value created in production. The regulating price of this, which is by assumption the direct price, is $2 per yard. Suppose now that at this regulating price, the expressed social need, i.e., the effective demand, for this product is only 40,000 yards of linen, which represents only 80,000 hours of labor time. Then the fact that the actual amount of total labor time devoted to linen production is greater than the amount socially necessary to meet effective demand means that the market price of the commodity will fall below its direct price of $2—to say $1.50 per yard of linen. The 50,000 yards actually produced will therefore sell for $75,000 in the market, and since $1 represents one hour of abstract labor, this means that the value realized in exchange, in the form of money, is 75,000 hours. And so we see that because the actual labor time devoted to this branch is greater than the labor time socially necessary to meet effective demand, a product representing a value of 100,000 hours is sold in the market for the monetary equivalent of only 75,000 hours. The "violation of this (necessary) proportion makes it impossible to realize the value of the commodity and thus the surplus-value contained in it."[15]

To summarize: Socially necessary labor time in the first sense defines the total value and unit social value of the commodity, and through the latter, the commodity's regulating price. Socially necessary labor time in the second sense, on the other hand, defines the relation between regulating price and market price. Both senses must be kept in mind if one is to understand exactly how social labor time dominates and regulates the exchange-process. We will see later that a failure to distinguish between these two real aspects of socially necessary labor time, and hence a failure to recognize Marx's own distinction between these two aspects, so confuses some Marxists that they end up abandoning the concept of the magnitude of value (as distinct from price) altogether.

3. Critique of the Neo-Ricardians

In what follows I will divide the main points of the Neo-Ricardian position, as summarized by Steedman, into four major groups and then address each in turn.

1. The Redundancy Argument

Figure 1 illustrates the first major argument marshalled by the Neo-Ricardians, which as Steedman notes, has been made "in various forms, by many different writers over the last 80 years," and in which he claims "no logical flaw has ever been found."[16] Such brave words clearly deserve a closer examination.

Steedman explains the argument as follows. The box on the left represents the physical production data and the real wage, and these "suffice to *determine* the rate of profit . . . and all prices of production," as illustrated by the path marked "(b)." At the same time, "the quantities of labor embodied in the various commodities . . . can themselves only be *determined* once the conditions of production are known," as illustrated by path (a). From this it follows at once that labor values therefore "*play no essential role* in the *determination* of the rate of profit (or of the prices of production)."[17] In other words, values are redundant

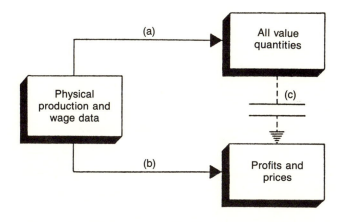

Figure 1.

in the analysis of exchange relationships.

Notice how often the word "determine" crops up: the physical production data *determine* values, and in conjunction with the real wage also *determine* prices of production. But what then determines this physical production data?

In Marx, the answer is clear: it is the labor process. It is human productive activity, the actual performance of labor, that transforms "inputs" into "outputs," and it is only when this labor is successful that we have any "physical production data" at all. Moreover, if the labor process is a process of producing commodities, then it is one in which value is materialized in the form of use-values. Thus both "inputs" and "outputs" are the use-forms of materialized value, and we can then say that in the *real* process, it is *values that determine the "physical production data."*

We also know, moreover, that in the *real* process of reproduction, the production of use-values *precedes* their exchange. Indeed, exchange itself is a process in which the different labor times involved in producing these use-values actually confront each other, and are eventually articulated into a social division of labor—through the medium of money prices. Thus it is *values that also determine prices*, in a double sense: prices are the forms taken by values in exchange, and the magnitudes of these values dominate and regulate the movements of their price forms. The latter point must of course be developed further, since we need to show not merely that prices of production and profits rest on the expression in circulation of value and surplus-value, but also that the former magnitudes are regulated by the latter. This we take up in the next section. Nonetheless, we may summarize the above argument in a diagram, figure 2, that serves as a contrast to figure 1.

How do Neo-Ricardians manage to miss so elementary a point? It is, I think, because of two fundamental weaknesses characteristic of their analysis. First, in spite of their protestations to the contrary,[18] they tend to view production as a

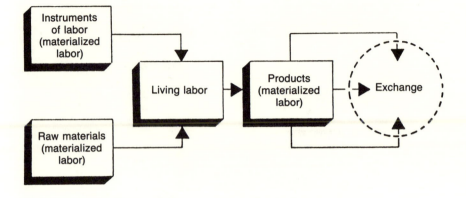

Figure 2.

technical process, as physical data, instead of a labor process in which human labor is objectified in use-values. Hence the characteristic emphasis of the Neo-Ricardians on distribution: once the labor process is seen as a technical process, only "distribution" appears truly social.

Second, they typically confuse the real process with its appropriation in thought. In the real process, as we have seen, social labor time *really* regulates exchange. The physical *data* are then a conceptual summary of the real determination, and if we then use the data to conceptually *calculate* values, we only capture in thought their real magnitudes. Such a calculation no more determines these values than does the calculation of the mass of the earth determine either the earth or its mass. It merely recognizes what already exists. This is a fundamental point in a materialist view of the world, and the eighty-year failure of the Neo-Ricardians to distinguish real and conceptual determination reveals their long attachment to an idealist method.

2. The Inconsistency Argument

Let us return for a moment to the Neo-Ricardian fork diagram in figure 1. In that diagram, the path (c) from value magnitudes to profits and prices is dotted to express its redundancy. But it is also blocked off, in order to represent the Neo-Ricardian argument "that one cannot, in general, explain profits and prices from value quantities."[19]

There are two basic components to this argument. The first is simply the redundancy argument repeated once again, in which Steedman insists that since he can *calculate* both value and price magnitudes from the physical data, the former cannot therefore determine the latter. For him, only algebra "explains" anything. We have already dealt with the superficiality of this type of reasoning.

The second element is more substantive, though it, like the first, is hardly new. In essence, this point has to do with the "transformation problem." In what follows I will therefore present both the problem and its treatment, though the main results I will utilize are developed by me elsewhere, and will merely be outlined here.

The basic issues are well known. Following Steedman's own analysis, we abstract from fixed capital and joint production,[20] and consider a given mass of use-values representing a given sum of values and sum of surplus-values. Then, with prices proportional to values (for simplicity in exposition, let $1 represent 1 hour of value), this mass of use-values will be expressed in exchange as a sum of direct prices and direct profits. Under these circumstances all money magnitudes are directly proportional to the corresponding value magnitudes, and therefore all money ratios are equal to the corresponding value ratios. In this case, the relationship between production and circulation is specially transparent.

Now consider the same mass of use-values, hence the same sum of values and surplus-values, exchanged at prices of production. We are considering, in other words, a change in the form of value alone, from direct prices to prices of production. Prices of production are therefore transformed direct prices, and since the latter are themselves the monetary (trans-)forms of value, prices of production are doubly transformed values.

The relation between the sum of prices and the sum of values defines the value of money. If we then keep the value of money constant in order to simplify the analysis, the sum of prices of production will equal the sum of direct prices. The sum of money prices will, in other words, be constant across the transformation. Nonetheless, individual prices of production (transformed direct prices) will differ from individual direct prices. Strictly speaking, one should refer to these differences as "price of production—direct price deviations." This is a very awkward term, however, and it is much simpler to follow Marx's usage and speak of "price-value" and "profit-surplus-value" deviations. I will therefore stick to this traditional usage, but with the clear understanding that the deviations we speak of are between money magnitudes.

It is evident that no change in the mere exchange ratios through which a given total product is distributed can alter the total mass of use-values so distributed. It follows immediately, as Marx points out, that no change in exchange ratios can alter either the sum of values or the sum of surplus-values; it can only result in a different kind of division of these totals.[21]

It does *not* follow that the *monetary* expression of these sums is invariant: even with the value of money constant, so that the sum of prices is constant, the sum of transformed profits (corresponding to prices of production) will in general differ from direct profits. The question is, given that circulation neither creates nor destroys values (assuming the whole product is sold), how is it that profits can differ from surplus-value?

When a commodity is sold at its direct price, the seller and buyer exchange equal values in commodity-form and money-form, respectively. But when prices deviate from values, a transfer of value takes place during the exchange process.

For instance, when a commodity sells at a price below its value (i.e., below direct price), the capitalist who sells the commodity receives a value in money-form that is less than the value he hands over in the form of a commodity, and vice versa for the buyer. Surplus-value is therefore transferred from seller to buyer.

To understand the general implications of this, let us first divide the total social production into three great branches (means of production, workers' articles of consumption, and capitalists' articles of consumption), and then, on this basis, analyze the effects of price-value deviations on the transfers of value in simple reproduction. To do this we will consider the effect of price-value deviations in each branch *taken singly*, holding the prices of the remaining two branches exactly equal to values. We are therefore momentarily allowing the sum of prices to deviate from the sum of values, though we will soon return to this equality. It is important to note that this is an analytical device only, not a description of an actual process.

Suppose the first branch raises its total price above its total value, with the other two keeping their prices equal to values. Then the gain in profits of the first branch is exactly equal to the rise in the sum of prices. This branch, however, sells means of production, which in simple reproduction are equal in magnitude to those used up as constant capital in all three branches. Therefore the price rise of the first branch, *which is the same thing as the rise in the sum of prices*, produces an exactly equal rise in the total cost-price of all three branches. But if the sum of cost-price rises as much as the sum of prices, the difference between the two, which is the *sum of profits*, is not changed at all. It follows therefore that though the first branch can alter its own profits by altering its price, other things being equal, this cannot in any way give rise to any change in the sum of profits. What is gained by one capitalist as *capital-value*, in the *form of profits*, is exactly offset by what is lost by the capitalist class as a whole as *capital-value*, in the form of constant capital. *The transfers of value therefore remain within the circuit of capital, so that within this circuit the net transfer of value is zero.*

A similar analysis can be conducted for the second branch, which sells workers' articles of consumption. Here, any rise in this total price is initially at the expense of the immediate buyers, who are the workers as a whole. But since we are considering a change in the form of value alone, the value of labor power and hence the real wage are held constant, so that any rise in the price of workers' means of subsistence is also a rise in the variable capital advanced by capitalists in all three branches for the purchase of labor power. Consequently, here too the sum of cost prices will rise exactly as much as the sum of prices, so that total profits remain unchanged. The second branch can alter its own profits, but only at the expense of the profits of the remaining two branches, because what it gains as capital-value in the form of profits is also lost by the capitalist class as a whole as capital-value in the form of variable capital. Once again, the transfers of value remain internal to the circuit of capital, with the consequence that the net transfer is always zero.

We come finally to the sale of capitalist articles of consumption, the third branch. A change in total price here, say a fall in total price below value, holding all other prices constant, means an equivalent fall in its profit below surplus-value, and of course an equal fall in the overall sum of prices. Thus far, this is similar to the previous two cases. But from here on the analysis differs, because the loss in *capital-value* due to profits being below surplus-value in the third branch appears as a gain in *revenue-value* to the capitalists who buy these articles of consumption. Though this loss in capital-value is indeed compensated by a corresponding gain elsewhere in social reproduction, this compensating effect disappears from the purview of the circuit of capital and is therefore not "charged," so to speak, against the fall in profit. It is this transfer of value between the circuit of capital and the circuit of revenue, through the process of exchange, that explains why price-value deviations can give rise to deviations between the sum of profits and the sum of surplus-values, *without violating the law of the conservation of value through exchange*.

The above results were explicitly derived for the case of simple reproduction only. However, as I show elsewhere, they can be extended to cover expanded reproduction also. Moreover, in this general form they hold true for any price-value deviations at all, not merely those arising from the formation of prices of production.

In most analyses of social reproduction, the circuit of capitalist revenue is not explicitly accounted for. Of course, under these circumstances it appears completely mysterious that as prices deviate from values, a given surplus-product and hence a given mass of surplus-value can manifest itself as a variable mass of profit.

However, once the *whole* of social circulation is analyzed, the mystery disappears. To the extent that price-value deviations give rise to transfers between the circuit of capital and the circuit of capitalist revenue, these transfers will manifest themselves as differences between actual profit and direct profits. Ironically, though this phenomenon is evidently a mystery to most Marxist discussions of this issue, it was no mystery to Marx himself: "This phenomena of the conversion of capital into revenue should be noted, because it creates the *illusion* that the amount of profit grows (or in the opposite case decreases) independently of the amount of surplus-value."[22]

None of this should come as any surprise once the difference between value and form-of-value has been grasped. Value and surplus-value are created in production, and expressed as money magnitudes in circulation. Since the circulation magnitudes are more concrete, they are necessarily more complexly determined than value magnitudes, for they express not only the conditions of production of value but also the conditions of its circulation. As such, the relative autonomy of the sphere of circulation necessarily expresses itself as the relative autonomy of price magnitudes from value magnitudes. Profits, in other words, depends not only on the mass of surplus-value but also on its specific mode of circulation.

The concept of the relative autonomy of circulation from production implies not only that profit can vary independently of surplus-value, *but also that this independence is strictly limited*. It is necessary, therefore, to show how value categories themselves provide the limits to the variations in their money-expressions.

Intuitively, it is evident from the preceding discussion that the overall deviation of actual profits from direct profits is the combined result of two factors. First, it depends on the extent to which the prices of capitalists' articles of consumption deviate from the values of these articles—that is, it depends on the manner in which surplus-value is distributed among capitalists, and on the resultant pattern of individual price-value deviations. And second, it depends on the extent to which this surplus-value is consumed by capitalists as revenue—that is, on the distribution of this surplus-value between capital and revenue. Even when prices deviate from values, the size of any transfer from the circuit of capital to the circuit of revenue will also depend on the relative size of the circuit of revenue. Where all surplus-value is consumed, as in simple reproduction, the deviation of actual profits from direct profits will be at its maximum. When, on the other hand, all surplus-value is re-invested, in maximum expanded reproduction, then there is no circuit of capitalist revenue and consequently no transfer at all: total actual profits must, in this case, equal total direct profits, regardless of the size and nature of individual price-value deviations.[23]

With only a little more effort, one can extend the preceding results on the sum of profits to the case of the rate of profit. It will be recalled that when all capital turns over in one period, as is assumed here, the rate of profit is equal in magnitude to the mass of profit divided by the cost-price. The sum of prices, on the other hand, is the sum of cost-prices and the sum of profits. Then, if with a constant sum of prices, individual price-value deviations cause the sum of profits to be larger than surplus-value, the sum of cost-prices will be correspondingly smaller than $C + V$. Then the average money rate of profit will be larger than the value rate of profit $\left(\dfrac{S}{C+V} \right)$ on account of both a larger numerator and a smaller denominator. Nonetheless, the general relation between the two is merely another expression of the total profit-surplus deviations analyzed above, and is therefore subject to the same fundamental determination.[24]

All this was based on arbitrary market prices. If we now confine ourselves to prices of production, we can be even more precise. Since the mass of profit and the rate of profit are so closely connected as far as these issues are concerned, it is sufficient to illustrate the argument for the latter.

We begin by noting that for given conditions of the labor process, the value rate of profit $r°$ can always be expressed as a steadily (i.e., monotonic) increasing function of the rate of surplus-value.

$$(1) \qquad r^\circ = \frac{S}{C+V}$$

where S = surplus-value, V = value of labor power. Let $L = V + S$ = value-added by living labor (if N = the number of workers employed, and h = the length of the working day in hours, then $L = Nh$). Let $k = \dfrac{C}{L}$ = the ratio of dead to living labor. Then

$$(2) \qquad r^\circ = \frac{\dfrac{S}{V}}{\left(\dfrac{C}{L}\right)\left(\dfrac{L}{V}\right) + 1} = \frac{\dfrac{S}{V}}{k\left(1 + \dfrac{S}{V}\right) + 1}$$

Since k depends only on the technology and the length of the working day h, when these conditions of the labor process are given, r° will vary directly with the rate of surplus-value. Thus the value rate of profit is a monotonic increasing function of the rate of surplus-value.[25]

In recent years, several authors have shown that when direct prices are transformed into prices of production, though the transformed money rate of profit r will in general deviate from the value rate (we have already seen how and why), nonetheless this transformed rate also is a monotonic increasing function of the rate of surplus-value.[26] But once it is recognized that the value rate of profit r° and the transformed rate r both increase as $\dfrac{S}{V}$ increases, it follows at once that they

must move together: *when the value rate of profit rises (falls) its reflection in the sphere of circulation, the transformed rate of profit, also rises (falls).*

Figure 3 depicts this intrinsic relationship. For the sake of illustration, it is assumed here that r° is larger than r, though of course it could equally well be the other way around.[27]

It is interesting to note that although Marx insists that the equalization of the rate of profit and the formation of individual prices of production are of great importance for individual capitals or subsets of capitals, he also insists that for the system as a whole the previously derived laws are basically unaltered. In a letter to Engels, after presenting the basic phenomena arising from the transformation process, Marx goes on to summarize what remains to be developed. "Further: the *changed outward form* of the law of value and surplus-value—which were previously set forth and which are still valid—*after the transformation of value into price of production.*"[28]

At all times and in all places, price is the outward form of value, the reflection

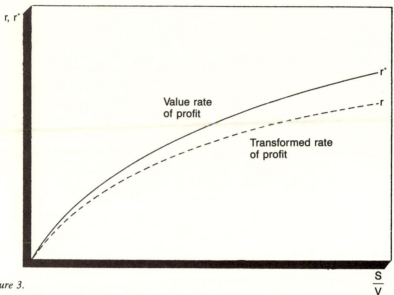

Figure 3.

of value in the sphere of circulation. What the transformation does, Marx argues, is to transform this outward form, to introduce into it certain fresh determination and new sources of variation, but to do so in such a way as to leave the intrinsic connections unchanged. Look again at figure 3. It illustrates this conception perfectly: in the relatively autonomous mirror of circulation, the transformed rate of profit appears *as a displaced image of the value rate of profit*, essentially the same in determination but somewhat different in exact magnitude. The autonomy of the sphere of circulation is expressed in this displacement of magnitude; on the other hand, the limited nature of this autonomy manifests itself precisely through the fact that it is the structure of value categories (the pattern of organic compositions, and the proportion of surplus-value that is converted into revenue) that provides the limits to this displacement effect. The variations in the form of value are thus shown to be conditioned and limited by the very structure of value itself.

The notion of relative autonomy, of variation within limits, is of course entirely absent from the Neo-Ricardian discussion. Given their own deep debt to orthodox economics, this should come as no surprise. Consequently, they have always insisted that the difference between value and its expression in circulation implies an inconsistency, a complete divorce of inner connection, between the two.

The money rate of profit, Steedman notes, is generally different from the value rate. From this he concludes that ''the latter ratio provides no adequate measure of either the rate of profit in a capitalist economy or the potential for accumulation in such an economy.''[29] This is the ventriloquist voice of his method speaking, not the algebra. It is, moreover, an obscurantist voice, precisely because it takes refuge in algebra in order to obscure the profound silence on the question of method.

Three further points should be made on this subject. First of all, even though we can establish that individual price-value deviations do not alter the fact that aggregate value magnitudes clearly regulate aggregate price magnitudes, it is not sufficient to stop here. Once we move to a more concrete analysis, then the individual price-value deviations and the transfers of value to which they give rise become quite important in their own right. For the analysis of the phenomena of competition, of regional and international differences, of development and underdevelopment, the relation of the parts to the whole is itself of paramount concern.[30] Once we consider these issues, then it becomes important to address the theoretical determinants of individual price-value deviations, in terms of both their directions (which dictate the directions of the transfers of value) and their magnitudes (which indicate how large such transfers are likely to be).

In addition, we also need to look at the empirical magnitudes involved. Indeed, this second issue is implicit in the issue of the theoretical determinants, since in Marx's method the purpose of theory is to grasp the structure of the real relations—which can be done only through the study of these real relations themselves.[31]

This in turn leads to the third point. Given that theory must be developed in conjunction with the "material of observation" which, precisely because it is *material*, can "weed out . . . hypotheses, doing away with some and correcting others until finally the law is established in a pure form,"[32] it follows that scientific abstraction must be what Marx calls a "determinate abstraction." Abstraction must be typification, the extraction from some aspect of the real of its "simplest characterization."[33]

In bourgeois social science, however, abstractions tend to be idealizations, not typifications. When Marx speaks of the reproduction of the moving contradiction that is capitalist commodity-production, a reproduction process that necessarily must occur by trial-*through*-error, he always speaks of a process of tendential regulation in which discrepancies and errors of one sort constantly produce those of an opposite sort. "The total movement of this disorder is its order."[34] Similarly, when he speaks of capitalist competition, he speaks of it as a *war* in which "each individual capital strives to capture the largest possible share of the market and supplant its competitors and exclude them from the market—*competition of capitals*."[35]

The Neo-Ricardians, on the other hand, are safely ensconced within equilibrium analysis, conducted on the assumption of "something like perfect competition."[36] These concepts do not merely idealize capitalist reality, they systematically and ideologically obscure it. Their pride of place in Neo-Ricardian analysis therefore highlights once again the profound limitations of this school of thought. It has been so successful in its struggle against Neoclassical theory not merely because it is better than its adversary, but also because it is so similar to it. With this in mind, we turn to the third major type of argument made by the Neo-Ricardians against the theory of value in Marx.

3. The Primacy Argument

In the previous section I argued that the quantitative difference between, say, the value and money rates of profit did not and should not obscure the more fundamental qualitative *and* quantitative relation between the two. Steedman does not see this, naturally, because his method does not afford him the concept of relative autonomy. But to this Steedman would reply: "Now if these profit rates differ, which is the significant one? Which will affect capitalists' decisions and actions? And which will tend to be made uniform, as between industries, in a competitive economy? The answer is self-evident; it is the money rate of profit which affects decisions and tends to be equalized. The 'value rate of profit,' used by Marx, is of no concern to the capitalists, it is unknown to the capitalists. . . . The implication is clear; $S/(C + V)$ is not a significant rate of profit in a capitalist economy, and it does *not* equal the actual, money, rate of profit."[37]

There are three levels of argument here. At the first, Steedman notes that all actual decisions are made in terms of money magnitudes. This is, of course, the point of departure for Marx also. Money prices and profits are the immediate regulators of reproduction, and the very object of the law of value is to discover their inner laws.

At the next level, Steedman goes on to say that because the value rate of profit is "unknown to the capitalists," "of no concern" to them, it is "*not* a significant rate of profit in a capitalist economy." How extraordinary it is to claim that only what "the capitalists know" is significant, in other words, that appearances are significant but essences are not! In one stroke Steedman throws out all science.

But there is a third level here, with an even deeper problem. Let us stop for a minute and ask what it is that these capitalists in fact "know."

Well, capitalists know that capitalism is an unplanned society, in which they are free to take their chances producing commodities in the hope of making a profit. And they certainly know that there is no guarantee they will receive this profit, *or any profit at all*, and even if they do, that they will be able to repeat it. They therefore know that prices and profits fluctuate constantly, and that there is never at any moment a *uniform* rate of profit, *so that prices of production never exist as such*. It follows from this that the prices, the individual profit rates, and even the average rate of profit, on which capitalists base their actual decisions, are never equal to prices of production and the uniform profit rate on which Steedman apparently bases *his* decisions.[38] The uniform rate of profit is of course "unknown to the capitalists," hence of "no concern to them," and therefore by his own argument it is "*not* a significant rate of profit in a capitalist economy."

Fortunately for him, the last proposition is not true. And that is simply because it is his argument itself that is not significant. But then if one argues instead that prices of production and the uniform rate of profit are important even though they never exist as such in circulation—precisely because they dominate and regulate the constantly fluctuating constellation of market prices and profit rates—then it is equally true that values and the value rate of profit are even more important because they in turn dominate and regulate prices of production and the uniform rate of profit. And this is just what Marx argues all along.

One might ask: how could Steedman make so egregious an error? Quite simply because he operates entirely within the concept of equilibrium. If one assumes that there is no contradiction between private independently undertaken labors and the social division of labor, so that the articulation of labor is *immediate*, then one can equally well assume that prices of production and the uniform rate of profit obtain directly in circulation. *But then the characteristic contradiction of capitalism has been spirited away altogether.* Once you replace the concept of tendential regulation with that of equilibrium, you have switched from abstraction as typification to abstraction as idealization. This is, of course, characteristic of vulgar economy, and is built into the basic mathematical formulations on which Steedman relies so heavily.

4. The Choice of Technique Argument

The Neo-Ricardian pattern of confusing tendential regulation with equilibrium, and of competitive battle with perfect competition, shows up even more forcefully in their analysis of the so-called choice of technique. Since I have discussed this issue elsewhere, I will only mention the central points here.[39]

Steedman begins by noting that capitalists in a particular industry often have the possibility of more than one method of production. The method chosen, he argues, is then the one that yields the highest rate of profit,[40] as estimated in terms of existing wages and prices. As always, these existing prices are exactly equal to prices of production, all rates of profit are exactly equal to the uniform rate, and equilibrium rules everywhere. Because capitalists choose the method with the highest rate of profit, no method will be adopted unless it is higher than their own existing rate of profit, and since this rate is identically equal to the uniform rate of profit, they will adopt a new method only if it yields a rate of profit higher than the uniform rate. It follows from this that the adoption of a new method in effect adds a new higher rate of profit to the existing rates (which by assumption are all equal to the uniform rate), and therefore ends up eventually raising the uniform rate of profit itself.

From a Neo-Ricardian point of view, this means that if we had knowledge of all the possible methods in all the different industries, we could assemble them into different combinations of one method per industry, and then argue that the particular combination that in practice would be adopted at a given real wage would be the one that yields "the highest possible uniform rate of profit."[41] So, the knowledge of the real wage and possible combinations of methods enables

Steedman to identify the combination that would yield the highest uniform rate. He therefore concludes that it is the real wage and the spectrum of possible combinations that "determine" the uniform rate of profit and the actual combination (physical data). And only when the actual combination is given, according to him, are values "determined." The "determination of the profit rate is thus *logically prior* to any determination of value magnitudes," so that when "there is a choice of technique, any attempt to ground the theory of the rate of profit on any value magnitudes must be ill-conceived."[42]

This whole analysis is a résumé of the characteristic confusions of the Neo-Ricardian school. To begin with, once it is recognized that market prices and profit rates can never exactly equal prices of production and the uniform rate of profit, then the whole process of reducing the question to one of selecting the combination that yields the highest uniform rate of profit falls apart. Suppose, for instance, that market prices differ from prices of production, so that industry profit rates differ from the uniform rate of the Neo-Ricardians. Then, precisely because calculations are being made in terms of prices that do not directly embody the uniform rate of profit, a new method in a particular industry can raise the industry's profit rate *and at the same time lower the uniform rate.* A production method that yields a higher than average rate of profit at one set of prices need not do so at some other set. Steedman himself emphasizes this possibility vis-à-vis the "inconsistency" between prices of production and direct prices, without noting that it applies with the same force to the "inconsistency" between market prices and prices of production.[43] Had he done so, however, he would have been forced to conclude on the basis of his own logic that prices of production and the uniform rate of profit are not significant on two counts: not only are they "unknown to the capitalists," etc., but their very use in analysis can lead us to false conclusions.

However, there is an even more basic error in Steedman's logic. Consider the fact that when capitalists evaluate methods of production, they do so not only on the basis of anticipated prices of the plant, equipment, materials, and labor power, but also on the anticipated performance of the labor process associated with this method (which will determine the anticipated relation between "inputs" and "outputs"), and finally on the estimated conditions of sale. Therefore, the profits they evaluate are themselves potential profits based on the potential creation of value and surplus-value in production, and on their estimated realization in circulation. So we may say that, *even in thought*, surplus-value regulates profit. Moreover, for this potential itself to be made real, actual value and surplus-value will have to be produced and then realized, so that *in practice also*, surplus-value regulates profit.

Lastly, I would argue that even the Neo-Ricardian description of the process whereby methods are evaluated is false. Steedman tells us that "each industry will seek to adopt that production method which minimizes costs."[44] On the surface, this is similar to Marx's argument that competition drives capitalists to increase the productivity of labor in order to lower cost-prices. But when Steedman speaks of "costs," he means *prices*, i.e., cost-prices *plus* profit. The Neo-Ricardian analysis, in other words, *is predicated on the treatment of profit as a "cost" of production.* Once profit is treated as what it truly is, an excess over all costs, then on top of everything else, the Neo-Ricardian claim that the profit rate cannot fall due to a rising organic composition is also falsified.[45] In the end, rather than being their strongest case, their treatment of the so-called choice of technique turns out to be the weakest of all.

4. Concluding Remarks

Recent events have led to a tremendous revival of interest in Marxian economic analysis. But this process has also produced its own specific problems, because as Marxian economics gains in respectability, the temptation to represent itself in "respectable" terms grows accordingly. And these terms, in the end, are almost always the wrong ones.

There is no question that Marxism must appropriate all modern developments. But to appropriate them involves much more than merely adopting them: it involves tearing them out of the bourgeois framework in which they appear, examining their hidden premises, and resituating them (when and if possible) on a Marxist terrain—a terrain that cannot be derived merely by algebraic variation or sociological transformation of the premises of orthodox economics. We must, and indeed we do, have our own ground to stand upon.

It is my contention that the Neo-Ricardian (Sraffa-based) tradition is by far too "respectable." Its roots in (left) Keynesianism are easy to establish, and its refuge in mathematical economics is quite revealing. Nonetheless, the claims made by this school must be addressed, and its real contributions must be separated out from what is merely part of its cloak of respectability. In this paper I attempt to do just that, by focusing on the central arguments involved. Secondary matters involving questions of fixed capital and joint-production are not treated here, in part because of their greater difficulty, and in part because of the astonishing weakness of the Neo-Ricardian formulation of these issues. An adequate treatment of these issues would require confronting these formulations themselves, in terms of both their internal consistency and their (external) adequacy to the relations they pretend to represent. Such an investigation is well beyond the scope of the present paper.

The Neo-Ricardians tell us that the concept of value in Marx is not only unnecessary in the analysis of capitalism, but also irreconcilable with the actual relations involved.

In order to address these claims, I have first attempted to set out how and why *labor* appears inextricably bound up with Marx's notion of value, why the magnitude of value is measured by abstract labor time, and why Marx argues that this magnitude *regulates and dominates* what he calls the "ever fluctuating exchange-relations between the products."

With this in mind, I then address the specific arguments made by the Neo-Ricardians, as summarized by Ian Steedman, concerning the redundancy of values, their inconsistency with respect to prices, and the primacy of the latter over the former. In all cases I utilize the same algebraic formulations as they do, and within this framework I demonstrate that there are a host of issues and results that the Neo-Ricardians remain unable to discover precisely because they remain so closely tied to the structure of orthodox economics. The concept of value, including the magnitude of value, illuminates the whole qualitative *and* quantitative analysis of price relations, uncovering relationships and causalities where the Neo-Ricardians see merely discrepancies. It informs and orders the analysis, thereby demonstrating precisely its scientific power.

By the same token, the logical contradictions and inconsistencies in the Neo-Ricardian analysis are thrown into sharp relief. For instance, Steedman's own logic, if correct, would lead one to conclude that not only values and the value of rate of profit, *but also* prices of production and the uniform rate of profit, are *not* "significant . . . in a capitalist economy." But of course his logic is not correct, and its correction reinstates both the latter and the former. It only goes to show that algebra is no substitute for logic. [. . .]

Notes

1. On the place of *Capital* in Marx's overall planned work, see R. Rosdolsky, *The Making of Marx's Capital* (London, 1977), ch. 2.
2. David McLellan's *Marxism After Marx* (New York, 1979) makes abundantly clear that very little of the history of Marxist thought depends on the specific analysis developed in *Capital*. Economics plays only a small role in all this, and even here a good part of the history is one of a series of struggles to justify the need to set aside the analysis in Marx, or at least "modernize" it by ridding it of unnecessary and outmoded concepts (such as value). Colletti's essay "On Bernstein and the Economics of the Second International" brilliantly analyzes this process of revision and its conceptual roots (L. Colletti, *From Rousseau to Lenin* [New York, 1972]). See also Perry Anderson's stimulating book *Considerations on Western Marxism* (London: NLB, 1976).
3. Anderson, *Considerations on Western Marxism*, p. 55.
4. Ian Steedman, *Marx After Sraffa* (London: NLB, 1977), ch. 14, pp. 205–207.
5. Marx to Kugelmann, July 11, 1868, in *Marx-Engels Selected Correspondence*, 3d ed. (Moscow, 1975), p. 196.
6. K. Marx, *Capital*, vol. 3 (New York, 1967), p. 880.
7. Colletti, *From Rousseau to Lenin*, p. 83.
8. Marx to Kugelmann, p. 196.
9. Marx, *Theories of Surplus-Value: Volume 4 of Capital*, part 2 (Moscow, 1968), p. 403.
10. Colletti, *From Rousseau to Lenin*, p. 87.
11. Marx, *Capital*, vol. 1 (Harmondsworth: Penguin Books in association with New Left Review, 1976), p. 139.
12. Ibid., p. 193.
13. K. Marx, *Capital*, vol. 3, pp. 179–80.
14. Ibid., p. 198.

15. Ibid., p. 636.

16. Steedman, *Marx After Sraffa*. The diagram is from p. 48, the quotes from p. 49, note 15.

17. Ibid., p. 14. In all these quotes, the emphasis on the word "determine" is mine.

18. Steedman states that "all production is assumed to be carried out by workers, in a socialized labor process" (ibid., p. 17). Nonetheless, he remains quite oblivious to the elementary implications of this assumption, and continues to speak of "physical conditions of production" *determining* "the quantities of labor embodied in the various commodities" (ibid., p. 14).

19. Ibid., p. 49.

20. Ibid., p. 50. Steedman notes that these general conclusions hold even when we abstract from fixed capital and joint production. We will therefore similarly restrict our analysis here, all the more so since a proper treatment of these two questions cannot be undertaken until the simpler ones have been addressed. The "choice of technique," on the other hand, will be treated in the next subsection.

21. Marx, *Capital*, vol. 3, p. 43.

22. Marx, *Theories of Surplus-Value*, part 3 (Moscow, 1971), p. 347. It is interesting to note that Marx discovers this phenomenon in connection with his analysis of differential rent, and not that of price of production. It is often forgotten by Marxists that differential rent also implies price-value deviations, since it is the marginal conditions of production that regulate the market price while it is the average conditions of production that always determine (social) value. Thus even when the regulating price is equal to value, it is in this case equal to the unit value in the marginal land, which is necessarily different (higher) than the average unit value. Thus the regulating price deviates from (average) value.

23. This result has been mathematically known for some time, *though not conceptually grasped*, as the equality of profits and surplus-value along the Von-Neumann ray. See A. Shaikh, "Theories of Value and Theories of Distribution," Ph.D. diss., Columbia University, 1973, ch. 4, sec. 4, and M. Morishima, *Marx's Economics* (Cambridge, 1973), p. 142.

24. For further details, see my unpublished paper "The Transformation From Marx to Sraffa (Prelude to a Critique of the Neo-Ricardians)," March 1980.

25. Shaikh, "The Transformation From Marx to Sraffa," sec. 3, 3.

26. Shaikh, "Theories of Value," ch. 4, sec. 4, and Morishima, *Marx's Economics*, p. 64.

27. The general shape of the functional relationship of r to S/V can be derived graphically from Morishima, *Marx's Economics*, p. 64, fig. 2. The relationship between r^* and S/V, on the other hand, follows simply from equation 2 in this paper. A much more detailed treatment of the theoretical and empirical relationship between the value rate of profit r^* and the transformed rate of profit r is provided in my paper "The Transformation from Marx to Sraffa," sections 3 and 4. In the aggregate, these two ratios turn out to be virtually indistinguishable.

28. Marx to Engels, April 20, 1868, in *Marx-Engels Selected Correspondence*, p. 194.

29. Steedman, *Marx After Sraffa*, p. 205.

30. See, for instance, my paper "Foreign Trade and the Law of Value," *Science and Society* (Fall 1979 and Spring 1980), in which I discuss the role of trade, capital flows, and transfer of value between capitalist regions.

31. In my paper "The Transformation From Marx to Sraffa" I establish on both theoretical and empirical grounds that the typical price-value deviation is $\pm$ 20 percent for both market prices and prices of production, with typical correlation coefficients (adjusted for heteroskedasticity) of about 93 percent. As I note in my paper, Ricardo seemed to have a vastly superior grasp of these relations than do the Neo-Ricardians!

32. Colletti, *From Rousseau to Lenin*, p. 42.

33. Ibid., p. 43.

34. K. Marx, *Wage-Labour and Capital*, reprinted in the *Marx-Engels Reader*, ed. Robert C. Tucker (New York, 1972), p. 175.

35. Marx, *Theories of Surplus-Value*, part 2, p. 484.

36. Armstrong and A. Glyn, "The Law of the Falling Rate of Profit and Oligopoly: A Comment on Shaikh," *Cambridge Journal of Economics* 3 (1979): 69.

37. Steedman, *Marx After Sraffa*, p. 30.

38. Steedman makes much of the fact that since direct prices differ from prices of production, the average profit rate in terms of direct prices (which is the value rate of profit) will differ from the average profit rate in terms of prices of production (which is, of course, the uniform rate of profit). But he does not seem to notice that this would also hold for any two sets of differing prices, so that in general the average profit rate in terms of market prices will *never* be equal to the uniform rate of profit.

39. A. Shaikh, "Political Economy and Capitalism: Notes on Dobb's Theory of Crisis," *Cambridge Journal of Economics* 2 (1978): 233–51. See also the debate surrounding the above article, and my rejoinder on "Marxian Competition Versus Perfect Competition: Further Comments on the So-called Choice of Technique," *Cambridge Journal of Economics* 4 (1980): 75–83.

40. Steedman, *Marx After Sraffa*, p. 64.

41. Ibid., p. 64.

42. Ibid., p. 65.

43. It is only in some recent unpublished papers that Steedman has begun to notice that the difference between actual market prices and theoretical prices of production "raises important questions for contemporary analysis." (Ian Steedman, "Natural Price, Market Price, and the Mobility of Money Capital," unpublished paper, 1978, p. 5).

44. Steedman, *Marx After Sraffa*, p. 64.

45. For a more detailed presentation of this argument, see the papers cited in note 39.

A Patriarchal Mode
of Production

NANCY R. FOLBRE

Contemporary analysis recognizes the possibility of coexisting modes of production—for example, feudalist forces and relations of production side by side with slave-holding forms of each—in the same social formation. Nancy Folbre uses that insight to recast dramatically the ongoing debate over the concept of patriarchy in feminist literature. Folbre argues that patriarchy can be understood as a mode of production with a logic of its own, and that it too can coexist with the more traditionally conceived modes of production of Marxist analysis. She offers this new conceptual foundation as a means of overcoming tendencies in more traditional Marxist analysis to treat gender issues as subordinate to those of class, and as a means of bridging the gulf between treatments of patriarchy and capitalism in much of feminist analysis. Folbre's article appears for the first time here.

> Hence property: the nucleus, the first form of which lies in the family, where wife and children are the slaves of the husband. This latent slavery in the family, though still very crude, is the first property, but even at this early stage it corresponds perfectly to the definition of modern economists who call it the power of disposing of the labor power of others.
>
> —Karl Marx, *The German Ideology*

The concept of patriarchy is central to the theoretical vocabulary of feminism.[1] It is a concept that has enabled feminists to move beyond a simple categorization of forms of sexual inequality toward an understanding of sexual inequality as a system. It is a concept that has inspired a large and significant body of empirical and historical research on women. Yet it is a concept that remains, in many important ways, vague and undefined.

This is not to say that specific definitions of patriarchy have not been proffered, nor to imply that such specific definitions have nothing in common. In fact, much of the recent feminist literature reveals a convergent emphasis on patriarchy as a system of control over women's productive and reproductive capacities. But this convergence has largely served to intensify a fundamental controversy. Is patriarchy a system of control over women that is analogous to but separate and distinct from capitalism? Or is it part of a single system of control over women that grows out of the class relations of capitalism and/or other modes of production?

Those who treat capitalism and patriarchy as dual systems often differentiate between them by the hypothesis that capitalists as a class benefit from one while men as a gender benefit from the other.[2] But as critics of the dual-systems approach have pointed out, the putative relationship between patriarchy and capitalism remains unclear. Dual-systems theorists have failed to provide an analysis of the internal logic or the laws of motion of patriarchy that could explain its interaction with other systems of modes of production, leaving themselves open to the criticism that patriarchy is an ahistorical theoretical construct.[3] By the same token, "single-system" theorists have not adequately explained why capitalism or other class societies take a patriarchal form.[4]

The terms "single system" and "dual system" themselves are symptomatic of a problem. Patriarchy may be a "system," or part of a "system." But what is a "system"? From the point of view of Marxian theory, capitalism is more than a system. It is a mode of production. Despite considerable controversy over its precise definition, this term connotes a strong emphasis on the social relations of production governing the expropriation of surplus labor time. And despite considerable controversy over the "internal laws of motion" of modes of production, the term implies a certain general logic of development and change.

I argue here that the patriarchal "system" that dual-systems theorists have described can be better understood as a patriarchal mode of production that can exist in articulation with other modes of production, but nonetheless has an internal structure and an internal logic of its own. My conceptualization of a patriarchal mode of production grows out of a feminist inspired redefinition of some of the basic categories of historical materialism, such as production, exploitation, and class. It also draws upon recent innovations that have dissociated contemporary Marxism from the economistic and deterministic tendencies of traditional historical materialism.

I begin by reviewing the motivation underlying the dual-systems approach, criticizing the conceptual dichotomies that have predisposed Marxists to treat gender inequalities as derivative of class inequalities, traditionally defined. For most Marxists, gender is to class as ideology is to economy, reproduction is to production, or domination is to exploitation, an indisputably important but nonetheless subsidiary category. Dual-systems theorists, as self-defined socialist feminists, have sought to place class and gender on a more equal footing, arguing that patriarchy has both ideological and economic elements, encompasses both reproduction and production, entails both domination and exploitation.[5] This argument, while not incorrect, is seriously incomplete, because it does not provide a coherent theoretical framework for analyzing patriarchy as a totality.

The concept of a patriarchal mode of production does not automatically provide a solution to this problem. In the second section below I argue that previous efforts to specify a patriarchal, household, or domestic mode of production have proved unsatisfactory partly because they have assumed that either patriarchy or capitalism must be "dominant" in the sense that only one class structure can prevail. Nonetheless, recent scholarship within the Marxian tradition has both modified the traditional definition of mode of production and emphasized the articulation of modes of production within social formations, setting the stage for a new conceptualization of a patriarchal mode of production. In the final section I define this mode of production, briefly describe its internal dynamics, and sketch some of the salient features of its articulation with other modes of production such as capitalism.

Dichotomies and Dualities

The intellectual history of the Marxian analysis of women's oppression is largely a theory of conceptual hierarchies. The succession of dichotomies, from ideology/economy to reproduction/production reveals a growing interest in material dimensions of women's oppression. But the primacy of categories such as economy, production, and exploitation within historical materialism places gender-based inequalities based on ideology, reproduction, and/or domination on a "lower" level of analysis. By excluding gender inequalities from its primary categories, traditional Marxism essentially predetermines the political subordination of feminist issues to class issues, narrowly defined.

Juliet Mitchell's *Psychoanalysis and Feminism*, for instance, gave rise to a new genre of Marxist feminist analysis in which women's oppression was pictured in ideological and psychological terms.[6] But while this conceptualization tempered the economism of traditional Marxist theory, it did so at the expense of a materialist analysis of women's oppression. Even those Marxists who stress the relative autonomy of ideology are reluctant to dissociate it from material relations altogether.[7] The mere lack of symmetry between gender and class is less problematic than the difficulty of explaining how and why patriarchal ideology emerges in the absence of any material determinants.

Partly as a result, Marxist-feminists have increasingly begun to locate women's oppression in a distinctive arena of material or economic life-reproduction, defined as the bearing and rearing of children and the care and nurturance of adults. Socialist feminists Gayle Rubin and Zillah Eisenstein were among the first to emphasize the relative autonomy of a sex/gender system or "mode of reproduction."[8] Lourdes Beneria argues that reproduction of the labor force is at the root of women's subordination and that women's role in reproduction essentially determines their role in production.[9] Wally Seccombe argues that the exclusion of reproductive labor from the economic base or infrastructure is the most serious flaw in the traditional Marxian concept of a mode of production.[10] In her recent book Lise Vogel reconstructs a Marxist "single systems" approach, assigning women's oppression to the sphere of social reproduction.[11]

But a theory of patriarchy based on mode of reproduction or an expanded definition of production encompassing the reproduction of labor power does not resolve the theoretical dilemma. Does the reproduction of labor power have a dynamic of its own? Or are the social relations of reproduction largely shaped by the social relations of production? Marxists and Marxist-feminists typically opt for the latter. Maria Dalla Costa and Selma James argue that women's reproductive labor lowers the cost of reproduction of labor power, subsidizing wages and therefore primarily benefiting capitalists.[12] Harold Wolpe, Carmen Diana Deere, and Immanuel Wallerstein apply similar reasoning to the effect of reproductive labor on wage rates in the third world.[13] Wally Seccombe argues that demographic changes resulting from changes in family, household, and kin structures are largely determined by the dominant mode of production and stage of proletarianization.[14] Reproduction and the social relations that govern it are treated as the consequence of forces operating in another realm.

The possibility that the social relations of reproduction could be causes, rather than merely effects, is often circumscribed by a reluctance to consider the possibility of exploitation within the realm of reproduction. Exploitation within the family could provide a material motive for certain forms of patriarchal control, but this form of exploitation was largely defined out of existence in the domestic labor debates.[15] Even those Marxists who argued that value was created in the household, i.e., that women's labor represented socially necessary labor time, neglected to explore the distribution of embodied labor hours between family members. In other words, they assumed that the exchange that takes place between a wage worker and a household worker, the exchange of household labor for a share of the wage, is necessarily an equal one.[16]

The tendency to restrict the domain of women's oppression to the political and ideological arena of "domination" and reserve the economic arena for class relations is characteristic of a large body of Marxist literature.[17] Samuel Bowles and Herbert Gintis, for instance, argue that domination is conceptually prior to exploitation.[18] But their emphasis on domination is reminiscent of radical feminist assumptions that the urge to dominate is somehow innate, unlinked to any material rewards. Even those Marxists who are sympathetic with Bowles' and Gintis's particular critique of the traditional Marxist tendency to simply reduce domination to exploitation are likely to remain predisposed to view forms of domination linked to exploitation as more intense and more persistent than "freestanding" forms of domination.

Stephen Resnick and Richard Wolff have gone further in the direction of analyzing the exploitation of women in Marxian theoretical categories, describing women as a "subsumed class" and sexism as a "condition of existence" for capitalism.[19] They distinguish between a subsumed class and a fundamental class by defining the former in terms of the distribution of surplus value and the latter in terms of the production of surplus value. Their dichotomy between production and distribution provides the rationale for the dichotomy between fundamental and subsumed class processes.

This approach provides a framework for analyzing material inequality between men and women in Marxian terms. But the very term "subsumed" conveys the conceptual hierarchy that persists despite Wolff and Resnick's epistemological insistence that class is merely a "point of entry." This conceptual hierarchy is asserted, not explained, and rests implicitly on the assumptions that production is a more basic category than distribution and, even more importantly, that production of surplus takes place only within "fundamental" class relations that clearly do not include relations between men and women.

Dual-systems theorists have found all the approaches described above unsatisfactory precisely because of the conceptual dualism that has separated and subordinated gender to class. Their emphasis on dual systems may be seen, in large part, as a critical response to dual categories. Heidi Hartmann, for instance, insists that not only does patriarchy have material dimensions but it embraces both production and reproduction. "The material base of patriarchy," she argues, "does not rest solely on childrearing in the family, but on all the social structures that enable men to control women's labor."[20] But what are these social structures, and how do they differ from the social structure that is capitalism?

The internal dynamics of patriarchy as a system remain unclear. Its historical dimensions are often emphasized, but seldom explained. Patriarchy is often described as preceding capitalism, but its interaction with precapitalist modes of production such as feudalism is seldom described. Dual-systems theory emphasizes the analogies between patriarchy and capitalism—men benefit from one, just as capitalists benefit from the other. But as long as patriarchy is a "system" and capitalism is a mode of production the analogy remains incomplete. It is this incompleteness that prompts the following consideration of the concept of a mode of production.

Modes of Production

The dual-systems dilemma cannot be overcome simply by the nomenclatural designation of a new mode of production. In fact, most previous efforts to conceptualize a patriarchal, domestic, or housework mode of production either internalize or invert the conceptual hierarchies described above.[21] Furthermore, the concept of mode of production, like the theory of historical materialism itself, has undergone substantial revision in recent years. The concept no longer implies, as it once did, an economistic or deterministic theory of historical change. It is precisely this shift of theoretical emphasis that lends the project of developing theoretical parallels between patriarchy and capitalism as modes of production a new plausibility and a new appeal.

Christine Delphy asserts that a patriarchal mode of production coexists with capitalism today and that women represent an exploited class within that mode.[22] But Delphy, like Shulamith Firestone, Mary Daly, and other radical feminists, espouses a theory that is simply the mirror image of traditional Marxism.[23] She writes, "It is not because capitalism buys and exploits the labor power of the husband that, at the same stroke, it exploits the wife. That is absolutely wrong.

Obviously, she is exploited by her relations of production, not by those of her husband.''[24] It never seems to occur to Delphy that a wife could be exploited by both sets of relations of production. In her view the class position of a woman's family cannot override or even mitigate her gender-class position. Delphy relegates class, as traditionally defined, to an even lower level of analysis than traditional Marxists relegate gender.

This work shares a common tendency to exacerbate, rather than to overcome the asymmetries to which Marxist-feminist analysis is prone. Its problem resides partly in their tendency to overlook the articulation and interpenetration of distinct modes of production. And this tendency arises, at least in part, from their failure to integrate the insights of a growing effort to revise and redeploy the basic concepts of historical materialism.

The meaning of the concept mode of production has evolved and is still evolving in conjunction with (1) a movement away from economistic versions of Marxism, (2) a movement toward a more flexible and less deterministic analysis of the ''laws of motion'' of modes of production, (3) a modification of traditional notions of ''dominance'' of one mode of production, and (4) a widening of the definitions of surplus and surplus expropriation or exploitation.

In the writings of Louis Althusser and Etienne Balibar, the mechanistic base/superstructure distinction of Bukharinesque Marxism virtually disappears.[25] Modes of production are no longer treated as synonymous with the economic base, but are described in terms of economic, political, and ideological dimensions. This description helps convey the meaning of a structural causality in which economic factors are determinant ''only in the last instance.'' Most contemporary Marxists accede to an extremely modest view of economic causality, emphasizing economic factors primarily in terms of the limits they set and the pressures they exert.[26]

Traditional assumptions regarding the ''laws of motion'' of capitalism as a mode of production are also being substantially revised. The basic tendencies first systematically described by Marx—steady proletarianization, concentration of capital, and susceptibility to crisis—still provide a basic framework of analysis. But many contemporary Marxists like Samuel Bowles and Herbert Gintis emphasize the ways in which political struggle and political consciousness condition economic processes.[27] David Gordon, Thomas Weisskopf, Richard Edwards, and Michael Reich offer detailed historical accounts of the ways labor market segmentation and racial and sexual discrimination shaped proletarianization within the United States.[28] E. P. Thompson beautifully illustrates the specificities and contingencies of English political history and argues that they may be better understood in terms of a certain ''historical logic'' rather than inexorable laws of motion.[29]

These theoretical innovations have had a significant impact on accounts of the coexistence and articulation of modes of production within social formations and within the ''world system'' as a whole. The writings of both Perry Anderson and

Immanuel Wallerstein, for instance, both go far beyond the traditional Marxian emphasis on a single mode of production.[30] In the field of economic development scholars like André Gunder Frank and Ernesto Laclau, despite their many disagreements, jointly render the notion of any automatic succession of "historically necessary" modes of production quite obsolete.[31] Pierre Rey argues persuasively that precapitalist class formations exercise considerable influence on capitalist societies.[32] The fact that capitalism often expands at the expense of other modes of production does not necessarily mean that it is dominant in the sense that its class relations supersede all others.

Despite the ongoing process of theoretical evolution, the theory of historical materialism retains a basic theoretical intent that distinguishes it from other social scientific theories, including many of those informed by feminist concerns. The concept of a mode of production asserts the relevatory power of a systematic consideration of the way in which economic surpluses are extracted, and consistently raises a heuristic question. Who benefits materially from a given set of social relations of ownership and control, and who is hurt? The commitment to asking this question has pushed Marxists well beyond their traditional preoccupation with inequalities between capitalists and wage workers toward a wider concept of surplus and surplus extraction. Many contemporary Marxist economists explore inequalities between advanced capitalist countries and underdeveloped dependent capitalist economies; inequalities within the working class based on race, gender, and occupation; and inequalities within the state owned, centrally planned economies that are commonly described as socialist.

Until recently these particular dimensions of inequality were pictured largely in political and ideological terms and explained largely by reference to the "underlying" economic dynamic of capitalist exploitation. But contemporary theories of imperialism dwell at length on the transfer of economic surplus between nations as a whole through the repatriation of profits and the unequal exchange built into the terms of trade.[33] The labor theory of value is being used to explain the transfer of surplus between workers implicit in the unequal access to education, skills, experience, and jobs that renders labor a very "heterogenous" commodity.[34] John Roemer's *General Theory of Exploitation* outlines a mathematical approach to exploitation that is applicable to exchanges that take place outside of capitalist relations of production, including those within and between so-called socialist economies.[35] Similarly, my own previous work argues the logical possibility of exploitation and unequal exchange within the family.[36]

From this perspective, the basic problem of Marxist-feminist theory, the problem of conceptualizing the relationship between distinct but related forms of oppression, appears by no means unique. It represents a problem intrinsic to the process of developing and extending the theory of historical materialism. This ongoing process entails continuing efforts to address the issues of economism, determinism, and dominance. It also requires an explicit effort to overcome the conceptual segregation of women's oppression described above. Marxism as a methodology can encourage as well as sustain redefinitions that accommodate the possibility that different types of production coexist, with correspondingly different means of production, different types of exploitation, and overlapping, sometimes contradictory class structures. The challenge lies in providing a rigorous conceptualization of noncapitalist modes of production and explaining their conflicts and complementarities with capitalism. The following discussion of a patriarchal mode of production represents a small but crucial step toward meeting this challenge.

A Patriarchal Mode of Production

A patriarchal mode of production can be defined as a distinctive set of social relations, including but by no means limited to control over the means of production, that structures the exploitation of women and/or children by men within a social formation that may include other modes of production, none of which is necessarily dominant. This definition is consistent with the broad version of contemporary historical materialism referred to above but is premised on a concept of production that includes household labor and childrearing, a concept of exploitation that applies outside as well as within capitalist relations and production, and a concept of a social formation in which distinct modes of production coexist. This definition provides a basis for exploring the analogies between patriarchy and capitalism. It also provides a basis for examining the differences between them. It is the differences between their internal logic and internal dynamics that are crucial to an analysis of their codetermination of certain aspects of historical change.

Like the term "capitalist mode of production," the term "patriarchal mode of production" singles out particular social relations rather than a particular type of labor (such as domestic labor or housework) or a primary site of labor (such as the family or household). Prominent among these social relations are relations of ownership and control over means of production. Patriarchal control over patriarchal means of production is analogous to capitalist control over capitalist means of production where patriarchal means of production can include: (1) capital, land, houses, farm or household equipment owned or controlled by patriarchs; (2) means of subsistence such as wages or other income that are controlled by patriarchs; and (3) means of reproduction, such as women's reproductive capacities, that are subject to patriarchal control. Relationships of ownership and control are seldom absolute, but must be understood in terms of systematic patterns of unequal power which are reproduced over time. The coexistence of patriarchal and capitalist means of production implies that individuals may enjoy privileged access to one means of production, may enjoy privileged access to both means of production, or may suffer disadvantaged access to both means of production.

Relationship to a specific means of production represents little more than a conceptual point of entry, for classes defined in these terms are by no means homogeneous. Within capitalism, for instance, nonclass factors such as type of occupation, section of employment, and trade unions membership exercise considerable influence.[37] Within the patriarchal mode factors such as age, marital status, and family size all impinge on patterns of inequality. Nonetheless, relationship to the means of production is an important category insofar as it defines a major dimension of power that often sets the stage for exploitation.

Exploitation, understood as the systematic expropriation of surplus labor time, cannot take place outside of relations of domination that lend meaning to the term "expropriation." Purely voluntary transfers of surplus labor time cannot be construed as exploitative. But one of Marxism's most important insights is that exchanges that appear quite voluntary may in fact be predetermined by differences in economic power. Physical force is seldom required to compel a worker to accept a wage, if the worker is denied other alternatives. Similarly a woman's choice to enter or remain within a patriarchal household may be involuntary in the sense that her realm of choice has been constricted by the exercise of patriarchal power.

Patriarchal domination makes patriarchal exploitation possible. But exploitation provides a motive for patriarchal domination, a motive that is neither abstract nor ahistorical, but specific to certain circumstances that define the potential risks and rewards of domination. Furthermore, the economic privilege that exploitation can confer effectively reinforces patriarchal domination. The nature and extent of exploitation is important not only in and of itself, but through its influence on the reproduction of patriarchal domination over time.

The nature and extent of exploitation within the capitalist mode is normally analyzed in terms of the extraction of surplus value, in the form of profit, from the wage worker. Like most participants in the domestic labor debates, most Marxists argue that work performed outside capitalist relations of production cannot be analyzed in terms of value or socially necessary labor time because there are no forces of competition operating to eliminate inefficient producers, and therefore no tendency for the average labor time spent producing a given good to converge to the socially necessary or most efficient amount.[38] Other Marxists take issue with this claim, arguing that non-capitalist production is conducted efficiently and can be conceptualized in terms of socially necessary labor time.[39]

Although this is an important debate, the concept of patriarchal exploitation does not hinge on the applicability of value theory to the household. Patriarchal exploitation can be defined in the same way Marxists have always defined exploitation in noncapitalist modes of production such as feudalism: in terms of surplus labor time, or the difference between the amount of time individuals work and the amount of time embodied in the goods they themselves consume. In the aggregate, the number of labor hours performed is equal, by definition, to the amount of labor time embodied in goods consumed (if savings are treated as deferred consumption). To say that a class is the beneficiary of a transfer of surplus labor time is to say that its members consume more embodied labor than they perform. Numerous time-budget studies showing that women tend to work much longer hours than men, when household as well as wage labor is taken into account, suggest that patriarchal exploitation can be analyzed in quantitative terms.[40]

The Marxian theory of exploitation rests on certain assumptions, not the least of which is the assumption that differences in the intensity of labor and the skill required to perform it can be taken into account. This difficulty seems less troublesome than the alternative Neoclassical economic assumption that any exchange that takes place outside of physical coercion necessarily leaves both parties better off. Neither embodied labor nor Neoclassical "utility" can be directly measured. But the possibility of arriving at some measure of exploitation, however imprecise, seems preferable to the misleading certainty of an approach that rules out the possibility of exploitation a priori.

A concern with material dimensions of inequality does not render subjective considerations unimportant. The Marxian critique of capitalism dwells at length upon the irrational and alienating aspects of capitalist production.[41] Marxian analyses of the role of families and schools in reproducing class inequalities parallel the work of feminist scholars like Nancy Chodorow who explain the ways in which childrearing practices cast male and female personalities into a patriarchal mold.[42] Sexuality cannot be analyzed in terms of labor hours, but neither can the "hidden injuries of class."[43] It may nonetheless be true that sexual and psychological oppressions can best be understood within the larger social contexts in which they emerge and thrive.

The symmetries between patriarchal and capitalist exploitation should not obscure the differences between the two. The primary site of capitalist exploitation is the capitalist firm; the primary site of patriarchal exploitation is the patriarchal household.[44] Production takes place at both sites, but it takes different forms. The household remains the only site where people and their labor power are produced, and this particular production has many complex implications.

Among the most important of these implications is the link between women's labor and the labor of their children. In certain circumstances patriarchs can appropriate surplus time directly from their children.[45] Even if both parents expect net economic benefits from rearing children, these net benefits may accrue primarily to patriarchs.[46] In certain circumstances patriarchs can appropriate surplus labor time from women by means of children. Even if patriarchs do not expect economic benefits from rearing children, they may ensure that the costs of rearing children are borne primarily by mothers. Thus patriarchal exploitation of women can take a form that is somewhat indirect.

Patriarchal exploitation, in all its forms, seems to be conditioned by the intimate character of family life. The stability of the patriarchal family as a unit to which most members belong for life may place certain limits on the degree of exploitation that can take place within it. On the other hand, the fact that many individual lives begin and end within the patriarchal family lends patriarchal exploitation the appearance of being both natural and inevitable. If patriarchy fails to generate surpluses comparable in size to those of capitalism, it nonetheless enjoys a uniquely powerful mechanism of social reproduction.[47]

Despite the differences between patriarchal and capitalist forms of exploitation, both are important to understanding the internal dynamics of their respective modes of production. Marxian theory rejects the notion that economic growth is a "natural" consequence of technical change and insists that it is determined in large part by the social relations of capitalist production. The organization of the patriarchal mode of production suggests that the high levels of fertility that can lead to rapid population growth are by no means "natural" but are in large part the outcome of patriarchal controls over women's activities. Just as capitalism provides an impetus to economic growth by rewarding those who "accumulate, accumulate," patriarchy can provide an impetus to population growth by rewarding the patriarch who "begets, begets."

The internal logic of patriarchal relations governing inequalities between men, women, and children within households may be highly complementary to other class-based relations of production governing inequalities between distinct households. Where production continues to be organized on a household or family basis and a surplus is extracted by political or military means from a specific class of households, as under feudalism, patriarchal forms of exploitation may not only be reinforced but themselves serve as reinforcers of the authority of the symbolic father, the lord, the king, or the pope. Far from being subsumed by struggles between feudal classes, patriarchy may significantly alter the trajectory of a social formation such as patriarchal feudalism through its impact on demographic change.[48]

The articulation between patriarchy and a mode of production such as capitalism is far more complex, because it often leads to changes in the basic organization of production. In the early stages of capitalism in the United States and England, families as a whole were employed and exploited. But capitalism, for the most part, utilizes individual rather than family labor.[49] Furthermore, commodity production grows partly at the expense of the patriarchal economy, providing cheap substitutes for the goods and services once provided by women and children. Historically, this process of substitution began with the manufacture and sale of textiles, and it remains underway today with the expansion of services such as fast foods restaurants and commercial child-care services.[50]

Many historians have noted that the early English factories competed with individual patriarchs for the labor of women and children, and that wage labor, however exploitative, increased the relative economic independence of women and children.[51] Both of these types of competition between patriarchy and capitalism probably weakened the economic incentives for patriarchal exploitation of women's childbearing capacities and contributed to the transition to lower fertility rates that generally accompanies the transition toward capitalism.[52]

But the decline in the relative economic importance of patriarchy's primary site—the household—does not imply that patriarchy was or is subsumed by capitalism, for at least three reasons. First, while capitalism transforms those patriarchal social relations that are not conducive to capital accumulation, it preserves and reinforces others. For instance, the patriarchal tradition of assigning women the least productive and most time-consuming tasks provided a means of segregating and disciplining the labor force.[53] Furthermore, capitalists proved as unwilling, if not more unwilling than patriarchs, to assume a major share of the costs of rearing children. The patriarchal ideology that childrearing merits only minimal remuneration (because it is not really work) serves to justify the consistent lack of public or state support for female-headed families.[54] By internalizing and incorporating certain aspects of gender-based inequality, capitalism has contributed in some respects to patriarchy's continuing viability.

Second, patriarchy has had and continues to have an economic basis in the organization of household production and women's unequal access to market income, and it continues to deliver substantial economic privileges to men. In the United States today women continue to earn an average of only $.60 for every dollar men earn, only slightly more than half of women are in the wage labor force, and most women wage workers continue to rear children and provide services to husbands and other family members within a patriarchal context.[55] Capitalism may have provided substitutes for many goods and services once provided within the home, but it is by no means clear that it will provide substitutes for all of them. Children are not yet widely available on the open market. And the lack of alternative sources of personal support leads many women to prefer the patriarchal family to the impersonal exploitation of wage labor.

Finally, the distribution of economic power and privilege in contemporary society seems consistent with the persistence of the kinds of contradictory class positions suggested by the intersection of patriarchy and capitalism as modes of production. For some women the privileges of family class counter-balance the liabilities of gender class, while other women are doubly or triply disadvantaged. Their "net" privilege or disadvantage is far too complex to be arrived at through a process of adding up, but some consideration of the diverse sources of oppression helps explain the divisions that have plagued and still plague the feminist movement. These divisions run too deep to be explained by a "false consciousness" or lack of consciousness of oppressive inequalities. They reflect awareness of different sorts of inequalities, and different sets of risks, faced by women in contradictory class positions. Despite their common gender class, women in the United States remain subdivided into different classes defined not only by access to the privileges of capital but also by access to the privileges of race.

In short, patriarchal capitalism may represent far more than either a single system or a dual system. It may represent a single social formation comprising two modes of production that interact with, as well as articulate, the other. This representation resolves the dual-systems dilemma but leaves open the possibility that other modes of production may coexist with patriarchy and capitalism within a social formation even more complex than patriarchal capitalism. It also accommodates the possibility that diverse social formations mutually influence each other within something resembling a world system.

Mode of production, social formation, world system—these are all theoretical constructs whose specific meanings remain to be developed through further historical and empirical application. But however vague they might seem, they hold far more specificity and substance than the much used term "patriarchal system." Until recently, the Marxian vocabulary has remained essentially disconnected from the feminist problematic. Once informed by this problematic, however, this vocabulary establishes new and vital connections between Marxist and feminist concerns.

Notes

1. In the fall of 1983 Jeanne Henn and I discovered that our conceptualization of a patriarchal mode of production has proceeded along similar lines, albeit with different emphases. I have learned a great deal from our discussions and from her manuscript, "Towards a Materialist Analysis of Sexism" (Dept. of Economics, Northeastern University, Boston, Massachusetts). I also received a great deal of very sound criticism and advice from Samuel Bowles, Ann Ferguson, Herbert Gintis, David Gordon, Tom Harris, Elaine McCrate, and Wally Seccombe. Thanks also to Julie Graham, Cindi Katz, Don Shakow, and Dan Wiener for their comments. My greatest debt is to my students at the New School for Social Research, 1983–84, prescient and supportive critics all.

2. Heidi Hartmann, "Capitalism, Patriarchy and Job Segregation by Sex," in *Capitalist Patriarchy and the Case for Socialist Feminism*, ed. Zillah Eisenstein (New York: Monthly Review Press, 1978); "The Family as a Locus of Gender, Class, and Political Struggle: The Example of Housework," *Signs: Journal of Women in Culture and Society* 6, 3 (Spring 1981): 366–94; Sheila Rowbotham, *Women's Consciousness, Man's World* (Harmondsworth: Penguin, 1974).

3. See, for instance, Michele Barrett, "It follows that although important dimensions of women's oppression cannot be accounted for with reference to the categories of Marxism, it is equally impossible to establish the analytic independence of a system of oppression such as the category of 'patriarchy' suggests," *Women's Oppression Today* (London: Verso Editions, 1980), p. 249. See also Mary O'Brien, *The Politics of Reproduction* (Boston: Routledge and Kegan Paul, 1981), p. 117.

4. Iris Young, "Beyond the Unhappy Marriage: A Critique of Dual Systems Theory," in *Women and Revolution*, ed. Lydia Sargent (Boston: South End Press, 1980).

5. Hartmann, "Capitalism, Patriarchy, and Job Segregation by Sex." See also Heidi Hartmann and Ann Markusen, "Contemporary Marxist Theory and Practice: A Feminist Critique," *Review of Radical Political Economics* (Summer 1980), pp. 87–94.

6. Juliet Mitchell, *Psychoanalysis and Feminism* (New York: Pantheon, 1974).

7. Barrett, *Women's Oppression Today*, p. 252.

8. Gayle Rubin, "The Traffic in Women" in *Toward an Anthropology of Women*, ed. Rayna Reitner (New York: Monthly Review Press, 1979); Zillah Eisenstein, ed., *Capitalist Patriarchy and the Case for Socialist Feminism* (New York: Monthly Review Press, 1979).

9. Lourdes Beneria, "Reproduction, Production and the Sexual Division of Labor," *Cambridge Journal of Economics* 3 (1979): 210. See also Maureen McKintosh, "Repro-

duction and Patriarchy: A Critique of Meillasoux, Femmes, Greniers, et Capitaux," *Capital and Class* 2 (1977).

10. Wally Seccombe, "Marxism and Demography," *New Left Review* 137 (January-February 1983).

11. Lise Vogel, *Marxism and Women's Oppression* (Rutgers: Rutgers University Press, 1984).

12. Maria Dalla Costa and Selma James, *The Power of Women and the Subversion of the Community* (Bristol: Falling Wall Press, 1970).

13. Harold Wolpe, "Capitalism and Cheap Labor in South Africa," *Economy and Society* (1972); Carmen Diana Deere, "Rural Women's Subsistence Production in the Capitalist Periphery," *Review of Radical Political Economics* 8, 1 (Spring 1976); Immanuel Wallerstein, "The Rural Economy in Modern World Society," in *The Capitalist World Economy* (Cambridge: Cambridge University Press, 1979), p. 127.

14. Seccombe, "Marxism and Demography."

15. Barbara Himmelweit and Simon Mohun, "Domestic Labor and Capital," *Cambridge Journal of Economics* 1, 1 (March 1977); Maxine Molyneux, "Beyond the Domestic Labour Debate," *New Left Review* 116 (July-August, 1979): 3–27.

16. Wally Seccombe, "The Housewife and Her Labour Under Capitalism," *New Left Review* 83 (January-February 1973): 3–24.

17. See, for instance, Barrett, *Women's Oppression Today*.

18. Samuel Bowles and Herbert Gintis, "The Class Exploitation Domination Reduction," unpublished manuscript, Department of Economics, University of Massachusetts, Amherst, Mass.; "Structure and Practice in the Labor Theory of Value," *Review of Radical Political Economics* 12, 4 (Winter 1981). See also Isaac Balbus, *Marxism and Domination* (Princeton: Princeton University Press, 1982).

19. Stephen Resnick and Richard Wolff, "Classes in Marxian Theory," *Review of Radical Political Economics* 13, 4 (Winter 1982).

20. Hartmann, "Capitalism, Patriarchy and Job Segregation by Sex."

21. See John Harrison, "The Political Economy of Housework," *Bulletin of the Conference of Socialist Economists* 2, 1 (Winter 1973): 35–52; Claude Meillasoux, *Maidens, Meal, and Money: Capitalism and the Domestic Community* (Cambridge: Cambridge University Press, 1981), p. 77; and John Caldwell, *Theory of Fertility Decline* (New York: Academic Press, 1982), pp. 17–179, 333–69.

22. Christine Delphy, "The Main Enemy," *Feminist Issues* 1, 1 (Summer 1980): 23–40; "A Materialist Feminism is Possible," *Feminist Review* 4 (1980): 79–105.

23. Shulamith Firestone, *The Dialectic of Sex*; Mary Daly, *Beyond God the Father: Toward a Philosophy of Women's Liberation* (Boston: Beacon, 1973); *Gyn-Ecology: The Metaethics of Radical Feminism* (Boston: Beacon, 1978).

24. Delphy, *Feminist Review*, p. 47.

25. Louis Althusser, *For Marx* (London: Allen Lane, 1969); Louis Althusser, Etienne Balibar, *Reading Capital* (London: New Left Books, 1970).

26. See, for instance, Raymond Williams, *Problems in Materialism and Culture* (London: Verso, 1980), p. 37; Gregor McLennan, *Marxism and the Methodologies of History* (London: Verso, 1981).

27. Samuel Bowles and Herbert Gintis, "Structure and Practice in the Labor Theory of Value," *Review of Radical Political Economics* 12, 4 (Winter 1981).

28. David Gordon, Thomas Weisskopf, Richard Edwards, *Segmented Work, Divided Workers*; Michael Reich, *Racial Inequality: A Political-Economic Analysis* (Princeton: Princeton University Press, 1981).

29. E. P. Thompson, *The Making of the English Working Class* (New York: Vintage, 1963); *Whigs and Hunters: The Origin of the Black Act* (New York: Random House, 1975); *The Poverty of Theory* (New York: Monthly Review Press, 1978). It may seem

unnecessarily provocative to cite E. P. Thompson as part of a larger theoretical project to which Louis Althusser has also contributed, but the differences between their respective approaches are far less significant than the similarities. See Perry Anderson, *Arguments Within English Marxism* (London: New Left Books, 1980).

30. Perry Anderson, *Passages From Antiquity to Feudalism* (London: New Left Books, 1974); Immanuel Wallerstein, *The Capitalist World Economy* (London: Cambridge University Press, 1979).

31. André Gunder Frank, *Dependent Accumulation and Underdevelopment* (New York: Monthly Review Press, 1979); Ernesto Laclau, "Feudalism and Capitalism in Latin America," in *Politics and Ideology in Marxist Theory* (London: New Left Books, 1977).

32. Pierre Rey, *Les alliances de classes* (Paris: Maspero, 1973).

33. Arrhiri Emmanuel, *Unequal Exchange: A Study of the Imperialism of Trade* (New York: Monthly Review, 1972); Samir Amin, *Class and Nation, Historically and in the Current Crisis* (New York: Monthly Review Press, 1980).

34. Bowles and Gintis, "Heterogeneous Labor and the Marxian Theory of Value," *Cambridge Journal of Economics* 1 (1977): 173–92.

35. John Roemer, *The General Theory of Exploitation* (Cambridge: Harvard University Press, 1982).

36. Nancy Folbre, "Exploitation Comes Home: A Critique of the Marxian Theory of Family Labour," *Cambridge Journal of Economics* 6, 4 (December 1982): 317–29.

37. Nicos Poulantzas, *Classes in Contemporary Capitalism* (London: Verso, 1978).

38. Himmelweit and Mohun, Molyneux, "Domestic Labor and Capital."

39. Folbre, "Exploitation Comes Home"; Deborah Fahey Bryceson, "Use Values, the Law of Value and the Analysis of Non-Capitalist Production," *Capital and Class* 20 (Summer 1983): 29–63.

40. A. Szalai, "Women's Time: Women in the Light of Contemporary Time Budget Research," *Futures* (October 1975); M. Walker, "Time Spent by Husbands in Household Work," *Family Economics Review* (June 1970): 8–11. See also Hartmann, "The Family as Locus."

41. Paul Baran and Paul Sweezy, *Monopoly Capital: An Essay on the American Economic and Social Order* (New York: Monthly Review Press, 1966); Harry Braverman, *Labor and Monopoly Capital: The Degradation of Work in the Twentieth Century* (New York: Monthly Review Press, 1974).

42. Nancy Chodorow, *The Reproduction of Mothering* (Berkeley: University of California Press, 1978); Samuel Bowles and Herbert Gintis, *Schooling in Capitalist America* (New York: Basic Books, 1975).

43. Richard Sennett and Jonathan Cobb, *The Hidden Injuries of Class* (New York: Knopf, 1972).

44. Herbert Gintis, "On the Theory of Transitional Conjunctures," *Review of Radical Political Economics* 11, 3 (Fall 1979): 23–31.

45. Nancy Folbre, "Of Patriarchy Born: The Political Economy of Fertility Decisions," *Feminist Studies*; Caldwell, *Theory of Fertility Decline*; see also Carl Mosk, *Patriarchy and Fertility: Japan and Sweden, 1880–1960* (New York: Academic Press, 1983), p. 32; S. Cheung, "The Enforcement of Property Rights in Children and the Marriage Contract," *Economic Journal* (June 1972).

46. Cheung, "The Enforcement of Property Rights." See also Carol Brown, "Mothers, Fathers and Children, from Private to Public Patriarchy," in *Women and Revolution*, ed. Lydia Sargent (Boston: South End Press, 1981).

47. Chodorow, *The Reproduction of Mothering*.

48. Nancy Folbre, "Patriarchy and Population in Western Europe," unpublished manuscript, Department of Economics, University of Massachusetts, submitted to *Population Studies*.

49. Neil Smelser, *Social Change in the Industrial Revolution: An Application of Theory to the British Cotton Industry* (Chicago: University of Chicago Press, 1959).

50. Clair Brown, "Home Production for Use in a Market Economy" in *Rethinking the Family*, ed. Barrie Thorne with Maily Valon (New York: Longman, 1982).

51. William Lazonick, "The Subjugation of Labor to Capital: The Rise of the Capitalist System," *Review of Radical Political Economics* 10, 1 (Spring 1975): 9.

52. Folbre, "Of Patriarchy Born"; Caldwell, *The Theory of Fertility Decline*.

53. Lazonick, "The Subjugation of Labor." See also Stephen Dubnoff, "Gender, The Family and the Problem of Work Motivation in a Transition to Industrial Capitalism," *Journal of Family History* 4, 2 (Summer 1979).

54. Nancy Folbre, "The Pauperization of Motherhood: Patriarchy and Public Policy in the U.S.," *Review of Radical Political Economics* (Fall 1985).

55. U.S. Department of Commerce, Bureau of the Census, *Statistical Abstract of the United States* (Washington, D.C.: U.S. Government Printing Office), table 683, p. 413.

Corporations, the State, and Imperialism

PAUL M. SWEEZY

Although not originally a Marxist concept, imperialism is today generally linked to Marx- ist interpretations of the international expansion of capitalism. That linkage owes much to V. I. Lenin's Imperialism: The Highest Stage of Capitalism, *in which Lenin analyzed the First World War in light of monopoly tendencies in capitalism, and state intervention on behalf of capitalist interests. Whether a theory of imperialism has yet been rigorously linked to Marxist theoretical foundations is a question that has been under intense debate in recent decades.*

Paul Sweezy provides an introduction to the concept of imperialism and defines it in light of both the modern corporation and the role of the state in global capitalism. Based on a lecture by Sweezy at Stanford University, this article appeared originally in Monthly Review, *the journal that he edits.*

The fact that the title for this talk was given to me by the organizers of this lecture series reflects what is doubtless a widespread conviction that corporations, the state, and imperialism are intimately interrelated both in theory and in practice. My assignment, I take it, is to attempt to throw light on the nature of these interrelations. And the most logical way to proceed is first to define the three concepts individually and then to inquire as to how they are related to each other.

1. Corporations are the typical twentieth-century units of business enter- prise—first and foremost in production but also in commerce and finance.

2. The state is the institution which makes the laws and enforces them through an apparatus of armed force (including police), courts, prisons, etc. The state has a definite territorial identity: the area in which it operates is a nation, and within the nation's borders it is said to be "sovereign." The two characteristic features of sovereignty are a monopoly of (a) the legal use of armed force, and (b) the legal creation of money.

3. Imperialism is the process by which the corporations and the state team up to expand their activities, their interests, and their power beyond their borders.

The essential components of the corporation are capital and labor. Capital is money and means of production *in relation to* living labor. Only in combination with living labor is capital "productive," i.e., only thus is a product turned out

Paul M. Sweezy, "Corporations, the State, and Imperialism," *Monthly Review* 30, 6 (November 1978), pp. 1–10.

which is sufficient to sustain the laborers and leave a surplus for the owners of capital.

How does it happen that the laborers are willing to play this role? Why don't they use their own money and means of production, keep the whole product for themselves, and eliminate the capitalists altogether? The answer of course is that as the result of a long historical process reaching back into the fifteenth and sixteenth centuries, the laborers have been separated from their means of production and are obliged to sell their labor power to capitalists as the only way to avoid destitution and starvation. In other words, the means of production have been concentrated in the hands of capitalists, which today means corporations, and the workers have been transformed into wage-earners. In the United States this process was compressed into the relatively short span of two centuries. When the United States became a nation, more than three quarters of the workers were self-employed (owned their own means of production); today perhaps as many as 90 percent work for others, mostly corporations. The question is, why do workers tolerate this state of affairs? There are of course several reasons, but the most important one which underlies all the others is the system of private property, deeply imbedded in the constitution and the laws and vigilantly enforced by the state.

Thus the corporations are completely dependent on the state for their very existence, and the state in turn lives off the surplus produced by the workers and accruing to the capitalists, which means in the first instance to the corporations. The state and the corporations thus exist in a condition of symbiosis, each deeply dependent on the other.

Coming now to the problem of imperialism, we have to ask why this symbiotic relationship between corporations and state should result in a process of expansion in which the two mutually support each other. In other words, why isn't the relationship a static one which simply reproduces itself without essential change from one period to the next? To answer this it is essential to understand the nature of a unit of capital, which is what a corporation is, in the overall capitalist economy.

Here we can call on an extremely useful pedagogical device, comparing capitalism to simple commodity production, a mode of production which never actually existed independently of other modes of production. It should be emphasized, however, that simple commodity production is in no sense an *imaginary* mode of production: its component elements have existed in many historical societies, and in some regions at certain times it has come close to realization as an integrated and coherent form (for example, in certain parts of North America in the century or so surrounding the American Revolution). The defining characteristic of simple commodity production is that producers own their own means of production and satisfy their needs through exchange with other similarly situated producers. Farmers owning their own land, implements, and animals produce more food than they need, weavers more cloth, tailors more suits, hatters more hats, shoemakers more shoes, etc. Each producer takes his surplus to market and exchanges it for money, and with the money so acquired he buys the products of the others which he requires to satisfy his family's needs. Symbolically, this process can be represented, following Marx, by the formula C-M-C where the first C stands for a specific commodity being marketed by its producer, the M for the money the producer gets in exchange, and the second C for the bundle of useful commodities which he buys with this money. Here, obviously, we are talking about a system of production for use. The link is indirect: producers do not use their own products (or at least by no means all of them), but nevertheless their purpose in producing is to satisfy their needs, not to add to their wealth. In such a society—and indeed this tends to be true of all precapitalist societies—anyone whose purpose is to amass wealth as such is looked upon as a deviant, a miser, not a rational person.[1]

Matters are radically different when we come to capitalism, a society in which the actual producers own no means of production, are unable to initiate a process of production, and hence must sell their labor power to capitalists who do own means of production and are therefore in control of the processes of production. Here the defining formula C-M-C loses its relevance and must be replaced by its "opposite," M-C-M. What this symbolizes is that the capitalist who is the initiator of the production process starts with money M. With this he purchases commodities C consisting of means of production and labor power which he transforms through a process of production into finished commodities ready for sale. When the sale has been completed he finds himself once again with money M: the circuit is closed.

In the C-M-C case the first and last terms can be, and indeed are normally expected to be, quantitatively equal, i.e., to have the same exchange value. The rationale of the operation lies not in the realm of exchange value but in that of use value: for the simple commodity producer the C at the end has a greater use value than the C at the beginning, and it is this increase in use value which motivates his behavior. Nothing of the sort exists in the M-C-M case. The first and last terms are both money which is qualitatively homogeneous and possesses no use value of its own. It follows that if the two Ms are also quantitatively equal, the operation totally lacks any rationale: no capitalist is going to lay out money and organize a process of production in order to end up with the same amount of money as he had at the outset. From this we can deduce that for capitalism to exist at all the M at the end must be larger than the M at the beginning. We can therefore rewrite the formula as M-C-M' where $M' = M + \Delta M$. Here ΔM represents more money or, as Marx called it, more value (*Mehrwert*), which is customarily translated into English as surplus value.[2]

So far we have been considering what happens in a given period, say a year: the capitalist lays out M at the beginning of the year and ends up with M' at the end. But this is only the start of an analysis: the capitalist does not wind up his enterprise at the end of a single production cycle. The enterprise continues to operate from one cycle to the next into the indefinite future, often outliving generations of its capitalist owners. And the enterprise which had a capital of M at the beginning of the first year starts the second with M', and this in turn becomes M'', M''', M'''', and so on and on in successive years. This is what Marx meant when he defined capital as self-expanding value. Of course, not every individual unit of capital succeeds in living up to its ideal: many fall by the wayside or are gobbled up by luckier or more efficient rivals. But this only increases the importance of "trying harder," and the harder they all try the more marked becomes capitalism's essential nature as an expanding universe. Considered as a whole, capital *must* expand: the alternative is not a relaxed and happy condition of zero growth, as some liberal reformists would like to believe, but convulsive contraction and deepening crisis.

Given the symbiotic relation between the corporate units of capital and the state, it is but a logical corollary that the state is as expansion-minded as the corporations. This does not mean that the state is necessarily fixated on its own expansion; it means simply that the state's primary concern is the expansion of capital, for the very simple reason that any faltering in this respect means crisis for the whole society including, of course, the state. How this primary concern of the state is implemented, however, depends on the circumstances of time and place.

In an earlier period of capitalist history when the individual units of capital were small and capitalist relations were expanding rapidly into a precapitalist environment, the domestic tasks of the state were relatively simple: helping to create a suitable wage-labor force through direct or indirect expropriation of independent farmers and artisans; providing infrastructure in the forms of roads, canals, and railways; and maintaining a reasonably orderly monetary and financial system. In the international sphere, the main task of the state was to assure for its own producers access to external markets on the most favorable terms possible—a task which involved continuous conflict with foreign states and led to innumerable commercial and colonial wars.

But as capitalism in a given area approaches maturity—i.e., as the size of the units of capital grows, taking on the corporate form with an attendant development of monopolies and oligopolies; as the precapitalist segment of the population dwindles; and as the problems of cyclical recessions and secular stagnation become increasingly serious—as these and other factors operate to multiply and intensify the obstacles to the continued expansion of capital, the role of the state takes on new dimensions of magnitude and complexity. Many of its new or enlarged functions have to do primarily with internal matters (e.g., fiscal and monetary policies), while others are essentially international.[3] Here our interest is mainly in the latter.

The starting point, as always, is the conditions and requirements of the expansion of capital (I keep insisting on this because it is the sine qua non of *any* understanding of how capitalist societies actually work). Starting in a single industry and contributing a small share of the industry's total output, the typical unit of capital grows by accumulation, acquisition, and merger to be large relative to the industry's total output—in other words, it grows faster than the industry as a whole and as a consequence conquers an increasing degree of monopoly power. But there comes a time when this process reaches a limit. Theoretically, it could continue until one firm controlled the whole industry, but this situation is rarely reached: the normal situation is oligopoly (a few sellers) rather than monopoly (one seller), with each of the oligopolists powerful enough to hold its own against its rivals. When this stage has been reached, the conditions of further expansion are basically altered. The achievement of oligopoly status usually brings greater profitability, hence ability to accumulate more rapidly, at the same time that possibility of expansion within the industry is restricted to the rate of growth of the industry as a whole. Under these circumstances accumulation increasingly takes the form of conglomeration (expansion into other industries which have not yet reached the same degree of maturity) and multinationalization (expansion beyond existing national boundaries). It is the latter which sets new tasks for the state.

There are two kinds of multinationalization which need to be distinguished. The first takes place within the developed core of the global capitalist system (interpenetration of each other's territory by national oligopolists), and the second takes place between the developed core countries and the underdeveloped periphery. The first kind, interpenetration, does not pose any particularly urgent problems for the state. It has taken place on a vast scale since the Second World War, with the main direction of movement being from the United States to Western Europe and, to a much smaller extent, Japan. In the last few years, however, there has been an increasing flow in the opposite directions, with European and Japanese firms setting up branches or affiliates in the United States. Since all these countries have well-developed capitalist systems and stable state structures, and since they are all deterred from putting obstacles in the way of this kind of capital movement by the credible threat of retaliation, the states involved have not found it necessary or useful to adopt policies or apply measures with respect to foreign capital greatly different from those in force domestically. (This has been less true of Japan which, for historical reasons, developed its own capitalism behind an elaborate screen of protective devices. But here, too, the mutual pressures of multinationalization have been slowly prying Japan open to foreign capital: Japanese "exceptionalism" seems to be more a matter of the past than of the present or future.)

When it comes to the other kind of multinationalization, however, matters are very different. It can be said without fear of exaggeration that the expansion of capital into the underdeveloped periphery on the scale desired, and in a real sense needed, by the oligopolistic corporations of the advanced countries would be totally impossible without the massive and unremitting application of the power of their states, either individually or collectively (including through such agencies as the International Monetary Fund and the World Bank), to the shaping and maintenance of an institutional setting and what is known as an "investment climate" favorable to the functioning of profit-oriented capitalist enterprise. This application of power takes place directly (as in Greece in the 1940s, Vietnam, and the Dominican Republic; or the recent French intervention in Zaire; or a long string of CIA-organized coups in Iran, Guatemala, Greece in 1967, Bangladesh, etc.) or indirectly through arming, financing, and politically supporting client regimes throughout the third world to repress their own people, and in some cases to act in addition as subimperialist gendarmes in their respective geographical regions. The enormous apparatus of power necessary to sustain this worldwide enterprise in geopolitical engineering is centered in the United States and benefits from important and sometimes vital support from the other advanced capitalist countries acting as junior partners; it involves the deployment of military bases with their complements of military personnel and weapons over three quarters or so of the surface of the globe; and its bitter fruit is a fearsome crop of increasingly numerous and brutal dictatorships seeking to make the world safe for capital, and in the process making it less and less habitable for human beings.

In the ideology of capitalism, of course, this very dark cloud has a silver lining. The repression, the suffering, the misery of the present are supposed to be temporary, unavoidable aspects of a transition from underdevelopement and backwardness to the promised land of full-fledged capitalism. And not surprisingly in this ideological fairy tale it is precisely the expansion of the multinational corporations—which we too have placed at the center of our analysis—which is supposed to provide the motor force. Wasn't it the accumulation of capital which led from the poverty of the Middle Ages to the affluence of today's advanced capitalist countries? And aren't the multinational corporate giants of our time infinitely more effective accumulators than the relative pygmies that pioneered the economic development of Western Europe, North America, and Japan? And if this is so, aren't we justified in looking forward to rapid progress and a happy ending?

The answer, unfortunately, is no—flatly and unconditionally. Multinational capital in migrating to the third world today has absolutely no intention or interest in transforming those societies. It plans to adapt to and exploit the conditions which exist there. Whatever transformation takes place is a by-product of this process and cannot but intensify rather than alleviate the tragic conditions which are already deeply rooted in a long history. The general case can be most effectively presented by means of a particular example, the expansion of foreign (predominantly U.S.) capital into Brazil, one of the biggest and potentially richest countries in the third world. Multinational corporations based in the advanced capitalist countries go to Brazil to supply and profit from markets which already exist and can be expected to grow with the general expansion of global capitalism. Some of these are domestic Brazilian markets, fueled by the spending of perhaps 20 percent of the population in the highest income brackets. Others are international markets for agricultural products, raw materials, and certain kinds of manufactured goods the costs of which can be kept low through the employment of cheap labor. But there is one market, potentially by far the largest, which does not exist and which the multinational corporations have no intention whatever of creating, the market which would burgeon along with a rising real standard of living for the Brazilian masses. The reason for what may at first sight seem a paradox is simple: for capitalists, both Brazilian and foreign, the masses are looked upon as costs, not as customers: the lower their real wages, the higher the profits from selling to the local upper class and the international market. The vicious dynamic at work here has resulted in a drastic decline in the level of real wages in Brazil since the military coup of 1964, amounting by some estimates to as much as 40 percent. A stunning illustration of what Marx called the general law of capitalist accumulation—growing riches on the one hand, deepening poverty on the other. And Brazil, far from being an exception, is a perfect example of what is happening and will undoubtedly continue to happen throughout the underdeveloped periphery of the world capitalist system.

I think you will agree with me that the conclusion to be drawn from this analysis is obvious. For the great mass of people living in the third world—and that means for well over half of the human race—who are the special victims of this stage of capitalist development, the only possible way forward is to break out of the straitjacket which has been imposed upon them by the raw power of the metropolitan centers and to enter upon their own self-reliant course of development. This means revolution, the most massive and profound revolution in human history. And that is the final term in the logic of "corporations, the state, and imperialism."

Notes

1. In Webster's unabridged dictionary the first meaning given for "miser" is "a wretched or severely afflicted person."

2. We are not concerned in the present context with the *origin* of surplus value but rather with (1) its presence as a necessary condition for the existence of capitalism, and (2) with some of its crucially important implications for the way capitalism functions.

3. An important point which cannot be developed in the present context is that internal policies of the state often involve significant conflicts of interest within the national ruling class which under certain conditions may become so serious as to impair or even paralyze effective state action—a problem which has received far less attention than it deserves in discussions of the Marxist theory of the state. Such conflicts are much less likely to be involved in the external policies of the state; the entire national capitalist class is normally interested in maximizing gains at the expense of foreign nations and peoples.

Marxist Perspectives
on Policy

Marxists are committed to progressive social change; for them change from capitalism to a democratic form of socialism is the paramount policy objective. Humanized capitalism is taken to be a contradiction in terms. Their analysis of capitalism provides both a basis for rejection of what they understand as an exploitative and inherently divisive system and a basis for their work for social transformation. Ernest Mandel has described this process of change as one involving progressive disalienation: the regaining by workers of collective control over the product of their work and over the organization of the work they do, and the elimination of divisions among the people involved in productive and reproductive work.

Socialism is understood to be a transitional step toward a communist society, one without internal contradiction. Whether that unrealized state of civilization is utopian or not—whether it is a vision or guide to action or an actual objective to be achieved—is a matter of debate, and a matter for history to determine. What matters to Marxists today is that capitalism be overcome, that the wage system be abolished, and that an irreversible transformation be established toward production for use rather than for profit.

The ways in which these broad objectives are translated into immediate goals vary with the historical conditions of the society in question. Central questions include the level of organization and solidarity within the working class and with its allies, the extent of development of meaningful democratic practice in the society, and the immediate ability to meet basic human material needs through noncommodity forms of production and distribution. Questions on strategy are many. They include whether or not social democracy, a constrained and regulated form of capitalism, constitutes a viable path to socialism. As long as people depend for survival on individual income from work, strategies to win full employment are important, even if capitalism cannot meet them. A more socialist strategy is to reduce individual dependence on wages and salaries, and to reduce the time devoted to material reproduction of life. Included as well is the question of the potential role in socialist politics for an expanding white-collar, but perhaps increasingly proletarianized, work force in advanced industrial societies. Indeed they include the question of how realizable radical social transformation is in the more industrial capitalist societies, and whether, given an increasingly international division of labor, it logically finds greater impetus in the third world.

Problems of capitalist society and programmatic recommendations to resolve them are too numerous to summarize fully here. A list of readings is provided below to facilitate further investigation of these issues. What follows is a sample of perceived problems, and related policy recommendations that flow from a Marxist perspective.

• Market distribution of commodities produced for profit is a hallmark of capitalism that is considered both alienating to those who produce them and wasteful of the human and natural resources used in their production and marketing. Planned production of at least the basic food, clothing, shelter, and medical and educational services necessary to sustain life is a basic socialist objective. A society would have as its goal the social distribution of these basic goods and services as a fundamental right of all citizens.

• Work in organizations producing goods and services should be organized democratically by those who perform it. If producing for basic human need, that work is guided by objectives set in a social and democratic planning process. If producing other goods to be distributed through markets, firms involved might have greater autonomy in setting their goals. Basic productive resources must be socially owned and publicly controlled.

• Racism and sexism have historical origins and psychological bases that reach beyond capitalism, but they are fundamentally useful to white males in power under capitalism. These forms of alienation stand in the way of working class organization to overthrow capitalism, and they are played upon to heighten divisions within that class. Capital is served by its ability to privatize child-rearing and other costs of reproduction and daily life, and men served by their ability to treat those tasks as subordinate and the province of women. With regard to both race and gender, the liberal tenet of equal opportunity cannot be realized under capitalism. Overcoming that oppressive social system would not assure the elimination of racism and sexism, but it is a necessary condition for the achievement of those goals.

• Capitalism is a system involving the degradation of the natural environment as well as the exploitation of human labor. The earth and its resources are privately owned, and this ownership is accompanied by the "right" to do almost anything with them. In addition to public ownership and control over resources, the socialist alternative stresses expanded use of public goods in defining and meeting the needs of daily life, including those of transportation (emphasis on public transit as opposed to the automobile) and leisure (public recreation facilities, support for the arts, etc.). Production for use rather than for profit assumes an emphasis on durable, long-lasting products as opposed to products with minimum life expectancy or planned obsolescence. Conservation of natural resources could then be part of a socialist quest for an ecologically sound life, rather than a threat to corporations' profits.

• Tensions in international relations are fueled by capitalism's unending quest for cheap labor and raw materials, a hospitable environment in which to take advantage of both, and spheres of influence to serve as potential markets for goods and services. The socialist alternative offers the potential for a system without capitalism's need for growth, a need frequently pursued most ruthlessly by the largest and strongest of capitalist nations.

Western Marxism involves a deep commitment to a more egalitarian and just order; one that would extend democracy into the economic realm, and expand it in the form of people's greater participation in the decisions that affect their lives. Seeking to overcome the close linkage between private wealth-holding and the exercise of power, it envisions a greater unity of our lives as producers, consumers, and citizens.

Suggested Reading

The following books represent a selection of significant contributions to contemporary Marxist analysis. They are generally available in university libraries, some are probably available in public libraries, or they can be ordered through bookstores.

Barrett, M. *Women's Oppression Today*. London: New Left Books, 1980.

Bowles, S., D. M. Gordon, and T. E. Weisskopf. *Beyond the Waste Land: A Democratic Alternative to Economic Decline*. New York: Doubleday, 1983.

Braverman, H. *Labor and Monopoly Capital: The Degradation of Work in the Twentieth Century*. New York: Monthly Review, 1974.

Cohen, G. A. *Karl Marx's Theory of History: A Defense*. Princeton: Princeton University Press, 1978.

Harvey, D. *The Limits to Capital*. Chicago: University of Chicago Press, 1982.

Horvat, B. *The Political Economy of Socialism: A Marxist Social Theory*. Armonk: M. E. Sharpe, 1982.

Mandel, E. *Late Capitalism*. London: New Left Books, 1975.

O'Connor, J. *Fiscal Crisis of the State*. New York: St. Martin's, 1973.

Ollman, B. *Alienation: Marx's Conception of Man in Capitalist Society*, 2d ed. New York: Cambridge University Press, 1976.

Reich, M. *Racial Inequality, Economic Theory and Class Conflict*. Princeton: Princeton University Press, 1981.

Sargent, L., ed. *Women and Revolution: A Discussion of the Unhappy Marriage of Marxism and Feminism*. Boston: South End Press, 1980.